CRITICAL PRAISE FOR THIS BOOK

This book fills a void, as it analyses, by means of original case studies, how the major agribusiness corporations respond to challenges posed by new regulation, environmental pressure, and market opportunities. Overall, it shows how corporate R&D and innovation is more driven by internal organizational imperatives (in particular profits and efficiency gains) rather than by societal and environmental concerns, consumer preferences, or competitors. Innovation and learning clearly appear to be a bottom-up (farm-level, SMEs), and not a top-down (corporate strategy) process. This excellent book is thus of value both to managers and activists. A must for anyone concerned with the future of corporate agriculture.

Matthias Finger, Professor and Dean, Swiss Federal Institute of Technology

One of the most pressing debates today in world agricultural policy relates to how we should consider corporate engagement with the environment. This book is a milestone in the analysis of this critical issue. Society needs to confront and resolve the issues presented in this book, which should be read by anyone with an interest in the environmental implications of our food system.

Dr Bill Pritchard, Senior Lecturer in Economic Geography, University of Sydney, Australia

KEES JANSEN &
SIETZE VELLEMA | editors

Agribusiness and Society

Corporate responses to environmentalism, market
opportunities and public regulation

Zed Books
LONDON · NEW YORK

Agribusiness and Society: Corporate responses to environmentalism, market opportunities and public regulation was first published by Zed Books Ltd, 7 Cynthia Street, London N1 9JF, UK and Room 400, 175 Fifth Avenue, New York, NY 10010, USA in 2004.

www.zedbooks.co.uk

Cover designed by Andrew Corbett
Set in Monotype Fournier by Ewan Smith, London
Printed and bound in Malta by Gutenberg Ltd

Distributed in the USA exclusively by Palgrave Macmillan, a division of St Martin's Press, LLC, 175 Fifth Avenue, New York, NY 10010

A catalogue record for this book is available from the British Library.
Library of Congress cataloging-in-publication data: available

ISBN 1 84277 412 3 cased
ISBN 1 84277 413 1 limp

Contents

Tables and figures

ONE | Agribusiness and environmentalism: the politics of technology innovation and regulation

KEES JANSEN AND SIETZE VELLEMA

§ By the start of the twenty-first century, agriculture had definitively lost its image as a natural and harmless activity. Consumer and environmentalist organizations in Europe, farmers' organizations in India and political coalitions in Brazil, are taking action against the introduction of genetically modified crops, which they view as a corporate appropriation of nature, an infringement of farmers' choice in seed selection and as an attack on agro-biodiversity.

Leading writers, cabaret performers and musicians in the Netherlands have launched cultural platforms against intensive pig-farming. Recent outbreaks of mad cow disease (BSE), foot and mouth disease, avian influenza, and other food scares, such as GMOs, pesticide residues and chemical food additives, have put organic agriculture definitively on the policy agenda, even though some prominent scientists fiercely condemn it as backward-looking. General discontent with the industrialization of agricultural production and food provision systems has put agribusiness and the food industry at the core of societal debates.

Life sciences industries, Monsanto in particular, are fiercely criticized for their biotechnology programmes. Pesticide industries are being charged with systematically contaminating the environment, their workers, our drinking water and the products we eat. Food producers are being criticized for promoting monocultures that lead to a higher use of agro-chemicals, an increase in soil erosion, a loss of agro-biodiversity and high energy use.

Growing discontent with conventional, industrialized agriculture is not only putting pressure on agribusiness but creating new opportunities for sustainable business strategies and opening up market niches for environmentally-friendly products. Supermarket chains turn towards organic and other environmentally-friendly foodstuffs as high-value products. Banana producers procure environmental certification for their bananas to enlarge, or at least maintain, their market shares in European countries. Food processing industries take up organic brands to lure green consumers seeking healthy foods. Research and Development (R&D) departments of agribusiness firms develop new technological tools for creating healthy food products or new farming methods.

The motives for agribusiness's responses to environmental concerns within society are thus diverse. These may include a strategy to lower social and political resistance by pressure groups against their production methods or products. Or it may be that firms have to comply with environmental regulations or improve their environmental management in order to avoid new and stricter regulations. These responses to external factors interact with internal ones: business managers who become adherents of the 'ecological paradigm' may be vital to the internalization of environmentalism in their firm (Vorley, ch. 2; Johnson, 1998). Last but not least, firms can profit from environmentalism if they succeed in capturing the green consumer. They can extend or renew their product range to include organic food (Lyons et al., ch. 5) or try to convince buyers that their products are more environmentally-friendly than those of their competitors in order to sustain or enlarge their market share (Jansen, ch. 7).

Given this multiplicity of responses it is not surprising that 'sustainable development' as undertaken by business has been evaluated in contrasting ways. Some authors argue that companies are genuinely committed to environmental issues, because firms have adopted environmental management systems, appointed board members with corporate environmental responsibilities and invested in improving environmental performance (Beloe, 1999; Shrivastava, 1996). Several chapters in this book describe how, over the last decade, the array of responses to environmental concerns has shifted from end-of-pipe or control technologies, including more rational use of polluting inputs such as pesticides, to sustainable technologies and the design of cleaner production methods, ranging from organic food to hi-tech integrated pest management in plantations with monocultures of high-value export crops (Jansen, ch. 7; Guthman, ch. 6; Lyons et al., ch. 5). Businesses have conceded that the environment is an issue they must address and have moved in different ways to accommodate it within their strategies (Blair and Hitchcock, 2001; Reinhardt, 2000).

On the other hand, a critical view is emerging among environmental movements that firms address environmentalism merely as a sophisticated 'greenwash' strategy, manipulating the definition of sustainable development, bringing trade and environmental agreements in line with corporate agendas to convince the public that firms have moved into a new era of 'green business' (Greer and Bruno, 1996; Bruno, 2002).[1]

This debate leads to the crucial question about the extent to which the industry is capable of carrying through profound changes in production processes and product development to become proficient in developing new, environmentally-friendly products and services. This book focuses on one particular issue in this debate: the interaction between internal corporate environments where efficiency, profit and share price considerations predominate, and external environments where consumer preferences, NGO pressures and government regulations are decisive. This book examines the permeable boundaries between agribusiness and society in an attempt to clarify what enables firms to be innovative and to change their business strategies in the context of a growing societal concern for the environment. It provides a sociologically informed analysis of the internal dynamics within agribusiness firms, the possibilities for interest groups to change agribusiness performance, the role of the public sector in innovation and the mode of regulation of agribusiness operations.

Agribusiness firms, particularly the larger ones, are major actors in shaping the future of socio-technological and environmental landscapes in agriculture and food provision worldwide because they are financially capable of investing in technological innovation and are able to assess the environmental impact of their operations. The diversity of agribusiness operations cannot be covered in one book, but some of the most contentious firms and topics are included in our analysis: among them, the biotechnology firms Monsanto, Calgene and Zeneca, the pesticide producers Ciba-Geigy, Dow and Shell, the banana companies Dole and Chiquita, and the food industries Uncle Tobys and Heinz Wattie. Guthman's chapter (ch. 6) complements the analysis of larger corporations that shape agricultural modernization at the input and output side of the farm, with a closer examination of the other element of agribusiness, namely the large growers and grower-shippers which are at the heart of constructing 'the factories in the field'.

Following corporate activities in diverse places (including the USA, Europe, Australia, Brazil, Sierra Leone and Central America) we will be able better to understand the operation of agribusiness in different socio-technical and regulatory environments. This also requires specific research into the issues of dominance of, and resistance to, agribusiness operations in developing countries. Various chapters analyse the impact of state regulation or political campaigning by non-governmental social movements on agribusiness performance. The topics addressed in this book include 'green' bananas, genetically modified tomatoes and soya, the new markets in organic produce, occupational health and pesticides, and access to justice.

The starting point of this book is the proposition that the emergence of environmentalism in the late twentieth century has reshaped performance and innovation in agribusiness. 'Environmentalism' is here not used in the sense of a social movement of environmental organizations; rather, as a term ending in -*ism*, it indicates principally a set of ideas. Environmentalism refers here to a set of guiding principles for the preservation and enhancement of the environment. This set of ideas is no longer unilaterally defined by environmental movements; it has become incorporated into government policy, has been internalized by companies, has become part of international agreements and has guided consumer behaviour. Despite the borrowing of the term 'environmentalism' by more and more actors, we assume that it still connotes a recognizable and distinct set of ideas, even though the precise meaning of these ideas will continue to be the subject of controversies.[2] This use of the term environmentalism implies that this book not only looks at how environmental pressure groups are changing agribusiness performance but also how companies respond to the environmentalism present in regulatory and market demands.

This is not to say that the changing behaviour of firms in agriculture and food can be solely attributed to shifting ideas, to the rise of environmentalism and public awareness about sustainability. Guthman's analysis of Californian organic agriculture (ch. 6) shows how agribusiness change is embedded in regional agrarian economies and reproduces structuring factors for the behaviour of individual firms. High land values push farms into a process of intensification. The organic farming movement criticizes such forms of intensification and intends to develop alternatives. However, it is precisely the success of organic agriculture in California, developing into an organic agribusiness sector, which further contributes to increasing land values. The chapters by Harvey (ch. 4), comparing how Monsanto and Zeneca approached the GM tomato, and Pelaez and Schmidt (ch. 10), analysing Monsanto's confrontation with a restrictive regulatory regime in a Brazilian state, emphasize the importance of specific configurations of market opportunities and public regulation. Complex configurations rather than environmental concerns per se seem to be the principal driver of the responses and strategies of companies.

The greening of agriculture is part and parcel of a redirection and further intensification of agro-industrialization, featuring both changes in the relation between agriculture and the food or pharmaceutical industries, and changes in the farming sector itself (Reardon and Barrett, 2000). The size and impact of agro-processing, distribution and provision of farm-inputs, undertaken by agribusiness firms, continue to expand. Increasingly, value is being added in processing, branding and marketing, and less in production, or, in other words, farm production value-added decreases relative to value-added by non-farm actors in the food chain (Cook and Chaddad, 2000; Pritchard, 2000).

The farming sector worldwide is undergoing changes in product composition, technology, and sectoral and market structures. The research focus, in both the private and the public sector, has shifted from farmer to food processing firms, from the public financing of research and development to private financing, and from the functions of plant and cropping systems (or animal and animal husbandry), to the functions of cells, proteins, enzymes and genes. With regard to market structures the shift in economic power from the production side to the retail side is remarkable. This shift has led, among other things, to diminishing returns in the pesticide industry and has given rise to intensified operations by corporate fresh food producers, increasingly defining themselves as food marketeers sourcing fresh produce on a global scale. These general developments make up the context wherein agribusiness and food industries take up environmentalism and decide on investments in technology innovation, the implementation of environmental standards and the inclusion of public regulatory measures into their operations.

The question as to how and to what extent environmentalism makes companies change their strategies and performance is approached from two angles in this book. First, the authors examine what leads firms to include environmentalism in their business strategies, to be innovative in technology development and to change performance in production processes. Part I, 'Agribusiness's Responses to Environmentalism in the Market', takes up the issue of the incorporation of environmentalist concerns into agribusiness strategies and their technology agendas as an expression of a politics of technology innovation. A particular point of concern is whether the growing incorporation of environmentalism into corporate strategies is changing the restricted pallet of choices and constraining variety in technology innovation, exemplified by the strong reliance on biotechnology or genetic engineering. Moreover, even apparently more environmentally-friendly technological alternatives such as organic farming seem to be shaped by the general process of agro-industrialization and its corresponding technological trajectories. The

greening of agriculture and food is in the first place an issue of technological innovation in production processes and product development.
Unlike the more conventional approaches of technology, technological
innovation is here not viewed as a neutral outcome of science nor as a
simple result of market forces. Below we will introduce the concept of
'politics of technology innovation' to explain the important influences of
institutional and social dynamics, negotiation and contestation, and history and power, on the pace and direction of technology innovation.

The focus on struggles around technology innovation is further
deepened in Part II, 'Regulating Corporate Agribusiness: New Roles
for the Public Sector', which examines how changes in regulation and
legislation and a redefinition of the tasks of the public sector may
impact on corporate behaviour. The issue of regulation is the second
angle from which we explore agribusiness–society relationships. The
analysis starts from the notion that the many subtle ways of restructuring the marketplace are often not recognized as such. Two decades
of deregulation and market-led innovation have raised the question as
to how governments, citizens and social movements can govern corporate practice and how the selection of technological options can be
supported by representative forms of decision-making. The classical
division between state-led and market-led development is increasingly
viewed as an unsatisfactory framework for a definition and a defence
of public interests. The search for new forms of regulating agribusiness
activities touches upon the balance of power between state, corporations
and social movements. This part discusses technological innovation in
relation to the rather limited scope of regulatory instruments, to the
shifting balance in public and private control over agricultural development, to the lack of democratic procedures for governing the selection
of technologies and opening up viable alternative technological trajectories, and to the lack of judicial instuments for making corporations
liable for the unwanted consequences of the technologies they create.
Part II calls for a new phase of rethinking and reconstructing public
regulation and intervention in agrarian development, after the phases
of state-led modernization and its demolition by a combination of its
own contradictions and free market ideology.

AGRIBUSINESS STRATEGIES AND ENVIRONMENTALISM

With the 1992 UNCED Earth Summit in Rio de Janeiro the business
community incorporated into their discourse the concept of 'sustainable development', developed earlier in the Brundtland report (WCED,

1987). At the follow-up summit in Johannesburg ten years later, corporations were at the centre-stage of the new environmentalism, and self-regulation of environmental performance was considered a core strategy within sustainable development. Agribusiness firms are heavily involved in the wider business and research initiatives that address environmentalism, such as the World Business Council for Sustainable Development <www.wbcsd.ch>. In particular, agribusiness corporations which sell technologies that are subject to environmentalist critique, including pesticides and genetically modified food, have undertaken efforts to participate in the so-called 'greening of agriculture' (cf. Vorley and Keeney, 1998). After years of strategy development and the initial implementation of sustainable agriculture programmes by agribusiness, it is time to take a critical look at where they are at this moment and to understand why some corporations are more successful than others in introducing environmentally-friendly innovations. For this purpose, this book tries to come to grips with the variety of possible business strategies and technological solutions that agribusiness firms and food industries propagate to solve environmental problems.

The chapters in this book show the wide range of responses and strategies adopted by agribusiness companies to cope with environmentalism. The first type is a rather defensive, or in any case reactive, one and claims that the firm's products and production processes are not harmful to humankind and nature. These claims are made to counter public unrest and criticism. Rosenthal (ch. 8) describes the fierce defences of Dow Chemical and Shell against indictments which intend to make them liable for the effects of their chemical products on the health of plantation workers in developing countries. Monsanto, the agro-chemical company that launched itself as a model for sustainable business based on life sciences, proves to be a case in itself and its history has become a model for understanding the pitfalls of innovation in biotechnology in a corporate environment. The Brazilian case, analysed by Pelaez and Schmidt (ch. 10), shows how hostilities between Monsanto and a large number of environmental groups and farmers' organizations reveal the company's limited capacity to convince stakeholders of its sustainability strategy. Environmental protest, however, was not the only cause of Monsanto's problems at the start of the twenty-first century. Harvey's comparison (ch. 4) of the different ways in which Zeneca and Calgene/Monsanto introduced GM-tomato products shows that a company's behaviour and performance have to be explained from its entanglement with a specific configuration of market opportunities and regulatory measures. In international markets the fate of these competing companies has been determined by a clash between the configurations in the USA and Europe. Vellema (ch. 3) analyses how Monsanto's construction of an acceptable form of environmentalism was hampered by its dependence on specific product lines and technologies, uncertainties about creating innovative products, and the institutional constraints resulting from financial pressures, in addition to the lack of public acceptance of the company's technological products. He argues that the demanding task for company management is to combine all aspects into a working configuration in order to establish a transition to sustainable business. Environmentalism is but one element of the more complex configurations.

Constructing an image of environmental friendliness is not always a defensive strategy. If it is combined with making substantial changes in production processes, it can be viewed as a different, second, type of response. Jansen (ch. 7) describes how banana companies have very rapidly reshaped their production systems in line with environmentalist thought, thereby seeking alliances with different sorts of certification agencies. They now use the image of a certified green quality banana as a key feature of their brands. Societal pressures led to a decrease in pesticide pollution and accidents with pesticides in their plantations as well as the implementation of integrated environmental management systems within the firm. Such forms of self-regulation, in close co-operation with credible auditors, not only address the issue of image and brand construction (market-driven), but may also be driven by cost reduction (less pesticide use) and the wish to convince regulators to move away from 'command-and-control' or 'mandatory' regulation and accept self-regulation.

An even more proactive, third, type of response is the development of new products which create or respond to new, alternative niche markets resulting from environmentalism and green consumerism. The clearest examples are the agribusiness activities in markets for organic agricultural products, discussed by Lyons et al. (ch. 5) and Guthman (ch. 6), and also the initial intentions of Ciba-Geigy (later Novartis, now Syngenta) to develop new products for smallholders in developing countries, described by Vorley (ch. 2). Lyons and her co-authors describe the relative ease with which Heinz Wattie and Uncle Tobys in Australia and New Zealand entered the niche markets for organic foods. Through an analysis of the contested meanings agribusiness ascribes to organic and other green labels, they illustrate corporate greening strategies, and the extent to which such strategies are impacting in Antipodean organic agriculture and food production.

What becomes clear is that environmentalism does have an impact on corporate practice. Yet most authors seem to agree that the incorporation of environmentalism usually leads to partial changes in the behaviour and performance of agribusiness companies and food industries. A major point the various authors make is that environmentalism does not imply a radical change in the overall business organization per se. Corporations such as Ciba-Geigy and Monsanto, which depend on creating innovative products, face more difficulties trying to achieve sound environmentalism along the technological paths of organic agriculture or agro-ecological agriculture. For them, responding to environmentalism tends to result in a defence of biotechnological innovation with arguments about the supposedly environmentally-friendly impacts of specific products, for example stating that genetically modified crops would decrease the use of herbicides or insecticides.

Several of the case studies in this book indicate that the creation and selection of sustainable solutions in agricultural production and food provision are related to the extent of institutional change in business organization. Food industries that operate closer to consumer markets tend to be flexible and able to grab the opportunities in 'environmentalist niches'. Correspondingly, their interactions with consumers, societal groups and regulatory agencies are of a different nature from the defensive responses by polluting agro-chemical industries and more controversial life sciences companies. The latter seem to have more difficulties in using environmentalism as a lever to construct a new business model or strategy from scratch.

Even in the search for organic niche markets, firms primarily build on older organization models. Guthman (ch. 6) discusses how agribusiness, upon entering Californian organic agriculture, reproduces structural patterns of agricultural modernization. These are not changed by organic labelling. Lyons et al. (ch. 5) argue that, in organic agriculture, innovation largely depends on learning by doing at farm level or by small enterprises, which are later taken up by larger industries. These industries develop their organic product lines with already existing techniques of organic farming, developed within the farming sector. Increasingly, organic food chains are the mirror of conventional food chains, with only a few specific adaptations in the production process at field level, with regard to fertilizer and pesticide use.

THE POLITICS OF TECHNOLOGY INNOVATION

The analysis of agribusiness in this book is not phrased in terms of a systemic orchestration of globalization by agribusiness corporations or food industries, and it intends to go beyond descriptions of agribusiness expansion and concentration (Bonanno et al., 1994; Goodman and Watts, 1997). Instead, it intends to disclose why firms make particular choices of technology use or market opportunities, and to unravel the concrete intricate interweaving of people, artefacts, codes and living things (Whatmore and Thorne, 1997). Consequently, corporate responses to environmentalism involve a wide variety of social actors, as well as non-human elements. Methodologically, this calls for in-depth investigations into concrete business practices and the interconnections with institutional, cultural, economic, political and material elements. This approach also makes technology a central focus of social analysis.

The premise of this book is that new technologies or combinations of technologies, resulting in new technological trajectories, are central for making a substantial shift towards sustainable agriculture. Most authors in this book share the proposition that technology innovation is neither an autonomous process driven by inner scientific logic nor a simple result of the operation of market mechanisms. On the contrary, there is space (albeit limited) for social choice (Coombs, 1995). The selection of technological solutions or innovation routes by agribusiness is not just a linear outcome of profit-maximizing strategies but is embedded in a complex set of external factors and internal aspects of agribusiness organization and strategies. Technology innovation is an outcome of the contested social choices of involved social actors with different views on what kind of technology should be developed. Exploring the relation between agribusiness and environmentalism raises a question about the politics of technology innovation. In the context of this book, this points to the involvement of different social groups in technology innovation and the conflicting interests that may arise when selecting and institutionalizing technological options. It furthermore indicates that such conflicts about innovation take place at different levels: within the firm, in the marketplace, in interaction with other social actors, and within the process of formulating regulation. Within firms, for example, research and development departments have to negotiate about technological futures with managers of other business units. When new products are launched on the market or otherwise released, they may generate conflicting views on their impact, now and in the future. Not only direct users or consumers may intervene but also other stakeholders such as nature conservationists. In the public domain, society raises questions about who defines the goals and who sets the preconditions for innovation. Here, societal organizations ask whether it should be agribusiness firms which define what new environmentally-friendly agricultural products should look like (Glover and Newell, ch. 9).

The concept of politics of technology innovation does not imply that interests are the only determining factor in technological change. The dramatic misfortune that Monsanto called down upon itself may partly be explained by the company's inability to construct biotechnologies that could really convince consumers (Harvey, ch. 4) and to the inter-action between the organization of technological competency inside firms and the appreciation of technology in the public domain (Vellema, ch. 3). The extent to which agribusiness can shape agricultural futures with biotechnology also depends on bio-organic processes that are far more difficult to manipulate and effectively control than biotechnology futurologists want us to believe by painting a promising future with biotechnology and environmentally-friendly agricultural production. Technology is not an entirely plastic entity that is shaped at will by technology developers.

The issue of path dependency is relevant here. The process of technology innovation follows certain rule-sets which are embedded in a complex of engineering practices, production process technologies, product characteristics, skills and procedures, ways of handling relevant artefacts and persons, and ways of defining problems. The cultural matrix of experts in the field, technical groups and managers involved as well as the complex selection environment, which includes, besides market forces, government regulation and institutions such as science and law, create stabilized interdependencies (Nelson, 1995; Rip and Kemp, 1998). Both the material and organizational properties of inno-vation make technology innovation 'path-dependent'.[3] Thus, in techno-logy innovation continuity of thinking and practice is as important as renewal and change. Vorley's chapter explores how Ciba-Geigy tried to incorporate environmentalist views into its overall corporate strategy. Vorley describes the history of a long-term proposal to restructure parts of Ciba-Geigy's pesticide business into a product unit provid-ing pest control services to resource-poor smallholders. His story ex-plores the tension between a more agro-ecological technological path – eventually implying that the pesticide industry shifts from an input industry that delivers crop protection products to a service industry that delivers integrated pest management – and a biotechnology path. Understanding how these tensions evolve requires insights into those factors that push towards a certain solution. It follows from Vorley's account that Ciba-Geigy closed down its projects on increasing small farmers' skills in integrated pest management, because these did not provide the short-term profits which shareholders sought. The general shift from dividend as the main target for shareholders to a rise in share prices increased the importance of technological promises and shortened the term in which shareholders expected a profitable return. This was conducive to biotechnological innovation and not to the more incremental agro-ecological or organic farming type of innovations. In the end, Ciba-Geigy put aside alternative technological routes and prioritized one main direction: biotechnology. Vorley's chapter should not be read as if technology innovation is only internally determined. Looking at path-dependency also implies raising questions about interaction with the external selection environment. Part II of this book not only explores what agribusiness firms can change of their own volition, but also where regulation through other social actors can shape technology innovation.

REGULATION AFTER THE SUSTAINABILITY DECADE

The emergence of the greening of business coincided with the ideological predominance of deregulation and privatization. Voices from different political stands pronounced that traditional views on state regulation, focusing on state-imposed constraints on undesirable behaviour, have become obsolete. Decisions about technology use and innovation – the core of environmental performance – have increasingly become controlled by corporate decisions. In a rather short period the locus of agricultural technology innovation has shifted from the public sector, with a predominant focus on farm enterprises, to the private sector – predominantly input and food processing industries. Although states still set some environmental standards, large enterprises have a more prominent stake in defining and imposing international standards (Finger and Tamiotti, 1999). This raises questions as to how the expansion of green business strategies relates to contemporary forms of public regulation and what can be expected from future public intervention in private activities.

The regulation paradox: the choice between state- and market-led change

Statism and Marketism can be viewed as two paths to Order (Busch, 2000). The idea that a choice can be made between the State and the Market as a preferred path to Order – in our case sustainable development of agriculture – is a paradox. The belief that the changed performance of economic actors can be a substitute for state regulations is mistaken, since it cannot rule out the centrality of social/public delineation of standards, rules and norms which makes it possible for economic actors to operate and for markets to exist. The nature of the paradox between state- and market-led development is clearly illustrated in the exemplary narrative of a recent book by environmental economists and engineers of the World Bank (World Bank, 2000). In the view of this group of policy researchers, new forms of regulation and public action are much more cost-effective than the conventional formal regulation based on monitoring, data analysis and record-keeping, and police action and enforcement. The latter are time-consuming and expensive. New forms of regulation and public action include environmental education, political mobilization of local communities to push for higher pollution penalties, governmental support for the conversion to clean production, and charging plants for the rate of pollution. These new forms of regulation are considered to be more attractive to developing countries with limited resources for environmental regulation. The World Bank study proposes the substitution of mediation, support in environmental management and training (the 'carrot' approach), and pollution charges and public disclosure, for conventional regulation in the form of penalties and restrictions (the 'stick' approach). They argue strongly in favour of clearer, simpler, transparent and information-intensive regulation.

On the one hand this report straitjackets the question of environmental regulation into a contemporary ideological framework of economic reform and deregulation which, according to the authors of the report, reduces pollution intensity by cutting subsidies for raw materials and encouraging international trade, privatization of state enterprises, more publicly traded firms, and larger firms and plants (World Bank, 2000). On the other hand, a closer look at the report's proposals reveals that these, in fact, conflict with the discourse of deregulation and free market. Many of the proposed actions require an increase in state intervention and a strengthening of state structures compared with the existing situation in most countries. The state should even become actively involved in innovation processes *within* firms. The proposals imply larger environmental agencies, which should be able to collect and interpret information, enact effective regulations and enforce these. In practice, this means more instead of less regulation. In this respect, there seems to be little ground for presenting conventional and new forms of regulation as an exclusive opposition.

Solving the paradox can be problematic. Welford (1997) denies the value of solving the paradox between market- and state-led development and brings forward new types of oppositions. He argues that the 'old' opposition has been superseded by an opposition between, on the one hand, *modernist constructs* emphasizing growth, globalization, materialism and consumption, and, on the other hand, *bio-regional green constructs* emphasizing values associated with connectedness, spirituality (as opposed to organized religion), individuality, community, sufficiency and simplicity. This carries with it a criticism of the tendency to translate all kind of social and ethical values into monetary values (Benton, 1999). Bio-regional green constructs stress that transnational corporations do not really intend to produce and trade sustainably, that is reducing growth in production, as this would undermine their *raison d'être*. The development of environmental departments, corporate environmental programmes and voluntary codes of conduct do not thwart the crucial tendency to expand markets and production activities, and increase sales of material products.

This view supposes that the bargaining power of governments and multilateral governmental agencies *vis-à-vis* corporate capital has declined (Greer and Bruno, 1996; Mulligan, 1999). Even though bio-regional green constructs call for more public and mandatory control of corporations and technology development, as well as a reversal of neo-liberal policy instruments, they generally provide few concrete proposals as to how regulation, meant to direct agribusiness's environmental performance and technology innovation, can be made more effective. Furthermore, calls for promoting alternative technology innovation tend to focus on local green alternatives and hardly make use of concentrated research and development institutions. In this view, alternatives to agribusiness expansion have, in the context of a weakening state, to come from grassroots organizations. These organizations can set in motion participatory processes of government and enforce the improvement of local and national laws and commitment to international agreements (Welford 1997). The central focus of social action is therefore on strengthening the organization of grassroots movements. Opposition means tackling corporate activities which endanger local communities and building up alternative bio-regional activities such as LETS (Local Exchange Trading Schemes). Environmentalists may also negotiate with the corporations for more and better stakeholder assessments and social and environmental audits in which the participation of civil society organizations (development NGOs, environmental organizations and other social movements) has to be increased (Karliner, 1997; Korten, 1999; Mullingan, 1999; Tokar, 1997; Welford, 1997).

Whereas the discussion of public regulation in bio-regional green constructs is rather limited, we find extensive discussions about the role, character and possibilities of environmental regulation in the ecological modernization approach. A central thesis in the ecological modernization approach is that environmental regulation, if well designed, can establish a positive relationship with economic competitiveness and growth (Gouldson and Murphy, 1998). The emergence of the green consumer points to a desired transition towards sustainable development. The latter requires a series of social and institutional transformations of science, markets, the role of the nation-state and a restyling of environmentalist ideology (Mol and Sonnenfeld, 2000). These transformations should bring about a shift from reactive control techniques (end-of-pipe) to anticipatory clean technologies, move the environment from the periphery to the core of business decision-making and develop strategic perspectives on both radical and incremental changes.

Similar to the bio-regional green constructs, the ecological modernization approach notices the contemporary weakening of sovereign regulatory public authority with regard to environmental issues. In contrast to the first approach, however, the currently favoured move from mandatory regulation to self-regulation or voluntary regulation, in which corporations take the lead and increase their power to control, is evaluated more positively. According to Midttun (1999), it forces industries to integrate environmental management more strongly into their business strategies. For governments of developing countries it reduces the costs of improving industry's environmental performance and reduces pollution while industry continues to grow (World Bank, 2000). Such a view on regulation contemplates an increasing importance of corporate economic agents as carriers of ecological restructuring.

It seems that the bio-regional green constructs either find the mentioned paradox irrelevant or reduce the issue of how to improve environmental regulation to the notion of giving more voice to environmental movements. They are less involved in rethinking the complexities of managing the state and shaping the larger economy. The ecological modernization approach is much closer to solving pragmatically the day-to-day problems of improving environmental regulation. The challenge taken up in this book is to bring into the analysis the dynamic nature of a capitalist economy and its underlying power relations (cf. Goldblatt, 1996), while recognizing the intricacies of regulating and steering business performance in the context of multiple business–society interactions.

Nowadays, many policy frameworks take up principles from the ecological modernization approach and propose combinations of mandatory and voluntary regulation. Furthermore, they expect much from environmentalist demands in the market (cf. Gouldson and Murphy, 1998). Several chapters in this book question the high expectations of such proposals (particularly Jansen, ch. 7, and Lyons et al., ch. 5). It is problematic to take green consumerism as evidence for an increase in consumer power and to propose it as an alternative for public regulation to shape green development. Green consumerism neither changes legal frameworks nor decision-making in technology development. It does not set standards but primarily causes some new standards to be set. Even though the power balance has shifted from the production to the consumption side, this does not imply an increase in the power of consumers to define the conditions under which their food is being produced and what technologies are being developed. Mainly large retailers have become proactive in setting product standards, not the majority of the consumers (Lyons et al., ch. 5). Both consumers and farmers generally develop reactive responses only. Consumers may stop buying certain food products but, in order to do this, alternative products first have to be known and available. They have little proactive voice in defining what will be put on the supermarket shelves. Likewise, farmers have little capacity to change the research and development agenda or the products of input delivering industries.

Another problem concerns the shifts in power relations brought about by the change from mandatory to voluntary regulation and the related question as to who sets the final bottom line of standards with which economic actors have to comply. Jansen's chapter (ch. 7) analyses the ways two companies, Chiquita and Dole Food, institutionalized two different forms of voluntary regulation by linking up with rather contrasting actor-networks: one of a populist-entrepreneurial nature and one of a scientific-bureaucratic nature. The banana companies took little notice of mandatory environmental regulation as long as only the Honduran government pressured for compliance with the standards. Only after market demand for 'green' bananas started to grow, did they initiate different forms of voluntary environmental regulation, which indeed had a clear impact upon internal organization as well as on cultivation practices in the plantations. What follows from Jansen's study, however, is that the possibilities of self-regulation are rather limited and, in fact, build upon standards set by mandatory regulation. Hence, the expansion of green business strategies has not ruled out the earlier question as to what extent and how public regulation should intervene in private activities, such as agribusiness operations, and the market. The search for hybrid forms of regulation thus still requires a strengthening of public capabilities and democratic control to balance corporate power.[4] So, contemporary trends of deregulation, self-regulation and soft regulation require the paradoxical condition of a 'strong state' (Leftwich, 2000), particularly in developing countries, which is knowledgeable and capable of collecting and interpreting relevant information and generating precision regulation. Although this book does not provide an overview of all possible regulatory instruments, it develops crucial arguments that underline the importance of a further rethinking and strengthening of regulatory frameworks.

New roles for the public sector

The idea of strengthening public regulation goes far beyond notions of modernization, management, governance or administration; it is decisively an issue of politics, that is about intervening in differences, conflicts, resources, power and control (Leftwich, 2000). Various chapters take up elements of this general point. Rosenthal (ch. 8) argues in favour of a more profound discussion about global access to justice in order to guarantee that agribusiness performance will change and become controllable in situations of underdevelopment. She describes the juridical struggles that took place after large numbers of banana workers from various developing countries sued, in the USA, pesticide producers and banana corporations for the use of the nematicide DBCP in banana cultivation when, according to the plaintiffs, the companies knew beforehand about the possible negative health effects of the use of such pesticides. Rosenthal makes the point that globalization is seen only in terms of opening up markets, and that corporations do not want to take the legal responsibilities for the injuries or pollution caused by their products or procedures in other countries.

Glover and Newell (ch. 9) further discuss liability strategies as proposed by Rosenthal. The limitations of public regulation in terms of including public concerns have prompted civil society actors to fill these governance gaps and to resort to litigation or liability strategies, public law challenges, or micro-surveillance and exposure. Such forms of 'civil regulation' expose the deficiencies of public regulation. Glover and Newell show that, in the controversies around possible risks in biotechnology development, governments respond mainly to business advocacy to focus on commercial and trade concerns, leaning towards regulation *for* business rather than regulation *of* business. The competition between different approaches to the regulation of the biotechnology sector raises the fundamental question of who decides what is the appropriate role of new technologies. How this question is handled influences to an important extent public trust in the ability of regulatory bodies to pass judgment on new technologies. Glover and Newell also conclude that while civil regulation constructs new normative frameworks, generates fresh expectations and brings into the regulatory process a wider circle of stakeholders, it can never replace the authority, legitimacy and enforceability of public regulation. Rather than pulling in different directions, civil and public regulations should, according to these authors, interact in a mutually supportive way with each approach building on the limitations of the other.

Pelaez and Schmidt (ch. 10) also explore the creation of links between public and civil regulation and argue that it is a contested issue and object of social struggle. They examine two modes of state intervention in the introduction of genetically modified soya in Brazil. The federal government actively favoured Monsanto's investments in Brazil and supported the introduction of genetically modified soybeans without any restriction. However, the local state of Rio Grande do Sul supported the view of a coalition of environmentalist and smallholder movements and issued a ban on the cultivation of genetically modified crops as part of an alternative regulatory regime. Monsanto's efforts to pressure the federal government in Brazil to break the restrictive regulation at the lower state level, by using both legal and illegal activities, were intended to split the coalition which sought alternative technologies for improving seed quality and tried to change public regulation. To date, this struggle within the Brazilian state is still ongoing.

Richards (ch. 11) explores from another angle the contested terrain in which linkages between civil society, public regulation and private interests are established or disrupted. In his chapter he argues that more is at stake than a simple opposition of public and private spheres: the public and the private can interweave in different ways and generate different imaginations of technological futures. The conventional technological cultures have either been security-driven (exemplified by the Green Revolution) or market-driven (exemplified by public–private partnerships around biotechnology). Richards warns us about technological monoculturalism in which the greening of agriculture and the provision of food security is left to agribusiness alone, closing off alternative technology paths. Richards makes the case for a strong public intervention in technology innovation and the development of alternative technology paths that form the basis for dialogue and negotiation with private corporations (cf. Vellema, ch. 3). In this view, regulation seems more than controlling the unintended consequences of new technologies generated by the private sector; it involves a proactive civic and public intervention to shape the direction of technology innovation. The struggle is to sustain the competition between differently configured cultures of technology, and to expect new projects to arise, triggered by new crises, shaped by new social energies and commitments.

It may not be strange that the shortcomings of self-regulation (Jansen, ch. 7), current justice systems (Rosenthal, ch. 8), civil society interventions (Glover and Newell, ch. 9; Pelaez and Schmidt, ch. 10) and market-driven definitions of technology agendas (Richards, ch. 11) become particularly salient in a context of underdevelopment. Even though many developed countries proclaimed the canon of deregulation, they often strengthened their public environmental regulation. They have included self-regulation and negotiated rule-making, but with mandatory, restrictive regulation as a stick that can be used if the former remain ineffective. But the development of that stick has remained weak in many developing countries. If agribusiness in this globalizing world increases its power to control the world's food provision and enlarges its effects on the use of the world's natural resources, what kind of public and civil regulation of these processes is required? At this juncture, many intellectuals of different disposition and inclinations consider such a question about the role of the public as an anachronism. This book shows that it is precisely contemporary economic and political processes which make this question more relevant than ever.

NOTES

The editors are grateful to Peter Oosterveer, Harro Maart and Julie Guthman for comments on earlier versions of this chapter (the usual disclaimers apply). We thank the Agrarian Questions Congress Organization and the Technology and Agrarian Development Group of Wageningen University, the Netherlands, for supporting this book project.

1. 'Greenwashing' is defined as the dissemination of information or disinformation so as to present an environmentally responsible public image without bringing about substantial changes in the production process (Bruno, 2002).

2. The diverse discourses, philosophies and basic assumptions of environmentalism have been analysed extensively elsewhere and will not be examined here (e.g. Milton, 1996; Yearly, 1996). Similarly, we will not go into discussions about agro-ecological alternatives based on small-scale, locally-oriented production and locally-oriented commercialization networks. Other relevant topics raised in some chapters but not explored in depth due to limited space are the global development of market chains and the increasing power of retail firms, the role of steering institutions such as the WTO, the influence of capital flows and the changing relationships between shareholders and firms.

3. The concept of path-dependency or technology trajectory may have an

unhappy resonance with technological determinism and internalism. This can be resolved only if we conceptualize the actual behaviour of a firm as a representation of a compromise between different, potentially contending courses of action, not as a sort of linear progression of technology development in which future innovations are predictable from earlier steps, but as an instituted process in which different institutional aspects interact (Harvey, 1999; MacKenzie, 1992).

4. Arguing likewise, Benton (1999) deconstructs the common assumption of a radical difference between market instruments and old-fashioned 'command and control' in environmental policy. He contends that this assumption is mistaken. Even though it may sound otherwise, there is 'an interesting consensus between neo-Marxist and neoclassical economists to the effect that left to themselves, capitalist market forces degrade their own environmental conditions'. Both standpoints now support the view that capitalist growth is not sustainable without effective extra-economic policy interventions to constrain environmentally damaging patterns of economic calculation (Benton, 1999: 215).

REFERENCES

Beloe, S. (1999) 'The Greening of Business?', *IDS Bulletin* 30 (3): 43–9.

Benton, T. (1999) 'Sustainable Development and the Accumulation of Capital: Reconciling the Irreconcilable?', in A. Dobson (ed.), *Fairness and Futurity: Essays on Environmental Sustainability*, pp. 199–229. Oxford: Oxford University Press.

Blair, A. and D. Hitchcock (2001) *Environment and Business*. London: Routledge.

Bonanno, A., L. Bush, W. H. Friedland, L. H. Gouveia and E. Mingione (eds) (1994) *From Columbus to ConAgra: The Globalization of Agriculture and Food*. Lawrence: University of Kansas Press.

Bruno, K. (2002) 'Greenwash + 10: The UN's Global Compact, Corporate Accountability and the Johannesburg Earth Summit'. CorpWatch/Tides Center <www.corpwatch.org/campaigns/PCD.jsp?articleid=1348> (7 October 2002).

Busch, L. (2000) *The Eclipse of Morality: Science, State, and Market*. New York: Aldine de Gruyter.

Cook, M. L. and F. R. Chaddad (2000) 'Agroindustrialization of the Global Agrifood Economy: Bridging Development Economics and Agribusiness Research', *Agricultural Economics* 23 (3): 207–18.

Coombs, R. (1995) 'Firm Strategies and Technical Choices', in A. Rip, T. J. Misa and J. Schot (eds), *Managing Technology in Society: The Approach of Constructive Technology Assessment*, pp. 331–45. London: Pinter.

Finger, M. and L. Tamiotti (1999) 'New Global Regulatory Mechanisms and the Environment: The Emerging Linkage between the WTO and the ISO', *IDS Bulletin* 30 (3): 8–15.

Goldblatt, D. (1996) *Social Theory and the Environment*. Cambridge: Polity Press.

Goodman, D. and M. Watts (eds) (1997) *Globalising Food: Agrarian Questions and Global Restructuring*. London: Routledge.

Gouldson, A. and J. Murphy (1998) *Regulatory Realities. The Implementation and Impact of Industrial Environmental Regulation.* London: Earthscan.

Greer, J. and K. Bruno (1996) *Greenwash: The Reality Behind Corporate Environmentalism.* Penang, Malaysia: Third World Network.

Harvey, M. (1999) 'Genetic Modification as Bio-Socio-Economic Process: One Case of Tomato Purée', CRIC Discussion Paper no. 31. Manchester: University of Manchester & UMIST.

Johnson, D. B. (1998) 'Green Business: Perspectives from Management and Business Ethics', *Society and Natural Resources* 11 (3): 259–66.

Karliner, J. (1997) *The Corporate Planet: Ecology and Politics in the Age of Globalization.* San Francisco, CA: Sierra Club Books.

Korten, D. C. (1999) *The Post-Corporate World: Life After Capitalism.* San Francisco, CA: Berrett-Koehler.

Leftwich, A. (2000) *States of Development. On the Primacy of Politics in Development.* Cambridge: Polity Press.

MacKenzie, D. (1992) 'Economic and Sociological Explanation of Technical Change', in R. Coombs, P. Saviotti and V. Walsh (eds), *Technological Change and Company Strategies*, pp. 25–48. London: Academic Press.

Midttun, A. (1999) 'The Weakness of Strong Regulation and the Strength of Soft Regulation: Environmental Governance in Post-modern Form', *Innovation* 12 (2): 235–50.

Milton, K. (1996) *Environmentalism and Cultural Theory. Exploring the Role of Anthropology in Environmental Discourse.* London: Routledge.

Mol, A. P. J. and D. A. Sonnenfeld (2000) 'Ecological Modernisation Around the World: An Introduction', *Environmental Politics* 9 (1): 3–15.

Mulligan, P. (1999) 'Greenwash or Blueprint? Rio Tinto in Madagascar', *IDS Bulletin* 30 (3): 50–7.

Nelson, R. R. (1995) 'Recent Evolutionary Theorizing About Economic Change', *Journal of Economic Literature* 33: 48–90.

Pritchard, B. (2000) 'The Tangible and Intangible Spaces of Agro-food Capital', Paper presented at the IRSA X World Congress of Rural Sociology, Rio de Janeiro, Brazil, July 2000.

Reardon, T. and C. B. Barrett (2000) 'Agroindustrialization, Globalization, and International Development: An Overview of Issues, Patterns, and Determinants', *Agricultural Economics* 23 (3): 195–205.

Reinhardt, F. L. (2000) *Down to Earth: Applying Business Principles to Environmental Management.* Boston, MA: Harvard Business School Press.

Rip, A. and R. Kemp (1998) 'Technological Change', in S. Rayner and E. L. Malone (eds), *Human Choice and Climate Change: Volume Two, Resources and Technology*, pp. 327–99. Columbus, OH: Battelle Press.

Shrivastava, P. (1996) *Greening Business: Profiting the Corporation and the Environment.* Cincinnati, OH: Thomson Executive Press.

Tokar, B. (2001) *Redesigning Life? The Worldwide Challenge to Genetic Engineering.* London: Zed Books.

Vorley, W. and D. Keeney (1998) 'The Greening of Industry versus Greenwash:

Introducing a Case Study', in W. Vorley and D. Keeney (eds), *Bugs in the System: Redesigning the Pesticide Industry for Sustainable Agriculture*, pp. 1–16. London: Earthscan.

WCED (World Commision on Environment and Development) (1987) *Our Common Future*. Oxford: Oxford University Press.

Welford, R. (1997) *Hijacking Environmentalism: Corporate Responses to Sustainable Development*. London: Earthscan.

Whatmore, S. and L. Thorne (1997) 'Nourishing Networks: Alternative Geographies of Food', in D. Goodman and M. Watts (eds), *Globalising Food: Agrarian Questions and Global Restructuring*, pp. 287–304. London: Routledge.

World Bank (2000) *Greening Industry: New Roles for Communities, Markets, and Governments*. Oxford: Oxford University Press.

Yearly, S. (1996) *Sociology, Environmentalism, Globalization: Reinventing the Globe*. London: Sage.

PART I

Agribusiness's Responses to Environmentalism in the Market

TWO | Reconciling shareholders, stakeholders and managers: experiencing the Ciba-Geigy vision for sustainable development

WILLIAM VORLEY

§ This is the story of a life science company's vision for sustainable development, and how a resulting initiative in the Plant Protection Division – the Farmer Support Team – flourished and then fell foul of the contradictions nested within that vision. The company was Ciba-Geigy, the Swiss life science multinational.[1]

This is a personal story that dates back over two decades. As with all personal stories, there is a risk of rewriting history to make oneself appear nobler and wiser than the facts justify. There is also the risk of casting a 'visionary' company as a greenwashing Goliath, that defends the status quo by 'injecting itself with tiny doses of the reality of these issues' (Edwards, 1995: 188). My intention is to do neither. The purpose of this chapter is to track how a company's vision for sustainable development allowed employees of Ciba-Geigy to succeed with an innovation in environment, safety and customer service. I then describe how the demise of that innovation reflects the wider contradictions that caused the downfall of the vision itself, and presents continuing problems for the company and industry in getting to grips with the larger issue of sustainable agriculture. I draw attention to how a corporation in a business sector undergoing rapid consolidation and change can find itself with serious contradictions between long-term aspirations for stakeholder value and the short-term reality of shareholder value, and how those contradictions can untangle a vision for sustainable development. The industry's experience with biotechnology is provided as evidence of how abandoning long-term vision in the interests of shareholder value may itself be a threat to corporate sustainability, even when 'sustainable development' has slipped off the public's radar.

CIBA-GEIGY

Ciba-Geigy was formed by the merger in 1970 of CIBA and J. R.

Geigy, two venerable Swiss pharmaceutical and chemical companies, with historic roots in dyestuffs which date back to the eighteenth century. Ciba-Geigy became Novartis in 1996 after merging with another old Swiss firm, Sandoz. The life science format has since been abandoned; in 2000 Novartis divested agro-chemicals and seeds as Syngenta, formed from the merger of Novartis Agribusiness and Zeneca Agrochemicals. Syngenta globally ranks first in crop protection, and third in the high-value commercial seeds market. Sales in 2001 were approximately US $6.3 billion. Syngenta employs more than 20,000 people in over fifty countries. The company is 'committed to sustainable agriculture through innovative Research and Technology'.

Between 1942, when Paul Müller working for J. R. Geigy discovered DDT's insecticidal properties, and 1999, when Novartis withdrew from production of its most toxic organophosphate insecticides, Ciba-Geigy's agricultural business was built around controversial chemicals. The issue managers had to struggle to support the cash-cow insecticides such as monocrotophos, and the herbicide atrazine, which began appearing in European drinking water supplies in the 1980s. A huge research effort has been committed to the discovery of selective and safe replacements that would not end up in water, would not harm beneficial insects and wildlife, and would have low mammalian toxicity.

The company was nevertheless sensitive to public opinion, having lived through a damaging and expensive scandal over its failure to withdraw the anti-diarrhoeal drug clioquinol from the market (Hansson, 1989), and having a continual drip of pesticides issues, including accusations of spraying children in Egypt with the DDT successor Galecron. The company took these criticisms seriously. Being head-quartered in one of the most environmentally conscious societies in the world, Switzerland, Ciba-Geigy was having acceptance problems on its own doorstep. It was becoming difficult to find top-quality employees from Switzerland prepared to work for the company, especially in the pesticides businesses.

Ciba-Geigy has been a longstanding actor and commentator on Third World development issues, with its own Ciba-Geigy Foundation for Third World Development (now Syngenta Foundation for Sustainable Agriculture).[2]

VISION 2000 — THE TRIPLE BOTTOM LINE

Ciba-Geigy's 'Vision 2000' grew out of an atmosphere of declining public acceptance. The chemical industry was facing unprecedented hostility following the poisoning of the Rhine in 1986 by the Sandoz warehouse fire, and the explosion at Union Carbide's plant in Bhopal India in 1984. Pesticides were under attack worldwide, and the mid- to late 1980s probably marked a record low point in the legitimacy of the chemical industry. At the same time, there was increased engagement by industry in the pre-Rio sustainable development debate, led by the Swiss industrialist Stephan Schmidheiny and the Business Council for Sustainable Development, an elite international grouping of business leaders that included Ciba-Geigy's then president, Dr Alex Krauer (Schmidheiny, 1992).

Vision 2000 was an early incarnation of the 'triple bottom line'.[3] It states simply: 'We want to ensure the prosperity of our enterprise into the next millennium by striking a balance between our economic, environmental, and social responsibilities' (Ciba-Geigy, 1992). These responsibilities were described as 'equal ranking' in the company's literature. Alex Krauer wrote in the *Ciba-Geigy Journal*: 'Businesses which are unable to recognize the signs of the times, or cling to outmoded attitudes and behaviour patterns because of technical or financial deficiencies, are fated to become the victims of the structural changes which environmental necessity has thrust upon us' (Krauer, 1992). In the 1991 annual report, Krauer and Ciba-Geigy chairman Heini Lippuner stated that Vision 2000 'provides forward-looking competitive advantages, without which sustainable success in a world of social and environmental change will no longer be possible'.

Vision 2000 stressed engagement 'in an open dialogue with the public'. As early as 2 October 1989, Krauer told the magazine *Der Spiegel* that, in agriculture, 'a "pact of reason" is necessary. What is required is a new solidarity between industry, the community and public officials … Even in the delicate area of biotechnology,' Krauer continued later in the interview, 'it is a matter of obtaining a societal consensus as to what should be allowed and what should be forbidden.' In this flurry of interviews and speeches[4] that were to be condensed into Vision 2000, Krauer spoke of entrepreneurial and socio-political goals becoming identical. 'Then', he said, 'society will again consider our entrepreneurial activities appropriate and meaningful, which are the prerequisites for acceptance. Beyond supply and demand, we have to be seen as serving people and society, instead of degenerating into something that is an end in itself.'

THE FARMER SUPPORT TEAM

Ciba-Geigy's pesticide business in developing countries had traditionally been based on large contracts with government projects, aid programmes and parastatal marketing boards such as the Sudan Gezira Board. A 'big project' paradigm grew around these large contracts in the late 1960s and 1970s, based on aerial applications of insecticides,[5] and lived on in the company even as the real world of small farm agriculture was changing. By the late 1980s, many parastatals were being broken up or privatized in response to economic reforms and structural adjustment programmes. There emerged a market of millions of small farmers making independent pest-control decisions under conditions of imperfect information and weak extension systems, served by distribution systems that involved huge numbers of salesmen from the multinationals and local formulators, marketing via independent pesticide dealers. Pakistan, the Philippines, Bangladesh and Indonesia were among the countries where Ciba-Geigy put these systems into place. The sales force had incentives for meeting targets, and received US-style training in selling skills. Ciba-Geigy was rewarded with market dominance in these countries.

I had joined the company in 1985, with a background in insect ecology, including two years in Malaysia researching problems associated with pesticide use in rice. This research was supported in part by Ciba-Geigy, and their products were among those tested for unwanted side effects on rice pests and their predators.

To a new employee in the company with an interest in peasant farming, this status quo was uncomfortable. Sales of organophosphates with the highest World Health Organization acute toxicity ranking in developing countries was becoming an issue, and epidemiological data were starting to point to the chronic health costs of their misuse (e.g. Loevinsohn, 1987; Pingali et al., 1994). The FAO Code of Conduct[6] was raising stakeholder expectations of industry commitment to reducing pesticide exposure and risk to farmers in developing countries. Companies and their industry association GIFAP (now CropLife International) were facing an uphill struggle of 'training' smallholder farmers in the safe use of pesticides, with advice based on measures (gloves, mask, respirator, visor, aprons and so on) which are in practice completely inappropriate from both a climatic and an economic perspective. The concept of Integrated Pest Management (IPM) based around an ecosystem concept rather than a 'pest wars' mentality, was beginning to make important headway in the public sector thanks to a committed group of rice ecologists and educators associated with the FAO and the International Rice Research Institute. The pesticide industry was being painted as a major constraint to IPM implementation, having scoffed at the concept throughout the 1970s and much of the 1980s, and having distorted the term towards integrated pest*icide* management (Thrupp, 1996).

Within Ciba-Geigy, IPM was seen by enlightened research and development staff as the future for pest control, though primarily as a market for new selective chemistry rather than a systematic business transition from pest control to ecosystem management. Meanwhile, the marketing of existing products proceeded as usual. I felt that this construction of environmental challenges only as a new product opportunity ignored the following facts: (i) farmers in developing countries continued to rely on older established products; (ii) use recommendations for those products were stuck in pre-IPM language, such as 'spray every 14 days once pests are first seen'; (iii) some of these old products were moderately selective and 'IPM-compatible'; (iv) the new generation of highly selective chemistry would be priced out of the reach of the vast majority of smallholders.

In the late 1980s, sections within the company were receptive to the need for reforming Ciba-Geigy's approach to IPM and small farmer sectors, and major resources were made available to me to develop a better understanding of the economics and ecology of using the company's products in small farmer cropping systems, especially in rice. This information was a good foundation for the Farmer Support Team (FST), which was approved by the management committee of Ciba-Geigy's Plant Protection Division in January 1991.

My efforts to establish a dedicated team to build small farmer skills in Integrated Pest Management (IPM) and safe use of pesticides had failed twice under the old pre-Vision 2000 order. The eventual approval of the establishment of a Farmer Support Team in 1991 demonstrates clearly how Vision 2000 ushered in a new fertile environment for innovation. The approved project proposal comprised a headquarters staff of three, an annual budget of SFr 2 million (about US $1.4 million) and matching funds from participating affiliate companies.

Our FST had humbler ambitions than taking Ciba-Geigy to the Promised Land of sustainable development. It was conceived to bring environmental and ethical product stewardship to small farmers in developing countries, and thereby to develop these markets qualitatively. The objective of the FST was to approach these small farmer markets as opportunities to build farmers' skills in maximizing the benefits and minimizing the risks from pest and pesticide management, and thereby to gain advantages in the marketplace and acceptance in society at large.

By helping to build small farmers' skills in IPM, the FST could fold in concepts of safety and application within an overall 'more benefits, fewer risks' message. This was a big break from traditional industry 'safe use' projects, which continue to promote safe handling of pesticides with very little evidence of sustained behavioural change. The FST was not embarrassed to call itself a marketing strategy, though one aimed at qualitative rather than quantitative growth.

In areas of unsustainable pesticide overuse, such as highland vegetable production, the FST sought actively to *reduce* market volume in order to slow or prevent the costly 'treadmill' of overuse and the rapid build-up of chemical resistance in key insects and fungi. Ideally, the frequent use of often highly toxic products at high application volume could, through training, be replaced with precise application of selective products in conjunction with non-chemical means of insect and disease prevention. Farmers and farm labourers were trained in pest ecology, the recognition of natural enemies, economic thresholds, pesticide application and safety. In low-input crops such as maize and millet, the FST stressed plant health and good agronomy before resources were spent on crop protection chemicals.

Once the FST was staffed and the concept developed, a request for proposals was sent out to all Ciba-Geigy affiliate companies with plant protection business interests, outlining the philosophy of the FST, and offering co-financing over five years and technical and organizational support to develop FST projects in their countries. From the many proposals received, nine were approved, three in Asia, two in Latin America and three in Africa. Local teams were formed and a series of annual workshops – whose participants included many non-Ciba resource personnel – allowed a global organization to be quickly built.

The FST saw itself as a temporary, devolved learning organization. The focus on small farmers in developing countries was seen as the first phase in a larger, longer campaign to test the 'IPM Plus' strategy throughout the company's operations. Building skills in affiliate companies was a break with Ciba-Geigy's centralized service operations, and allowed the FST to bypass a tradition of top-down management. Cost sharing by the affiliates developed a strong sense of local ownership. Use of consultants from outside Ciba's area of core experience allowed the import of knowledge and skills into a company that had, through its tradition of life-long employment, become intellectually inbred.

Thanks to the FST staff, impacts in the field were often rapid. In Indonesia, for example, a group of trained vegetable farmers surveyed in 1994 had been able to reduce application frequency from ten treatments at high volume to between four and eight treatments at low-medium volume. In Pakistan, only one case of pesticide poisoning was reported to doctors in the FST area in 1993, as compared with sixty-seven in an equivalent area without FST intervention. In the Dominican Republic, there was a genuine turnaround in the prospects for sustainable pest and disease management in the infamous Constanza valley.

The FST was not without criticisms of 'greenwash' (Greer and Bruno, 1996). This was, after all, an industry with a low and declining public legitimacy. A legacy of opposing or co-opting IPM (Vorley and Keeney, 1998b) had foreclosed on a whole range of opportunities for collaboration with key stakeholders. Our team also made some mistakes: we should have insisted on external auditing, and at least one FST project engaged in dubious partnerships with local academics in support of questionable 'IPM' recommendations. Generally, though, the programme created a new attitude in Ciba-Geigy to a farm sector that had been considered as issue-rich and profit-poor.

SUSTAINING THE FARMER SUPPORT TEAM IN A PERIOD OF RAPID CHANGE

The first big challenge to the Farmer Support Team came soon after its creation, when another cornerstone of Vision 2000 – the separation of the divisions into semi-autonomous business units (in the case of Plant Protection, into Insect Control, Weed Control, Disease Control and Seed Treatment Business Units) – was implemented. With financial transparency, it became clear that the smallest business unit, Insect Control, was expected to shoulder the financial burden of the FST, since FST was seen as most central to managing issues with their 'black cow'[7] products. Weed Control and Disease Control managers saw little benefit from the FST, having a different set of issues from those addressed by a focus on IPM and safety. Developing countries were rather trivial as a proportion of their total sales, and even then business was concentrated on the plantation rather than smallholder sector. Business unit leaders outside Insect Control began to demand hard short-term market development goals in exchange for continued funding.

In order to diversify funding from within the company, a presentation was made to the board of the Ciba-Geigy Foundation for Third World Co-operation, requesting matching funds in support of the FST. The proposal was rejected, with board members commenting that the Foundation 'was not there to fund what company Divisions should be doing already'.

In early 1993, there was a shock in the division. The division leader, who had vigorously championed the implementation of Vision 2000 within the division through courageous targets for biological and IPM-compatible products, was replaced by a turnaround specialist, latterly of the Plastics and Additives Division. Shareholder pressure was at work. Clearly the division's high costs, especially labour, were a drag on shareholder value. There was a growing feeling within the division that the financial responsibility of the Vision 2000 triad was 'more equal' than the social and environmental goals.

The Farmer Support Team was one of the first easy targets. One year after the team had received huge exposure in the glossy annual report (Ciba-Geigy, 1992) and when the success of the FST was being hailed in internal company media (Ciba-Geigy, 1994a, 1994b), business unit leaders seemed prepared to abandon the concept. These pressures were also felt in local divisions, and staff from Pakistan to Colombia began to see FST as a risky career option. The team was saved by a deliberate guerrilla tactic of bringing the international team members to the Basle headquarters, and directly confronting senior management with the benefits of FST activities. A direct appeal to rescue this child of Vision 2000 was also made to Dr Krauer.

The FST is still active around the world, and with new leadership has managed to achieve some institutional stability. The concept has been regionalized, expanded and applied as a way of doing business, and the FST has taken on the task of challenging mind-set in the company's functions and structure. But frustration within Syngenta about the apparent gap between the corporate vision of sustainable agriculture and the reality of reduced investments in the sector has continued, illustrated by the departure of two key personnel in the past year.

VISION 2000 IN THE YEAR 2002

Over a decade since the launching of Vision 2000, the 'prosperity of the enterprise' was 'ensured' only by cutting off one of Ciba-Geigy's life science legs – the Agricultural Division – as Syngenta, the 'world's first dedicated agribusiness company'.

Despite the hype, it is clear that the Agricultural Division was dropped from the core pharmaceuticals business because of a steep decline in the strategic value of pesticides, seeds and crop biotechnology, and a perception that, as a maturing industry, the agricultural business would be a drag on the performance of the Pharmaceutical Division. Syngenta has continued sharp reductions in its global workforce on top of the 1,100 job losses announced by Novartis in the June 1999 'project focus' and the 3,000 from the restructuring carried out after the merger with Sandoz in 1996. Vision 2000 has disappeared from the company's communications. There is no monitoring of success in meeting the goals of the vision. Instead of a company-wide commitment, enquiries about sustainable development are now channelled to the largely philanthropic Syngenta Foundation for Sustainable Agriculture.

VISION 2000 IN HINDSIGHT

Why was Vision 2000 such a potentially short-lived window of innovation in building more sustainable business practices?

Vision 2000 was a strictly top-down affair. All employees were sent on training courses where, through a series of videos and exercises, we 'got' the vision. I found this idea of jumping through hoops to be highly patronizing, and had worked up quite a head of steam by the end of the 'training' programme. Surely, I thought, effective vision was built up from the grassroots of a company, rather than delivered by trickling down the organizational pyramid, from top management to laboratory assistants. But while there were many cynical remarks about Vision 2000, few if any of my colleagues shared my concerns about how it was delivered.

Weisbord and Janoff (1995: 36) describe a similar experience of a 'visioning exercise' undertaken by a large company:

> One troubled corporate giant planned to put thousands of people through a training event staged by a prestigious business institute, incorporating every new idea on customers, markets, service and empowerment. To the proposal of several staff that the company should substitute future searches – on the theory that the people could get the company out of the box if given a chance – top management turned a deaf ear. Nobody could imagine anything useful happening that wasn't prescribed by experts. The chance that people might *do* exactly what was needed, or that collectively they had enough skills and knowledge, was far outside the frame of reference in the executive suite.

Vision 2000 was foisted on a company with an extreme uniformity of perspective, partly achieved through a culture that separated employees' personal values from their professional positions and rhetoric (Cairncross, 1995). Uniformity of perspective was actually increasing, because of the very low rate of recruitment into this mature industry. Organizations with uniformity of perspective are characterized by a tendency to search for the familiar when faced with ambiguity and uncertainty (Knowles and Saxberg, 1988).

The Plant Protection Division translated Vision 2000 as a shift from hard pesticides to soft pesticides (selective chemicals and 'natural' compounds), and pointed a fundamentally unchanged operation – chemists, toxicologists, product managers, salespeople and issues managers – in that direction. Vision 2000 was merely a course correction on an unquestioned voyage of pest control; the researchers kept researching, the salesmen selling, the lobbyists lobbying. The FST was, in retrospect, approved as an issues management exercise and a bridge to keep old products alive until the newer products started generating good revenue. Had there been no 'black cow' products, there probably would have been no FST.

At the corporate level, Vision 2000 was translated into the eco-efficiency of production processes. It was thus the domain of the Corporate Safety and Environment Division, focusing on clean production of the existing product range (fewer 'bads'). Corporate Environmental Reports, published since 1993, are the stuff of process engineering: energy savings, CFC emissions, waste reduction and emergency response.

Vision 2000 appeared to be a statement for what the company *didn't* want to be (a big, bad chemical company), rather than a view of what it wanted to be, based on strategic renewal of the underlying theory of the company.

By the mid-1990s, Ciba's corporate vision already looked like a brief *affaire*, cut short by the austere interventions of financial institutions and the need to generate short-term returns to push through merger plans and compete for investor finance against soaring hi-tech stocks. An interview by the magazine *CASH* in 1999 with Thomas Dyllick, professor of environmental management at the University of St Gallen in Switzerland (Müller and Vontobel, 1999), spelled out how corporate visions for sustainability are trumped by the immediate and overriding need to enhance shareholder value:

CASH: In enterprises today, environmental matters no longer have the same value as in the eighties. A consequence of the recession or changing values?

DYLLICK: I believe that there has been a generational change. Environmental activities in the enterprises are linked strongly to the consciousness and commitment of the top management. One must realise that their priorities have changed. Share performance has become the all-dominating yardstick, and the new bosses orient themselves very much more strongly to it than their predecessors. In recent years environmental activities were clearly scaled back. They are content with a moderate performance.

CASH: How is this manifested?

DYLLICK: The environmental job positions were thinned out, the people were retired or they became independent advisors, there are fewer resources for environmental protection. There is also clearly less management attention. Think of the Vision 2000, developed for Ciba-Geigy by Alex Krauer after Schweizerhalle.[8] Ecological and social targets were set across the whole enterprise. Such a thing does not happen these days.

CASH: Must dead fish once more float down the river?

DYLLICK: I do not wish for that. But it would surely increase attention again.

VISIONS FOR SUSTAINABLE DEVELOPMENT AND THE BIOTECHNOLOGY EXPERIENCE

The struggle to protect and 'mainstream' the Farmer Support Team is after all a small story in a large company. Except for occasional star billing in company literature, the world of Ciba-Geigy hardly noticed the team. But I judge the industry's failures in the development of crop biotechnology to derive from exactly the same set of circumstances: namely, the failure to create an appropriate vision of sustainable development due to uniformity of perspective, and the failure to talk the visionary talk due to pressures of maintaining shareholder value. Far from being trivial, mistakes with crop biotechnology are the key factors behind the dramatic drop in the strategic value of agribusiness sectors within life science enterprises which led to Novartis's disengagement from agriculture.[9]

Until wide literacy is built within a company, even the most enlightened top-down vision will be based on a narrow set of opinions, usually with the old filters of uniform perspective in place. The experience of Monsanto is especially relevant here. Under the banner of 'doing well by doing good', Robert Shapiro, CEO of Monsanto from 1995 to 2001, established a vision for the company based on a narrow view of sustainable development. Shapiro's perspective of the coming breakpoint or discontinuity in the crop protection business was that the chemical industry was becoming obsolete, and that biotechnology would rescue society from the 'more food from less land' dilemma. Shapiro apparently surrounded himself with a handful of like-minded biotechnology enthusiasts, so there were few voices in that inner circle to provide a reality check (Kilman and Burton, 1999). This is reminiscent of the failed ventures by ICI and BP in the 1970s to develop manufactured protein sources in the belief that world hunger was due to a shortage of protein.

A wider vision, based on a concept of sustainable development that grows out of new literacy, cross-fertilization at the grassroots and an understanding of the whole agrifood system, may have seen the breakpoint very differently and predicted the folly of a top-down research-driven vision (Vorley and Keeney, 1998a). These wider forces include a shift in political influence in the agrifood chain from farming to consumer sectors, the emergence of environmental liability issues around biotechnology, deteriorating faith in science and the globalization of advocacy.

The events since 1995 are well known (see Harvey, ch. 4, and Vellema, ch. 3). Unlike the directors of Ciba-Geigy, Shapiro acted boldly on his vision, and for a couple of years took Wall Street along with him. But by the end of 1999, Monsanto was a humbled force. Subsumed into Pharmacia & Upjohn (now the Pharmacia Corporation), Monsanto's pharmaceutical division Searle has been asset-stripped, and the agricultural business has become a separate business, with part sold off.

Stuart Hart, business professor at the University of North Carolina, points to how Monsanto's operational processes undermined the vision. Hart considers that Shapiro was naïve to believe that if you simply put out a vision, people would get behind it. 'Monsanto paraded a lot of sustainability stars [such as Paul Hawken] through its corridors,' says Hart, 'but the rank and file never internalized what the stars had to say.' Hart concludes that duties at Monsanto 'were flying in all directions, sometimes 180° away from the sustainability cause. Tactics like hiring detectives to spy on farmers were clearly at odds with the driving vision. And the company's inability to listen was pathological' (Frankel, 2000).

Indeed, Monsanto had managed to ostracize just about all of its key stakeholders. At the same time as it was promoting its GM technology as feeding the hungry and saving the environment, Monsanto appeared to be attempting to (i) wrest control of the world's seed stock, and then render the seeds of those crops sterile so that they could not be collected and saved; (ii) gag media criticism; (iii) threaten farmers with legal redress if they replanted farm-saved GM; (iv) indoctrinate Europeans about the benefits of GM technology, with a huge PR campaign; and (v) play trade hard-ball with the European Union over acceptance of their GM products.

Drawing on Monsanto's experience, Carl Frankel (2000) points to the need to 'align company vision with organisation structures and incentives, communications and empowerment strategies. Unless vision is integrated with strategy, it will wither.'

Consultant Paul Gidding says:

> Monsanto didn't get into trouble because sustainability was a core strategy or because it had a high profile around the issue. The company's problems stemmed from its failure to integrate business strategy and sustainability. Shapiro had a vision around sustainability – a 'new economy' idea. But he didn't have a 'new economy' strategy for making it happen. Monsanto applied 'old economy' ideas – PR campaigns, government power relationships and the like ... Until companies realize sustainability is not just a bunch of new product ideas but a new way of doing business, they will continue to fail. (Frankel, 2000)

Ciba-Geigy, though less aggressive by comparison than Monsanto, also forgot its Vision 2000 pledge on obtaining a societal consensus around biotechnology. By 1996, word on the street was that 'Companies like Monsanto and Ciba-Geigy have begun to act as though people are a peculiar irritant to their achievement of their aims of making money from selling [biotechnology] products to farmers.'[10]

VISION 2000 AND SUSTAINABLE AGRICULTURE

The failure of Ciba-Geigy's Vision 2000 to create an organizational culture of learning and innovation around sustainable development, aside from a few fragile initiatives like the Farmer Support Team, is reflected in the events of 1993 and early 1994 when the Plant Protection Division faced a much more complex challenge: to respond to the emerging rubric of *sustainable agriculture*. The shrinking of opportunities for innovation and out-breeding in relation to the demise and compromise of Vision 2000 meant that the experience of the Farmer Support Team failed to influence the role that Ciba-Geigy in particular and agribusiness in general are playing in sustainable agriculture.

Uniformity of perspective meant that searching for the familiar within 'sustainable agriculture' was leading Ciba-Geigy into a very narrow, self-justifying orthodoxy. Low-input farming is low-yield farming. Efficient agriculture is sustainable agriculture. First World farmers are famine fighters. Plant protection is food protection. The next era of crop protection will be high-technology 'precision' agriculture and protection via the seed with biotechnology. The public is irrational and needs to be nursed out of its misconceptions through 'effective communication'. Statements on sustainable agriculture were caught up in avoiding unsustainability rather than promoting sustainability. Sustainability seemed to be a pet that everyone wanted to stroke but nobody wanted to feed. When it was discussed, it was seen as an issue that might affect the company's business, rather than an objective around which business should be realigned.

I was of the opinion that Ciba-Geigy must throw its net forwards and wide to catch the right approach and the right 'products', in order to be able to realign its activities to remain economically and politically healthy in the decades ahead. We could then see the sustainable agriculture movement not as a threat to our future business but as our future business opportunity. In autumn of 1993 I was approached by the company to lead a project on sustainable agriculture, involving extensive interviews with key 'influencers', the movers and shakers of sustainable agriculture. I was disappointed to learn how closely the goals of this work revolved around issues management and sustainability as a threat to business, rather than sustainability as an opportunity. In the turmoil of restructuring and a 'back to basics' philosophy, there was neither the opportunity to commit personnel and resources to speculative future-oriented activities which were not related to core business, nor the credibility to collaborate closely with other institutions working in sustainable agriculture. Vision 2000 seemed a long way off. It was primarily this failure that caused me to resign from Ciba-Geigy at the end of January 1994, after over eight years with the company.

THE FARMER SUPPORT TEAM IN CONTEXT

Thanks to Vision 2000, the Farmer Support Team, as a temporary, parallel organization within a large multinational agribusiness, encouraged creative thinking and developed a cadre of people who had the potential to assist the organization to move from chaos to order as it began a new phase of its existence (Knowles and Saxberg, 1988). But the FST organization, at least up to 1994, had not transformed the corporation. This may in part have been due to the 'hair shirt' phenomenon (Richardson, 1992) in which a closed group of committed people hog the action and salve the conscience of the system, but leave most people out. This form of organization can thus be a constraint to systematic merging of personal and professional ideas across a company, as they can politicize rather than democratize ideals.

But the main constraint to the FST was also the main constraint to Vision 2000; that is, that a general vision for sustainable development that excludes the majority of its workforce and does not challenge the underlying theory of the company is itself unsustainable. Such a vision cannot survive internal or external shocks, such as a merger or the loss of key products.

In the case of Ciba-Geigy, a weak vision was imposed on a company within a mature, consolidating industry, with devolved management, uniformity of perspective and short-term financial objectives. Under these conditions

- new ideas and their promoters are under very high short-term pressure to succeed
- fluctuating signals from management make it dangerous to run with a long-term concept
- managers are afraid to associate themselves with groups not focused on the 'key product/key country' status quo
- there is no time for strategic thinking
- non-core objectives such as sustainable development are sidelined to industry associations or marginal 'hair shirt' groups, or are retrofitted on to the status quo

The industry is therefore weakened, and becomes progressively less courageous as it heads towards generic commodity status.

NOTES

1. 'Life science' is 'a technological platform that includes complementary pharmaceutical, chemical, and biotechnological capabilities' (see Kalaitzandonakes, 1998; Vorley, 1999).

2. <www.syngentafoundation.com>

3. Concern with not only the traditional bottom line of profitability, but also goals related to environmental protection and meeting social needs (see Utting, 2000).

4. Opening lecture at the 15th Autumn Seminar of the Ciba-Geigy Central Research Laboratories, 16 October 1989. See also A. Krauer, 'Plädoyer für den gesunden Menschenverstand: Ökologie im Verbund mit qualitativem und quantitativem Wachstum', *Neue Zürcher Zeitung*, 24/25 March 1990: 26.

5. The BIMAS Project in Java, Indonesia (1968 to *ca.* 1970), in which 400,000 ha of smallholder rice paddies were treated by twelve planes with the insecticide diazinon; the Gezira Cotton Project in the Gezira irrigation scheme in Sudan (1968 to *ca.* 1978) in which up to 75,000 ha of cotton farmed by tenant cultivators were

treated with DDT and then monocrotophos (with DDT mixtures and Nogos as emergency back-ups) (CIBA, 1968); the 'Taona Zina' Project in Madagascar (1982 to *ca.* 1984). The Gezira project, which at its peak in 1976/77 employed sixty-three expatriates, 300 local staff using seventy cars, fourteen planes, and applied 750 tons of insecticide (Ciba-Geigy, 1977), failed due to the ecological inflexibility of 'big project' methods. Pest control failed due to pesticide resistance and the emergence of uncontrollable secondary pests, especially the whitefly *Bemesia tabaci*. The Madagascar project fell foul of different interpretations of IPM between Ciba-Geigy and the Swiss academic partner, but the Ciba-Geigy Foundation for Third World Co-operation continued to justify the intervention from an benefit-cost standpoint (Leisinger, 1986).

6. In 1985 the FAO adopted the International Code of Conduct on the Distribution and Use of Pesticides to raise industry marketing and distribution practices.

7. Typology of Beaumont et al. (1993).

8. The Sandoz warehouse fire at Schweizerhalle near Basle in November 1996, which severely damaged biota in the Rhine for at least 400 km.

9. Other factors that brought down the agribusiness star were: (i) a downturn in the global farm economy forced deep price competition in the pesticides business. The relentless slide of power and profits down the agrifood chain to processing and especially retail sectors meant that suppliers to farming were in a cost-price squeeze familiar to their farming customers; (ii) a wave of mergers and consolidation in the pharmaceutical industry meant that, in order to match competitors such as Merck and Glaxo Wellcome, life science companies were struggling to focus on improving the profitability of their pharmaceutical businesses, which typically had operating margins running at three times that of agro-chemicals. It was clear to many observers of the industry that the agro-chemical business itself was not sustainable.

10. *Independent*, 21 October 1996.

REFERENCES

Beaumont, J. R., L. M. Pedersen and B. D. Whitaker (1993) *Managing the Environment*. Oxford: Butterworth-Heinemann.

Cairncross, F. (1995) *Green, Inc.* London: Earthscan.

CIBA (1968) 'Island in the Sand', *CIBA Journal* 44/1967–68: 14–17. Basle, Switzerland: CIBA Ltd.

Ciba-Geigy (1977) 'Das Gezira-Baumwollproject', *Ciba-Geigy Magazine* 4/77: 22–5.

— (1992) *Annual Report 1991*. Basle, Switzerland: Ciba-Geigy AG.

— (1994a) 'Das Farmer Support Team der Division Pflanzenschutz', *Ciba Streiflichter* 1. Basel Switerzland: Ciba Communications, Ciba-Geigy AG.

— (1994b) 'Umweltgerechter und ganzheitlicher Pflanzenbau auch ausserhalb von Europa', *Ciba-Zeiting* 3/94: 18–19.

Edwards, D. (1995) *Free to be Human: Intellectual Self-defence in an Age of Illusions*. Totnes: Resurgence Books.

Frankel, C. (2000) 'Food, Health and Still Hopeful', *Tomorrow* March/April 2000: 6–8.

Greer, J. and K. Bruno (1996) *Greenwash: The Reality Behind Corporate Environmentalism*. Croton-on-Hudson, NY: Third World Network & APEX Press.

Hansson, O. (1989) *Inside Ciba-Geigy*. Penang, Malaysia: International Organization of Consumers' Unions.

Kalaitzandonakes, N. (1998) 'Biotechnology and the Restructuring of the Agricultural Supply Chain', *AgBioForum* 1 (2). <http://www.agbioforum.missouri.edu/agbioforum/vol1no2/>

Kilman, S. and T. M. Buton (1999) 'Biotech Backlash is Battering Plan Shapiro Thought was Enlightened', *Wall Street Journal*, 21 December 1999.

Knowles, H. P. and B. O. Saxberg (1988) 'Organisational Leadership of Planned and Unplanned Change: A Systems Approach to Organisational Viability', *Futures* 20: 252–65.

Krauer, A. (1992) 'Sustainable Development – A Window of Opportunity for Progressive Companies', *Ciba-Geigy Journal* 2: 6–11.

Leisinger, K. (1986) 'Multinational Companies and Agricultural Development. A Case Study of "Taona Zina" in Madagascar', *Food Policy* 12: 227–41.

Loevinsohn, M. E. (1987) 'Insecticide Use and Increased Mortality in Rural Central Luzon', *Lancet* 8546: 1359–62.

Müller, A. and W. Vontobel (1999) 'Interview "Wir müssen handeln, diskutiert haben wir lange genug": Thomas Dyllick über Umweltmanagement und die vernachlässigten Potenziale im Umweltschutz', *Cash* 18, 7 May: 49.

Pingali, P., C. Marquez and F. Palis (1994) 'Pesticides and Philippine Rice Farmer Health: A Medical and Economic Analysis', *American Journal of Agricultural Economics* 76: 587–92.

Richardson, T. (1992) 'Leading Search Conferences: Reflections on Managing the Process', in M. R. Weisbord (ed.), *Discovering Common Ground*, pp. 317–24. San Francisco, CA: Berrett-Koehler.

Schmidheiny, S. and the BCSD (1992) *Changing Course: A Global Business Perspective on Development and the Environment*. Cambridge, MA, and London UK: MIT Press.

Thrupp, L. A. (1996) *New Partnerships for Sustainable Agriculture*. Washington, DC: World Resources Institute.

Utting, P. (2000) *Business Responsibility for Sustainable Development*, United Nations Research Institute for Social Development Occasional Paper no. 5, Geneva: UNRISD.

Weisbord, M. R. and S. Janoff (1995) *Future Search: An Action Guide to Finding Common Ground in Organisations and Communities*. San Francisco, CA: Berrett-Koehler.

Vorley, W. T. (1999) *Thirty Cabbages: Greening the Agricultural 'Life Science' Industry*, Gatekeeper Series no. 82. London: International Institute for Environment and Development.

Vorley, W. and D. Keeney (eds) (1998a) *Bugs in the System: Redesigning the Pesticide Industry for Sustainable Agriculture*. London: Earthscan.

Vorley, W. and D. Keeney (1998b) 'Solving for Pattern', in W. Vorley and D. Keeney (eds), *Bugs in the System: Redesigning the Pesticide Industry for Sustainable Agriculture*, pp. 193–215. London: Earthscan.

THREE | Monsanto facing uncertain futures: immobile artefacts, financial constraints and public acceptance of technological change

SIETZE VELLEMA

§ Technology plays an ambiguous role in achieving sustainable development: it has the potential for solving serious environmental problems and it has already been demonstrated to be a major source of environmental problems (Schot, 2001). Analogously, agribusiness, as a major driver of technology development in food and agriculture, has the potential both to bring environmental progress and to produce harm to the environment. Hence, for understanding the relationship between technology and sustainable development it is relevant to investigate how agribusiness firms manage technical change. The analysis in this chapter, with a particular focus on the rise and fall of the American agro-chemical multinational company Monsanto, intends to disclose a pattern for how agribusiness firms manage the many-sided process of technical change.

Monsanto's strategy and technologies led to a fierce public debate about the preferred technological direction for realizing sustainability in agriculture and food. The actual introduction of Monsanto's techno-logical products led to public criticism on the supposed radical impact and risks of the technology and revealed contrasting perspectives on the desired futures and the value of technological novelty. This chap-ter, however, does not intend to solve the contradictions surrounding biotechnology and genetic engineering. Rather it takes an interest in investigating how real companies construct technologies and shape the world. The position taken in this chapter is that, in contrast to enter-ing the ideological debate on which technology is better or worse, we should explore how technological progress is restricted by technological, financial, institutional and cultural boundaries (cf. Basalla, 1988).

In the late 1980s and increasingly in the 1990s, a number of agro-chemical companies adopted a strategy to transform their enterprises into life science industries. Their strategic considerations were largely steered by the wish to materialize the opportunities offered by genetic engineering and biotechnology. The agro-chemical companies aimed high: both in terms of corporate profits and in terms of societal benefits brought by new technologies. In the publicity and fanfare accompanying new agro-biotechnologies, leading life science companies such as Monsanto and Astra Zeneca constantly emphasized the potentials of biotechnology for protecting the environment, providing healthier food and medical applications and securing access to food for people in developing countries. Monsanto's ambition was to contribute to a sustainable level of food provision for the world's rapidly growing population by integrating established technologies such as herbicide use and breeding techniques with advanced biotechnology. In October 2000, the company's website <www.monsanto.com>, it stated that many of its products aimed at helping farmers to produce improved crops – crops that yield more and better food – while at the same time limiting the resource consumption and strains on the environment that accompany traditional agricultural production methods.

Monsanto's corporate executive officer in the 1990s, Robert Shapiro, was an outspoken proponent of exploiting biotechnology's capacity to 'revolutionize agricultural practices'. He reasoned that, if used well, the combination of information technology and biotechnology could accomplish the abolition of hunger and the lightening of the environmental burden in our society. Shapiro was considered to be a pioneer in the evolving life science industry and was jokingly baptized the Bill Gates of biotechnology. He strongly believed something similar to what had happened in the IT-sector could occur in the biotechnology industry due to a combination of improved scientific research about genes, the seemingly endless number of possibilities for genetic modification and the increased capacity to process and use genetic information (i.e. genomics).

To achieve these ambitious goals, Monsanto adopted what can be called a linear model of innovation. In this model (see Figure 3.1), science provides the basics for new technologies that, eventually, will serve the market with new uses and improved practices and provide consumers with improved and acceptable (food) products. To expand its own competencies, Monsanto had to acquire a large number of biotechnology and seed companies for which it borrowed large sums of money in the stock markets. In its efforts to convince investors of its life science paradigm, Monsanto sketched a bright future of the technological path it had taken. Monsanto formulated this strategic paradigm at the intersection of the accumulation of technological capability, competitive behaviour and its organizational design (Metcalfe and Boden, 1992).

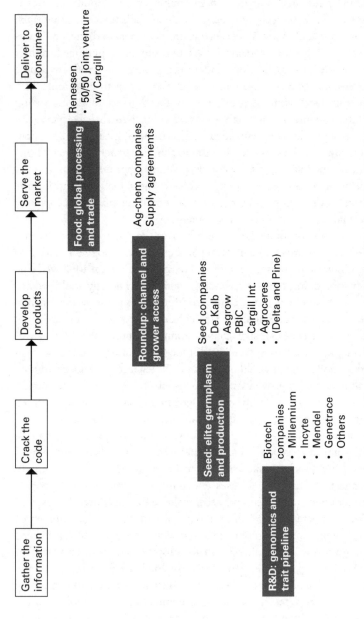

FIGURE 3.1 Monsanto: a linear model of innovation combined with a series of acquisitions.
Source: <www.monsanto.com> (March 2000).

The following analysis of Monsanto's proactive management of technological change centres on three areas relevant for the realization and commercial exploitation of new technical products. First, to substantiate its claim of improving environmental performance in agriculture and human health in food provision, the company had to come up with convincingly 'better' technologies or tools that out-competed existing technologies in the eyes of users of agro-biotechnologies, mainly farmers and consumers of food products. To this end, it had to build new technological capabilities, to acquire skills and to translate biological and technical knowledge into commercially viable commodities. Second, Monsanto had to create financial and political alliances in order to be able to purchase and link a range of mainly seed companies and biotechnology venture enterprises to its new strategy. It had to convince investors of the probability of profits, cost reductions and efficiency gains. And, finally, the company had to find an acceptable institutional modality for introducing and diffusing its new technological products into society. Here, the company entered the terrain where its internally formulated technological agenda had to interact with the external selection environment.

For the analysis of technical change it is relevant to emphasize that technology is not merely a tool rooted in a set of (routine) activities that transform raw materials or, in the case of agriculture (Benton, 1989), regulate biological transformation processes. Technology is also part of a configuration that embodies rule-setting regimes and many interactions with intended and unintended outcomes. And, technology intervenes in policy and debate because its symbolic and ideological elements associate a thing or a tool with modernity, progress and rationality or, in contrast, with danger, evil or artificiality. In this broader interpretation, technology is a configuration that works or does not work (Rip and Kemp, 1998), depending on how agribusiness firms manage the multiple facets of technical change. In the following, success or failure of agribusiness's contribution to sustainability is examined by looking into the ways in which Monsanto achieved technological innovation, created access to financial resources supporting this innovation, and managed feedback loops from society reflecting on the nature of the innovation.

RUNNING INTO CONTROVERSY: THE PROBLEM OF TECHNOLOGICAL IMMOBILITY

Originally Monsanto was a chemical company known for a variety of products such as chemical warfare products, especially Agent

Orange widely used in Vietnam, industrial materials such as PCBs and synthetic fibres, and Nutrasweet, an artificial sweetener widely used by food companies such Coca-Cola. This analysis concentrates on the company's role as a major producer of (chemical) agricultural inputs; especially its herbicide Roundup, commercialized since 1976, which sells all over the world. After numerous research activities in the late 1980s, in the period from 1992 to 1998 the company implemented a life science strategy and, in order to realize this, assembled financial resources and technological capabilities. The paragraphs below discuss three questions that seriously steered the outcome of Monsanto's strategy. What are the benefits for users of the technology, i.e. farmers? What are possible risks for consumers and the environment? Who owns and controls the technology?

What are the benefits for farmers?

A major factor motivating Monsanto to develop and to market new agricultural biotechnologies was that its patent on glyphosate, the active ingredient in its biggest profit-maker, the herbicide, Roundup, was due to expire in the year 2000. A broad-spectrum herbicide Roundup was one of the world's best-selling herbicides; the market for weedkillers is worth US $14.3 billion a year. Roundup's global sales were five times higher than those of its next largest competitor. In 2000, about 20 per cent of Monsanto's overall revenue came from patent-protected glyphosate weedkillers.[1] The company's worldwide agro-chemical sales continued to increase, largely due to the growth of sold volumes of Roundup.[2] The continuous profits from the sales of Roundup supported the company's early investments in biotechnology in the 1980s. However, due to the expiration of the company's long-time patent on Roundup's active ingredient, glyphosate, the reliable profit-maker was in danger, especially since glyphosate is easy to produce and agrochemical companies were able to launch competitive product lines.

Compared to the European life science companies such as Novartis or Astra Zeneca, Monsanto invested heavily in agricultural biotechnology rather than in pharmaceuticals (Bijman and Joly, 2001). Consequently, Monsanto's market orientation was primarily directed towards farmers and agro-chemicals (Harvey, ch. 4). Monsanto built on its existing product lines in crop production for developing the following types of products. First, it introduced Roundup Ready soybeans, canola, cotton and other crops resistant to the Roundup brand family of non-selective herbicides. Second, the company developed a growing range of insect-protected crop seeds, including Bollgard and Ingard insect-protected cotton, YieldGard and Maisgard insect-protected corn, and NewLeaf insect-protected potatoes.

Biotechnology provided Monsanto with a tool to sustain its large market share in the growing market for herbicides. Roundup is a broad-spectrum herbicide that kills plants indiscriminately. In Monsanto's Roundup Ready varieties, a gene from a micro-organism made the plants tolerant to direct spraying with the herbicide Roundup. Initially, the Roundup Ready varieties were well received. The rapid adoption of the genetically engineered herbicide-resistant varieties resulted in a planted area of around 35 million ha, especially in the USA, Argentina and Canada (Rafi, 2000; Weiss, 1999),[3] which made Monsanto number one in the field of agricultural biotechnologies. In particular, Roundup Ready soybeans were adopted much faster than envisioned in the original time-frame (soybeans are usually produced in herbicide-dependent production systems) (Deutsche Bank, 1999). As an explanation for the favourable reception, seed companies claimed that herbicide-tolerant crops offer effective options for controlling pests, reducing chemical pesticide use and, consequently, lowering production costs (USDA Economic Research Service, 1999).

At the same time, however, Roundup Ready crop varieties, especially soybean, became a source of controversy among some agronomists. The rapid adoption looked remarkable because under most conditions RR soybeans produced lower yields than comparable but non-engineered varieties (6–7 per cent difference; Benbrook, 1998). Roundup Ready varieties, as a whole, seemed to have been rather variable in yield and disease reaction (Blaine, 1999a, 1999b). Scientists also reported that modified soybeans were cracking up in the heat; crop losses of these modified soybeans could reach up to 40 per cent in hot soils (*New Scientist*, 20 November 1999). Also the qualities of Roundup itself, applied in a herbicide-dependent crop system, were discussed. Alan Blaine observed that Roundup needed some help on some weeds (Blaine, 1999a), and questions were raised as to whether a cropping system designed around the application of a single herbicide would be sustainable and profitable in the end. Competitive alternatives were available in conventional soybean seed as well as in herbicide-resistant varieties, now also distributed by competing companies.

Competing companies used the observed possibility of lower yield to advocate alternatives to the Roundup-dominated regime. American Cyanamid Company, for example, argued that Roundup on RR soybeans was only one weed-control option. The company stressed that growers should choose seed varieties that had the best all-round genetic package and then plan weed control to optimize yields. This argument was linked to the fact that soybeans are naturally tolerant to many Imidazolinone (IMI) herbicides, introduced by the company in 1985. Pioneer HiBred, the world's largest producer of maize seed, decided after tedious negotiations it would not proceed to work on Roundup Ready technology because Monsanto's proposed restrictions and charges outweighed the benefits for farmers (*New York Times*, 19 November 1997).

In addition to these agronomic doubts about the performance of Monsanto's costly varieties, the launching of Roundup Ready soybeans in 1996 led to mounting concerns about the life science industry's manoeuvres to increase its control over agriculture and to marginalize small producers of biopesticides (Jenkins, 1999). Monsanto's most controversial action was to demand that farmers who bought a bag of Roundup Ready seed should pay a special 'technology fee' and sign a contract which stipulated that they would not use any of the harvested crop as seed for the next year (Mendelson, 1998). This broke with a long tradition in American farming in which soybeans were saved from harvest and used for the next planting (*Agrarisch Dagblad*, 20 March 1996). Moreover, the contract required farmers to apply only the Roundup formulation of glyphosate, and Monsanto representatives were allowed to inspect and test farmers' fields (Grain, 1997). Together with the general controversy over biotechnology products, Monsanto's policing of farmers gave rise to a widespread uneasiness about the benefits to farmers brought by Monsanto's first-generation products (Weiss, 1999).[4] The mixed picture of the benefits of genetically engineered crops like Roundup Ready soybean made it difficult for farmers to decide what option would best serve their interests.

What are the risks for consumers and the environment?

The environmental impact of genetically engineered crops became an issue after the wider public received signals about the unintended consequences of the use of *Bacillus thuringiensis* (Bt) in genetic engineering, a crucial step for Monsanto's insect-protected crop lines (Jenkins, 1998). Bt is a bacterium that normally lives in the soil and which affects lepidopterans (butterflies and moths) and is fatal to insects such as corn borers, attacking commercially important crops such as maize. The insertion of the Bt-gene, which codes for the toxic protein, gives plants the ability to make a toxic protein, and, hence, protect themselves. This technology seemed to be appropriate for reducing the amount of pesticides sprayed in intensive agriculture. In most commercial crops the use of Bt genetic engineering is tested; almost all biotech research to develop microbial insecticides is directed at the Bt bacterium (Grain, 1995). Monsanto controlled Bt cotton and Bt potatoes and was eyeing huge profits in the highly competitive Bt maize market.

However, the monarch butterfly threw a spanner in the works. A national symbol in the USA, and sometimes called the Bambi of the insect world, it appeared in full colour on the front page of the *New York Times*, revealing public concern for its wellbeing. Fears were raised after *Nature* published the results of research conducted by Cornell entomologist John Losey. He discussed the possible threat to the butterfly posed by Bt-crops after observing that half of the monarch butterfly larvae died four days after eating milkweed plants dusted with pollen from genetically engineered Bt corn.[5] Although Losey explicitly stated that the lab-based results were preliminary, the paper generated intense public debate about the possible risks of Bt crops (Pew Initiative, 2002). The arguments that Bt is, technically speaking, a special case, and that the risk to monarch butterflies is fairly small, could not prevent the controversy surrounding the environmental impact of Bt crops gradually becoming a liability to life science companies (Kraaijeveld, 1999).

Exposure of the potential risks of Bt technology spurred on the growing public distrust of the life science industry. A retrospective study of the Pew Initiative shows the emergence of concerns about the way in which scientific questions are raised and resolved in a highly politicized environment, the role of scientific journals and the mainstream press in building the controversy, and the adequacy of regulatory bodies in reviewing potential risks (Pew Initiative, 2002).

The safety of genetically modified foods became even more controversial after Arpad Pustzai spoke about his research indicating that genetically modified potatoes harmed the immune system and the internal organs of rats.[6] Although Pustzai also acknowledged that his findings were preliminary but nevertheless important enough to be made public, the validity of the research immediately became the subject of a widely publicized debate. Successive events revealed that much had happened behind the scenes, e.g. suppression of the debate and Monsanto's partial financial support to Pustzai's employer, the Rowett Institute, which eventually distanced itself from Pustzai (Levidow, 2002). Furthermore, public understanding of technological risks was embedded in an increasing concern over food safety following several scandals such as 'mad cow' disease and dioxin contamination. As a result, genetic modification was linked to an eroding confidence in scientific practices and in the direction of technological development.

Monsanto's response was to place the responsibility for risk assessment primarily in the hands of regulatory bodies. Monsanto's director of communication, Phil Angell, said to the *New York Times*: 'Monsanto should not have to vouchsafe the safety of Biotech food. Our interest is in selling as much of it as possible. Assuring its safety is the FDA's (Food and Drug Administration) job' (Pollan, 1998). Yet the company cannot be absolved from securing safety in uncharted terrains, especially because, 'there is still a lot we don't understand about gene expression', according to the co-director of Monsanto's potato subsidiary, Naturemark (in *Rachel's Environment and Health Weekly*, no. 637, 1999).

As Monsanto's life science strategy evolved, the company ran into deep water. In a competitive business environment and in the midst of public controversies, the company had to find a way to deal with the fact that it did not know all the answers. It appeared that the possibility of unintentional effects caused by modern technologies importantly shaped the public debate, and disagreements in the scientific community about safety tests further fuelled public outrage.[7] As a result of these controversies, scientific integrity, professional liability and the credibility of experts were no longer taken for granted by the general public. This certainly affected an industry so strongly dependent on knowledge and science; especially because trust-securing mechanisms were not yet in place.

Who owns and controls the technology?

Trust in the life science industry, and in Monsanto in particular, was further eroded due to a clash of views with respect to control and ownership of the technology. A driving concern for Monsanto was the need to recover its research and development expenses and to secure profits for its financiers. The company estimated that it takes ten years and about US $300 million to create commercial products such as Roundup Ready soybeans. For every new kind of engineered seed that makes it to field trials, around ten thousand have failed somewhere along the development pipeline. Monsanto believed it had found a technical solution for the problem of proprietary rights and profits in a package of genes making seeds sterile; this has come to be known as 'terminator technology' (Rafi, 1999), but was more neutrally described as Genetic Use Restriction Technology (GURT). When inserted into seeds, genes ensure that the plants lose their germinative capacity. Monsanto tried to acquire the company holding the patent on the technology: the cotton seed company Delta and Pine which collaborated closely with the US Department of Agriculture. The Roundup Ready soybean had already made a noise in the world, but GURT or terminator technology really fanned the flames (Rafi, 1999; Glover and Newell, ch. 9).

Protests against Monsanto's potential use of GURT were especially damaging to the company's public relations campaign which focused on the positive contribution of Monsanto's life science strategy to farming in developing countries. This positive image was placed in a critical perspective by news stories and campaigns by NGOs and other organizations. The use of GURT only to protect proprietary seeds was strongly protested by farmers' organizations and by countries such as Zimbabwe and India. Due to sterile seeds, critics said, small farmers would no longer be able to save seed and to develop adopted varieties and they would become totally dependent on the commercial seeds provided by companies like Monsanto. In the UK, the PR company hired by Monsanto strongly advised against highlighting the potential benefits for agriculture in developing countries, apparently acknowledging the weakness and perhaps the wrong timing of this argument. Nevertheless, Monsanto decided to link its technological enterprise to the betterment of human life. The company's legitimacy was thus seriously undermined by the potential threat of terminator technology.

The visit of Gordon Conway, president of the Rockefeller Foundation in New York, a leading institution of the Green Revolution, and committed to helping the rural poor by providing access to modern technologies, to the boardroom of Monsanto accelerated the controversy surrounding terminator technology. Shapiro wanted to consult Conway after the furore sparked by this technology in Europe. The Rockefeller Foundation was expected to be an ally because it had put more than US $100 million into public research into GM crops. But the opposite happened: Conway decided to hold the powerful corporation accountable to the public and he informed the press about what he was going to say in the privacy of the boardroom. He lectured the board for an hour and urged them to change track. 'In Europe it had alienated millions, he believed, and was threatening a trade war and long term damage to the prospects of the poor. The corporation with a reputation of arrogance and secrecy was seen to be responsible for meltdown of confidence in science and big business and a backlash against US agriculture' (Vidal, 1999). Conway argued that the possible adverse consequences for billions of farmers in the developing world outweighed any social benefits in protecting terminator technology.

As a result of this public campaign against terminator technology, pressure on Monsanto increased. In October 1999, the company announced in an open letter to Conway that it had decided 'not to commercialize sterile seed technologies [...] Though we do not yet own any sterile seed technology, we think it is important to respond to those concerns at this time by making clear our commitment not to commercialize gene protection systems that render seed sterile' (Shapiro, 1999a).[8] Notwithstanding Monsanto's stand not to commercialize sterile seed technologies, the need for companies to protect and gain a return on their investments in agricultural innovation is real and this problem has not yet been solved.

The problem of technological immobility

The above shows that Monsanto created images of technologies realizing ambitious goals such as environmentally-friendly modes of production or healthy food for everybody, but that its actual technology strategy was not congruent with this endeavour. Due to the need to deliver short-term profits the company stayed close to its experience in agro-chemicals. The discussion above confirms that 'Roundup is the engine that's driving Monsanto', as argued by Paul Raman, a chemical analyst for the investment banking firm S. G. Warburg & Co. (Steyer, 1996). In trying to pursue its high-profile investment strategy, Monsanto could neither escape from the biological properties of agricultural crop production (Goodman, 1999; Goodman et al., 1987) nor from the routines and trajectories in its own organization (Dosi, 1982). Monsanto's life science strategy reshaped the form of agricultural technologies to some extent, but their function in modern agriculture largely remained the same. Marketing of the company's technological commodities and of its life science strategy was further troubled by controversies over the benefits and risks of new plant varieties. In addition, Monsanto's efforts to control the use and distribution of its technological products stirred up criticism among a diverse group of political actors: leading public institutes, farmers' organizations and governments.

THE BOTTOM LINE: INVESTORS' APPRECIATION OF AN
INDEBTED COMPANY

In 1998 Monsanto completed several critical steps in establishing a life science strategy. The company's strategy required the shaping of R&D capabilities leading to technologies across a broader but related product scope (Bjornson, 1998). To enhance its technical capabilities, Monsanto directed its corporate strategy to buying of or merging with seed and biotechnology companies, the costs of which rose to US $8.5 billion.[9] The company acquired two of the world's top ten seed companies: De Kalb: an old family company, for US $2.3 billion and the international seed business of Cargill for US $1.4 billion. Also in

1998, it paid more than $500 million for the UK-based Plant Breeding International. Monsanto also intended to take over the world's largest cottonseed company, Delta and Pine; the pending purchase of Delta and Pine would add another $1.8 billion to its investments.

Through this series of transactions the company's management believed it could complete the network it needed in major crops to compete successfully in the global agricultural marketplace. Basic to the acquisition strategy was that leading seed companies would give Monsanto access to their mature marketing and distribution assets and that their incorporation would create a synergy through which products could be introduced faster in the realm of food, nutrition and health. In a span of two months, Monsanto catapulted itself to become the world's second largest seed company, but this expansion was made possible by external financial resources.

Monsanto funded its seed company acquisitions through a series of financing transactions and a combination of divestitures and cost reductions (especially retrenchments). It had to raise up to $4 billion in a series of financing transactions, which would include the issuance of approximately $1 billion of common stock, $500 million of adjustable conversion-rate equity security units, and approximately $2.5 billion of long-term, unsecured debt. Divestitures of businesses were expected to generate gross proceeds of $1 billion. Monsanto also announced a restructuring of the company that could eliminate 700 to 1,000 jobs, with an additional 1,300 to 1,500 job reductions resulting from divestiture of other entities (AgBiotech, 1998).

Monsanto's financiers expected the company to deliver a return on investments by connecting its business operations to its technological capabilities. Initially, institutional investors reacted positively to the company's ambitions and, in general, the market values of agricultural seed and biotechnology firms increased in the 1990s. Many of the mergers in the life science industry were supported by investors and the stock value of these corporations reflected expectations about the profitability of newly developed genetic traits and of the synergies whereby research capabilities and technology were shared across multiple product lines. However, in the life science industry, fast marketing of new products and expensive and continuous innovation have to realize profits. This is a demanding and difficult strategy to pursue, and it is uncertain whether the strategy can meet the expectation of high financial returns in the short run (Bjornson, 1998).

Due to Monsanto's dependence on external financiers, the actual results of its life science strategy had an immediate effect on judgements and decisions in the stock market. In the spring of 1999, Monsanto's financial figures continued to show a substantial increase in earning (5 per cent) and income (28 per cent).[10] But the company's optimistic prospects disappeared over the summer due to a combination of consumer concerns over GM products, food industries' demands for labelling, the refusal of angry farmers to plant GM crops, and the introduction of a segregation in the grain and soybean markets. The two-tier grain market endangered sales of genetically modified crop varieties and obstructed the advantage of price premiums for value-added GMO seed. 'Don't expect the food manufacturers and retailers to take a bullet for GMOs,' Deutsche Bank wrote in its report, 'GMOs are dead' (Deutsche Bank, 1999). The Deutsche Bank was also troubled by the fact that an industry leader such as Du Pont steadfastly refused to forecast publicly when biotechnology would yield a return on investment. Before, the investment community accorded only positive attributes to genetically modified corn and soybeans, such as innovation, productivity and progress, but now GMO crops have become 'a liability rather than a drive of growth' (Deutsche Bank, 1999). The general concerns over biotechnology had truly rattled the institutional investors.

It was the critical analysis of the world's largest bank, the Deutsche Bank, which really cut the ground from under Monsanto's feet. In 1999, the bank repeatedly advised institutional investors not to invest in life science industry as a whole or even to sell their shares. Investors drove down the stock prices of agricultural life science companies during 1999. Hardest hit was Monsanto, both because of its sometimes careless advocacy of the life science strategy and because of its indebtedness after the takeovers in the seed sector. The company was anxious to keep its 'A' status, but the two Deutsche Bank reports wounded Monsanto's glamorous strategy. The bank was prepared to believe that GMO crops were safe, but it viewed the 'perception wars' as lost by industry. 'Industry fully believes that it has science on its side, but science may not be enough,' the bank wrote (Deutsche Bank, 1999). Monsanto spent billions of dollars on acquisitions, millions on R&D and on publicity, but fast results failed to appear. With its high-cost life science strategy, Monsanto had become fully dependent on shareholders and investors and ran into the quicksand of short-term investment interests. Shapiro's passionate advocacy of the life science strategy exceeded his company's coffers and Wall Street's patience.

Robert Steyer, journalist for the *St Louis Post-Dispatch* in Monsanto's home town, wrote about the position Shapiro ended up in:

He is being roughed up by the quick-score behavior of big-time money managers who control about 80 percent of Monsanto's stock. 'Once that pressure starts, you can't afford to have the institutional investors dumping their stock,' said a former Monsanto executive who requested anonymity. 'Many people look at life science as providing some sort of short-term dividend, but that's never been the case,' said Sano Shimoda, presenting BioScience Securities, in Orinda, California, an agribusiness research firm. 'Life sciences is a long-term strategy.' Several bigger companies – such as DuPont and Novartis – have the money to carry on the life sciences concept if Monsanto gets carved up. But these companies still view life sciences as a collection of components rather than as a unified business that weaves together all of the units. (Steyer, 1999)

Shapiro's desire to buy seed companies stretched Monsanto's balance sheet, resulted in high debts and weakened its stock price, despite big revenue infusions from the herbicide Roundup and from the arthritis drug Celebrex.

The financial markets pressured the company to look for a way out, while, preferably, realizing the maximum value for investors (Martinson, 1999). Many financial analysts believed that Monsanto had no choice but to seek protection in a larger enterprise to sustain financially the company's life science strategy. Shapiro talked to many drug and chemical companies before embarking on an ill-fated merger plan with American Home Products Corp. in 1998 (Steyer, 1999). Only after three successive failed attempts did Monsanto find its new partner, just before the year 2000: the pharmaceutical firm Pharmacia & Upjohn (*New York Times*, 21 December 1999). In this merger, Monsanto's pharmaceutical division Searle, which brought in big revenues from the arthritis drug Celebrex, and not the Agricultural Division appeared to be the most attractive asset.[II] After the merger, Monsanto made a new start as a company exclusively devoted to agriculture (Verfaille, 2000); the strategy for the Agricultural Division was importantly modelled on a Roundup-based trajectory and profits had to be secured by a reduced price designed to result in increased sold volume. As a result, financial analysts regarded the agricultural business of Monsanto as a possible sleeper, an out-of-favour business that was too important to dump but too much of a liability to keep whole (Associated Press, 20 December 1999).

CONFRONTATION WITH THE PUBLIC DOMAIN: TECHNOLOGY IN AN IDEOLOGICAL BATTLE

In 1999, doubts aired by investors gradually confronted Monsanto with the uncertain future of blazing a new trail. For different reasons,

Monsanto's investors, farmers' organizations and closely related NGOs, such as Rafi, or environmental groups, such as Greenpeace or Friends of the Earth, felt uncomfortable with the prominently advocated trust in a new technology. Since the 1980s, environmental movements and farmers' organizations have pointed at the tendency towards concentration in the agro-industry and in the last few years they have labelled the life science industries as monsters producing 'Frankenstein' food for their own profits and for the mere interests of their shareholders. Making the technological future in the areas of food, health and agriculture dependent on a few multinational firms would diminish the control and influence of actual users of technology, of consumers of food products and of buyers of medical drugs.

As a result of these criticisms, the life science industry had to operate in a situation in which the organization of technology development and the possible threats of new technologies had become politicized. At the end of the 1990s, public campaigns and lobbying gave weight to a widespread 'No' to biotechnology. Peter Melchett, chief executive of Greenpeace, said in reply to Shapiro's speech to the Greenpeace Business Conference in 1999:

> Everything we've actually seen of GM food and farming so far is bad and is taking us in the wrong direction, it is the latest and the least acceptable aspect of the industrialization and intensification of agriculture. A truly visionary holistic life science combining the fundamental goal of achieving agricultural production while sustaining life in all its rich diversity does already exist, it is directly in tune with public values, it works by making the most of natural processes, it produces food of the highest quality and it brings premium prices for farmers, it's called organic agriculture [...] People know what kind of world they want for themselves and their children, they know how they want companies to behave and they know how they want their food to be produced and you, Bob, I believe, are blocking that progress.[12]

So, the juxtaposition was there: on one side the 'hard-core bio-technologists' and on the other side the 'soft humane ecological agri-culturists'. Both contrasting views seemed to believe that the respective technological paradigms would lead the way to the betterment of human life and ecological soundness.[13] This situation brought about another crucial test for Monsanto: it had to show its ability to communicate in an arena with different views on the future and to manage various interactions with governments and other stakeholders. This required other skills than developing new technologies. It meant that the company had to seek dialogue and exchange with organizations and people outside its bounded institution. How did Monsanto handle the dialogue about technological alternatives and choices?

When Monsanto started to invest in biotechnology in 1986 it was both lobbying for regulations and guidelines from US government agencies and carefully consulting environmental, farmer and consumer groups to build confidence in the new technology. Earle Harbison, president and CEO at Monsanto during the late 1980s, told the *New York Times*: 'We recognized early on that while developing lifesaving drugs might be greeted with fanfare, monkeying around with plants and food would be greeted with skepticism' (Eichenwald, 2001). The company anticipated concerns and sought dialogue and consultation with the stakeholders. But when Harbison retired in the early 1990s, the entrance of Robert Shapiro dramatically changed this dialogue. When the new management team took over, the company's careful go-slow strategy changed into an offensive one, dismissing concerns in society as the 'insignificant worries of the uninformed'. Confident that worries about the new technology had been thoroughly disproved by science, it began championing bioengineered agriculture, marketing products that primarily benefited farmers rather than general consumers, and opposing regulatory measures such as labelling of genetically modified food. This became the company's message to the outside world, but how was this related to decision-making and day-to-day practice inside the corporate buildings?

How the company, as an institution, thinks and works is difficult to investigate but a television documentary by Wolfgang Herles (1998), broadcast by the German ZDF, left ajar the door of Monsanto's headquarters in St Louis, Missouri, USA.[14] The documentary is instructive for answering the question how Monsanto's management and in particular Robert 'Bob' Shapiro projected and handled the process of technological change. At the beginning of his career Shapiro had combined his activities as a folk singer and anti-war activist with the position of teacher, and he marched in the 'War Against Poverty' of President Johnson. However, the events of the 1960s shattered his faith in political reforms and he landed up in business where he tackled complex challenges. As a director of Nutrasweet, a profit-making division of Monsanto, letters from diabetic children who could finally eat sweets convinced him that companies were able to do things that were beneficial to people. New products and technologies not only served to generate profits, he discovered, but they could also mean something for the world. In this sense Shapiro's corporate style represents progress, which contrasts sharply with the predilection for the past expressed by so many of the opponents of biotechnology (Schulman, 2000).

The atmosphere inside the offices reflected Shapiro's confidence in his vision that everything would be different. Open offices were supposed to help to use resources economically. The absence of neckties, casual styles and informal meetings typified, according to the CEO, the new combination of profit and philosophy characteristic of the life science industry. Small placards urged employees to take time to smell the roses or to sit back, relax and watch the world go by. During meetings Shapiro stimulated his employees to think about the kind of company that can navigate its way creatively – 'a different type of enterprise'. In his office, symbols confirmed his trust in the innovative strength of the life science company: a small bowl with shrimps represented a self-sustaining biosphere. A framed quotation of the American general George Patton revealed his management style: 'A good plan executed now is better than a perfect plan next week.'

During the 1990s, Monsanto aired its image of technological progress for a better world in various media and political arenas. It constructed a culture of environmental responsibility. Advertisements announced that the company's new emphasis on genetic engineering aimed at feeding the world and saving the environment from unsustainable agricultural practices. Shapiro saw this project as environmentally enlightened, using terms like 'sustainable development' and 'holistic solutions'. He saw the results of the life science programme in the company as environmentally good: less need for pesticides, weed control without disturbing the soil and greater food production from less land (Knox, 1999). Monsanto would leave behind its history of being entrenched in the chemical industry. The invention of the life science strategy supposedly meant a clean break.

However, environmentalists who went to the corporate headquarters in St Louis at Monsanto's invitation to give seminars and lectures on many aspects of sustainability, returned disappointed (Hawken, 1999). Invited environmentalists ran into collision with the company's scientists who seemed to ridicule the implications of sustainability. Paul Hawken, a businessman with an environmental record, complained that Monsanto never took sustainability seriously: 'Although I refused initially, I accepted [Monsanto's invitation] reluctantly for a simple reason: if Monsanto could change, then any company could.' He continued:

> I don't know of any new [Monsanto] products that came about because of any environmental commitments, and the old underlying divisional

culture of ramming products into the marketplace without consulting a broader stakeholder community about effects, values, science, and other potential concerns – with the arrogance that entails – remains intact. What exists now is a company without clear leadership, with divisional heads consistently putting their foot in their mouth, and a product line that is truly unnerving.[15]

This suggests that the actual contribution of the company in addressing environmental concerns or societal needs was difficult to measure.

Michael Muston, president of Mycogen Seeds, one of the leading venture companies in the development of Bt and hence linked to most life science industries, acknowledged the moderate advance achieved in the last decade: 'Now I consider Bt and glyphosate resistant beans to be very useful – and very practical – applications of biotechnology. These first two pioneering traits do exemplify a noteworthy point however, that is we tend to first use new technology in very conventional ways. In so doing, it is difficult to stray far from the obvious and, thus the first agriculture uses of biotechnology were not necessarily the most creative' (Muston, 1998). In addition, Gould (1997) argues that Bt's exceptional nature – it is a toxic protein that makes it transferable to other plants – explains why it is attractive to commercial enterprises. But this also shows that Bt represents a contingent, simple solution to a specific crop production problem rather than the first result of the supposed technological synergy in the life science industry. The above suggests that most technological change in the life science industry was essentially a step-by-step process, and not the radical change envisioned by Shapiro.

Despite this unruliness and the tardiness of technological advancement, Shapiro consistently acted as a leading proponent of technological progress.[16] In his address to the Greenpeace Business Conference, one of the company's main and most influential critics, Shapiro expressed his consistent belief in the benefits of technological change:

[...] we started with a conviction that bio-technology was a good technology, was and is safe and useful, valuable, we've been working on it for twenty years and that's the source of that conviction [...] We've behaved then as though this is or should be a debate and the unintended result of that has probably been that we have irritated and antagonized more people than we've persuaded, our confidence in this technology and our enthusiasm for it has I think widely been seen, and understandably so, as condescension or indeed arrogance, because we thought it was our job to persuade, too often we've forgotten to listen. (Shapiro, 1999b)

Only after the strong expression of public criticism and the loss of confidence in the financial markets was Shapiro prepared to acknowledge that he had been naïve in trying to win fast approval for innovative technologies. He promised a new dialogue with society in a search for common ground: 'The underlying premise of dialogue is pretty straightforward, in this case it is that there are both real benefits to the use of bio-technology and at the same time there are real concerns about its use. If you don't believe that there are real benefits then there is no room for dialogue, if you don't believe that there are real concerns there's no room for dialogue' (Shapiro, 1999b).

From a company's perspective, the tension between seeking an open dialogue and advocating the benefits of a new, but complex, technology is not easy to resolve. After the merger with Pharmacia, the newly appointed president and CEO Hendrik Verfaille, a Monsanto veteran who had worked his way up in the herbicide industry, spoke about the company's new pledge:

> This is a story about a company more closely identified with this technology than any other. This is a story about a company that didn't always represent this technology the way it should have. This company did do many things well. It got the science right – no small achievement in and of itself. The science is solid, and it's world-class. This company got the safety studies right [...] The company understood this new technology could transform the marketplace – and that the future, including the immediate future, was in the integration of chemicals, traits and seeds [...] I would like to be able to say that this story ends with 'and they lived happily ever after.' But that, of course, is not what happened. The company – my company, Monsanto – had focused so much attention on getting the technology right for our customer – the grower – that we didn't fully take into account the issues and concerns it raised for other people. We thought we were doing some great things. A lot of other people thought we were making some mistakes. We were blinded by our own enthusiasm. We missed the fact that this technology raises major issues for people – issues of ethics, of choice, of trust, even of democracy and globalization [...] When we tried to explain the benefits, the science and the safety, we did not understand that our tone – our very approach – was seen as arrogant. We were still in the 'trust me' mode when the expectation was 'show me.' And so, instead of happily ever after, this new technology became the focal point of public conflict, the benefits we saw were jeopardized, and Monsanto became a lightning rod. (Verfaille, 2000)

This quotation confirms the general idea that Monsanto's way of interacting with the public domain had prevented its business strategy from becoming a success. One important cause of Monsanto's trouble was that it had adopted a technology-driven business model. In this model, the relationship between technology and society was a unilateral one; the company's management consistently propagated technology development as the source of societal progress, specifically by bringing about fundamental changes in agricultural practice and food provision. The company's stubborn position in the confrontation with its critics made technology instrumental in an ideological debate about the future of agricultural production and food provision rather than the foundation for an economically viable, socially acceptable and environmentally sustainable strategy. The analysis shows that saying 'No' to certain technological developments may push for a dialogue about technological alternatives. It remains uncertain, however, whether a mere 'No' to genetic engineering or biotechnology will open ways to act constructively in shaping alternative corporate structures and technological strategies.

CONCLUSIONS

Undeniably, technological change will be part of a transition to sustainable agricultural production and safe and healthy food provision. By using the opportunities offered by biotechnology and genetic engineering, Monsanto tried to create an acceptable version of agribusiness environmentalism and it was championing a single progressive agricultural biotechnology supposedly serving both corporate targets as well as the public good (cf. de Wilde, 2000). The fierce opposition from environmental movements, farmer's organizations and sometimes governments is often depicted as the root cause of the erosion of Monsanto's strategy. This chapter does not explain the dynamics of corporate behaviour from an opposition between environmentalists and agribusiness firms; rather it presents Monsanto's strategy as an uncertain bet on the company's capacity to translate a radical narrative of the technological future into a profitable business strategy and a socially acceptable enterprise with real benefits for the environment.

The case study of Monsanto exposes the limits of the company's capacity proactively to manage and steer a process of technological change. This chapter suggests that Monsanto overestimated its ability to develop and introduce a new set of biotechnologies creating a sustainable future. A major hindrance for the company's success was the fixed and irreversible nature of technology. Monsanto built on its history as an agro-chemical company, selling Roundup herbicide, making the management of technological change strongly path-dependent and revealing the predominance of incremental changes. Monsanto was not successful in truly changing the technological substance of agricultural production and food provision.

Financial pressures did not allow the company to experiment in niche markets, demonstrating the viability of the technology or learning from other firms and sectors. Monsanto was forced to sell a high-profile promise in order to find funding for its strategy, based on the appropriation of knowledge through mergers and acquisitions. The company's dependence on the financial markets meant that it had to deliver short-term shareholder value and, consequently, was forced to launch commercially successful products in haste. The difficulty experienced in quickly producing commercial and financial results was not acceptable to Monsanto's financiers.

In the implementation of its life science strategy the company had to find a balance between the uncertainty of innovatory search activities and the continuity and path-dependency of the common, robust technologies inside its own complex organization (Coombs et al., 1992). It seems that as a complex and hierarchical institution Monsanto could not simply set aside its history, that is, the ways in which its previous innovations and technological products affected subsequent innovations and channelled technical change in particular directions (Harvey, 1999). In such situations, managers, researchers and engineers continually make strategic and ad-hoc decisions and manoeuvre within a selected range of options, out of which they construct a world of technological progress, environmentalism and profitability (MacKenzie, 1992).

Furthermore, the form of environmentalism constructed by Monsanto was not readily accepted by the wider public or by environmentalist groups in particular. Increasingly, biotechnology and genetic engineering became a compelling social and environmental concern and occupied a central place in public controversies (Tokar, 2001). In 1999, the suggested ill-effects of technological growth were central to the public debate about biotechnology, and in particular about genetically modified crops, and the impact of technology and science became politicized. The critics of the corporate life science strategy succeeded in bringing forward the notion that corporate managers might have taken a wrong turning.

Monsanto had not reckoned with the continuous interaction between its own practices and the responses to and acceptance and uses of its technological products in areas outside the boundaries of its own organization. It appears that the development and introduction of agricultural biotechnologies are part of both the fabrication of and the opposition to a corporate technology agenda. Monsanto's straightforward view on technology development left little or no space for feedback loops from society and end-use markets.

NOTES

I am indebted to Jeroen Breekveldt for his endless patience in exploring the World Wide Web, for a period of eight months in 2000, and tracing the bits and pieces of information about the events revealing corporate strategies in the 1990s. The Technology and Agrarian Development Group, Wageningen University, encouraged the publication of this research.

1. *The Times*, 1 September 2000.

2. After the merger with Pharmacia, Roundup was maintained as a major profit generator for Monsanto's Agricultural Division mainly based on increased sales volumes and lower prices. Data provided by the company in March 2000 show that volumes almost tripled between 1994 and 1999, while prices declined approximately 30 per cent in the same period. <www.monsanto.com/monsanto/investor/literature/financial/sldo13.htm>

3. Rafi used Wood Mackenzie, agrochemical industry analysts based in the UK, and Clive James, International Service for the Acquisition of Agri-Biotech Applications (ISAAA), as sources for projecting trends in the life science industry. Mackenzie released a global review and forecast on GM seeds in January 2001 entitled 'Seeding Growth'. For more information: <www.woodmac.com>

4. Weiss (1999) argues that Monsanto could have done things differently. Weiss discusses the example of AgrEvo that also sells engineered canola in Canada yet has chosen not to place restrictions on seed use. Its plan is to make money on its herbicide Liberty rather than on its Liberty-tolerant seeds. The more seeds sold, blown or given away, the better. Monsanto, however, does not have that option because of the expiring of its Roundup patent.

5. Josey reported his findings in the Scientific Correspondence section in the 20 May 1999 issue of the journal *Nature*. The report was peer-reviewed by two outside reviewers.

6. Pustzai expressed his concerns about the safety of GM food in a television interview (BBC, 'World in Action', August 1998).

7. This chapter's task is not to determine why some risks became politicized and emphasized while others remained latent (Tansey and O'Riordan, 1999).

8. Also in this open letter from Monsanto CEO Robert B. Shapiro to Rockefeller Foundation president Gordon Conway (4 October 1999) the company stated that '[i]t is also important to understand that the technical and business utility of sterile seed technology is speculative. The specific technology over which Monsanto would gain ownership through its pending merger with DeltaPine Land is developmental, at least five years away from any possible commercialization, and may or may not prove workable in a commercial setting.' Its announcement about

abandoning the terminator technology also resulted in an end to the pending merger negotiations with Delta and Pine. Delta and Pine accused Monsanto of breach of contract and filed a law suit in which it claimed US $1 billion of alimony.

9. *NRC Handelsblad*, 29 September 1999: 18.

10. Source: <www.stockmasters.com> (August 1999).

11. The newly formed company became the world's eleventh largest drug company controlling top-selling medicines to treat ailments from arthritis to glaucoma: 60,000 employees, sales of US $17 billion, and investments in pharmaceutical research and development of US $2 billion.

12. <www.biotech-info.net/business_conf.html> (March 2000).

13. The ideological course of the debate on biotechnology was the thorn in Conway's flesh when he addressed the board of Monsanto: 'Admit that you do not have all the answers. Commit yourselves to prompt, full, and honest sharing of data. This is not the time for a new PR offensive but for a new relationship based on honesty, full disclosure, and a very uncertain shared future' (*Guardian*, 9 October 1999). In the *Financial Times* (4 May 2000) Conway ridiculed the lack of subtlety in the current GM debate: 'The environmental activists draw a hard line – it is all bad – while the biotech companies say it is all good. They have become like professional wrestlers, with the whole thing made worse by PR men on both sides.'

14. A film by Wolfgang Herles (1998), '*Das Gen-monopoly: Wie Monsanto Furcht und Hoffnung Sät* (The Gene-monopoly: How Monsanto Sows Fear and Hope)', broadcast by ZDF (10 May 1998).

15. He reveals his experiences, after being invited to Monsanto's office in St Louis, in *Rachel's Environment and Health Weekly* 668, September 1999 (<www.rachel.org/bulletin>).

16. The website of the Biotech Knowledge Center, sponsored by Monsanto, still echoes ideological controversies about the direction of technical change:

REFERENCES

AgBiotech (1998) *AgBiotech Newsletter* 156.

Basalla, G. (1988) *The Evolution of Technology*. Cambridge: Cambridge University Press.

Benbrook, C. (1998) 'Evidence of the Magnitude and Consequences of the Roundup Ready Soybean Yield Drag from University-Based Varietal Trials in 1998', *AgBiotech InfoNet Technical Paper* 1. <www.biotech-info.net/RR_yield_drag_98.pdf> (September 2000).

Benton, T. (1989) 'Marxism and Natural Limits: An Ecological Critique and Reconstruction', *New Left Review* 178: 51–86.

Bijman, J. (1999) 'Innovation Challenges for the European Agbiotech Industry', *AgBioForum* 4 (1): 4–13. <www.agbioforum.missouri.edu>

Bijman, J. and P. B. Joly (2001) 'Innovation Challenges for the European Agbiotech Industry', *AgBioForum* 4 (1): 4–13.

Bjornson, B. (1998) 'Capital Market Values of Agricultural Biotechnology Firms:

How High and Why?', *AgBioForum* 1 (2): 69–73. <www.agbioforum.misso uri.edu>

Blaine, A. (1999a) *Agronomy Notes*, 03/06/99. <www.ext.msstate.edu/newsletters/ agronotes/> (September 2000).

— (1999b) *Agronomy Notes*, 08/01/99. <www.ext.msstate.edu/newsletters/ agronotes/> (September 2000).

Coombs, R., P. Saviotti and V. Walsh (1992) 'Technology and the Firm: The Convergence of Economic and Sociological Approaches', in R. Coombs, P. Saviotti and V. Walsh (eds), *Technological Change and Company Strategies: Economic and Sociological Perspectives*, pp. 1–24. London: Academic Press.

DeGregori, T. R., 'Genetically Modified Nonsense', *Reference* 2769, 27 January 2000. <www.biotechknowledge.com/showlib_biotech.php3?2769> (February 2000).

Deutsche Bank (1999) 'GMOs are Dead', unpublished report.

Dosi, G. (1982) 'Technological Paradigms and Technological Trajectories: A Suggested Interpretation of the Determinants and Directions of Technical Change', *Research Policy* 11: 147–62.

Eichenwald, K. (2001) 'Biotechnology Food: From the Lab to a Debacle', *New York Times*, 25 January 2001 (<www.nytimes.com/2001/01/25/business/25 FOOD.html>)

Goodman, D. (1999) 'Agro-Food Studies in the "Age of Ecology": Nature, Corporeality, Bio-Politics', *Sociologia Ruralis* 39 (1): 17–38.

Goodman, D., B. Sorj and J. Wilkinson (1987) *From Farming to Biotechnology: A Theory of Agro-industrial Development*. Oxford: Basil Blackwell.

Gould, F. (1997) 'Integrating Pesticidal Engineered Crops into Mesoamerican Agriculture', in A. Hruska and M. L. Pavón (eds), *Transgenic Plants in Mesoamerican Agriculture*, pp. 6–36. Tegucigalpa: Zamorano Acedamic Press.

Grain (1995) 'Engineered Bt: From Pest to Market Control', *Seedling*, December.

— (1997) 'Roundup Ready or Not', *Seedling*, March.

Harvey, M. (1999) 'Genetic Modification as a Bio-Socio-Economic Process: One Case of Tomato Puree', *CRIC Discussion Paper*, no. 31.

Hawken, P. (1999) 'Monsanto and the Natural Step Revisited', *Rachel's Environment and Health Weekly* 676, November (<www.rachel.org/bulletin>).

Jenkins, R. (1998) 'Bt in the Hot Seat', *Seedling*, September.

— (1999) 'The Bt Story', *Genet News*, 17 November (<www.gene.ch/genet/1999/ Nov/msg00035.html>)

Knox, N. (1999) 'Pharmacia & Upjohn, Monsanto Intend to Merge', *Associated Press*, 20 December.

Kraaijeveld, K. (1999) 'Biotechnologie zet Novartis klem', *NRC Handelsblad*, 2 June.

Levidow, L. (2002) 'Ignorance-based Risk Assessment? Scientific Controversy over GM Food Safety', *Science and Culture* 11: 61–7.

MacKenzie, D. (1992), 'Economic and Sociological Explanations of Technical Change', in R. Coombs, P. Saviotti and V. Walsh (eds), *Technological Change and Company Strategies: Economic and Sociological Perspectives*, pp. 25–48. London: Academic Press.

Martinson, J. (1999) 'Monsanto Pressured to Sell off GM Assets', *Guardian*, 22 October.

Mendelson, J. (1998) 'Roundup the World's Biggest-Selling Herbicide', *Ecologist* 28 (5): 270–5.

Metcalfe, M. J. and S. Boden (1992) 'Evolutionary Epistemology and the Nature of Technology Strategy', in R. Coombs, P. Saviotti and V. Walsh (eds), *Technological Change and Company Strategies: Economic and Sociological Perspectives*, pp. 49–71. London: Academic Press.

Monsanto (1999) 'Background Statement: Gene Protection Technologies'. <www.monsanto.com/monsanto/gurt/statement.html> (April 1999).

Muston, M. J. (1998) 'Ten Integrated Steps to Success', Iowa State University, Integrated Crop Management Conference, 17 November 1998. <www.mycogen.com/pressrelease.asp?ID=8> (October 2000).

Pew Initiative (2002) *Three Years Later: Genetically Engineered Corn and the Monarch Butterfly Controversy*, Pew Initiative on Food and Biotechnology. <www.pewagbiotech.org/resources/issuebriefs/monarch.pdf> (December 2002).

Pollan, M. (1998) 'Playing God in the Garden', *New York Times*, 25 October 1998.

Rafi (1999) 'Traitor Technology: The Terminator's Wider Implications', *RAFI Communiqué*, Jan./Feb. 1999. <www.rafi.org>

— (2000) 'Speed Bump or Blow-Out for GM Seeds? Stalling Markets, Taco Debacle & Biotech Bail Outs', *Geno-Types*, 21 December.

Rip, A. and R. Kemp (1998) 'Technological Change', in S. Rayner and E. L. Malone (eds), *Human Choice and Climate Change: An International Assessment*, vol. 2, pp. 327–99. Washington, DC: Batelle Press.

Schot, J. (2001) 'Towards New Forms of Participatory Technology Development', *Technology Analysis and Strategic Management* 13: 39–52.

Schulman, B. J. (2000) 'Eco-kapitalisten komen zichzelf tegen', *NRC Handelsblad*, 13 May.

Shapiro, R. (1999a) 'Open Letter to Rockefeller Foundation President Gordon Conway', 4 October. <www.monsanto.com> (November 1999).

— (1999b) 'Address to Greenpeace Business Conference'. <www.monsanto.com/monsanto/mediacenter/speeches/99oct6_Shapiro.html> (October 1999).

Steyer, R. (1996) 'Monsanto Makes Bestseller Better', *St Louis Post-Dispatch*, 21 January.

— (1999) 'Monsanto Faces Its Option', *St Louis Post-Dispatch*, 14 November.

Tansey, J. and T. O'Riordan, 'Cultural Theory and Risk: A Review', *Health, Risk and Society* 1 (1): 71–90.

Tokar, B. (2001) 'Introduction: Challenging Biotechnology', in B. Tokar (ed.), *Redesigning Life? The Worldwide Challenge to Genetic Engineering*, pp. 1–16. London: Zed Books.

USDA Economic Research Service (1999) 'Genetically Engineered Crops for Pest

Management', 25 June. <www.ers.usda.gov/Topics/View.asp?T=100400> (May 2000).

Verfaille, H. (2000) 'A New Pledge for a New Company, Remarks at Farm Journal Conference', Washington, DC. <www.monsanto.com/monsanto/layout/media/speeches/11–27–00.asp> (February 2001).

Vidal, J. (1999) 'How Monsanto's Mind was Changed', *Guardian*, 9 October.

Weiss, R. (1999) 'Monsanto's Gene Police Raise Alarm on Farmers' Rights, Rural Tradition', *Washington Post*, 3 February: A01.

Wilde, R. de (2000) *De voorspellers: een kritiek op de toekomstindustrie*. Amsterdam: De Balie.

FOUR | The appearance and disappearance of
the GM tomato: innovation strategy, market
formation and the shaping of demand

MARK HARVEY

§ Calgene's FlavrSavr tomato and Zeneca's tomato purée were the
'world's first genetically engineered whole food' (Martineau, 2001;
Harvey, 1999a, 1999b, 2000; Harvey et al., 2002).[1] With the development and introduction of the GM tomato, both companies entered new
terrain. Calgene, a US-based venture biotechnology company now incorporated in Monsanto, was mainly oriented towards the application
of genetic modification in agriculture. Also Zeneca, a major European
agro-chemical and life science company now part of Syngenta, centred
most of its efforts on providing technical solutions in the production
of broad acre crops. What was new about the modification of the tomato was that it changed the nature of the crop as food, rather than the
crop as cultivated and commercially linked to use of pesticides, as is the
case with soybeans, cotton or rape seed. The first GM tomato went on
sale to consumers in the USA in 1994, the second in the UK in 1996.
Within two years, both had disappeared; Calgene had been taken over
by Monsanto (1996), and the market for GM food in the UK had been
closed down (1998).

Remarkably, protest movements raising alarm about the potential
harm of GM crops for the environment or human health had only an
indirect impact on the disappearance of the GM tomato in the United
Kingdom, and none at all in the USA. The significance of this particular GM innovation is that environmental issues were *not* central or
directly implicated. Genetic pollution is not a significant risk because
of the reproductive incompatibility between domesticated and wild
species (Jones, 2000). There were no issues of super-weeds or genetic
drift of pesticide tolerance, as no pesticides or pesticide tolerance traits
were involved. The case of the GM tomato shows that it is important
to recognize the heterogeneity of GM innovation and not to put GM
into one basket, as a device to demonize all GM technologies. So, if

the role of environmentalism was only marginal, what does explain the rise and fall of the GM tomato?

What is particularly interesting about this appearance and disappearance is that it was the *same* innovatory genetic modification, applied to the *same* fruit, resulting in a tomato product, one fresh and the other processed. And yet both disappeared for very different reasons: different business strategies of the firms involved, different markets, different regulatory systems, important differences in actual product quality, and, perhaps above all, different consumers.

The argument of this chapter at root involves the clash between different varieties of capitalism, expressed in this empirical case in what may be termed the 'Monsanto-Zeneca thesis'. The fundamental argument is that clashes between different varieties of capitalism are fundamental to the dynamics of innovation and socio-economic change. The Monsanto-Zeneca thesis can be summarized as follows: *When two or more configurations of different regulatory regimes, different market and business and inter-firm strategies, and different macro-social consumer demand characteristics come into conflict, the consequences create disruption and turbulence for those configurations that in turn induce further structural change as a condition for further innovation.*

The comparison of the very different failures of Calgene's FlavrSavr tomato and Zeneca's tomato purée, based on the same technological innovation, serves as an interesting 'experiment' on the significant socio-economic structural variables at play in order to support this thesis. As will be seen, the experiment is made more intriguing by the ways in which the Calgene and Zeneca trajectories were intertwined. The contrast between the two can be summarized in these terms. Calgene failed to establish a consumer market for a GM food product even within its own business context, and the GM tomato was then dumped by Monsanto on its acquisition of Calgene. *It was strictly a business failure.* This was almost a confirmation of Monsanto's first agrifood-oriented technology strategy: forget consumers, target farmers (see also Vellema, ch. 3). Zeneca succeeded, at least initially, in establishing a consumer market for a GM food product within an UK business context (and was well advanced towards establishing a European market for a new generation of nutrient-dense tomatoes). A strong consensual marketing policy of open information, labelling and segregation, co-operative and strategic relations between Zeneca and retailers, and an attractive product at an attractive price, a long-term consumer-oriented vision, was followed by successful sales in comparison with the non-GM alternative. But Zeneca's best-laid plans were then undermined by the clash of configurations, when Monsanto-style GM products and agri-oriented technologies disrupted and eventually destroyed the market for GM food products in the UK, at least in the short run.

This clash of configurations remains most clearly evident in the issue of segregation and labelling, currently before the World Trade Organization disputes procedures. The issue was straightforward: Monsanto's initial policy of no segregation, no labelling of GM crops meant no consumer choice of whether to buy or not to buy foods derived from genetically engineered crops. The current Monsanto policy of shifting the cost and onus of segregation and labelling on to producers and consumers of GM-*free* foods underscores a much more fundamental – or configurational – attitude. For Monsanto, those who want segregation and labelling will have to pay the market price for it. For Monsanto, regulation for segregation constitutes a restraint of trade, an interference in the market. For Europe, full information is necessary for informed choice, and uninformed choice is no choice. Information empowers consumers, lack of information (not knowing whether or what GM is involved) undermines choice and potentially destroys markets. Segregation and labelling are *either* enshrined by market regulation deemed necessary to give consumers choice (European configuration) *or* a response to a consumer preference expressed through the premium price paid by consumers in an unregulated market (US configuration). In the latter alternative, segregation and labelling are a luxury for which only those prejudiced against GM may choose to pay (Chataway and Tait, 2000)[2] – granted that GM foods have passed all the regulatory hurdles within the US regulatory regime that demonstrate ecological and nutritional safety.

This chapter tries to explain the disappearance of the GM tomato by answering the question, what happens if two configurations are incommensurable or even clash. But before doing so it is worth stressing two key aspects of the analytical approach adopted here. First, by using the term 'configuration' between aspects of firm behaviour, markets, demand and regulation, it is suggested that these are analytically interdependent dimensions. A firm's existence, let alone strategy, is intelligible only within the context of distinct organizations of markets, patterns of demand and regulatory architecture – and the same goes for each of the other terms in relation to the others. Second, the concept of demand and of consumers adopted here is far from the methodological individualism of marginal utility preference or satisficing rationality. Instead, major differences in consumers' relation to food, including demand for, or trust in, food, result from major societal differences. There can be little doubt that political campaigns and alliances between different pressure groups, as well as concerted action between governmental and business groups such as retailers, have also played a major role in shaping demand for GM foods. These are not factors exogenous to markets; they are at the very core of any integrated analysis of market formation and of socially generated demand.

The case study presented in this chapter follows the trajectory of the technology on both sides of the Atlantic. Several phases are distinguished. The analysis starts with the phase of direct competition between Calgene and Zeneca, eventually leading to the 'splitting of the GM tomato'. After the split, the separate trajectories of the FlavrSavr and GM tomato purée from scientific laboratory to retail product are summarized and contrasted. The failure of the FlavrSavr is then contextualized within the broader US configuration, exemplified by Monsanto's innovation strategy. The destruction of the market for GM tomato purée in the UK is explained in terms of both the clash of configurations and the forces shaping demand.

For the Zeneca part of the story, a research project on the tomato involved interviews[3] with key informants in public science laboratories, Zeneca, Safeway and Sainsbury's, Greenpeace, the Soil Association, Friends of the Earth and Genewatch. Interviews were supported by a wide range of additional qualitative materials, from US GM tomato patent documentation to Select Committee reports of the House of Lords. For the Calgene and Monsanto story, the sources are mainly secondary, although important information on the FlavrSavr is provided by a detailed personal account of one of the scientists working for Calgene for much of the period concerned (Martineau, 2001).

THE SPLITTING OF THE GM TOMATO

From the outset, the choice of the tomato and of the particular genetic modification technology by both Calgene and Zeneca was high risk and extremely uncertain. It is striking that the two companies had no background in the market or the business of producing, distributing or retailing tomatoes. As one of the leading scientists put it: 'In the general scientific sense, we knew where it was going. And in the commercial sense absolutely no idea ... They [Zeneca] had no tomato business whatsoever. They didn't come to us saying we need to know about tomatoes. They said we need to know about plant genes. The tomato system is as good as any for finding out about plant genes' (interview, Don Grierson, Nottingham University).

Zeneca had been committing itself towards its core business activity focused on broad acre crops, buying up seed companies, and still focusing on its historical core business closely linked to agro-chemical pesticides.[4] Calgene, as a nascent biotechnology company, also had no experience in this area, and was exploring many other genetic modification alternatives also more oriented towards agribusiness. It had acquired Stoneville Pedigree Seed, and was developing genetically engineered crops resistant to the herbicide bromoxynil in partnership with Rhone Poulenc, a strategy very similar to Monsanto's with Roundup Ready and glyphosate: 'All the indications were that Calgene science and Calgene business were coming together nicely to produce what was expected to be the company's first genetically engineered product: BromoTol cotton seed' (Martineau, 2001: 1–2).

The GM technology involved in the tomato departed significantly from many of the contemporary technologies being developed for resistance to pests, as with Bt maize, or for use in conjunction with agro-chemicals as with Roundup Ready and glyphosate. It was not just a question that these technologies were oriented towards crop yield and quality, and were in competition with other systems of cultivation (traditional agrochemical or organic). Genetic modification in the case of the tomato affected the way the plant developed and involved suppressing or 'silencing' the gene that controlled the process of ageing or ripening in the tomato, the polygalacturanase gene (pTOM6). This gene programmed the collapse of cell walls in the pectin chain. Suppressing the gene delayed or prevented normal ageing or ripening processes. Similar genetic modification was being developed in relation to another aspect of senescence, the gene controlling the production of ethylene (pTOM13), the 'silencing' of which produced a tomato that never aged. The technique involved in both cases was the reintroduction of cloned tomato genes back into the tomato,[5] which had the effect of suppressing the expression of these genes, and even destroying the specific genetic material concerned. It is worth stressing that *no* genetic material foreign to the tomato was involved in achieving this result, unlike some other genetic modification technologies. The identification and suppression of both genes added considerably to the scientific understanding of the processes of senescence, but at the same time promised an entirely different market than agribusiness and competing technologies of cultivation. The outcome of this technology was to affect the quality of the fruit, rather than the process of cultivation. At the outset, no one anticipated exactly what the product market would eventually be, but it was certainly downstream of farmers.

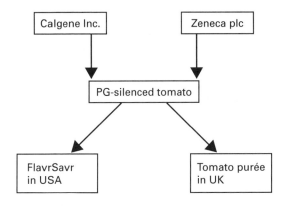

FIGURE 4.1 Two separate trajectories in the GM tomato

A key to understanding the development of the GM tomato was the initial phase of intense competition between scientists at Calgene and at Nottingham University and Zeneca. There was a race both to publish and to patent the identification of the polygalacturanase gene. Both sets of scientists were anxious to be the first, and yet there was a great contrast between the two, which shaped future developments. Calgene was a relatively small biotechnology firm, a spin-off from the University of California in Davis, with Roger Salquist, a venture capitalist and ex-submarine commander from the US Navy as CEO. Its commitment to the race put a great deal at stake for this type of bio-entrepreneur. In the UK, Zeneca, one of the leading agro-chemical and life science companies, was pursuing a strategy of open collaboration with public science institutions and had established a long-standing relationship between Wolfgang Schuch, their leading scientist, and Don Grierson with his team at the University of Nottingham.[6]

What for Calgene was almost a make-or-break venture was for Zeneca the early stages of a long experimental process of innovation that was far from dependent on the success of this first project. In the event, a number of patents were granted to both Calgene and Zeneca teams with closely related technologies between March 1986 and November 1987. Grierson, however, was the first to publish on two occasions, and did so before patents had been granted (Redenbaugh et al., 1992; Martineau, 2001: 21, 30–1, 37; interviews with Don Grierson and Wolfgang Schuch).

The matter was further complicated by Campbell's Soup Company's ownership of the seed variety on which experimentation was undertaken in the USA. By such complications, history is made. Initially, Campbell's prohibited Calgene from entering into the tomato business on their own account at all. Only in 1991 did they relax these terms and allow Calgene to develop its genetic modification technology under licence for the fresh tomato market, to avoid competition in Campbell's processed tomato business (Martineau, 2001: 11, 126). In these circumstances, a deal was negotiated between Calgene and Zeneca to split the GM tomato. Calgene was to develop the FlavrSavr for the US market while Zeneca was eventually to produce tomato purée for the UK market, with the tomato genetically modified in identical ways (see Figure 4.1).

Before passing on to the two separate trajectories, there is one further critical aspect to the splitting of the GM tomato. The US fresh tomato industry had long developed a cultivation and distribution system in which tomatoes were mechanically harvested, picked green and subsequently ripened by exposure to ethylene gas (Busch et al., 1991; Friedland and Barton, 1976; Friedland, 1975). It is widely recognized that 'early picking hurts the taste' (*Sacramento Bee*, 2002).[7]

Genetic modification which allowed the tomato to ripen on the vine, while at the same time being robust enough to be harvested mechanically, was thus seen to offer a breakthrough in the quality of fresh tomato flavour, while retaining low-cost large-scale production methods. By contrast, Europe and the UK have a fresh tomato market where fruits ripen on the vine, whether in open field or under glass, and are hand-picked when ripe. The genetic modification for fresh tomatoes thus offered little promise of creating a new market for high-quality tomatoes. Innovation in this respect would not have transformed this market in the way it potentially might have done in the USA, because of the initial difference in cultivation processes and markets. Innovation thus can be understood only in relation to the existing structures of markets to be transformed: demand side is already present for the supply side.

FLAVR DOES NOT SAVR CALGENE FROM DEATH OR MONSANTO

The trajectory of the FlavrSavr is analysed in four phases, from research and product development, to market introduction and disappearance, to facilitate comparison with the Zeneca story.

Phase 1. The lock-in to fresh tomato

As has been shown, Calgene's commitment to the tomato was initially far from evident. Indeed, until 1988 there had been a strong likelihood that either cotton or canola would prevail and, even then, there was still a possibility that Calgene would produce a BromoTol tomato with the same agribusiness orientation for GM+pesticide cultivation (Martineau, 2001: 56). Moreover, Campbell's Soup financed most of their research on the tomato.

Nevertheless, Calgene was under increasing financial pressure through the 1980s to find a GM product to start generating income. By 1988 it had progressed much further technically with the tomato, and specifically with the polygalacturanase gene, than with canola or cotton. A severe financial crisis in that year led to the sale of seed companies and to redundancies in the scientific staff. Calgene considered two main business options: to remain as a biotechnology company which traded in licences of its cloning and GM technology, or to become a vertically integrated company producing products for the end market in its own right. Given the squeeze from Wall Street to achieve significant returns, BromoTol technology would have restricted the company to an alliance with the dominant partner producing the related pesticide, and hence at a disadvantage for capturing a significant share in the value chain. In a strategy that foresaw escaping from the restrictive terms of the Campbell's contract, the option of producing a GM tomato requiring no chemicals therefore seemed the attractive alternative. Further tilting the balance towards the FlavrSavr tomato was growing political opposition both from Al Gore at the White House to bromoxynil because of risks to farmers' health, and from Jeremy Rifkin at the Campaign for Pure Food.

This combination of financial constraints and pressures, power relations between agro-chemical and small biotech, and the political risks involved with bromoxynil strongly affected Calgene's decision to commit its main resources to the tomato. From 1988, that commitment was to maximize returns to R&D by engaging the company in the development, production and distribution of the GM tomato. It was an all-or-nothing strategy to enter the tomato business, based on the conviction that the biotechnology would conquer the market: 'It was hoped a successfully introduced FlavrSavr tomato could open the door for the entire agricultural biotechnology industry' (Martineau, 2001: 9).

Phase 2. Pioneering regulatory science
The decision taken, Calgene then embarked on the as-yet uncharted process of acquiring regulatory approval for a GM food to be sold to consumers. This process, which took a further four years, was in-

tegral to the final development of the FlavrSavr tomato as a product rather than a simple requirement to be met. After initial questions over whether a less stringent approval was needed for genetic engineering as a processing technique than for a new food, Calgene opted for the latter more exigent test. As a consequence, it was essential to genetically engineer a tomato with *demonstrably* stable genetic characteristics over generations. Furthermore, the use of an antibiotic marker (*kan-r*) for the inserted PG clone produced enzyme changes, risked creating antibiotic resistance, and could possibly cause mutagenesis in other genes (pleiotropy). The theoretical possibility existed that this would result in genetic instability, health damage and changed expression of some of the tomato's vital nutritional components, such as vitamins A or C. A FlavrSavr had therefore to be developed with a demonstrably stable gene construct where genes were continuously and consistently sited at one chromosomal locus (Martineau, 2001: 122)[8] over generations. Finally, once all this had been achieved in the design of the tomato gene construct, it had to be proved safe for human consumption, by testing to prove that there were no traces of any DNA material or related protein products other than those normally found in a tomato, especially from the *kan-r* gene.

In short, the final GM tomato was considerably altered and technologically developed to meet these regulatory conditions (Redenbauch et al., 1992). The FlavrSavr approval process then became a standard for the Food Advisory Committee of the FDA, for the introduction of all subsequent GM foods, earning it the reputation among opponents as the 'Trojan horse' of genetic engineering (Mayer and Rutovitz, 1996).[9] But, critically, from a regulatory standpoint, Calgene was faced with a transparent, single and integrated regulatory regime,[10] operative for the one market that the company targeted, the US domestic market.

Phase 3. Instituting a business and a market

Within three days of receiving FDA approval for the FlavrSavr, the new tomato went on sale in a limited number of stores, mostly in California, on 21 May 1994: 'They sold like hot cakes [sic] … State Market resorted to limiting customers to two FlavrSavr tomatoes a day' (Martineau, 2001: 192). But Calgene's attempt to transform itself from a biotechnology company into a tomato producer and distributor was visibly flawed even at this moment of first launch. In 1991, as part of the new business strategy, Calgene had created Calgene Fresh Inc. as a vehicle for its tomato business: 'A key to the plan was that Calgene Fresh would charge a premium for its tomatoes of two or three times the price of "gassed green" fruit because of their higher quality. It was a novel idea, since there were essentially no premium tomatoes on the market at the time' (Martineau, 2001: 135).

To create a new market thus required a double shift, the establishment of both a premium quality and a GM food market. To achieve the first shift, Calgene created a brand for a premium range, MacGregors: 'The name would stand for farm-stand fresh, great-tasting tomatoes from the good old days' (Martineau, 2001: 138).

There was no recognition of a contradiction between a market niche created for the hallowed-traditional and one for the frontier-scientific – the hottest hi-tech tomato from pre-industrial farms. Calgene also began forming a business organization for supplying the GM tomatoes on a twelve-month basis, with supplies from Mexico and California, through partnerships with Gulfstream Tomato Growers Ltd and Meyer Tomatoes Inc. At the same time major and much more heavyweight competitors were establishing markets with much higher coverage in the USA. DNA Plant Technology Corporation (DNAP) had developed a similar tomato using somaclonal variation without gene insertion that had no need for regulatory approval. Meyer went into a competing partnership with them to produce and distribute their VineSweet tomato, and in 1993, a year before the launch of the FlavrSavr, broke ties with Calgene. Simultaneously, Monsanto was also exploiting its developed distribution system to supply over 1,000 stores with their Premium Ripe tomato, also not GM, and played in a league above Calgene that had established entry into only seventy stores by the end of 1994. Finally, the Campbell's Soup Company, the main external funder of the R&D of the FlavrSavr, announced that it would not use genetically modified foods in any of its products: 'Calgene employees felt betrayed' (Martineau, 2001: 160).

From this struggle to transform its business and market, analytically, several key aspects are involved. First, Calgene itself was small fry in big tomato business, encountering powerfully positioned competitors. Second, creating a new manufacturer-brand in a fragmented retail market structure requires considerable resources and large-scale production facilities lacked by Calgene. On both these counts, it is doubtful that Calgene had developed an assessment of the multiple economic power relations, and relied too heavily on a naïve belief in a winning technology. Third, the creation of product differentiation in an established consumer market and the introduction of a technologically radically new product are two different processes that can be combined only with great difficulty.

Phase 4. End of business, end of market: Monsanto swallows Calgene

From the moment of the product launch, Calgene was in severe financial circumstances, and went to the capital markets for more stock in October 1994. The business base was contracted, a new CEO appointed, and a new more national roll-out of the FlavrSavr attempted in May 1995 to 1,700 stores from New England to California. But the premium price was still high, twice that of any other tomato. Worse, one of the key reasons for the high price was beginning to emerge. There was a high level of wastage because at the retail end much of the produce was of poor quality. Substandard FlavrSavr tomatoes had to be sold, outside the MacGregor brand, to fast-food outlets such as Burger King. A major reason for the high waste was that the new GM tomato was inadequately engineered for the existing distribution systems. It was simply the wrong technology for the job. The silencing of the PG gene slowed down rotting once ripe, but not ripening.[11] They were ripening too quickly, becoming soft and easily damaged. Tomatoes would stay firmer for longer once on the supermarket shelf, but would not get to the supermarket shelf in consistently good enough shape using distribution systems established for 'gassed green' tomatoes. Calgene's share values had halved by early 1995, making the company prey to acquisition by one of its main competitors in the new premium market, Monsanto. After buying a 49 per cent share in the company in July 1995, Monsanto took a majority share in July 1996, and the remaining stock in January 1997. After gaining control, Monsanto dumped the FlavrSavr business: it did not fit the Monsanto model of GM technologies at that time. The FlavrSavr, the business of producing it and the market for selling it, failed to become economically instituted within the prevailing US system.

Martineau's insider account – one of progressive disillusionment – betrays some of the symptoms of the problems that beset Calgene: it was a 'firm's eye' view of the world. The main problems with Calgene for her were that the business model was misguided ('Calgene had no business in that business,' pp. 223–4); and that the technology was the wrong technology for an existing market ('Because it was a back-end benefit, the FlavrSavr was at best of marginal value to a fresh market tomato business,' p. 224). With a better business strategy and the correct technology, Martineau argues, Calgene might have prospered, instead of becoming the much-cited model of what not to do.

But the above analysis suggests a quite different perspective. From the outset, Calgene was embedded in a complex pattern of inter-firm power relations characteristic of the structure of US business and biotechnology, and within a particular structure of fragmented retailing. The view of technology and markets was not just Calgene's 'mistake', its own peculiar supply-side vision of markets created by superior technologies. It was a vision typical of, and sustained by, the configuration of US consumer markets and inter-firm, supply chain and retailing systems. And it was a vision, as will be seen, that was shared by Monsanto.

THE ZENECA STRATEGY

As with the FlavrSavr tomato, the development of genetically modified tomato purée can be analysed by contrasting it to Calgene in each of four similar phases.

Phase 1. A long period of pre-market scientific collaboration between public science institutions and Zeneca

One of the conspicuous differences between Calgene and Zeneca was the time-scale in which they operated. In Calgene, the science was in-house and costed to the balance books from the start, so accelerating the push to market. Looked at overall, from the main university scientist's first engagement with tomato and genetic modification in 1974, there was a span of twenty-two years before a product appeared on the supermarket shelves. Although the UK science was if anything slightly ahead of that of the US team, the period from patent to market was also more extended: in the USA from 1986 to 1994, in the UK from 1986–87 to 1996. As already noted, the initial collaboration between Zeneca's chief scientist, Wolfgang Schuch, and Don Grierson aimed to develop the fundamental science, seen primarily as a pre-market requisite that could have any number of eventual product outcomes. The decision to concentrate on the PG gene was taken only four years after their collaboration had started. The interaction between the two sets of scientists was one which was based on developing complementary capabilities, co-development of science and techniques of genetic modification, and agreements over IPR, publication for academics, patenting for the company (Harvey, 1999a).

Phase 2. A development of the model of a distributed innovation process

The collaboration between Zeneca and the Grierson laboratory at the University of Nottingham became part of an evolving strategy of innovating through collaborative relationships (Coombs et al., 2001). Wolfgang Schuch of Zeneca said in an interview: 'The core concept of collaboration had to be re-created, but now in an intercorporate environment. This whole business of being involved in the academic interaction, we actually did again with PetoSeed, in an industrial interaction. I think the issues in principle were exactly the same, only now we had to work with another company.'

Again in contrast to Calgene, Zeneca set about establishing a network of firms with distinct capabilities in the tomato business in order to develop the final, as yet undefined, product. It had been proved that the suppression of the PG gene produced a higher-quality taste and, for processing purposes, a much more viscous or denser-juiced tomato. The fact that Calgene had already obtained regulatory approval for the cultivation of GM tomatoes in the USA, and Zeneca's existing contacts within the tomato seed and processing business, led them to develop partnerships with PetoSeed and Hunt-Weston, the first for the cultivation and second for the processing. To anticipate, the decision to cultivate under the US regulatory regime was seen as a transitional step, prior to the much more complex and obstacle-ridden path of gaining regulatory approval in a European context. Zeneca, at least by 1997, had quite clearly understood that in the long term it was not viable to produce genetically modified foods from one regulatory regime in the market of another regulatory regime, particularly if these were in conflict over the criteria to be applied (interview with Poole, Zeneca director of communication). In the process, Zeneca was developing a sensitivity to operating within the very different contexts of the USA and Europe, negotiating its way, for example, through conflicts in perspectives and assumptions between UK retailers and US producers. They had a range of interactions stretching way beyond the horizons of a Calgene, or even a Monsanto.

It is worth emphasizing that the particular trajectory of the GM tomato towards purée was shaped by the nature of the innovation processes as distributed between specific collaborators in specific intermediary markets stretching across wide geographical spaces. Zeneca's decision to use Californian tomatoes and process them in the USA had a significant impact on the decision to develop the GM tomato for purée. Processing in the USA was undertaken normally by hotbreak technology, which was ideally suited for purée. In retrospect, Zeneca realized that a much better product would have been diced tomatoes, where consumer benefits were much more evident, than in purée produced under the hotbreak technology that was quite destructive of flavour. The 'mistake', however, was clearly conditioned by the circumstances pushing Zeneca to initiate the cultivation and production in the USA.

Phase 3. Instituting the market.

Having defined the product and established the partnerships necessary for its development, Zeneca then moved towards a strategy for the creation of markets for GM food products in the UK. Once more, the contrast between Calgene and Zeneca, and more particularly the market environments within which they were operating, could not have been greater. Given the power and integration of supermarkets within the UK, expressed most clearly by the innovation occurring through supermarket private-label products (Harvey et al., 2002), it was recognized that the strategy of collaboration had also to include major retailers. At the same time, the Institute of Grocery Distribution, the principal industry representative organization for the food retailing trade, were involved in order to establish a collective policy among retailers and producers on a general strategy towards the introduction of GM products. Labelling, segregation and information to enable consumer choice were considered a prerequisite of market formation, rather than a regulation of the market imposing external costs. This could be seen as recognition that informed consumer choice was an important societal consumer norm in this matter. Strong collaboration with retailers brought producers – and indeed product development – much closer to consumers, given that retailers' business lies in dealing directly with consumers. Individual choice was not counterposed to general rules and norms, as was the case for the Monsanto vision of markets.

But the collaboration with retailers established by Zeneca went further than setting these norms for trading in GM foods. After initially considering branding the GM tomato purée under the manufacturer's label, they decided to approach all major retailers with a view to trading under the supermarkets' private labels. In the event, two major retailers, Sainsbury's and Safeway, collaborated with Zeneca to develop the final product under retailer brands. Moreover, an unprecedented agreement was reached between these two retailers that there would be a joint launch, and that they would sell the GM tomato purée at the same price in the same format, with only the label of the retailer distinguishing the product.

In short, the launching of the first GM food in the UK was seen as a pre-competitive exercise in establishing a new market trusted by consumers (interviews at Zeneca, Safeway, and with Gavin Bailey, ex-Sainsbury's): 'We needed to get a consensus built, such that retailers and the food industry wanted to do this. It was a good introduction for the food industry' (interview, Simon Bright, Zeneca).

It was a process of collaboration whereby mutual trust in confidentiality, in Zeneca's ability to supply the product, had to be developed. This market preparation took two years from inception to product launch, demonstrating the strategic importance that was attributed to it by all those involved (Sadler, 2000: 27–8, 85).

'It is a classic example of working with a supplier, a textbook example, quoted throughout the industry on how retailers and suppliers should work together. That was a major contributory factor to the tremendous success that this product has had' (interview, Tony Coombs, Safeway).

Phase 4. The market in operation

The new GM tomato purée went on to the supermarket shelves in early 1996 and, until it was withdrawn in late 1998, sold nearly 2 million cans. Where both GM and non-GM products were in store, the former outsold the latter by two to one (Tony Coombs, Safeway). The costs of production of the purée were substantially lower than the non-GM equivalent, largely through a 40 per cent reduction in wastage, as a result of the higher viscosity and processing quality of the GM tomato. Although the quality was generally regarded as superior, however, the product was not sold as a premium quality. Nor was it sold at a premium price, but at a price 15 per cent lower than that of non-GM tomato purée. The contrast with the MacGregor premium-priced FlavrSavr tomato was complete.

But it would be a mistake simply to suggest that Zeneca made the right strategic decisions, and Calgene made the wrong ones. For example, Calgene did not have the equivalents of a Safeway or a Sainsbury's to collaborate with, let alone pre-competitively to launch a product as a market creation exercise. Further, it is quite clear that Zeneca did not expect to recoup the full costs of development of this first pilot GM commodity through its sales. Zeneca had the luxury of being able to consider the costs of market formation as a long-term investment which did not require immediate returns from the sale of the first 'proof of concept' product. Calgene, on the other hand, was financially constrained by a much shorter time-horizon, with almost the whole future of the company vested in the success of obtaining an immediate income stream from the sale of the FlavrSavr. In short, the nature of the economic agents involved *and* of the existing market structures strongly conditioned strategic options. Options available for Zeneca simply did not exist for Calgene.

Up to this point, the trajectories of the FlavrSavr tomato and GM tomato purée have each been analysed within their respective configurations, the conditions for failure within the USA and the conditions for success within the UK. To understand the eventual collapse of the UK market for GM foods, it is necessary to consider a higher-level dynamic, the interaction between different configurations. Hence, this section investigates the Monsanto-Zeneca thesis introduced earlier. There are essentially two claims to the Monsanto-Zeneca thesis. It is claimed, first, that Monsanto (and its acquisition, Calgene) inhabited a quite different, multidimensional world from that of Zeneca, and that the contrast between each firm exemplifies the difference in those worlds; and second, that when trade or business activity occurs across and between different configurations where rules and norms are in conflict, the activity of a firm from one configuration can seriously disrupt attempts to construct norms and rules for markets in another configuration. The 'disruptive' firm according to one set of norms and rules then tends to be stigmatized as the 'miscreant', whereas the source of the conflict lies at the configurational level, rather than at the individual firm level. It was a commonly held view among those involved in constructing a market for GM foods in Europe that Monsanto played a significant role in undermining their best efforts. But it is important to avoid scapegoating an individual company when the issues involve much more than firm behaviour.[12]

In their original strategy for launching the second-generation GM tomato, a nutrient-dense tomato with potential health benefits,[13] Zeneca had already planned to switch production and collaboration to Europe for a product designed for a European market. It was considered that importing Californian tomatoes, grown under the US regulatory system, was not viable in the long term, particularly in the context of growing conflict between Europe and the USA within the WTO over regulatory regimes (interview, N. Pool, Zeneca). In an assessment undertaken by the Institute for Grocery Distribution, Sadler argues that the success of GM tomato purée was to be centrally undermined by the introduction of Monsanto's GM soya and Bt corn (Sadler, 2000: 29). They contributed to the destruction of a carefully constructed market for GM foods. But markets are complex formations, and their destruction is also a complex process. Consumer attitudes in the USA and Europe were markedly different, but so also, and perhaps more significantly, was trust in regulatory authorities, governments and food authorities. After salmonella, e-coli and above all BSE, the *institutional* conditions of trust had been severely undermined in Europe (Food Standards Agency, 2002), whereas in the USA a 1999 poll discovered that 76 per cent had a great deal or a fair amount of trust in the FDA (Sadler, 2000: Appendix 7). However, market formation has much more than consumer attitudes atomistically conceived. In the UK especially, but elsewhere in Europe, organized public opinion involved a rare combination of diverse strands opposed to the introduction of GM crops, from the organic movement, through to nature conservancy organizations, the British Medical Association and − Prince Charles (Harvey, 1999; Harvey et al., 2002). Active and organized opposition to GM foods is a significant constitutive aspect of the institution and de-institution of markets and systems of food provision.

A further dimension to these institutional conditions of trust, it must be emphasized, was the role that major players, notably retailers, had in the UK organization of food supply. Retailers, because of their business role, can even assume the mantle of voicing consumer interest and, given power, can have a powerful shaping role in end markets. Here the contrast with the Monsanto business environment, rather than with Monsanto as such, is of great significance. In the UK, retailers were in a strong position as primary consumer trust institutions to both create and destroy the markets for GM foods. Iceland plc, the British retailer, in deciding to source its 'private-label' products from GM-free soya processing plants in Brazil and Canada (Sadler, 2000: 63), demonstrated that integrated supply chains front-ended by retailers were a dominant form of inter-firm organization within the UK food provision configuration. They were therefore able to proclaim their products as GM-free, thus putting intense competitive pressure on other retailers and food manufacturers supplying them to do likewise. By contrast, Monsanto considered that its market generally stopped with the farmer, and that they had no control over the farmers to whom seeds are sold (Chataway and Tait, 2000: 20), let alone processors, distributors or retailers. Chataway and Tait, on the basis of many high-level interviews conducted at Monsanto, considered that their 'innovation and marketing strategy had the farmer at its core' (p. 38): 'Monsanto lacks experience with, or adequate acknowledgement of, consumers and public opinion. Traditionally, final consumers have not been considered important stakeholders and the complexities of public opinion have not overly concerned strategists' (p. 39).

On the basis of this structurally different relationship between biotechnology companies (such as Monsanto or Zeneca), farmers, retailers and consumers, it can be argued that a very different orientation towards GM technology innovation also emerged. Essentially, for Monsanto, innovation had very little to do with end market formation, let alone active shaping of that market. In this they followed a very similar pattern to that demonstrated by Calgene, in an overriding belief in a supply-side, technology-driven view of markets. The Monsanto CEO, Robert Shapiro, notoriously declared to an annual general meeting of shareholders that Roundup Ready GM technology had been the 'most successful launch of any technology ever, including the plough' (*Guardian*, 9 October 1999).

Given a superior technology driving down prices of outputs from farmers, farmers will be forced by competitive pressures to adopt GM, and given the option for cheaper food, consumers will act with their purses and choose the cheapest option. Only regulation will get in the way of market forces (Chataway and Tait, 2000: 35). This vision of the economic world is not so much that of neo-classical economics as of a world in which intermediate markets are serially structured in relation to end markets, and where consequently firms supplying products to intermediate markets can do so without consideration of end markets.

The clash of configurations which underpins the stigmatization of Monsanto was thus one where the business orientation of a firm from the US configuration created consternation and bewilderment to firms within the European configuration, and no doubt vice versa. How dare Europe suffocate the free play of market forces and suppress technological innovation! How could Monsanto behave so badly as to ignore consumer choice and public opinion!

A final dimension to the clash of configurations is that of regulatory regimes. The development of regulatory regimes is itself a complex process, and beyond the scope of this chapter to analyse. But it is clear that the gulf between US and European regulatory regimes has widened in the years following the first approval of the GM tomato. The widening also gave rise to increased conflict within the WTO. The major change has arisen in Europe, and this cannot simply be attributed to governmental policy, but to many of the influences already considered: political lobbies, greater salience of consumer power, the trust crisis in food provision, retailers as a powerful business lobby and so on.

The key emergent difference since the acceptance of the GM tomato under the EC Directive 90/220/EEC has been in relation to labelling, because effectively it segments the market in two: GM and non-GM foods (below a threshold). The directive requiring labelling, hence segregation, for Roundup Ready soya and Bt maize came into operation in May 1998, and the EC Regulation 1139/98 also set a threshold for 'identity preserved' streams of non-GM crops. More stringent regulations for the introduction of novel foods have also been developed (EC Regulation 258/97), covering both environmental and human health concerns.

But in addition to these broad parameters to the clash in regulatory regimes, an important difference of another order distinguishes the US from the European configuration. The USA is a unitary regime at the Federal level. Europe has a high level of regulatory complexity, where European-level regulation constitutes only one scale of regulatory regime. Each national government can, and to date has, implemented its own GM regulatory systems. As a consequence, from a regulatory standpoint, there is no single European market for GM foods.

This regulatory complexity stands in stark contrast to the USA (Schuch and Poole, 1993; Lindemann, 1993; House of Lords, 1998), and creates a further source of tension where discrepancies occur between national and European-level regulation. Conflicts between the US and European-level regulatory regime may induce further conflicts between the different levels of European regulatory regimes. This two- or multi-tier characteristic of the European regulatory configuration is therefore an additional aspect of the clash of configurations, related to regime complexity.

To sum up the discussion on the Monsanto-Zeneca thesis, the opposed dimensions of the two configurations are summarized in Table 4.1 below:

TABLE 4.1 Two opposed configurations

Agribusiness-production oriented	v	Food/consumer oriented
Single US regulatory regime regimes	v	Multi-layered European regulatory
Lower-power supermarkets	v	High-power integrated supermarkets
US consumer trust cultures	v	UK-European consumer trust cultures
Growing farmer doubts	v	Political alliances opposed to GM

The 'clash of configurations' is thus a multidimensional one, with Monsanto and Zeneca inhabiting quite different worlds in terms of business orientation, power relations between firms up and down the supply chain, socio-structural aspects of consumer markets, innovation and technology strategic possibilities and regulatory regimes. In the particular case in question, the institution of a market for GM tomato purée in the UK, and eventually the creation of wider markets for GM foods, including nutrient-dense foods, was undermined as much by this clash as by the internal dynamics within the UK and European configuration. Indeed, there is clearly an interaction between inter- and intra-configurational dynamics.

CONCLUSION

The 'silencing' gene in a tomato might at first sight appear to be the technical consequence of a scientific revolution of great potential that will ultimately be expressed in a multitude of different products, a transformation of both food and agriculture. But, this apparently singular genetic science and technique was shown to involve a wide variety of complex interactions from inception through all subsequent transformations. It never really was singular. Competition, scientific and commercial, between differently instituted dynamics in Calgene and Zeneca meant variety was already present in the initial conditions. As we learn from chaos theory, 'sensitive dependence on initial conditions' can produce massive divergences (Gleick, 1998).

Firms were engaged within existing configurations of capital, intermediary and end-product markets. Relative power between different types of firms matters: retailers, biotechnology companies, manufacturers, farmers and so on. Powerful retailers in a United Kingdom context have resulted in fully integrated food-provisioning supply chains led and orchestrated by the front-end, closest to consumers. Powerful agribusiness in the USA and relatively regional or fragmented retailers (with the possible exception of WalMart) have resulted in a much more segmented food-provisioning system, in which a biotechnology plays to its main market, farmers. Firms see the world, make strategies, develop rationales, from within the power configuration they centrally inhabit.

Furthermore, the atomistic conception of consumers makes it hard to understand that consumers relating to fragmented and low-power retailers are very different from consumers relating to powerful integrated national retailers selling their own-label GM-free produce. Consumer politics and organized lobbies are not 'interferences' in otherwise economic processes, but constitutive of them. And, as Polanyi argued long ago (1957/1944: 68), markets and regulation are original partners not latter-day opponents.

Tracing the contrary trajectories of the US FlavrSavr tomato and the UK GM tomato purée demonstrated the complex nature of the development of science, technology and business strategy *within* their respective configurations. The institution and collapse of their respective markets was shown to be radically different. At the next level of analysis, it was shown that there are strong interactions between the internal dynamics of a configuration and dynamics of conflict between configurations. The ultimate conclusion that may be drawn is that the development of science and technology within capitalism is a consequence of the multiple, fissured and contradictory nature of capitalist processes, rather than that of a single engine of universal science linked to a single engine of capital grinding out one inevitable global future.

NOTES

1. Calgene was a small US biotechnology spin-off company from University of California at Davis founded in 1980 with venture capital; Zeneca, originating from ICI, was a large UK-based multinational life science company that, in the wake of the market turbulence described in this chapter, split into two, a pharmaceutical division that merged into Astra-Zeneca, and a biotechnology division that merged into Syngenta.

2. ' "There are lots of people in the world who will offer you GM-free soya and corn ... but they are charging a price for it ... The only way you can get hold of it is to pay a premium and at the moment retailers are unprepared for that ... Market forces will prevail." (Senior Monsanto Manager)' (Chataway and Tait, 2000: 34–5).

3. I am grateful to my colleague, Dr Steve Quilley, for undertaking the interviews with organizations involved in eco-politics. The interviews were conducted in 1998–99.

4. Indeed, for Zeneca much of its business activity, including development of GM technologies, remained linked with agro-chemicals, although as a combination of technologies designed to reduce pesticide dependence (Tait and Chataway, 2000).

5. The reintroduction was achieved by use of *Agrobacterium tumifíciens* Ti plasmids, and could involve either reversing the DNA sequence to form anti-sense DNA, or by adding a copy of the same tomato gene back into the nucleus. The term 'gene silencing' was adopted to cover both techniques.

6. It is a strategy which has continued and expanded, notably with Syngenta (the agro-biotechnology progeny of Zeneca) at the John Innes Centre in Norwich (interviews in October 2000).

7. The *Sacramento Bee* (2002) has long taken an interest in the creation of a biotechnology hub in the area around Sacramento, and has tracked the fate of Calgene closely. In losing Calgene, it reported that 'Davis lost a golden opportunity to become a hub of the biotech industry'. A new genetic modification, this time to the rin gene, was claimed by the US Department of Agriculture, Cornell

University, in April 2002, which once more promises to solve the US problem of gassed fresh tomatoes. 'For understanding tomato ripening and eventually taste, this could be the Holy Grail,' claimed the scientist Jon Giovannoni.

8. This was demonstrated by use of the Southern blot technique.

9. 'Following the FlavrSavr™ decision, FDA has not conducted comprehensive scientific reviews of foods derived from bioengineered plants' (Beru, 2000).

10. In 1992, the FDA published a policy statement relating to all new GM foods: 57 FR 22984.

11. As part of the fundamental science, the genetic basis for the expression difference between ripening and rotting became better understood.

12. At the same time, many transnational corporations (including Zeneca) are quite capable of adapting to very different economic, business and regulatory cultures, and it is not being argued here that Monsanto is generally representative of all biotechnology companies in the USA.

13. This genetic modification was designed to increase the expression of the naturally occurring lycopene in tomato, with possible benefits for the alleviation of cardio-vascular disease and prostate cancer (Harvey, 1999; Harvey et al., 2002).

REFERENCES

Beru, N. (2000) 'Foods from Genetically Engineered Plants. The FDA's Experience: 1992 to the Present', in C. Fairbairn, G. Scoles and A. McHughen (eds), *Proceedings of the 6th International Symposium on the Biosafety of Genetically Modified Organisms* (8–13 July), pp. 65–70. Saskatoon: University of Saskatchewan.

Busch, L., W. B. Lacy, J. Burkhardt, and L. R. Lacy (1991) *Plants, Power and Profit. Social, Economic and Ethical Consequences of the New Biotechnologies*. Oxford: Basil Blackwell.

Chataway, J. and J. Tait (2000) *Monsanto Monograph*. Annex C11, PITA Project, European Commission <http://technology.open.ac.uk/cts/pita/AnnC11-mono-monsanto.pdf> (21 May 2003).

Coombs, R., M. Harvey and B. Tether (2001) 'Analysing Distributed Innovation Processes', CRIC Discussion Paper no. 43 (forthcoming in *Industrial and Corporate Change*). Manchester: Centre for Research on Innovation and Competition.

Food Standards Agency (2002) 'Consumer Attitudes to Food Safety' <www.food standards.gov.uk/> (November 2002).

Friedland, W. H. (1975) *De-Stalking the Wily Tomato: A Case Study in Social Consequences in Californian Agricultural Research*, Research Monograph no. 15. Davis: University of California.

Friedland, W. H. and A. E. Barton (1976) 'The Harvesting Machine Saved Tomatoes for California', *Society* 13: 34–42.

Gleick, J. (1998) *Chaos. The Amazing Science of the Unpredictable*. London: Vintage.

Harvey, M. (1999a) 'Genetic Modification as a Bio-Socio-Economic Process: One Case of Tomato Purée', CRIC Discussion Paper no. 31. Manchester: Centre for Research on Innovation and Competition.

— (1999b) 'Cultivation and Comprehension: How Genetic Modification Irreversibly Alters the Human Engagement with Nature', *Sociological Research Online* 4 (3).

— (2000) 'Genetically Modified Food: A Suitable Case of an Economic Sociology Treatment', *Economic Sociology Newsletter* 1 (3): 6–11.

Harvey, M., S. Quilley and H. Beynon (2002) *Exploring the Tomato: Transformations of Nature, Society and Economy*. Cheltenham: Edward Elgar.

House of Lords (1998) 'EC Regulation of Genetic Modification in Agriculture', Select Committee on European Communities. Second Report.

Jones, S. (2000) *Almost Like a Whale: The Origin of Species Updated*. London: Anchor.

Lindemann, J. (1993) 'Marketing Transgenic Food Crops in the U.S.: Regulatory Issues', in J. I. Yoder (ed.), *Molecular Biology of Tomato: Fundamental Advances and Crop Improvement*. Lancaster, PA: Technomic Publishing.

Martineau, B. (2001) *First Fruit. The Creation of the FlavrSavr Tomato and the Birth of Biotech Food*. New York: McGraw-Hill.

Mayer, S. and J. Rutovitz (1996) 'Trojan Tomatoes: Genetically Engineered for Delayed Softening or Ripening.' Greenpeace draft report, unpublished.

Polanyi, K. (1957 [1944]) *The Great Transformation. The Political and Economic Origins of Our Time*. Boston, MA: Beacon Press.

Redenbaugh, K., W. Hiatt, B. Martineau, M. Kramer, R. Sheehy, R. Sanders, C. Houck and D. Emlay (1992) *Safety Assessment of Genetically Engineered Fruits and Vegetables. A Case Study of the Flavr Savr™ Tomato*. Boca Raton, FL: CRC Press.

Sacramento Bee (2002) 'New Tomato Has Its Skeptics', *Sacramento Bee* 13 April 2002<www.sacbee.com>

Sadler, M. (2000) *GM Foods Past-Present-Future...? Industry's Approach, Consumer Attitudes, Expectations for the Future*. Letchmore Heath: Institute of Grocery Distribution.

Schuch, W. and N. Poole (1993) 'The Evolution of the Regulation of Genetically Modified Organisms in Europe', in J. I. Yoder (ed.), *Molecular Biology of Tomato: Fundamental Advances and Crop Improvement*. Lancaster, PA: Technomic Publishing.

Tait, J. and J. Chataway (2000) *Zeneca Agrochemicals Monograph*. Annex C16, PITA Project, European Commission <http://technology.open.ac.uk/cts/pita/AnnC16-mono-zeneca.pdf> (21 May 2003).

Yoder, J. I. (ed.) (1993) *Molecular Biology of Tomato: Fundamental Advances and Crop Improvement*. Lancaster PA: Technomic Publishing.

FIVE | Contrasting paths of corporate greening in Antipodean agriculture: organics and green production

KRISTEN LYONS, DAVID BURCH, GEOFFREY LAWRENCE AND STEWART LOCKIE

§ Over the last few decades, and throughout the world, the corporate sector has sought to establish its environmental credentials by integrating environmental and social justice issues into its corporate policy agendas and practice. Such restructuring is particularly evident throughout agriculture and food systems, where food processors and retailers appear to have taken note of the lessons to be drawn from the growth of the organic food sector. The growth of organic production has led the corporate sector to address – in various ways and to different degrees – 'green' issues in shaping the trajectory of this development. For some corporate actors, the influence of 'green' concerns has been manifest in little more than expressions of concern and statements of intent, which are designed to disguise current unsustainable practices. For others, in contrast, it is reflected in the restructuring of food production systems in ways that support the production of organic food, the development of environmental codes of practice and other initiatives which represent a new policy direction.

In this chapter we analyse the different strategies of corporate greening which have emerged throughout the agrifood sector in the Antipodes. In particular, we focus on two food companies – Uncle Tobys in Australia and Heinz Wattie in New Zealand – and examine the specific greening practices of these firms, and the impacts of such practices on producers, consumers and others engaged in food networks. An examination of these changes in the agrifood sector illustrates the various ways in which firms are responding to broader social and environmental challenges facing the agriculture and food industry. In particular, the analysis of these cases draws attention to the role of the production and processing sectors in Australia and New Zealand in developing strategies of corporate greening. This marks a significant contrast to strategies of greening occurring elsewhere, including the UK where retailers have taken the lead in shaping the trajectory of systems of agriculture and food production. The findings from this chapter indicate that while food companies play a significant role in the Antipodean organic food sector – manifest in different ways across each of these locations – their entry to organics, to date, has not heralded a radical transformation of agricultural practices. While growth in the organic sector presents an opportunity to address those environmental and social problems that have emerged alongside the current farm crisis, the activities of food processing companies in the Antipodes have gone only part way to address these challenges.

GREENING AGRICULTURE AND FOOD IN AUSTRALIA AND NEW ZEALAND

The organic food industry is currently the fastest-growing food sector worldwide. With consumption growth rates calculated at 25 per cent annually, the industry is estimated to reach 15 per cent of total food consumption by 2005 (Kinnear, 1999). In Australia and New Zealand, the industry has undergone sustained growth over the last ten years, increasing in value from AUS $28 million in 1990 to AUS $200 million by 1999 in Australia, and from NZ $1.1 million in 1988 to NZ $60 million in 2000 in New Zealand (Kinnear, 1999; OPEG, 2000; Saunders et al., 1997). Alongside this increase in the value of industry output, the number of certified producers in Australia utilizing organic methods has also increased substantially, from 491 producers in 1990 to an estimated 2,000 by 1999 (Kinnear, 1999). Similarly, in New Zealand the number of organic farms has increased from 89 to an estimated 300 by 1997 (Saunders et al., 1997). As a part of this growth, the organic industries across each of these locations have become increasingly integrated with conventional food systems, evidenced by the increased interest in organics shown by food firms, government departments and research institutions.

This apparent greening of food and agriculture in Australia and New Zealand must be understood within the context of the social, economic and environmental crises that are currently being experienced by rural communities. The rapid growth in the organic sector – and the involvement of corporate actors in this sector – reflects, at least in part, a response to the problems emerging from these contemporary farm crises. Foremost among these problems include a decline in farm numbers; increasing poverty and indebtedness as only a small group of highly productive farms earn commercial rates of return on investment; poorer health indicators than for the wider population; and land and water degradation which impose substantial immediate costs while threatening longer-term productive viability (Lockie and Bourke, 2001). Constant shifts in demand raise new threats and opportunities. A joint report issued by Australia's National Farmers' Federation and the Australian Conservation Foundation in April 2000 estimated that environmental degradation associated with agriculture in Australia costs in excess of AUS $2 billion annually and could rise to over AUS $6 billion annually by 2020 (Madden et al., 2000). The amount of land affected by salinity alone could rise from 2.5 million to 15.5 million ha unless action is taken. This is somewhat akin to an increase from an area the size of Belgium to an area the size of England and Wales. It is difficult to tell how much of New Zealand's agricultural lands is affected by erosion, salinity and other problems, as national data do not exist (Ministry for the Environment, 1997). Nevertheless, there is little reason to think that the situation is not similarly serious.

There is, in some respects, nothing new about environmental degradation, or attempts to address it, in Australian and New Zealand agriculture. Extensive soil erosion was a major political issue in both countries as far back as the 1890s and 1930s (Bradsen, 1988; Ministry for the Environment, 1997). By the 1970s over half of all agricultural lands in Australia required treatment for soil or vegetation degradation (DEHCD, 1978). There is also little new in the dominant approaches governments are taking to these issues, which focus on voluntary action on the part of landholders supported by research and education services provided by government (Bradsen, 1988; Ministry for the Environment, 1997). Even Australia's much-vaunted National Landcare Program, which is represented by government as a major investment in rural land degradation, is focused on encouraging voluntary action by providing limited financial support to community environmental groups (Lockie and Vanclay, 1997). In the absence of more overt intervention, Landcare has been represented by some of its critics as a triumph of marketing over substance that does little to help cash-strapped farmers make anything more than incremental changes in farming practice (Lockie, 1997a, 1999). Despite this, over 30 per cent of Australian farm businesses have at least one employee who is a Landcare group member (Mues et al., 1998) and the concept has spread to New Zealand, South Africa and elsewhere.

There are, however, at least two dimensions to the current phase of 'greening' that do appear to be novel. The first of these is the discourse of 'sustainable development' that circulates within contemporary agriculture, and the clear link that is made in these discourses between agricultural productivity and the conservation of natural resources. In contrast to the early days of soil and water conservation in Australia and New Zealand, when strategies to protect resources were believed to have few immediate or obvious economic benefits, most contemporary strategies offer improved profitability in the short and long terms (Barr and Cary, 1992). 'Conservation farming', for example, also known as minimum, reduced or no-till farming, uses synthetic herbicides in preference to mechanical tillage as a means to reduce soil disturbance, compaction and exposure while also reducing labour and increasing production (Barr and Cary, 1992). The second novel dimension is the development of discourses of food and environmental safety that stress, respectively, the impacts on human health and the impacts on other species and ecosystems of synthetic pesticides, fertilizers and veterinary drugs. More and more consumers, it seems, are not simply concerned about the fate of the countryside, they are worried about what the food they eat is doing to themselves.

At face value, the spectacular growth in the production and consumption of organic food in Australia and New Zealand, as in other parts of the world (notably Europe, the United States and Canada), supports the view that opposition to synthetic pesticides and fertilizers among consumers is growing. This trend challenges the dominant approach to soil and water conservation, that is, of replacing mechanical pest control with chemical controls. But it is also important to acknowledge a range of other factors and trends that militate against the shift towards organic production. First, the vast majority of farmers are sceptical of the ability of chemical-free farming systems to operate profitably and effectively, despite their own reservations about chemical use (Lockie, 1997b). Second, while high levels of financial support are made available to assist in the improvement of 'conventional' farming systems, there is little institutional support and research to assist farmers in making the move towards organics. In the face of constantly deteriorating terms of trade, most find farming a risky enough activity without abandoning their most accessible means of support (Lockie, 1997b). Third, there are a number of alternative means to reduce chemical residues or demonstrate product safety which stop short of full conversion to organic production. For example, integrated pest management (IPM) strategies reduce chemical use through more careful monitoring of pest populations and the use of both chemical and alternative means of control, while quality assurance (QA) systems such as developed by the International Organization for Standardization (ISO) allow tracking of produce from farm to consumer and provide guarantees that farmers have followed all the necessary procedures to reduce the risk of residues. Increasingly, large retailers and processors in Australia require farmers to adopt certified QA procedures (Lockie, 1998). Fourth, there is some evidence to suggest that many consumers of organic foods do so principally out of concern for the effects of chemical residues or genetically-modified organisms on their own health and well-being, rather than a concern for the environment (Lyons, 2000, 2001). Unless these consumers can be convinced either that looking after the environment and looking after themselves are essentially one and the same thing, or that organic certification is substantially more trustworthy than the alternatives, there is every possibility that they may favour those foods produced via certified IPM or QA processes – particularly when cheaper – over organics.

It should be no great surprise that not only is the greening of agriculture a complex and contested process, but that there is not always a direct relationship between the greening of food production and the greening of food consumption. Programmes such as Australia's National Landcare Program and technologies such as 'conservation farming' demonstrate how successfully discourses of sustainability have been incorporated within conventional agriculture while displacing concerns about chemical use to the realm of food safety and quality assurance. By promoting a discursive link between environmental and personal health – as illustrated in varying degrees by the activities of Uncle Tobys and Heinz Wattie, as discussed below – the organic industry seeks to challenge this displacement. However, it is arguable that the ways in which these discourses are taken up by corporate capital in their own greening strategies depend upon, and are critical to, perceptions of a separation between environmental sustainability and resource use on the one hand, and food safety and the use of agro-chemicals on the other. This is clear when we examine the pathways towards corporate greening in Australia and New Zealand, and compare these with that in Europe.

CORPORATE CAPITAL AND GREENING

The involvement of corporate capital in the agrifood sector of most industrialized countries, including Australia and New Zealand, has been an important impetus in expanding the size of the organic industry. These firms have engaged in discourses around the notion of 'clean and green' production, including organics, with the aim of addressing the two issues discussed above, that concerning sustainable development and that relating to food safety (Burch et al., 2001). Many corporations point to the adoption of concepts such as the 'triple bottom line', involving not just profitability as the main determinant of corporate effectiveness, but also embracing environmental responsibility and social equity, as evidence that they are committed to the adoption of sustainable production practices (Elkington, 1998). In this regard, the corporate sector has argued that it, too, has an interest in sustainable development, in part because consumer groups expect corporations to behave responsibly, and in part because companies are able to make savings by minimizing waste and better managing their use of scarce resources.

Such claims are not uncontested, and many critics have argued that this projection of 'corporate greening' is merely a public relations exercise – or a 'greenwash' – aimed not at making substantial changes to current practice but, rather, designed to improve a company's image at a time when many consumers and citizens are becoming increasingly concerned about large-scale environmental degradation (Beder, 1997; Greer and Bruno, 1996; Welford, 1997). From this perspective, capitalist enterprises are unable to change their behaviour because their main priority is still the maximization of profits for the benefit of their shareholders.

In terms of this debate, we take the view that it is not possible to generalize across all instances on the basis of *a priori* assumptions about the capacity of capitalist institutions to embrace the principles of sustainable development. The situation may well vary from company to company, from sector to sector and from country to country, and each case must be decided on its merits (Lawrence, 1999). In Australia and New Zealand, many food companies now produce a range of organic products, including breakfast cereals, frozen vegetables, baby foods, honey, pasta and soy products, which are distributed throughout both the domestic and international markets (Burch et al., 2001; Lyons, 1999, 2001). In Australia, Uncle Tobys, Berrivale and Sandhurst produce a range of organic breakfast cereals and fruit beverages, while in New Zealand, Heinz Wattie's Australasia, Talley's Frozen Foods and McCains Foods process frozen vegetables, Only Organic Baby Food Ltd distributes a range of baby foods, and New Zealand Biograins retails cereals and oilseeds (see Lyons, 1999, 2001; Monk, 1998). An examination of a selected food firm across each of these locations provides a context in which to assess the specificities associated with the involvement of two food processing companies in organic agriculture, and the degree to which this involvement represents a genuine shift to 'green production'.

A detailed analysis of case material avoids the problem of over-generalizing about the capacity of the corporate sector to respond to consumer concerns about environmental degradation and/or food safety. By focusing on the specificities of each case, the case study approach allows claims to corporate greening to be decided on their merits. To this end, this chapter will now overview the activities of Uncle Tobys in Australia and Heinz Wattie in New Zealand prior to assessing the implications of their involvement in organic production for Antipodean organic food and agriculture, and for our understanding of green production more generally.

Uncle Tobys

Uncle Tobys is the brand name of a range of cereal products manufactured by Australia and New Zealand's largest food company, Goodman Fielder. This diversified company produces a wide range of food lines marketed under a variety of brand names: edible oils (Meadow Lea, Praise and Crisco), milling and baking (Wonder White and Nature's Fresh), poultry (Steggles), pastry (Pampas) and gelatine. Until 1999, Goodman Fielder also owned a poultry processing company called Steggles and, along with its baking operations, supplied leading food chains such as McDonald's with ingredients, including chicken McNuggets, buns and crumpets. Goodman Fielder dominates a range of sectors in the Australian food industry, although with the sale of Steggles in 1999, and the acquisition of Defiance baking operations and New Zealand's biggest baker, Ernest Adams, it has come to concentrate on a few core activities in milling and baking. In the period 1999–2000, the company made a profit of $130.9 million (Goodman Fielder, 2000). The company produces only one line of organic products, the Uncle Tobys brand of breakfast cereal called Organic Vita Brits.

Uncle Tobys has been producing a rectangular breakfast cereal biscuit called Vita Brits, made from conventionally-produced raw materials, since 1935. In 1991 the conventional product was replaced by 'Organic Vita Brits'. The release of this organic breakfast cereal was Uncle Tobys' first overt 'green production' strategy, and signalled a substantive shift from its reliance on predominantly conventional food production systems for the supply of inputs for its broader range of processed foods. However, in 1997, the company withdrew from the organics market. This withdrawal was related to the increasing cost of sourcing organic wheat and what Uncle Tobys identified as limited consumer interest in Organic Vita Brits. Uncle Tobys did, however, continue to produce Vita Brits using conventionally-produced inputs. In 1999, the company reintroduced the organic line of Vita Brits, so that both product lines are now marketed. Organic Vita Brits currently retail at a small premium (less than 5 per cent) above the price of the conventional counterpart. Despite this product differentiation, Uncle Tobys markets both its organic and conventional products as healthy and nutritious (Lyons, 1999).

Uncle Tobys has employed various additional marketing strategies to promote its organic product, and to define aspects of 'green production' systems. Uncle Tobys began to source organic wheat in 1990 for processing its breakfast cereal for market release the following year. To source organic wheat, Uncle Tobys established verbal contract relationships with producers located in regions that were in close proximity to its processing plants in Victoria and Queensland. With its subsequent re-entry into the organics market in 1999, Uncle Tobys centralized the production of Organic Vita Brits to the Victoria plant, and thus dissolved agreements with producers previously supplying the Queensland operation. All producers supplying Uncle Tobys have been involved in the organic industry for some years, and are certified 'Level A' by the National Association of Sustainable Agriculture Australia (NASAA), one of the largest organic certification organizations in Australia. Uncle Tobys does not encourage conventional wheat producers to convert to organic practices, preferring to source organic wheat from established organic farms. In addition, Uncle Tobys processing plants are also certified by NASAA. Organic Vita Brits provides a relatively simple product for Uncle Tobys to produce organically, as it requires only one organic input: wheat. In contrast, most Uncle Tobys products require a range of inputs, including fruits, nuts and other grains and, as such, would be more difficult to produce organically. Consequently, Uncle Tobys remains uninterested in producing any other organic food. Goodman Fielder has to date taken no steps to convert other cereal products – marketed either under Uncle Tobys or its other cereal brand, Bluebird Foods – to organic production. To date, all Organic Vita Brits have retailed on the domestic markets, except for small quantities exported to New Zealand (Lyons, 1999).

Heinz Wattie

Heinz Wattie Australasia is one of the world's leading food processors, and is most well known for brands including Heinz, Watties and Weight Watchers, as well as Ore-Ida, the Budget Gourmet and StarKist. Heinz Wattie Australasia was formed in 1998 after the merger of Heinz Australia and Heinz Wattie. Heinz Wattie first entered into 'green production' in 1991 by way of processing frozen organic peas, carrots, sweetcorn and potatoes in New Zealand. Producers currently contracted to supply Heinz Wattie with organic vegetables are centrally located around a number of processing plants, with the most concentrated area under organic pea production at Canterbury, in the South Island of New Zealand. All producers supplying Heinz Wattie with organic produce are required to obtain organic certification from Bio-Gro New Zealand – the leading certification agency in New Zealand – and processing plants are also certified by Bio-Gro. As part of a strategy to ensure a continual supply of vegetables from farms in close proximity to processing facilities, Heinz Wattie developed a Grow Organic with Watties programme in 1990, which aimed to encourage conventional producers to convert to organic production, and to support them during this transition process. This programme provides information on Bio-Gro certification standards, as well as advisory services from Heinz Wattie field officers. The development of this programme to encourage and support producers throughout conversion to organic farming practices contrasts with the case of Uncle Tobys, who provided little or no support services to producers, but rather preferred to source inputs from already established organic farms. The success of the Heinz Wattie programme for the New Zealand organic industry is reflected in the area converted to organic production, which in 1998 represented 15 per cent of the total land contracted by Heinz Wattie nationwide (Anon., 1998). Heinz Wattie currently has contracts with fifty certified organic producers, who farm an area of 2,500 ha (Heinz Wattie, 2000). Heinz Wattie organic frozen vegetables are retailed throughout Japan, Europe, the United States, South Africa, Australia and New Zealand.

CONSTRUCTING 'ORGANICS': FOOD PRODUCTS AND
CORPORATE IDENTITY

The entry of Uncle Tobys and Heinz Wattie to the organic industry represents, at least in part, a response to the various pressures exerted by consumers and others in the food production sector. Not least among these is the pressure to 'green production' methods, so as to address, or at least make some attempts to address, those social and environmental problems facing rural communities, as well as attending to some of the concerns expressed by consumers about food safety. As an outcome of such dynamics, a number of changes are evident throughout Antipodean corporate food production sectors (in contrast to the retail sector evidenced in the UK).

To begin, corporate support for organic production systems (as evidenced by Heinz Wattie and Uncle Tobys) represent a significant departure from dominant cultural values and beliefs about farming, including those that prioritize conventional input-intensive farming methods. As discussed earlier, the priority still accorded to conventional farming methods derives from the belief that such methods can offer some solutions to agro-environmental problems. The evidence for this is to be found in the extensive government and industry support for chemical-intensive farming methods in Australia and New Zealand, while organic methods have been overlooked, and often criticized and ridiculed (Lyons, 2001). Corporate participation in the organic industry thus appears to represent a substantial departure from traditional techniques of food production. The participation by corporate actors in the organic industry has been manifest in material and symbolic transformations of the practices of these firms. That is, corporate food firms have altered aspects of both their food production systems, as well as the meanings of such systems and the foods they produce. It is important to note at this point that an array of actors – including farmers, certification agencies, consumers and others – play a key part in determining the material and symbolic character of organic food and agriculture. Each of these actors is also active in constructing meanings surrounding organic food and agriculture (see Lyons, 2000). This chapter, however, focuses specifically on the symbolic meanings which corporate actors associate with organic food in order to examine the various strategies companies engage in to construct meanings of environmentally-related symbols – including organics – and in turn, the ways in which they have associated such symbols with their products. Uncle Tobys and Heinz Wattie have, to varying degrees, embodied these meanings as part of a corporate philosophy.

Between 1991 and 1997, and from 1999 to the present, Uncle Tobys undertook two broad marketing strategies that signified attempts to associate environmentally-related symbols with its product. These strategies signified an attempt to shape understandings of organic and 'green production' more generally. The first of these strategies – manifest through packaging, advertising through television and print media and promotional material – involved constructing a connection between the self, the environment and the consumption of its product (Lyons, 1999, 2000). As part of this process, Uncle Tobys utilized environmental signifiers to reshape both its product, as well as that of its corporate image. In order to illustrate this theme, packaging and promotional material include various signifiers, such as the NASAA certification logo that ensures all ingredients are produced according to the strict guidelines stipulated by this organic certification organization. Additionally, boxes of Organic Vita Brits utilized the slogan 'Organic Food: Healthy For You, Healthy For The Environment', and listed the benefits of organic farming practices for the environment. An important additional greening strategy Uncle Tobys undertook was the sponsorship of Landcare Australia Ltd, entitling it to use the Landcare logo on boxes of Organic Vita Brits. The 'caring hands' mark that signifies Landcare has been endorsed widely within the corporate world as an indicator of environmental concern, and has consequently been adopted by many corporations including Monsanto, BP and Broken Hill Petroleum (BHP) (Lockie, 1997a). Thus, this signifier enabled Uncle Tobys to associate both its product, and concomitantly its corporate image, with a healthy environment. This meaning of organics concurred with those meanings associated with other 'green production' labels applied to Antipodean agriculture – including the Landcare programme, IPM and conservation farming – which also promoted environmental integrity and environmental sustainability. An important point to note here is that the adoption of an organic label required Uncle Tobys to alter its production system – that is, to source organic wheat and process their product following organic certification standards. Support for the Landcare programme, however, was in the form of a financial contribution, and did not require any alterations to production methods. Green production in this context thus represented only a symbolic, rather than a material, shift in corporate practices.

A second and closely linked discourse utilized by Uncle Tobys sought to associate organic food, and concomitantly its corporate image and green production more generally, with health. Slogans such as 'Organic Food: Healthy For You, Healthy For The Environment' suggested a commitment not only to a healthy environment, but also to healthy bodies. These symbolic constructions indicated that the consumption of Organic Vita Brits contributed to a healthy diet and good health. Well-known Australian beach and surf lifesavers, signifying safety and health (see Fiske et al., 1987), are also employed to promote Organic Vita Brits, further reinforcing this linkage. With the re-release of its organic product in 1999, Uncle Tobys further expanded the connection between healthy bodies, Organic Vita Brits, and its corporate image. In particular, Uncle Tobys was an official sponsor of the Sydney 2000 Olympic Games, and its owner, Goodman Fielder, committed over 1,000 tonnes of food to athletes, officials and guests throughout the Olympics. By these actions, Uncle Tobys and its parent company have assisted in attaching meanings associated with health and fitness to both their products, as well as the companies themselves. The use of healthy bodies – including that of high-profile Australian swimmer Lisa Curry-Kenny – to promote environmental initiatives such as Landcare, and later Coastcare, further strengthened this relationship, as well as associating a healthy environment with personal health (Lyons, 1999).

Heinz Wattie, in contrast, engages to a much lesser extent than Uncle Tobys with these signifiers. Heinz Wattie does, however, indicate its products are certified 'organic', thus appealing to similar consumer concerns. To date, demand for its products has outstripped supply – particularly throughout Japan, the West Coast of America and Europe – and while it is clear that such foods are highly sought-after, it is less well understood why consumers demand these foods. In addition to this promotion of its product, Heinz Wattie has also indicated a broader corporate commitment to environmental concerns and, in particular, has adopted a corporate environmental philosophy which is monitored by its environmental programme called 'Environmental Honesty' (Anon., 1996). The adoption of this programme illustrates Heinz Wattie's attempt to position itself as an environmentally responsible company. The corporate greening strategies undertaken by Heinz Wattie illustrate a somewhat more holistic approach to greening production than those undertaken by Uncle Tobys. While both companies sourced organic inputs, Heinz Wattie has developed an environmental programme to address the more general environmental problems related to the company.

These case studies of Uncle Tobys and Heinz Wattie show how each of these firms has actively sought, first, to shape understandings of 'green production', and, second, to attach these meanings to its organic products. Uncle Tobys' promotion of its organic product illustrates the importance of both the maintenance of environmental integrity during food production, alongside the health aspects of foodstuffs themselves. This firm's endorsement of Landcare and Coastcare programmes reiterates the importance which Uncle Tobys places on the environmental integrity of production. However, alongside Uncle Tobys' re-entry to the organic market in 1999, its marketing more closely focused on those meanings associated with the health benefits of organic foods (Lyons, 1999). While the company initially sought to attach meanings associated with both the environment and health to organic foods, recent marketing has promoted health and fitness.

However, before we attempt to evaluate the experiences of these companies, there is one important observation that needs to be considered. There is a significant difference that emerges when we analyse corporate greening in Australia and New Zealand, and compare it with experiences elsewhere, particularly in Europe. This difference relates to the sources of the pressure for companies to adopt sustainable practices; that is, in who takes the lead in shaping changes in the food production sector. This is significant because it may allow us some insight into the nature and form of corporate greening strategies, and whether or not any particular policy or action involves a meaningful commitment to sustainability, or whether it is a 'greenwash' (or even something else).

THE RETAIL SECTOR AND GREENING

In terms of 'green production', the experiences of the agrifood sector in the UK and Europe are very different from those emerging in Australia or New Zealand. While organic farming is expanding everywhere at a rapid rate, in the case of the UK much of the stimulus for this has come from the retail sector, and the supermarket chains in particular, which have placed a good deal of pressure on agrifood processors and producers to introduce environmentally sustainable practices that deliver safe foods and reduce the environmental impacts of farming. Thus, UK-based retail chains such as Sainsbury's, Iceland and Tesco have well-developed environmental management policies which go beyond a commitment to the marketing of organic produce. In the case of Sainsburys, for example, such management policies extend over the entire range of its operations, and the company produces an annual environment report which not only documents past progress but also sets new targets for the year ahead (Sainsbury, 2000).

In the area of product sourcing, for example, Sainsbury's impinges directly on the agrifood production system, imposing what it claims are environmentally responsible policies through the standards and requirements it imposes on those farmers and food processors who supply the company's own-brand products. Sainsbury's began to do this in 1991, when it introduced its integrated crop management (ICM) protocols for all UK fresh and frozen fruit and vegetables. The ICM protocol is a mutually agreed programme which specifies best practice for crop production and which works to achieve the reduction of agro-chemical inputs, and the company has plans to ensure independent verification of similar standards in the case of overseas suppliers. In addition, in 2000, the company was trialling an environmental management system which would apply to the more than 1,200 own-brand suppliers in 2001. Sainsbury's also encourages wildlife conservation by sourcing from suppliers who have implemented Farm Biodiversity Action Plans (FBAP), and, in 2000, also began to sell seafood sourced from fisheries which have been certified as sustainable by the Marine Stewardship Council (MSC). All-in-all, only 251 suppliers, out of a total of 3,000, were not producing under ICM, FBAP or similar guidelines. These initiatives are separate from the company's policy of marketing fully certified organic produce, which it first started to sell in 1986 (Burch et al., 2001).

It may be argued that such action is a 'greenwash' marketing tool, and is simply designed to generate a more favourable image for the company in the minds of the public. However, as has been argued elsewhere (Burch et al., 2001), in the case of Sainsbury's, there appears to be a significant difference in corporate outlook which results in changes in behaviour which are meaningful, but limited by external constraints – a 'partial greening' in other words. Whatever the case, the evidence suggests that, in Europe, the retail sector has taken the lead in shaping policy and behaviour at the farm level. By way of contrast, in Australia and New Zealand, the retail sector has not behaved in the same way, and there is little evidence of any broad-based or sustainable push to encourage suppliers to meet 'clean and green' standards in their management of the natural resource base. Of course, the supermarkets do insist on quality standards relating to *consumption*, and there has been some moderate interest on the part of supermarkets in selling a limited range of organic products already being produced (Monk, 1998). But even where retailers are marketing their own-brand supermarket labels, a situation that usually gives them a good deal of control over downstream production and processing, there has been no concerted attempt to impose environmental management standards of *production* on suppliers, in the ways that Sainsbury's and other retailers have done in the UK.

Instead, the impetus to what is claimed to be 'green' production in Australia and New Zealand has come from the production sectors themselves, and in terms of corporate greening, from companies such as Heinz Wattie and Uncle Tobys. Why is there this difference and is it of any importance? There does seem to us to be some significance in the fact that the impulse to green production comes from different sectors. While it is true that the retail sector is probably more closely attuned to expressions of consumer preferences than the production sectors, supermarket chains in the Antipodes have been spared some of the numerous and extreme food scares that have been so prevalent in Europe and elsewhere. Consumers in Australia and New Zealand appear to be more likely to believe the message put out by government and industry, that food supplies are already 'clean and green' and safe to eat (Alexander and Fry, 1994). More important than that, though, are the implications of the point made earlier in this chapter. Government initiatives such as Landcare and the greening strategies adopted by the corporate sector have succeeded in incorporating a discourse of sustainability into conventional agriculture while disassociating this from concerns about food safety. In other words, in the Antipodes, the link between environmental sustainability and resource use, and food safety and the adoption of conventional farming methods, is not well articulated.

In Europe, by way of contrast, many recent food scares have been seen to be directly related to the adoption of intensive methods of production, and there is a clear link established between the viability of the natural resource base and the quality and safety of products. The retail sector in Europe is usually the first point of contact for expressions of consumer concern about food safety, and while the production sectors obviously experience great disruption and loss of income when major food scares such as 'mad cow' disease emerge, the supermarket chains, operating in a highly competitive environment, clearly see some benefit in moving downstream in order to impose standards on both the quality of food and the sustainability of the production base. In a situation in which the standard of food is so closely related to the sustainability of the resource base – in terms of chemical residues, animal health and so on – there are clear incentives for retailers to get involved in the food production system. This is more so the case where major retailers such as Sainsbury's depend upon the sale of high-quality 'own brands' for the larger part of their total turnover. In this context retailers, not producers, become the guarantors of quality, and it is not surprising to see the retail chains moving downstream in order to ensure the foods they market under their own labels are produced to the highest standards and in ways that are both sustainable and safe.

As a consequence of these distinctions, the main impetus to 'green production' in Europe comes from the retail sector, while in Australia and New Zealand, it comes from the production sectors, which have subscribed to organic production methods largely as an aid to marketing rather than a commitment to sustainable production methods. But there are other consequences that emerge from the distinctions outlined above, which enable us to evaluate the extent of the commitment of companies like Uncle Tobys and Heinz Wattie to meaningful change.

FIRST AND SECOND PHASE GREENING

Worldwide, environmental and health discourses are increasingly influencing the shape of food production and consumption. Responding to changes in community perceptions towards, and attitudes about, foods the industry has begun to employ 'green' signifiers aimed at convincing consumers not only of the healthy nature of the product they are consuming, but also of the environmental credentials of the firms involved in food production. Whether this is simply 'greenwashing' (see Beder, 1997) is a matter of some importance. Burch et al. (2001) argue that the organic sourcing policies of Uncle Tobys and Heinz Wattie herald the move towards corporate greening, but only to a limited degree. Although these companies are adhering to certified standards in the production of organic foods, there are problems with other aspects of the total production and distribution system which raise serious questions about the sustainability of the company's activities. For example, the frozen vegetables are packaged in resource-intensive and non-renewable plastic bags, in the same way as the conventionally-produced lines. Moreover, unlike organic produce – which is grown to be sold in local markets – these corporate organic lines are mostly exported and therefore have to travel thousands of 'food miles' before they reach the consumer. There is, then, a considerable amount of non-renewable energy used in transporting and distributing the 'organic' product. Uncle Tobys, in particular, has illustrated no commitment to expanding the organic industry, or increasing its range of organic products. Burch et al. (2001) conclude that what we are witnessing in the case of both Uncle Tobys and Heinz Wattie is first phase, or partial, greening. Second phase, or full, greening might be deemed to be occurring when the agrifood companies subject the total process of production, processing and distribution to some kind of environmental audit. This might occur when they 'reach forward' in the off-farm aspects of processing and delivery, ensuring that food processing is undertaken in accordance with consumer demands for correct labelling, packaging is made from recyclable products, and that high energy-using processes for moving foods are replaced with more energy-efficient forms of transport. Alternatively, second phase greening might be deemed to occur when the supermarkets or fast-food companies selling a product 'reach backwards' into the chain of production to ensure that soil loss is minimized, animal welfare is enhanced and chemicals are either banned or their use is reduced.

On the basis of this formulation, it can be argued that there is evidence of second phase greening occurring in Britain and other European nations. In the UK, companies such as Sainsbury's and Tesco appear to be accepting responsibility for the delivery of environmentally-friendly products to increasingly discerning consumers. In doing so, retail companies are not only meeting consumer demands, but are also conforming to the tough regulatory frameworks that have emerged in an era of BSE and foot and mouth scares (Johnson, 1998). However, the activities of companies such as Uncle Tobys and Heinz Wattie suggest that what is occurring in Australia and New Zealand is first phase greening, and that the corporate sector there has little, if any, commitment to wider questions of sustainability.

The extent to which the move to organics is bound up with wider concerns about sustainable development is another point of interest in this discussion. Leaving aside the definitional difficulties associated with sustainability (see Drummond and Marsden, 1999; Paehlke, 1999), it can be stated unambiguously that governments in Australia and New Zealand are committed to the *principles* of sustainability. But there is also growing evidence that governments are relying on voluntary and 'self-help' means to bring about change. Landcare, highlighted earlier in this chapter, is one example. Another is the development of 'self-help' models, where limited funding is devolved to local catchment groups for expenditure on 'on ground' works, such as water and soil catchment management (see AFFA, 2000).

Apart from displaying the symbol of Landcare on corporate publicity materials, as a sign of strong commitment to the ideals of sustainability, few corporations have provided large-scale funding to communities to encourage a 'greener' future. Yet, according to Barr and Cary (2000), it is unlikely that 'community action' by itself will generate the needed changes in rural areas. These authors believe there is only a certain extent to which the 'stewardship ethic' can be harnessed to drive the profound changes necessary in thought and behaviour. Barr and Cary (2000) also highlight an apparent 'truism' of Australian agriculture: that there is a strong tendency for farmers to perceive environmental problems to be greater on neighbouring properties than on their own (many thereby having a 'justification' for inaction). Finally, the authors remind us that, as a voluntary activity, Landcare is unlikely to inspire more people to join the movement (the one-third of farmers currently engaged is unlikely to increase). A more important criticism is that there is no evidence that the Landcare approach leads to a fundamental alteration to productionist agriculture (see Gray and Lawrence, 2001; Lockie, 1999). Under present landowning laws, many producers believe they have rights to do as they wish with their 'own' resources, even where those resources are rivers, streams and biodiversity (Reeve, 2001). Despite the extraordinary amount of voluntary activities that have been undertaken by members of Landcare groups to address environmental degradation – in particular tree planting, fencing, pasture establishment and farm planning (Curtis and De Lacy, 1997) – a number of factors limit the impact of co-operative community action. These include the contradictions between such action and the highly individualized under-standings of property rights that dominate rural Australia (Reeve, 2001); the pressures placed on producers by tightening terms of trade to lift profitability by intensifying production (Lockie, 1999); and the huge amount of government and corporate research and education devoted to supporting the high-input agenda (Lockie, 2001). Thus, while it appears that Landcare groups have made significant inroads in dealing with some of the more pressing environmental externalities generated by current agricultural practices, they have done so in a way that will support the continued intensification of input use that many believe will lead to accelerating environmental problems (Lockie, 1999).

Will a 'sustainable organics' agenda be introduced in the Antipodes? As Lyons (1998) has reported, many new, corporate-linked, organic growers see themselves as old-fashioned organic growers, some of whom are quite happy to be labelled as 'greenies'. What we might suggest is happening is the emergence of a division among organic producers based on particular conceptions of the 'meaning' of organic and its place in a more sustainable agriculture (Lyons and Lawrence, 2001). The more that organics become a corporate-commercial reality, the less inclined will the 'new' producers entering the industry be to accept the old, and strict, parameters of production. As suggested else-where, organic growers who cherish the 'anti-' global/corporate world have good reason to be concerned that a corporate-linked organics is a trick to convince consumers that they are receiving 'clean and green' foods. This is despite the fact that the downstream system remains largely untouched, and the use of energy and production of wastes is no different from that of any other commodity within industrial agri-culture (Burch et al., 2001).

Many of the new organic producers are drawn to the industry for its profit-making potential. While this is a legitimate motivation within a system of capitalist production and exchange, it is not one that shares the discourses, images, ideas and philosophies that accord with those producers who believe organics is *the* sustainable future for Antipodean agriculture.

CONCLUSION

This chapter has illustrated the various strategies of green production undertaken between corporate actors, and across various agrifood sectors. It is apparent that Uncle Tobys and Heinz Wattie have engaged with organic production in diverse ways, and these have resulted in varying degrees of success in 'greening' their production systems. Furthermore, the actions of each of these companies located in the Antipodes diverge from those undertaken in other parts of the world – notably Europe, where impetus for green production has arisen largely from the retail sector. The drivers for such change in turn impact on the adoption of green strategies and their implementation. For example, the greening that has occurred throughout the European retail sector has resulted in alterations to production, processing, packaging and transport of food products. The retail sector has thus linked the various elements comprising the food system, and has addressed concerns at each of these points as part of their greening strategy. In contrast, Uncle Tobys and Heinz Wattie have altered specific activities situated at a discrete location in the food system. These activities have included sourcing organic inputs, as well as sponsorship of the Landcare and Coastcare programmes in Australia, and the development of an Environmental Honesty programme in New Zealand. While the activities of these firms represent an important part of the shift to greener production, they overlook the impacts that derive from other points in the food system.

Despite the 'partial' greening of food production facilitated by the entry of these corporate actors into organics, their involvement has been integral to the recent rapid growth of the organic food industry. Throughout the history of Antipodean agriculture (and that occurring elsewhere), chemical-intensive systems of food provision have been normalized. This is evidenced most specifically throughout the policies and research agendas of government departments. Corporate support for organics has, therefore, challenged some broadly held assumptions that have historically marginalized and inhibited the growth of the organic industry. Corporate actors have thus been essential for the rapid growth of the organic sector in Australia and New Zealand. The long-term implications of this involvement for the industry remain to be seen. To date it is evident that a bifurcation has developed between growers who support the formalization of the organic industry – including the entry of corporate actors and government departments – and those who oppose such changes, but rather value organic systems for their supply of non-processed foods to local markets.

The cases of Uncle Tobys and Heinz Wattie also illustrate those meanings of organics constructed around their organic products. Broadly speaking, both these companies associated two discourses with their organic product: that of environmental sustainability, and food safety and health. The case of Uncle Tobys revealed the privileging of health among these meanings as part of the marketing of Organic Vita Brits. The failure to connect (and to maintain a connection) between each of these meanings further magnified divisions with the organic industry. Importantly, the inability of these corporate actors adequately to conceptualize the relationship between food, the environment and health, suggests they also fail to contribute to a radical rethinking of food systems. As such, their involvement makes, at best, only a small contribution in shifting towards more socially just and environmentally responsible systems of food provision.

REFERENCES

AFFA (Agriculture, Fisheries and Forestry – Australia) (2000) *Steering Committee Report to Australian Governments on the Public Response to 'Managing Natural Resources in Rural Australia for a Sustainable Future'*. Canberra: AFFA.

Alexander, H. and R. Fry (1994) 'Showing the World the Way: The World Market for Clean and Green Products', *Agricultural Science* (January): 39–44.

Anonymous (1996) 'Watties Frozen Foods – Certified Organic Frozen Vegetables', *Food Australia* 38 (8): 352–3.

— (1998) 'Organic Land Grows', *Grow Organic* (March): 1.

Barr, N. and J. Cary (1992) *Greening a Brown Land: The Australian Search for Sustainable Land Use*. Melbourne: Macmillan.

— (2000) *Influencing Improved Natural Resource Management on Farms: A Guide to Understanding Factors Influencing the Adoption of Sustainable Resource Practices*. Canberra: Bureau of Rural Sciences.

Becker, E. and T. Jahn (eds) (1999) *Sustainability and the Social Sciences*. Paris: UNESCO.

Beder, S. (1997) *Global Spin: The Corporate Assault on Environmentalism*. Melbourne: Scribe Publications.

Bradsen, J. (1988) *Soil Conservation Legislation in Australia: Report to the National Soil Conservation Program*. Adelaide: University of Adelaide.

Burch, D., K. Lyons and G. Lawrence (2001) 'What Do We Mean by "Green"? Consumers, Agriculture and the Food Industry', in S. Lockie and B. Pritchard (eds), *Consuming Foods, Sustaining Environments*, pp. 33–46. Brisbane: Academic Press.

Campbell, H., J. Fairweather and D. Steven (1997) *Recent Developments in Organic Food Production in New Zealand: Part 2, Kiwifruit in the Bay of Plenty*. Dunedin: University of Otago.

Curtis, A. and T. De Lacy (1997) 'Examining the Assumptions Underlying Landcare', in S. Lockie and F. Vanclay (eds), *Critical Landcare*, pp. 185–200. Key Papers no. 5. Wagga Wagga: Centre for Rural Social Research, Charles Sturt University – Riverina.

DEHCD (Department of Environment, Housing and Community Development) (1978) *A Basis for Soil Conservation Policy in Australia: Commonwealth and State Government Collaborative Soil Conservation Study, 1975–77*. Canberra: AGPS Press.

Drummond, I. and T. Marsden (1999) *The Condition of Sustainability*. London: Routledge.

Elkington, J. (1998) *Cannibals with Forks: The Triple Bottom Line of 21st Century Business*. Gabriola Island, BC: New Society Publishers.

Fiske, J., B. Hodge and G. Turner (1987) *Myths of Oz*. NSW: Allen and Unwin.

Goodman Fielder (2000) *Goodman Fielder Annual Report*. Sydney: Goodman Fielder.

Gray, I. and G. Lawrence (2001) *A Future for Regional Australia: Escaping Global Misfortune*. Cambridge: Cambridge University Press.

Greer, J. and K. Bruno (1996) *Greenwash: The Reality Behind Corporate Environmentalism*. Penang: Third World Network.

Heinz Wattie (2000) *Heinz Wattie's Australasia*. <http://www.organicsnewzealand.org.nz/members/heinzwattie.htm>

Johnson, D. (1998) 'Green Businesses: Perspectives from Management and Business Ethics', *Society and Natural Resources* 11: 259–66.

Kinnear, S. (1999) 'Overview of the Organic Industry in Australia', Paper presented at *Farming for the Future. Organic Produce for the 21st Century*, Mackay, Queensland, 22–23 September.

Lawrence, G. (1999) 'Agri-food Restructuring: A Synthesis of Recent Australian Research', *Rural Sociology* 64 (2): 186–202.

Lockie, S. (1997a) 'Beyond a "Good Thing": Political Interests and the Meaning of Landcare', in S. Lockie and F. Vanclay (eds), *Critical Landcare*, pp. 29–44. Key Papers no. 5, Wagga Wagga: Centre for Rural Social Research, Charles Sturt University – Riverina.

— (1997b) 'Chemical Risk and the Self-Calculating Farmer: Diffuse Chemical Use in Australian Broadacre Farming Systems', *Current Sociology* 45 (3): 81–97.

— (1998) 'Environmental and Social Risks, and the Construction of "Best-Practice" in Australian Agriculture', *Agriculture and Human Values* 15 (3): 243–52.

Lockie, S. (1999) 'Community Movements and Corporate Images: "Landcare" in Australia', *Rural Sociology* 64 (2): 219–33.

— (2001) '"Name Your Poison": The Discursive Construction of Chemical-Use as Everyday Farming Practice', in S. Lockie and B. Pritchard (eds), *Consuming Foods, Sustaining Environments*, pp. 140–58. Brisbane: Academic Press.

Lockie, S. and L. Bourke (eds) (2001) *Rurality Bites: The Social and Environmental Transformation of Rural and Regional Australia*. Sydney: Pluto Press.

Lockie, S. and F. Vanclay (eds) (1997) *Critical Landcare*. Key Papers no. 5, Wagga Wagga: Centre for Rural Social Research, Charles Sturt University – Riverina.

Lockie, S., K. Lyons and G. Lawrence (2000) 'Constructing "Green" Foods: Corporate Capital, Risk and Organic Farming in Australia and New Zealand', *Agriculture and Human Values* 17 (4): 315–22.

Lyons, K. (1998) 'Understanding Organic Farm Practice: Contributions from Ecofeminism', in D. Burch, G. Lawrence, R. Rickson and J. Goss (eds), *Australasian Food and Farming in a Globalized Economy: Recent Developments and Future Prospects*, pp. 57–68. Melbourne: Monash Publications in Geography no. 50.

— (1999) 'Corporate Environmentalism and Organic Agriculture in Australia: The Case of Uncle Tobys', *Rural Sociology* 64 (2): 251–65.

— (2000) 'Situated Knowledges, Science and Gender: A Sociology of Organic Agriculture in Australia and New Zealand'. PhD dissertation, Central Queensland University.

— (2001) 'From Sandals to Suits: Green Consumers and the Institutionalisation of Organic Agriculture', in S. Lockie and B. Pritchard (eds), *Consuming Foods, Sustaining Environments*, pp. 82–94. Brisbane: Academic Press.

Lyons, K. and G. Lawrence (2001) 'Institutionalisation and Resistance: Organic Agriculture in Australia and New Zealand', in H. Tovey and M. Blanc (eds), *Food, Nature and Society*, pp. 67–88. Aldershot: Ashgate.

Madden, B., G. Hayes and K. Duggan (2000) *National Investment in Rural Landscapes: An Investment Scenario for NFF and ACF with the Assistance of LWRRDC*. Australian Conservation Foundation and National Farmers' Federation.

Ministry for the Environment (1997) *The State of New Zealand's Environment*. Wellington: Ministry for the Environment and GP Publications.

Monk, A. (1998) 'The Australian Organic Basket and the Global Supermarket', in D. Burch, G. Lawrence, R. Rickson and J. Goss (eds), *Australasian Food and Farming in a Globalized Economy: Recent Developments and Future Prospects*, pp. 69–82. Melbourne: Monash Publications in Geography no. 50.

Mues, C., L. Chapman and R. Van Hilst (1998) *Landcare: Promoting Improved Land Management Practices on Australian Farms*. Canberra: Australian Bureau of Agricultural and Resource Economics.

OPEG (Organic Producers Exporters Group) (2000) *OPEG Member Survey: 1999–2000*. <http://www.organicsnewzealand.org.nz/documents/survey2000>

Paehlke, R. (1999) 'Towards Defining, Measuring and Achieving Sustainability: Tools and Strategies for Environmental Evaluation', in E. Becker and T. Jahn (eds), *Sustainability and the Social Sciences*, pp. 245–63. Paris: UNESCO.

Pugliese, P. (2001) 'Organic Production and Sustainable Development: A Multi-faceted and Promising Convergence', *Sociologia Ruralis* 41 (1): 112–30.

Reeve, I. (2001) 'Property Rights and Natural Resource Management: Tiptoeing Round the Slumbering Dragon', in S. Lockie and L. Bourke (eds), *Rurality Bites. The Social and Environmental Transformation of Rural Australia*, pp. 257–69. NSW: Pluto Press.

Sainsbury (2000) *Environment Report 2000: Working Towards a Better Environment.* London: J. Sainsbury plc.

Saunders, C., J. Manhire, C. Campbell and J. Fairweather (1997) *Organic Farming in New Zealand: An Evaluation of the Current and Future Prospects, Including an Assessment of Research Needs.* MAF Policy Technical Paper. Canterbury: Department of Economics and Marketing, Lincoln University.

Welford, R. (1997) *Hijacking Environmentalism: Corporate Responses to Sustainable Development.* London: Earthscan.

SIX | Room for manoeuvre? (In)organic agribusiness in California

JULIE GUTHMAN

Care about social justice issues? Labor and employment practices by agribusiness, health problems related to pesticides by farm labor and the security of the small family farmer are related issues. If corporate farms continue their takeover of our food supply, then these businesses and their giant trading corporate partners can set the price of basic food commodities, dictate the wages and working conditions of farm workers and put family farms out of business through the consolidation of land holdings and economies of scale. Polluting farming practices and poor labor conditions are cheaper and are more likely to occur if corporations are allowed to continue taking over our food production. Preserving the family and small scale farm that can employ alternative methods and that can produce food for local consumption ensures food safety and is more environmentally sound than industrialized farming methods, and the organic industry is made up of primarily small sized producers. We have not fully addressed the issues of sustainability within the growing organic industry, but that question may become moot if these laws are passed. Lower standards will allow for a greater take over of organic farming by agribusiness and put the small producer out of work and off the land.

Claire Cummings (Board of Directors of Food First and Community Alliance with Family Farmers; Marin Food Policy Council), Commentator on Food and Farming on KPFA public radio, in response to the first set of organic rules proposed by the US Department of Agriculture, 1998

§ The last several years have been nothing less than extraordinary in exposing the public health, environmental and moral risks of industrialized agriculture. Each new round of news stories, whether about genetically engineered foods, 'mad cow' disease, foot-and-mouth disease, E. coli contamination or what have come to be routine pesticide scares, reinforces agriculture's prominence in contemporary environmental politics. Contemporaneously, organic agriculture has been positioned as the idealized alternative to industrial agriculture, both in social as well as ecological terms. And if the agent of agro-industrialization is profit-driven agribusiness, it is but a small step of logic to assume that organic farming is peopled by value-driven, small-scale family farms.

Despite, or perhaps because of, this positioning, organic food production and distribution has become one of the most dynamic and profitable segments of food provision. Playing on the increased public awareness of agriculture's ills, agribusiness firms are entering the organic marketplace, hoping to capture some of the above-average profits of an innovative field and be well-positioned in market share should demand for organic food continue to grow. Yet, agribusiness involvement in organic agriculture seems to be inherently contradictory, as it represents the industrialization of agriculture that organic consumers seem to be rebelling against. How, then, do we assess the presence of agribusiness in the organic sector? Does it necessarily dilute the meanings and practices of organic agriculture, or does it help spread ecological practices to a wider audience? And what does it mean for those small-scale, family farms that putatively populate the sector?

In this chapter, I consider how agribusiness has shaped organic agriculture in one of its key centres: California. Countering the image of a collection of small independent farms, I intend to document the form and extent of agribusiness involvement in the California organic sector. Yet the more important question I will address is how such involvement affects both standard setting and practices within the sector and, therefore, what environmental outcomes might evolve. Ultimately, I will argue that agribusiness participation in actual production – while falling short of organic ideals – is less critical than how agribusiness writ large drives wider processes of agro-industrialization. For the conditions set by agribusiness undermine the ability of even the most committed producers to counter the social and ecological effects associated with these processes. That being the case, it sheds doubt on the possibility of multiple paths to sustainability.

This chapter draws from the first extensive and in-depth social science study of organic production in California.[1] Although California's unique agrarian history and disproportionate amount of land available to produce crops belie any claims of representativeness, its prominence in the burgeoning organic produce industry cannot be denied. California was ground zero for both the counterculture and the yuppie explosion that put organic food on the proverbial map. It is also where US regulations for organic production first evolved and the site of several key institutions that have been critical in diffusing the techniques (and idioms) of organic farming. Today it holds more organic farms than any other state in the USA (extrapolated from Klonsky and Tourte, 1998), is second to Idaho in the amount of certified organic cropland, and grows 47 per cent of the certified organic vegetables and 66 per cent of certified fruit (Economic Research Service, 2000b). Given its particular crop mix, it is highly probable that California currently tallies more organic crop value than any other *country* in the world.

In the following section, then, I examine more fully the contradictory aspects of agribusiness involvement in organic agriculture, specifically drawing out what threats this may pose to the organic movement. Recognizing that the impact of agribusiness on organics in large part depends on how it is defined, I then attempt to create a working definition, particularly as it applies to conditions within California. Using a narrower definition than is common in the agrifood literature, I document the actual extent of agribusiness involvement in California's organic agriculture, showing how it has affected the structure of the sector and suggesting what the trends are for further involvement. The next section considers some of the empirical evidence regarding agribusiness influence on rules and regulations, and on other growers, as well as actual practices. Finally, the last section touches on the larger problematic, which is agribusiness's ability to shape agrarian structures in ways that affect all producers, making formal participation in organics less the issue than it appears at first glance.

IS AGRIBUSINESS INORGANIC?

It is impossible to divine a singular argument and meaning for organic agriculture. The organic movement grew from heterogeneous philosophical and historical roots (Harwood, 1990; Peters, 1979) and many of the ideas that are the basis of vernacular meanings of organic are not necessarily complementary (see also James, 1993 on the multiple meanings brought to organic). Such unresolved tensions continue to surface in ongoing battles around the regulation of 'organically grown food'. Not only are some facets more privileged than others (e.g. an emphasis on what inputs are used over how and where food is marketed), the very idea of state regulation remains a source of tension (see Guthman, 2000; Tovey, 1997; cf. Michelsen, 2001) especially among those who see organic production as an alternative to a hegemonic food system.

Still, for many who identify with the organic movement, the heart of organic farming is a critique of the industrialization of agriculture (Ikerd, 2001; Michelsen, 2001; Tovey, 1997; Vos, 2000). For Ikerd, this means an opposition to technical processes of specialization, standardization, centralization and, one would have to add, intensification: the speeding up and control of biological processes in the name of productivity. Accordingly, organic production should embrace regionally tailored, family scale, polycultural cropping and husbandry practices that privilege natural rhythms and balances. For others, the meaning of organic farming goes far beyond production practices. As Tovey notes, few in the movement see organic farming 'as inseparable from social issues, which range from rebuilding rural communities to avoiding exploitation of workers, overcoming the rural–urban or food producer–food consumer divide, creating an alternative lifestyle and alternative ways of relating to others and to nature' (Tovey, 1997: 25).

For agribusiness, involvement in organic agriculture raises its own set of contradictions. To embrace the organic critique is to call into question its own production methods (Barham, 1997; Clunies-Ross and Cox, 1994). The potential to disparage the vast majority of the food supply with any suggestions that organic food is safer or healthier is one of the reasons that state support in the USA for organic agriculture has been so slow in coming. There is also the question of profitability. If agribusiness success has been predicated on overcoming obstacles of distance and durability, through canning, freezing, cool chains and so on, as Friedmann (1994) so eloquently argues, then the organic movement's oft-voiced appeal to the seasonal and fresh undermines such success. Likewise, if agribusiness profitability relies on commodifying inputs and processes that were once produced on the farm or in household kitchens (Goodman et al., 1987), then an embrace of farm self-sufficiency and whole food consumption is equally problematic.

In short, agribusiness involvement in organic agriculture seems an oxymoron – antithetical to its very meaning – making it inorganic, in a way of speaking. Yet, there *is* agribusiness involvement in organics, notwithstanding the occasional stubbornness of those who see movement vitality in denying it (e.g. Michelsen, 2001). While the extent of such involvement is largely an empirical (and comparative) question, and, in part, turns on what definition of agribusiness is employed, the co-existence of two apparent opposites – agribusiness and organic agriculture – is the point of departure for my analysis. Accordingly, the more important question is how agribusiness penetration bears on the transformative potential of organic agriculture. Does agribusiness involvement promote organic agriculture by enabling it to reach a broader public, a claim of ecological modernization theorists (see Jansen and Vellema, ch. 1)? Do they co-exist, the former acting as a shallow form of organic agriculture, as suggested by Coombes and Campbell (1998)? Or does agribusiness hijack organic agriculture, as suggested in Buck et al. (1997)?

Not to be dismissed as an academic debate, these arguments are vociferously made within the community of organic practitioners. With the lines often drawn between the newcomers to the sector (or the buyers that drew them in) and the 'old-timers' or 'lifestyle' farmers – a debate that is echoed around the world (Padel, 2001) – in the USA (as witnessed at several industry conferences), the former argue that their participation helps the sector to grow, giving broader access to safer and healthier food. The latter group, suffering from the competition that rapid new entry has wrought, argue that 'organic' has much deeper meanings than the inputs that are used, having to do with a way of life, a special relation to nature and a commitment to values, very much echoing Tovey's (1997) sense of the movement. Meanwhile, those who are involved in advocacy, technical support and certification – i.e., those who have worked hard to promote organic farming – take the middle ground, recognizing that there are different levels of commitment to organic precepts and reminding the increasingly self-protective movement farmers that the original point *was* to change agriculture.[2] Their earnestness notwithstanding, this growing polarization between an 'organic industry' and an 'organic movement' is increasingly mapped on to notions of agribusiness and small-scale family farming.[3]

In an earlier paper based on preliminary research, my colleagues and I claimed that the most high-value crops and the most lucrative segments of organic commodity chains were being appropriated by agribusiness firms, many of which were abandoning the more sustainable agronomic and marketing practices associated with organic agriculture (see Buck et al., 1997). The strong form of hijacking suggested in this article posed three related threats to organic agriculture from agribusiness. The first, following Clunies-Ross (1990), was a political threat of lowering standards, or, as we perhaps too bluntly put it, 'commandeering the organic label' so as to dilute the meaning of organic. A second was a direct economic threat, such that agribusiness was in the position of substantially undermining the livelihoods of existing, presumably more committed, producers. A third was that agribusiness would practise organic farming in a more shallow way, effectively lessening some of the distinctiveness of organic versus conventional farming.

In consideration of the political threat, organic agriculture is primarily regulated by national and sub-national systems of certification, such that independent and/or state-sanctioned agencies verify that organic producers and marketers are in compliance with agreed-upon rules of what constitutes organic practice. Clearly, how these rules are defined makes a huge difference in who can participate in organic production and how. In terms of crop production, for example, virtually all systems of certification disallow the use of most synthetically-produced pesticides and fertilizers but some enjoin growers to go much further in making the farm a self-sustaining environment, by, for instance, implementing complicated crop rotations, recycling all nutrients and relying on biological pest control. A regulatory focus on inputs is much more likely to encourage entrants who can substitute allowed materials for disallowed materials, at least in crops where there are efficacious substitutes, while a process focus creates some significant obstacles to cookie-cutter organic practices (Guthman, 1998; Rosset and Altieri, 1997).

The concern that agribusiness firms will play a too prominent role in setting these standards suggests there are identifiable class-like interests in defining standards a certain way. Clunies-Ross (1990) was first to note a tension between what she calls the purists and the pragmatists in the British context. The Soil Association, representing the old-timer purist growers, wanted their standard to be the UK standard. This was threatened when a newer association, which represented more commercially-minded growers, not only attempted to rid organic farming of its 'muck and mystery' by giving certification a 'scientific' basis; but also developed a second, highly watered-down grade to help farmers in the transition period. This must be contrasted with the New Zealand case, where it was the organic export industry (the more corporate subsector) which was first to institutionalize fully a national standard. Left out of the process, the more lifestyle-oriented growers began to seek another, presumably deeper, form of accreditation. From this, Campbell and Liepins (2001) conclude that there is no inevitable watering down of standards from agribusiness participation, as there is always room for resistance and reconfiguration. Goodman (1999) and Vos (2000), too, see standard-setting as a site of discursive contestation, pointing to resistance on the part of consumers and committed producers who with 275,000 public comments stopped a potential hijacking of organic meanings when the USDA proposed a federal standard in 1997 far afield from what the organic industry had originally envisioned.

Others have treated rule-making as a less specifically instrumental process but one which none the less has important political content.

Tovey (1997: 33) argues, for example, that state involvement in the Irish case has had the effect of 'disregard[ing], ignor[ing], or repress[ing] the ideological content of the movement' by subsuming it under broader efforts of environmental preservation of the countryside, which, she argues, is antithetical to food production. Allen and Kovach (2000) posit that standardization supports a logic of commodification which inherently undermines the environmental benefits of organic agriculture, despite social movement contestation. Michelsen (2001), in contrast, finds no contradiction in institutionalization; on the contrary, he argues that it has given discursive space to alternative agriculture in the policy world.

The economic threat we spoke of in our earlier paper had two dimensions to it, reflecting two different mechanisms of agricultural industrialization. What we called appropriation and substitution draws from the work of Goodman et al. (1987) and is a relational definition. Appropriation refers to the process by which products and processes once integral to on-farm production are refashioned as inputs, making way for more factory-like production on the farm; substitution refers to processes by which post-production value-added becomes a high proportion of the total value of the commodity to the point where industrial processes may wholly substitute for rural products. Together they represent a general tendency for capital to carve up and usurp farm processes most easily and profitably moved into the factory (to be reconfigured as farm inputs or food manufacture), leaving the rest to on-farm producers. In parallel fashion, there is a potential for off-farm agribusiness actors to marginalize existing organic producers by extracting their surplus profits in this way.

What we called conventionalizing was less specified, but generally referred to the way that highly capitalized on-farm actors could out-compete existing organic producers by adopting industrial methods that play upon scale economies, re-creating, in other words, 'factories in the field' (McWilliams, 1971, original 1935). As processes become more specialized, standardized and centralized (following Ikerd 2001), scale economies are favoured, making it more difficult for less capitalized growers. This technical understanding of the industrialization of agriculture is crystallized in the well-known maxim of 'get big or get out'.

Carried to an extreme, the economic or second threat we posited would manifest in the third threat of agro-ecological enfeeblement. Were existing and/or more movement-driven producers to continue to farm with dedication to agro-ecological methods, they could be put out of business competing with growers who employ scale economies and a shallower form of organic agriculture. Alternatively, they could become contract farmers, with production practices dictated to them (Watts, 1993). Or they could simply follow suit and allow their practices to become industrialized. In any of these cases, economic marginalization would undercut the ability to practise a deep form of organic farming (as would enfeebled rules).

It is the implication of such strong tendencies that led our critics to accusations of universalizing and linearity (see Campbell and Liepins, 2001; Coombes and Campbell, 1998; DuPuis, 2000; Michelsen, 2001). Coombes and Campbell, for example, in an effort to accentuate resistance and agency, made the argument that lifestyle producers can exist simultaneously, even synergistically, with agribusiness producers. The New Zealand organic export sector is undoubtedly industrial, centred on durable fresh fruit crops (kiwis and apples) or frozen vegetables and controlled by exporters or processors respectively, that bring new commercial growers into organic production. Yet it has left the lifestyle growers, who cater to the small home market, to practise organic agriculture the way they see fit. If anything, they claim, the export sector helps the lifestyle sector by raising awareness of organic farming. Moreover, as simple commodity producers, i.e. family farmers who produce for the market but obtain virtually all their labour from within the family (Friedmann, 1978), the lifestyle growers produce a more diverse and harder-to-grow set of commodities, precisely because their class position allows them to take such risks.[4]

While the possibility of multiple paths to sustainability suggested by Coombes and Campbell seems a powerful retort to our original article, they pay little attention to another dynamic of capitalist agriculture: competition. To be sure, the spectre of competition reveals a fourth potential threat from agribusiness, thus far barely touched on in the current debate. First, though, it is important to clarify what is meant by agribusiness.

DEFINING AGRIBUSINESS

Agribusiness refers to the systemic way 'in which the activities of farming are integrated into a much larger industrial complex, including the manufacture and marketing of technological inputs and of processed food products, under highly concentrated forms of corporate ownership and management' (Whatmore, 2000: 10). While this suggests a *process* of agro-industrialization, it has become a convenient shorthand to treat a specific set of transnational corporations (TNCs), namely those involved in agro inputs and/or food manufacture and distribution, as agribusiness. This is the sense in which agribusiness is primarily used in this volume.

Given this sort of definition, TNC activity per se remains limited in the production of organic inputs (appropriation), although smaller agro-input firms are actively involved in producing allowable fertilizers and biological agents. Since many are funded by venture capital, it seems only a matter of time until the major agro-chemical firms acquire organic product lines. Whether this is greenwashing or inspired ecological modernization on the part of industrial actors remains to be seen (see Lyons et al., ch. 5; Jansen and Vellema, ch. 1). TNC activity is more apparent in the downstream end of food production (substitution). In the USA, General Mills is the most deeply involved, with its outright acquisition of Small Planet Foods, the owner of the Muir Glen (organic processing tomatoes) and Cascadian Farms (organic frozen fruits and vegetables) brands, and its introduction of Sunrise, an organic breakfast cereal. Gerber, Kellogg, Mars, Heinz and Dole own or sell at least one organic product. Whole Foods supermarkets and (all-organic) Horizon Dairy are publicly traded corporations, albeit not necessarily transnational in their distribution.

A focus on TNCs, however, does not do justice to the Californian situation. Fruits, vegetables and nuts have historically been major crops in California and currently comprise more than half of the total value of crops sold. More importantly, fruit, nut and vegetable crops accounted for 92 per cent of total organic sales and 74 per cent of organic land in production (Klonsky et al., 2001). Produce production has historically been co-ordinated by mid-size firms involved in both production and marketing, 'grower-shippers' and packers, as they have come to be known, who cater to the particularities of specific crops (Friedland, 1984). Accordingly, big players are not always that big (many are family-owned) although there have been waves of TNC activity.[5] TNCs, moreover, are rarely directly involved with on-farm production.

To exclude large growers and grower-shippers from the definition of agribusiness due to their comparatively small revenues and low capitalization is to relinquish the factories in the field as an important frame of reference for the industrialization of agriculture and one that has characterized Californian agriculture from the very beginning of the American period. Thus, for the purposes of this chapter, I use a definition of agribusiness that brings us back to the farm, to highlight the extent to which certain organizational forms involved in actual production are straying from what many consider the organic ideal.

At the same time, there is no simple commodity production, i.e. the ideal-typical family farm, to speak of in California, especially in fresh fruits and vegetables. This has an historical basis, having to do with how waves of migrants, mostly from the Pacific Rim and Mexico, were recruited, racialized and politically marginalized, creating an abundant reserve of cheap harvest labour. Indeed, the availability of this labour is what enabled California to become a world centre of produce production. What this means is that virtually all Californian farmers are capitalist producers, either employing their own wage labour or contracting for labour. Many, however, are equally tied into marketing (or credit) arrangements that appropriate surplus, creating important contradictions in their class position (Mooney, 1983).

The dearth of true family farms in California poses further difficulties in defining agribusiness. Unlike the New Zealand case (Coombes and Campbell, 1998), or the American Midwest (Friedmann, 1978), one cannot make a division based on the relations of production. Nor does a divide between corporate and family-owned farms have much salience. Many family-owned farms form closely-held corporations to obtain certain tax and liability privileges, and some of the largest grower-shippers in California are family-owned operations. There are distinctions between growers who market their produce independently and those who are tied into others through marketing or production contracts. Yet this distinction does not map on to scale, as many of both the largest and smallest farms are under contract.

Without a compelling relational definition, agribusiness must be defined as a matter of degree, making it a rather muddy category, if still an important one. An ideal definition would include a composite of variables, such as revenues, capitalization, land in production, vertical integration, separation of ownership and management, and corporate ownership. Given that most of this does not constitute publicly accessible data, one is forced to rely on various proxies, which, in this study, began with land[6] with on-line databases, interviews and news stories filling in some of the other variables for key players.

Finally, as the concept of agribusiness is applied to organics, the divide is often made between the old guard and new entrants, between lifestyle-oriented and commercially-driven players (Campbell and Liepins, 2001; Clunies-Ross, 1990). While there is some utility to this, as all studies recognize that recent growth in organics has necessarily come from conventional growers converting to organic, there is slippage too. In my research I met growers who had been involved with organics for over twenty-five years who were dubious about its benefits, and I met those who were still part of major conventional operations who were quite taken with organic philosophy. By the same token, as organic food provision becomes more competitive, it has encouraged some movement-oriented growers to become very business-oriented. So to posit these groups as wholly separate not only reifies a dualism, as it assumes that there is a clear mapping between old and new in their scale and practices, it also ignores the possibility for change. Most significant to my argument, it ignores the possibility of a 'homegrown' organic agribusiness.

For this argument, then, agribusiness refers to two separate groups: (i) large-scale industrial farmers, many of whom are tied with marketers through contracts; and (ii) firms that sell and market the products of others (many of whom have substantial land in production, too). The first group tends to be made up of conventional growers, many of whom are only partially organic. The second tends to be made up of old guard players who, at least once upon a time, identified themselves as part of the organic movement. Both groups have the potential to lower the bar, the first through conventionalization, the second through appropriation and substitution.

AGRIBUSINESS TAKEOVER?

At first glance, the California organic sector appears to be dominated by small farmers, in keeping with the organic imaginary. In 1997, the median organic farm size was 5 acres (2 ha) and median sales were $8,000 (Klonsky et al., 2001). Yet, of the 1,533 growers who comprised the organic sector in 1997, seventy-six had more than 1,000 acres (or 400 ha) in *total* crop production, putting them in the top 6.4 per cent of all Californian growers (Department of Finance, 1997). This reflects that mixed operations are wholly allowable by US organic standards, even though the state-collected data that were the basis of these particular statistics include only the organic portion of operations. Looked at from the perspective of gross sales (see Table 6.1), another measure of scale, over one-half the value of organic production was captured by the 2 per cent of growers who grossed over one million dollars that same year (Klonsky et al., 2001). These figures do not even include the sales of others' products, bringing the sales of some of these players into the $25–100 million dollar range – highly unusual for farming operations.

As for the other pole in the sector, most of the 79 per cent of organic growers with sales of less than $50,000 are not full-time growers, or at least do not receive their primary income from organic farming. Nor

TABLE 6.1   Organic growers by sales class 1997–98

Sales class ($)	Growers	% of growers	% of sales
0–9,999	860	56.1	2
10,000–49,999	347	22.6	6
50,000–99,999	116	7.6	5
100,000–499,999	158	10.3	24
500,000–999,999	25	1.6	10
1,000,000 and over	27	1.8	52
TOTAL	1,533	100.0	99

Source: Klonsky et al., 2001.

are they mainly independent farms. While some are market gardens and commercial orchards that provide a modest living, many more are one hectare or less fruit orchards, held as residential real estate, but operated through one of several large fruit packers. Importantly, many of the independent farms that identify with the organic movement are mid-size in sales, say in the range of $100,000 to $1,000,000 per year (making them quite large by agricultural census standards).

Put together, these statistics provide evidence of a bi-polar industry structure, with a handful of large firms capturing most of the revenue and a large number of small operations capturing relatively little. But what can be said about the presence of agribusiness? Table 6.2 lists the ten largest *growers* in the state who have attempted organic production. For most of these growers, organic production is only a minor portion of their operation, as is the case of the many other agribusiness growers who rank below them in size. Some of these growers do not even sell their organically grown crops as organic, which would put them in the smallest-scale category in Table 6.1.

Table 6.3, in contrast, lists those growers with substantial interest in organics. With the exception of Grimmway Farms, perhaps, one begins to see that this is an entirely separate set of players.[7] Some were conventional firms that converted to organic early on (in the 1970s or early 1980s), including those who converted when a new generation took over the family business. In contrast, the wildly successful Earthbound Farms/Natural Selection Foods is a case of homegrown agribusiness. Earthbound was started by Myra and Drew Goodman, self-proclaimed 'hippies' who met at the University of California at Santa Cruz and started growing organic berries and lettuce in 1984 on their newly-acquired 1 ha farm. At first they sold to area restaurants;

TABLE 6.2 Ten largest growers with organic acreage 1997 (ha in brackets)

Parent company: operating entities (on permit)	Primary crops grown	Total acreage – parent co. (ha)	'94 pesticide use permit[h] (ha)	Organic acreage[i] (ha)
American Protection Industries: Paramount Citrus Association, Paramount Farming	citrus	88,500[a] (35,815)	12,942 (5,238)	33 (13)
Cadiz International: Sun World International/ Superior Farms	citrus, grapes	61,000[b] (24,686)	16,380 (6,629)	133 (54)
Abatti Family: Alex Abatti, Jr Farming	wheat, alfalfa, vegetables, melons	54,000[c] (21,854)	18,847 (7,627)	?
Salyer Family: SK Foods/SS Farms	cotton, vegetables	27,000[d] (10,927)	28,588 (11,569)	300 (121)
Grimmway Enterprises: Grimmway Farms	carrots	24,380 (9,866)	24,380 (9,866)	2,000 (809)
Gill Family: American Farms/Rio Farms	vegetables	21,167 (8,566)	21,167 (8,566)	136 (55)
Harris Farms	livestock, wheat, vegetables	20,000[e] (8,094)	14,678 (5,940)	419 (170)
Gallo Vineyards	wine grapes	10,000[f] (4,047)	7,720 (3,124)	2,769 (1,121)
Double D Farms	field crops, vegetables	8,000[g] (3,238)	1,800 (728)	380 (154)
Sunview Vineyards	grapes	7,639 (3,091)	7,639 (3,091)	99 (40)

Sources: a: *Los Angeles Times*, 1986; PR Newswire, 1987; b: Carnal, 1996; c: pesticide use permits (CIRS database), all Abatti holdings; d: Stevenson, 1987, before Boswell buy-out; e: Groves, 1991; f: Zwerdling, 1993; g: grower interview; h: CIRS database; i: CCOF, 1997.
Note: Growers with separate entities/overlapping ownership have been combined, including family holdings.

then they came up with the idea of bagging their lettuce mixes for roadside stands and eventually retail. The company grew rapidly on its own until 1996, when it entered into a series of mergers and renamed itself Natural Selection Foods. In 1999, it teamed up with Tanimura and Antle, the largest conventional lettuce grower-shipper in the world, which bought one-third of the company. Natural Selection continued to grow geographically, with at least 1,600 acres (648 ha) in production in Baja, California, where they grow off-season lettuce and tomatoes; they continued to grow in market share by buying out or contracting with some of their erstwhile competitors. By 2001, they had 7,000 acres (2,833 ha) in organic production, 2,000 (809) more in transition, and were in contract with dozens of other large growers. Natural Selection remains the biggest supplier of speciality lettuces and the largest grower of organic produce in North America (Earthbound Farms, 2001).

While Tanimura and Antle clearly saw an opportune investment, most conventional agribusiness entry is more hesitant and protracted. Why are they entering at all? A key factor is that conventional growers are increasingly concerned about the regulatory environment affecting agriculture, including the changing acceptability of pesticide use. Agribusiness growers, in particular, frame it as a fear of 'having their tools taken away' and the need to find alternative strategies for pest and disease management. This was the motivation of Grimmway Farms, which became involved in organics when it bought out competitor Yurosek and Sons. Of Yurosek's 7,000 or so acres (2,833 ha), 1,800 acres (728 ha) had already been converted to organic production at the time of the 1995 purchase. With carrots being its sole cash crop, Grimmway was no doubt interested in substitutes for methyl bromide, a soil-disinfectant widely used in carrot production that is facing an international ban in the coming years. Still, it sees organics as a place to experiment with new techniques and not necessarily its ultimate home (grower interview).

Other growers are turning towards higher-value crops, allowing a higher return on less land, in the face of changing national support for agriculture and newly emerging trade regimes. While most value-seeking conversions have been among smaller growers, in areas where cotton once was 'king', organics have been a road out of a once important but now failing agribusiness sector. This was clearly the case for Denny Duncan, owner of Cal-Organics. In the early 1980s, his Kern county farm was doing so poorly that he began looking for a niche market, fearing that he would lose the land his father had owned since 1946: 'We were looking for things to grow on a smaller scale that had a

TABLE 6.3 Major organic farming operations based in California 1997

Parent company: operating entities (on permit)	Primary activities	Estimated organic acreage[a] (ha)	Estimated contract acreage (ha)	Estimated sales (in 1,000s)
Earthbound Farms/Natural Selection	salad mix grower-shipper	2,800 (1,133)	2,000 (809)	$50,000
Pavich Family Farms	fruit (dried and fresh) and vegetable grower-shipper	3,860 (1,562)	500 (202)	$40,000
Lundberg/Wehah	rice grower-processor-distributor	3,500 (1,416)	?	$25,000
Cal Organic	vegetable grower-shipper	2,000 (809)	1,100 (445)	$20,000
Bornt & Sons	vegetable grower-shipper	1,200 (486)	500 (202)	$15,000
Pure Pak	vegetable grower-shipper and processor	1,200 (486)	0	$10,00
Timber Crest Farms	fruit grower, processor and shipper	450 (182)	0	$9,000
Loma Vista/Santa Lucia Farms	contract vegetable grower	1,100 (445)	0	$6,000
Heger Organic Farms	fruit and vegetable grower-shipper	1,100 (445)	0	$3,000

Sources: a: CCOF and CIRS databases; sales and contract acreage are estimated on the basis of interviews, news stories and extrapolation. Exact sources are not disclosed to protect proprietary information.

Note: The Table excludes three major wine grape growers who do not market their wines as organic.

higher return and possibly save the family farm.' Duncan entered into organics in 1984, planting 10 acres (4 ha) of lemon grass for Celestial Seasonings. By 1990, newly formed Cal-Organic was the largest organic farm in the world in both sales and acreage (2,560 acres; 1,036 ha) (Fost, 1991). It is rumoured that Duncan has formed a strategic alliance with an even larger grower-shipper.

For others still, entry is serendipitous and experimental. Sun World International, for example, is only peripherally involved in organic production, primarily as an experiment, and has actually taken some acreage out of organic production (grower interview). At one time the second largest citrus marketer in California behind Sunkist, in 1995 Sun World filed for bankruptcy. It was eventually purchased by the Cadiz Land Company, which is publicly held and trades on the NASDAQ. Since the main thrust of Cadiz's business has been buying up Mojave Desert land with water reserves hoping eventually to market the water (Carnal, 1996), the organic operations have become even more marginal.

Mainly, agribusiness growers have responded to specific requests to grow organically. Recent years have seen unprecedented growth in the downstream end of organic food provision, particularly the burgeoning (and consolidation) of a new retail sector referred to as 'super-naturals': health food supermarkets that carry a full line of grocery items. These retailers have not only heightened demand for fresh produce, they have deepened demand for all kinds of end products. Meanwhile, those industry leaders who are increasingly involved in marketing, handling and brokering have a keen interest in seeing mainstream retail establishments consistently carrying organic products, and expanding what they call the mass market for organics. Accordingly, many of the larger-scale conventional growers have been brought into organic by intermediary buyers, including the organic industry leaders, who themselves want to work with so-called professional growers to ensure consistent supplies. Some recruits, like the Gills of American Farms/Rio Farms (Table 6.2), are outright sceptical about organics and are involved solely at the initiative of Natural Selection (grower interview).

In sum, it is not exactly the case that conventional agribusiness growers have intentionally taken over organic agriculture. While some have entered to seek value or position themselves for further growth, others merely want to experiment with organic techniques or, even less proactively, have been brought in as contractors to grow certain crops for buyers. Accordingly, conventional agribusiness entry is hesitant, protracted and there is a significant amount of exit as well. Instead, the pioneers of the organic industry have grown and expanded effectively to become agribusinesses, selling others' products and gaining a significant amount of market share. Some of these firms became leaders by the historic accident of having been involved in flagship commodities such as salad mix; others aggressively pursued growth strategies while the industry was in its infancy, first by expanding their own production, later by bringing these new growers in through 'co-operative arrangements'.[8] But in either case – whether led by conventional agribusiness or by a homegrown organic industry – the effect is the same: the organic sector in California has become more oligopsonistic (where a few buyer firms have control) in its structure than the conventional one.

AGRIBUSINESS INFLUENCE

How, then, does this pattern of agribusiness entry affect organic agriculture as a movement? What is the empirical evidence regarding the political, economic and ecological threats to organic agriculture predicted in Buck et al., especially in so far as agribusiness arose from the ranks of the movement? Let us start with the political threat, where the influence of homegrown agribusiness is most stark.

Political influence

First it must be said that the very existence of agribusiness participation in the sector points to the fact that broader and/or antidotal meanings of organic farming are not codified in existing rules and regulations. It is true that significant difference remains among private certifiers and national systems in terms of both allowable practices, i.e. what counts as 'organic', and the nature of enforcement. Yet, in general, standards focus on production processes only, already compromising a more holistic vision of organic. This, as I have argued elsewhere (Guthman, 1998, forthcoming), was inherent in the rule-making process, which necessarily entailed a rationalization and simplification of organic meanings, an unintended consequence, perhaps, of the necessity for transparency in the interests of trade.

The key question for these purposes, however, is to what degree was agribusiness instrumental in shaping the rules. In the USA, the public debate precipitated by the USDA's first iteration of proposed federal rules for organic production illustrates that there has been plenty of contestation within the politics of standard-setting. Yet the disjuncture between the USDA's first proposal and the recommendations of the National Organic Standards Board, the latter of which better reflected the wishes of the organic community, was mistakenly read, I believe, as deliberate evisceration by conventional (TNC) agribusiness.[9] This is seen in the opening quote of this chapter. With the possible exception of Monsanto's influence on the biotechnology issue (see Broydo, 1998), there is little evidence of direct agribusiness lobbying, although the true story has yet to be documented. Apparently convinced by the outpouring of public comments, the USDA gave in to a rule much closer to what organic players wanted with little fight. Conventional agribusiness players in the Californian sector also had little truck with the National Organic Standards Board position. Indeed, they deferred to the organic community, recognizing that the organic label had to have meaning for consumers if they were to receive a price premium.

Although conventional agribusiness has been fairly removed from defining organic, this is not to say that interest politics have not played a role. On the contrary, the making of the rule was highly politicized, as has been standard-setting by private certifiers from the beginning. For example, the fact that Chilean nitrate, which is disallowed by IFOAM, remains allowable for up to 20 per cent of farm nitrogen needs is a direct result of earlier battles *within* the boardrooms of key private grower-run certification agencies, where organic industry pioneers (including those mentioned above) took strong stands on this and other materials they felt were critical to their success. Even today, one of the critical points of unfinished business in the US rule is the definition of 'access to pasture' for livestock standards. Horizon Dairy, which does not generally range feed its cattle, is using its considerable clout within the organic industry to shape the new rule such that long-term pasturing will not be a requirement of organic livestock production.

Growers who contest the direction the rule-making has taken are looking to recapture the deeper meanings of organic farming by developing labels that go 'beyond organic' in areas such as wildlife habitat, farm size and local marketing practices. In that way, codification has enhanced the division between an organic movement, which seeks to retain the holistic meanings of organic farming, and an organic industry, which seeks to bring organic to a broader audience. But it is not so much a watering down of standards by conventional agribusiness, as an attempt by a homegrown organic industry to redefine them in ways that detach them from a politics of scale, precisely in order to 'level the playing field'.

Undermining livelihoods

Nor does the pattern of agribusiness involvement point to a clear case of marginalization of existing, movement-oriented producers. Although the organic industry is highly oligopsonistic, with buyer firms catering primarily to the 'mass market' for organics, many growers are not a part of that system. Like the New Zealand case (Coombes and Campbell, 1998), growers who sell to the industry leaders are pulled in from the ranks of conventional growers, both large in the case of commodity crop growers and small in the case of orchardists, while the lifestyle and other independent growers have a vibrant system of their own (although occasionally movement growers sell to the industry players, often later to complain they 'got burned'). Many in this latter group are highly successful, relying primarily on direct marketing through farm stands, farmers' markets and subscriptions (where consumer-members join and get a regular box of food) and/or selling to upscale restaurants.

That said, there are some key differences from the New Zealand case. While California's role as the 'salad bowl of the nation' (and occasionally the world) is no less true for organics, much organic food grown in California is eaten in California. Accordingly, industrial producers potentially compete with independent producers. Salad mix, once the flagship product of organic producers, went from being a speciality commodity to just a commodity over the course of about five years, virtually concurrent with Natural Selection's growth. Retail prices dropped about 200 per cent, squeezing many of the high-end 'niche' growers out of the market. Increased surveillance regarding food safety, particularly after sixty-one illnesses were linked to bags of salad mix found to be tainted with E. coli H157:H7 (*Food Chemical News*, 1998), also forced growers to get big (to pay for more frequent inspections and elaborate washing equipment) or get out.

Agro-ecology

Substantial variation in the ease of growing organically makes agribusiness involvement commodity-specific. In general, agribusiness is involved in 'easy-to-grow' crops – crops, that is, that can be grown on an industrial scale. In some cases, this ease directly stems from hard-fought battles around allowable inputs. Sulphur dust, for example, was deemed allowable because it is mined from natural sources, although it causes more farmworker sickness than any other input in California (Pease et al., 1993). Nevertheless, because Californian organic standards have allowed grapes to be treated with sulphur dust to control fungus, organic wine and raisin grapes have seen massive entry from conventional growers, packers and wine-makers. Likewise, Chilean nitrate was deemed allowable because it comes from bird guano, although soluble nitrogen increases soil sodium levels and is a known source of groundwater pollution (Conway and Pretty, 1991). The quick fix of Chilean nitrate has enabled shippers to find desert growers who would willingly grow a winter crop of salad mix. These examples show the articulation between agribusiness influence on the rule-making and its environmental outcomes.

Californian agribusiness growers also tend to practise a shallower form of agro-ecology (Guthman, 2000). Not only are they more inclined to rely on input substitution, they are more likely to do large plantings of single crops because they are economically tied to production contracts and even a minimal temporal or spatial rotation entails operating at a loss or developing additional markets. For similar reasons, they may release predator insects (including via helicopters), implementing a biological pest control of sorts, but they rarely plant non-cash crops to act as trap crops, beneficial insect harbours or fertility enhancements.

This is not to say that smaller and/or movement farmers necessarily practise a deeper form of organic agriculture. There is actually wide variation in organic practices, and basically only two kinds of growers have adopted a wholly integrative production style, incorporating practices such as on-farm compost-making, mulching, polycultural or mosaic planting and applying green manure. One is made up of hobby farms and micro-market gardens, which may be important ideologically but constitute a minute portion of the organic sector in terms of acreage and sales. The other is a more visible, if loose community of mid-size working farms, comprising about 5 to 10 per cent of the organic farms in the state. In their case, the employment of agro-ecological precepts is very much entwined with their marketing strategy, as well as ideological commitment. Direct marketing, through subscription boxes and farmers' markets, requires as diverse a crop mix as possible, with the timing of harvest smoothed, always to have an array of choices for the buyer. It also draws enough of a revenue margin to pay for these practices. In other words, there are no growers tied into marketing contracts who practise this type of organic farming. At the same time, this diverse (and ecologically conscientious) type of operation tends to be strikingly intensified, pulling two to five crops, including a cover crop, from a given piece of land in any given year.

The existence of high levels of intensification even on farms of the most value-oriented organic growers is a reminder that all organic farmers operate within a larger political economy. Costs of land, labour, credit and so forth reflect not only high levels of intensification, but also state support in the socializing of risk that has characterized agro-industrialization. Prices reflect a logic of competition. How much 'room for manoeuvre', as Michelsen (2001) puts it, do organic farmers have under these conditions?

THE VALUE OF LAND IN THE LAND OF VALUE

At first glance, the considerable involvement of agribusiness in the Californian organic sector does not pose a significant problem for organic agriculture. Although the organic industry has influenced organic standards in ways that protect its interests, and has helped spawn a shallower form of organic agriculture ecologically speaking, as I have described it thus far, it has not had a substantial impact on the livelihoods and practices of movement-driven farmers. In other words, these two subsectors do not necessarily exclude each other.

Yet it bears questioning whether *prima facie* existence of agribusiness involvement in organics tells enough of the story. For, if the 'problem' with agribusiness is interpreted to be its social and ecological effects rather than its scale per se, the crucial issue is how and to what degree are agribusiness practices replicated with alternative agricultures. Apparent co-existence becomes suspect to the extent that agribusiness brings to organic its own particular logic of agro-industrialization. In what follows, then, I argue that the conditions set by agribusiness undermine the ability of even the most committed producers to practise a purely alternative form of organic farming.

First, there is the issue of competition. Research into the economics of organic farming already acknowledges that organic food may cost more to grow because organic farmers effectively internalize costs that have been progressively externalized with modern farming (Jackson, 1990; Lampkin and Padel, 1994). Unless all farmers are required to abandon potentially harmful practices, as Lampkin and Padel (1994: 439) argue, this process of 'internalizing' social and environmental costs can be sustained only in a competitive environment through the market (premium prices) or through agricultural policy support.

In California, where there is no policy support other than a legal definition of organic, organic farmers depend on price premiums. Yet in the last decade the organic sector has been plagued with rampant price competition. Particularly in the easy-to-grow commodities where agribusiness has expanded, movement-driven growers have seen their price premiums disappear. As a consequence, many independent movement growers have staked their livelihoods on crops whose very nature (and skills needed to grow them) put them out of reach of the large grower-shippers. Heirloom tomatoes are one such crop, as the very nature of an heirloom varietal is one that is not amenable to an industrial way of farming. They are low yield, hard to handle, highly perishable and otherwise delicious. Some farmers now operate at or below cost (subsidized by outside income); others have simply gone out of business.

Perhaps the better indicator of the multiple and complicated regulatory and market forces that influence the cost structure of farming is land value. Land values in and of themselves are not determinative, but they do capture signals from all spheres that affect agriculture, from technological development to consumer demand to land use planning, into one measure of expectations. Moreover, they reflect the past, in that way accounting for the historical legacies of agribusiness.

California has been at the forefront of agricultural intensification. Led by various configurations of real estate speculators and large farmers, the first state-developed irrigation projects made possible the shift from extensive grain crops to fruit trees in the late nineteenth century; later projects supported intensive vegetable production in desert-like areas (see, e.g., Leibman, 1983; Pisani, 1984; Worster, 1985). Besides providing farmers with a massive subsidy (with many today paying less than full market price), by affecting what could be grown, irrigation dramatically affected agricultural land values in California. In the post-war years, coastal vegetable producers took the lead in intensification. Adopting practices that speed up crop turnover, including faster-growing varietals, greenhouse and transplant operations, and heavy use of nitrogen fertilizers – all derived from a synergistically related agro-input industry – allowed them to harvest up to five crops per year. For their part, landowners encouraged this sort of innovation. Where once they incorporated fallowing requirements in lease clauses, these covenants were abandoned when they recognized that enhanced productivity would increase ground rents (FitzSimmons, 1986; Harvey, 1982), another mechanism by which technological innovations were capitalized into land values.

Accordingly, average agricultural land values started to diverge from the rest of the USA at the end of the nineteenth century and dramatically took off in the 1960s when technological development enabled mass, year-round vegetable production (statistics gathered from Agricultural Research Service, 1958; Economic Research Service, 2000a; Pressly and Scofield, 1965). Within California, agricultural land values became differentiated on the basis of the crop value of the highest-value crop grown in any given region. Today, for example, central coast vegetable land trades at $27,000 per acre; southern California citrus land at $19,000 per acre, and central valley field crop land at $4,300 per acre (Cal ASFMARA, 2000). Add to this the extensive nature of urban growth in California affecting the value of almost all of California's harvest acreage (Blank, 2000: 4).

At the same time that various forces of modernization have pushed on land values, past patterns of exploitation, also led by agribusines, have been 'locked in' by land values. For example, through local farming organizations as well as individual growers, agribusiness actively participated in the political construction of the farm labour market by, among other things, often violent squelching of union activity, lobbying to exempt farm labour from federal labour laws, and deliberate employment of illegal immigrants (Daniel, 1981; McWilliams, 1971, original 1935; Mitchell, 1996; Thomas, 1985; Wells, 1996). The availability of cheap harvest labour, in turn, made labour-intensive speciality crop production viable. Yet, as expectations of depressed agricultural wages continued to be imputed into land values (Ball, 1980), extant land values reproduced the need for low-cost labour.

Agricultural land values have reinforced other sorts of social relations as well. Given the various ways that agribusiness extracts surplus through mechanisms of appropriation and substitution, farmers have become unwillingly dependent on buyers, perhaps entering into contracts as a way of minimizing the risk of selling their crops at next to nothing. Or they have been compelled to intensify production by, for example, adopting higher-yielding varietals, forgoing fallow periods or growing higher-value crops. Therefore, these social relations are entwined with and reinforce environmental problems. They have made farmers dependent on all manner of inputs to speed up and control biological production, contributing to the environmental externalities of soil erosion, nutrient depletion and toxic run-off, as well as the public health costs of cancer, endocrine disruption and so forth.

Of the many consequences of agro-industrialization, the one that most affects organic farmers – indeed, has driven growers to organic farming – is the constant pressure to adopt technologies or cropping systems that create more crop value per hectare. When land values are capitalized based on the highest value of crops produced and the most rapid turnover time and cheapest cost at which they can be produced, it clearly shapes what can be produced and how. So, in a place where all three of those factors have been escalated to an extreme, alongside the urban pressure, all growers are compelled to extract a tremendous amount of value from any piece of land just to meet their land costs.

In short, the imperative of agricultural intensification, resulting from long-term *processes* of agro-industrialization, poses the largest threat to an ecological farming strategy. Deep organic farming generally depends on rotations of marginal-value crops for fertility and non-commodity crops for pest control. Many growers simply cannot afford to take land out of crop production to allow these agro-ecological processes to take hold. Price premiums may compensate for the additional costs in the short run, but, again, an inexorable logic of competition has already eroded these premiums. As for the social issues, few organic farmers in California have even begun to address the farm labour issues that plague California's agro-industrial complex.

CONCLUSION

As back-to-the-landers and other cultural dropouts, perhaps some organic farmers were once content to exist 'outside the system' by supplying their own food or trading it locally. But for most within the movement (and the industry), organic farming was seen as a way to *change* agriculture (Michelsen, 2001). To the good, organic farming has been squarely brought into the market, with all the opportunities and threats that entails. For, along with a larger market, growing interest has wrought heightened competition and the substantial entry of agribusiness, representing the industrialization of agriculture that consumers seem to be rebelling against.

Broadly speaking, almost any organic farming in California is bound to be agribusiness farming, reflecting the agrarian structure of California, where true independent family farms, or simple commodity producers, are the exception. Yet, even though most organic farms in California are formally capitalist farms, the structure of the sector is bi-polar, with a few firms receiving most of the revenue and many small operations generating little. For the purposes of this chapter I focused on two sorts of enterprises to describe organic agribusiness in California: large-acreage farmers, many of whom are tied with marketers through contracts and have only partially converted to organic production; and large-revenue firms that both grow their own crops and market the products of others, and are heavily into organics. Some of the firms in the first group moved into organics to seek value or to experiment with new techniques in the face of a changing regulatory climate; most, however, were brought in by buyers from the second group. Since many in the latter group came up through the ranks of the organic movement, I refer to them as homegrown agribusiness. As part of a larger US organic industry, they are the ones driving what is going in with organic agribusiness.

With the best intentions of growing the sector, the industry leaders have helped put the organic sector on a difficult course. Not only is the vast majority of organic acreage in California farmed by those with light commitment, price competition is eroding the margins that committed producers depend on. Moreover, the conditions all growers face due to processes of agro-industrialization make conventionalization much harder to resist because it is embedded in land values, seriously constraining the ability to employ agro-ecological methods.[10] So while there is resistance, contestation, and so forth, against the industrialization of organic agriculture, there are also structural obstacles and internal contradictions to the spread of a deeper form of organic agriculture, giving organic farmers very little room to manoeuvre. In that sense, the threat that agribusiness would dilute the meanings and practices of organic agriculture has in some respects already been borne out. To deny this is to deny a critique of agricultural industrialization that the organic movement ostensibly gets its juice from.

NOTES

1. The study itself involved compiling survey and archival data on all 1,533 growers who comprised the official organic sector in 1997. The qualitative portion of the study was based primarily on interviews with 150 growers, attendance at industry conferences and interviews with regulatory agents, technical experts and industry advocates. Interviews were conducted in all major growing regions within the state and the interview sample was purposely stratified according to crop mix, scale of operation and certification status to evaluate the ways in which these variables mattered in terms of practice. Approximately one-half of those interviewed were so-called mixed growers (i.e. growers with both conventional and organic operations) to better understand the dynamics of conversion to organic production (albeit several of the 'all-organic' producers once converted themselves). The research was supported by grants from the National Science Foundation (SBR-9711262), the Association of American Geographers, and the University of California's Sustainable Agriculture Research and Education Program (UC-SAREP).

2. It is surely striking that at the 2001 Organic Regulatory Conference held in Oakland, California, there were movement growers speaking against state funding for conversion support.

3. Much of this debate is lost on organic consumers, who either assume that all organic farming fits its bucolic images or do not exactly care how the food is produced as long as it is 'pesticide-free'. While anecdotal as scholarly evidence, these are the two responses I consistently hear (and overhear) in markets, informal social situations and classrooms, from a wide range of organic consumers.

4. In Watts's (1993) thinking, this would make them prime targets for contract farming should the exporters wish to diversify.

5. For instance, in the late 1960s and 1970s, United Fruits, Castle & Cooke, and Coca-Cola were all active in the Salinas Valley produce industry (FitzSimmons, 1986). Dole continues to procure and ship Californian fruits and vegetables and much of the Californian wine industry is currently controlled by large multinational beverage companies.

6. Hectares were derived from California's pesticide use permits, which are required for all agricultural pesticides, including those allowed by organic rules. Pesticide use data have been collected and catalogued by the California Institute for Rural Studies.

7. Besides those players listed in Table 6.3, there are a few conventional firms that have developed sizeable organic operations. These include Missionero, Frank Capurro & Sons, Victor Packing and Rainbow Valley Orchards.

8. These range from brokering on a commission or per box basis, to share contracts, to forward contracts, to custom grow contracts where buyers pay for all expenses plus a guaranteed profit to the grower.

9. The so-called Big Three (the proposed allowance of genetically engineered organisms, irradiation and sewage sludge in organic practices) galvanized the most public attention, but there were dozens of other issues that were equally insidious for those who were intimately involved in organic production and marketing. Coming out of the blue, inclusion of the Big Three was interpreted by some as a botched attempt by the Clinton administration to address several unrelated regulatory problems in one fell swoop.

10. The policy implication of this argument is that some sort of subsidy for land is needed to encourage ecological farming. Yet this kind of state support is not even being considered in the USA. For that matter, organic farmers in the USA borrow too much ideologically from notions of agrarian democracy, and particularly an American idea of independence, to embrace such state support.

REFERENCES

Agricultural Research Service (1958) 'Current Developments in the Farm Real Estate Market: November 1957 to March 1958', Washington, DC: USDA.

Allen, P. and M. Kovach (2000) 'The Capitalist Composition of Organic: The Potential of Markets in Fulfilling the Promise of Organic Agriculture', *Agriculture and Human Values* 17 (3): 221–32.

Ball, M. (1980) 'On Marx's Theory of Agricultural Rent – a Reply to Ben Fine', *Economy and Society* 9 (3): 304–26.

Barham, E. (1997) 'Social Movements for Sustainable Agriculture in France: A Polanyian Perspective', *Society and Natural Resources* 10 (3): 239–49.

Blank, S. C. (2000) 'Some Facts About Farmland Values', *Agriculture and Resource Economics Update* 3 (4): 3–4.

Broydo, L. (1998) 'Engineering an Organic Standard', *Mother Jones* (May/June).

Buck, D., C. Getz and J. Guthman (1997) 'From Farm to Table: The Organic Vegetable Commodity Chain of Northern California', *Sociologia Ruralis* 37 (1): 3–20.

Cal ASFMARA (2000) 'Land and Lease Values'. <www.calasfmra.com/landvalues /2000/> (7 December).

Campbell, H. and R. Liepins (2001) 'Naming Organics: Understanding Organic Standards in New Zealand as a Discursive Field', *Sociologia Ruralis* 41 (1): 21–39.

Carnal, J. (1996) 'California's Cadiz Land Co. Acquires Sun World International Inc.', *Bakersfield Californian* (16 July).

CCOF (1997) 'Certified Organic Membership Directory and Product Index', Santa Cruz: California Certified Organic Farmers.

Clunies-Ross, T. (1990) 'Organic Food: Swimming against the Tide?', in T. Marsden and J. Little (eds), *Political, Social and Economic Perspectives on the International Food System*, pp. 200–14. Aldershot: Avebury.

Clunies-Ross, T. and G. Cox (1994) 'Challenging the Productivist Paradigm: Organic Farming and the Politics of Agricultural Change', in P. Lowe, T. Marsden and S. Whatmore (eds), *Regulating Agriculture*, pp. 53–74. London: David Fulton.

Conway, G. R. and J. N. Pretty (1991) *Unwelcome Harvest: Agriculture and Pollution*. London: Earthscan.

Coombes, B. and H. Campbell (1998) 'Dependent Reproduction of Alternative Modes of Agriculture: Organic Farming in New Zealand', *Sociologia Ruralis* 38 (2): 127–45.

Cummings, C. (1998) 'Some Questions About the Organic Standards'. <organic-certification@listserv.oit.unc.edu> (6 February).

Daniel, C. (1981) *Bitter Harvest: A History of California Farm Workers, 1870–1941*. Ithaca, NY: Cornell University Press.

Department of Finance (1997) 'California Statistical Abstract', 38th edn. Sacramento: State of California.

DuPuis, E. M. (2000) 'Not in My Body: rBHG and the Rise of Organic Milk', *Agriculture and Human Values* 17 (3): 285–95.

Earthbound Farms (2001) 'About Us'. <www.ebfarm.com> (13 August).

Economic Research Service (2000a) 'Statistical Bulletin, no. 855, Farm Real Estate Values'. <www.usda.mannlib.cornell.edu/> (7 December).

— (2000b) 'U.S. Organic Agriculture'. <www.ers.usda.gov/whatsnew/issues/ organic> (21 November).

FitzSimmons, M. (1986) 'The New Industrial Agriculture', *Economic Geography* 62 (4): 334–53.

Food Chemical News (1998) 'California Gourmet Salad Processor Charged with Food Safety Violation', *Food Chemical News* (19 January).

Fost, D. (1991) 'Organic Food Movement Bearing Fruit: Recent Growth Raises Industry Hopes that it May Yet Compete as Agribusiness', *Washington Post* (13 October).

Friedland, W. H. (1984) 'Commodity Systems Analysis: An Approach to the Sociology of Agriculture', in H. K. Schwarzweller (ed.), *Research in Rural Sociology and Development*, pp. 221–35. London: JAI Press.

Friedmann, H. (1978) 'World Market, State, and Family Farm: Social Bases of

Household Production in the Era of Wage Labor', *Comparative Studies in Society and History* 20 (4): 545–86.

— (1994) 'Distance and Durability: Shaky Foundations of the World Food Economy', in P. McMichael (ed.), *The Global Restructuring of Agro-Food Systems*, pp. 258–76. Ithaca, NY: Cornell University Press.

Goodman, D. (1999) 'Agro-Food Studies in the "Age of Ecology": Nature, Corporeality, Bio-Politics', *Sociologia Ruralis* 39 (1): 17–38.

Goodman, D., B. Sorj and J. Wilkinson (1987) *From Farming to Biotechnology.* Oxford: Basil Blackwell.

Groves, M. (1991) 'Brand 'Em Podnuh: Harris Ranch Shifts to Selling Beef under Its Own Label', *Los Angeles Times* (29 July).

Guthman, J. (1998) 'Regulating Meaning, Appropriating Nature: The Codification of California Organic Agriculture', *Antipode* 30 (2): 135–54.

— (2000) 'Raising Organic: An Agro-Ecological Assessment of Grower Practices in California', *Agriculture and Human Values* 17 (3): 257–66.

— (forthcoming) *Agrarian Dreams? The Paradox of Organic Farming in California.* Berkeley: University of California Press.

Harvey, D. (1982) *Limits to Capital.* Chicago, IL: University of Chicago.

Harwood, R.R. (1990) 'A History of Sustainable Agriculture', in C. Edwards, R. Lal, P. Madden, R. Miller and G. House (eds), *Sustainable Agricultural Systems*, pp. 3–19. Ankeny, IA: Soil and Water Conservation Society.

Ikerd, J. E. (2001) 'Farming in the New Century: Is Organic Farming Sustainable?' Paper presented at 21st Annual Ecological Farming Conference, Asilomar, CA, 24–27 January.

Jackson, W. (1990) 'Agriculture with Nature as Analogy', in C. A. Francis, C. B. Flora and L. D. King (eds), *Sustainable Agriculture in Temperate Zones*, pp. 381–422. New York: John Wiley and Sons.

James, A. (1993) 'Eating Green(s): Discourses of Organic Food', in K. Milton (ed.), *Environmentalism: The View from Anthropology*, pp. 205–18. London: Routledge.

Klonsky, K. and L. J. Tourte (1998) 'Organic Agricultural Production in the United States: Debates and Directions', *American Journal of Agricultural Economics* 80 (5): 1119–24.

Klonsky, K., L. J. Tourte, R. Kozloff and B. Shouse (2001) 'Statistical Review of California's Organic Agriculture 1995–1998'. Davis: University of California, Agricultural Issues Center.

Lampkin, N. and S. Padel (eds) (1994) *The Economics of Organic Farming.* Wallingford: CAB International.

Leibman, E. (1983) *California Farmland: A History of Large Agricultural Land Holdings.* Totowa, NJ: Rowman and Allanheld.

Los Angeles Times (1986) 'Briefly: Mobil Said It Will Sell a Farming Subsidiary', *Los Angeles Times* (1 April).

McWilliams, C. (1971) *Factories in the Field.* Santa Barbara, CA: Peregrine Smith.

Michelsen, J. (2001) 'Recent Development and Political Acceptance of Organic Farming in Europe', *Sociologia Ruralis* 41 (1): 3–20.

Mitchell, D. (1996) *The Lie of the Land: Migrant Workers and the California Landscape*. Minneapolis: University of Minnesota Press.

Mooney, P. H. (1983) 'Toward a Class Analysis of Midwestern Agriculture', *Rural Sociology* 48 (4): 563–84.

Padel, S. (2001) 'Conversion to Organic Farming: A Typical Example of the Diffusion of an Innovation?' *Sociologia Ruralis* 41 (1): 40–61.

Pease, W. S., R. A. Morello-Frosch, D. S. Albright, A. D. Kyle and J. C. Robinson (1993) 'Preventing Pesticide-Related Illnesses in California Agriculture: Strategies and Priorities', Berkeley: California Policy Seminar.

Peters, S. (1979) 'The Land in Trust: A Social History of the Organic Farming Movement'. PhD dissertation, McGill University, Montreal.

Pisani, D. J. (1984) *From the Family Farm to Agribusiness: The Irrigation Crusade in California and the West 1850–1931*. Berkeley: University of California Press.

Pressly, T. J. and W. H. Scofield (eds) (1965) *Farm Real Estate Values in the United States by Counties, 1850–1959*. Seattle: University of Washington Press.

PR Newswire (1987) 'Texaco Completes Sale of Its California Agribusiness Operations', *PR Newswire* (2 February).

Rosset, P. M. and M. Altieri (1997) 'Agroecology Versus Input Substitution: A Fundamental Contradiction of Sustainable Agriculture', *Society and Natural Resources* 10 (3): 283–95.

Stevenson, R. W. (1987) 'Farming in a Corporate Age', *New York Times* (11 September).

Thomas, R. J. (1985) *Citizenship, Gender, and Work*. Berkeley: University of California Press.

Tovey, H. (1997) 'Food, Environmentalism and Rural Sociology: On the Organic Farming Movement in Ireland', *Sociologia Ruralis* 37 (1): 21–37.

Vos, T. (2000) 'Visions of the Middle Landscape: Organic Farming and the Politics of Nature', *Agriculture and Human Values* 17 (3): 245–56.

Watts, M. J. (1993) 'Life under Contract', in M. J. Watts and P. Little (eds), *Life under Contract*, pp. 21–78. Madison: University of Wisconsin Press.

Wells, M. (1996) *Strawberry Fields: Politics, Class, and Work in California Agriculture*. Ithaca, NY: Cornell University Press.

Whatmore, S. (2000) 'Agribusiness', in R. J. Johnston, D. Gregory, G. Pratt and M. Watts (eds), *Dictionary of Human Geography*, p. 10. Oxford: Basil Blackwell.

Worster, D. (1985) *Rivers of Empire*. Oxford: Oxford University Press.

Zwerdling, D. (1993) 'California's Vineyards Discovering Organic Farming', *National Public Radio* (1 November).

PART II

Regulating Corporate Agribusiness:
New Roles for the Public Sector

SEVEN | Greening bananas and institutionalizing environmentalism: self-regulation by fruit corporations

KEES JANSEN

§ Self-regulation by agribusiness is increasingly seen as the *pièce de résistance* for realizing a true shift to sustainable agriculture. Self-regulation means that private sector organizations themselves define the objectives, procedures, time frames, instruments and monitoring programmes for the improvement of environmental performance. Many policy-makers at the recent World Summit on Sustainable Development in Johannesburg in 2002 viewed self-regulation as the principal win-win solution for sustainable development, thus provoking disapproval from civil society organizations and independent scientists. In this view, self-regulation fits well into the contemporary policy discourses of deregulation and privatization since it can perfectly substitute mandatory or command-and-control regulation by the state. In contrast to the latter, self-regulation is supposed to be more flexible and efficient to improve environmental performance because it uses the advanced knowledge, informational advantages and entrepreneurial dynamism of the industry, avoids putting constraints on competitiveness, and creates a sense of mutual responsibility instead of perpetuating corporate self-interest (e.g. Bennett, 1999; Gouldson and Murphy, 1998). Approaches of environmental regulation that move away from command-and-control regulation – with its emphasis on monitoring, data analysis and police action – are viewed as particularly relevant for developing countries as these approaches are supposedly more cost-effective, feasible and less time-consuming (World Bank, 2000). Postmodernist perspectives consider self-regulation as the answer to the increased complexities arising from globalization processes, and 'the announcement of the death of modern mandatory regulation' (Middtun, 1999).

These views are contested by a second perspective that questions to what extent profit-seeking companies will be able or willing to improve their environmental performance if externally imposed restrictions are lacking. This perspective supposes that, in general, self-regulation is a form of 'greenwash', i.e. disinformation to present an environmentally responsible public image (Bruno, 2002; Greer and Bruno, 1996; Korten, 1999). A core problem of self-regulation is the lack of accountability. The issue these critics put forward is how to bring corporate behaviour under democratic control at the national and international level.

Quite likely the discussion between these contrasting perspectives will become even more heated over the next years. But is self-regulation greenwash by definition or is it possible to discern different forms of self-regulation and environmental performance of corporations thereby judging some better than others? An equally relevant question is whether the emphasis on self-regulation is justified in the context of a weak state – as present in many developing countries – or whether development efforts should instead focus again on improving the regulatory capacity of the state. The stalemate in the discussion between devotees of self-regulation and fervent corporation critics cannot be solved without reconsidering the relationships between self-regulation by industry and external pressures, for example by state regulation or civil society organizations. To find answers to these intriguing issues we need more empirical research into concrete cases of self-regulation.

One possible relevant case for deepening this discussion is the efforts of the banana companies Chiquita and Dole to bring a certified green banana to the market. This chapter compares the process of certification, auditing and restructuring of banana production in Chiquita and Dole's plantations in Honduras.[1] It particularly focuses on the interaction between technological change and the nature of the chosen alliances with certification agencies. It addresses the following questions. Which changes in environmental performance, internal organization, production systems and external linkages have been brought about through self-regulation by Chiquita and Dole? Why did Chiquita and Dole opt for different forms of environmental labelling and did this lead to diverse effects? What are the limitations of these forms of self-regulation and how do they relate to mandatory regulation?

IMAGES AND INTERNATIONAL MARKETS

The banana sector has been the subject of fierce environmentalist criticism with regard to massive pesticide intoxication (Jiménez, 1995; Wheat, 1996) and deforestation (Lewis, 1992), as well as of social criticism. In the early 1990s, over 16,000 banana labourers and ex-labourers of twelve different countries became involved in a class action lawsuit filed in the USA, arguing that exposure to the nematicide DBCP in the late 1970s had sterilized them (see Rosenthal, ch. 8). The International Water Tribunal in 1992 denounced Dole's pesticide contamination in Costa Rica. The activist journal *Multinational Monitor* listed Dole in its 1994 list of 'Ten Worst Corporations' and Chiquita in its 1995 selection. The *Cincinnati Enquirer* published in 1998 a series of controversial articles questioning Chiquita's business practices (Gallagher and McWhirter, 1998), and these were succeeded by a series of legal battles with the company. Several websites critically follow the comings and goings of the banana corporations.[2] The call for a boycott has been in the air for a long time. In the midst of these activist campaigns, the banana companies intensified their efforts to create an image of a 'nutritious, wholesome, and good tasting' banana. Certifying their bananas as environmentally-friendly products is seen as a major contribution to this image. Environmental certificates encode in one message to the consumer their good intentions, strict morality, good practices, transparency and submission to independent control. Visitors to Chiquita and Dole's internet sites will certainly come across their claims of environmental responsibility.[3]

The market arena of internationally traded dessert bananas is dominated by three very large companies (Dole, Chiquita, Del Monte), which account for 65–70 per cent of world exports, and two large companies (Noboa, Fyffes), which control another 16–17 per cent (Andreatta, 1997; Kasteele, 1998). An enormous expansion of production area without the expected growth of demand led to overproduction in the 1990s.[4] Furthermore, since 1993 a European trade regime intended to protect EU producers (Canary Islands, Martinique and Guadeloupe) and banana-producing ACP countries (the African, Caribbean and Pacific Group of States which developed a partnership with the European Union) with a complex quota system. In this world-market banana crisis, market prices tended to fall below production costs (Chambron, 1999; Kasteele, 1998).[5] The companies responded to the fall in prices with major restructuring of their organizations. There was a general pressure to eliminate workers' social guarantees and reduce salaries, non-profitable plantations were abandoned, and contracts with contract farmers were renegotiated or terminated. Moreover, tax reductions were negotiated in various exporting countries.

To some extent Chiquita and Dole responded differently to the crisis and the new EU trade regime. Chiquita reacted late to the EU trade regime, possibly anticipating that the regime would not hold very long, but also because of financial limitations. Once the regime was installed

Chiquita fiercely opposed it. The close links between Chiquita and US politicians and administrators were a major force behind US complaints to the WTO and the EU–USA banana trade conflict, which lasted until spring 2001. Dole, instead, approached the European market more pragmatically. It invested successfully in banana production and trade in the Canary Islands and former European colonies, and developed strategic joint ventures with European distribution networks, thus increasing access to banana licences in Europe (Kasteele, 1998). It also made agreements with Fyffes in order to use other channels to locate its bananas. Dole effectively combined sourcing of dollar bananas, EU bananas and ACP bananas to obtain the EU banana quota. This difference in strategy contributed to an increase of Dole's market share in Europe at the cost of Chiquita's share, particularly in Germany.[6]

In the established banana markets of the USA and the EU, successful 'branding' is seen as a prerequisite for success in the struggle over market shares. For Chiquita, its well-known brand is its main asset. Furthermore, a brand that links 'high-quality' and 'wholesome food' with 'environmental-friendliness' may be instrumental in counteracting the image of the banana as a symbol of environmentally and socially unfriendly monocultures as projected in activist campaigns. Chiquita was the first to seek labelling by joining the ECO-OK green label initiative of the Rainforest Alliance, a US-based environmental movement. Dole followed and expanded its ISO 9000 quality system to the field of environment by registering for the ISO 14001 label, designed by the International Standard Organization (ISO). As will be explained below, seeking certification and green labels was not simply a social construction of images. It led to, and could only be a result of, organizational change as well as innovations in production methods within the firms.

HONDURAN PRESSURE TO IMPROVE ENVIRONMENTAL PERFORMANCE

The international critique of banana production has its roots in a long history of local struggles between workers, nationalist social groups and the banana companies. Honduran scholars have fiercely criticized the multinational fruit companies for their involvement in the suppression of labour unions (Argueta, 1992; Barahona, 1994; MacCameron, 1983), in dominating national political projects (Flores, 1979), in their control of national territory and natural resources (Del-Cid, 1976; Murga Frassinetti, 1978), and in sabotaging or subsuming alternative projects of co-operative production (Posas, 1985, 1992; Slutzky and Alonso, 1980).[7]

On these waves of an anti-imperialist critique of foreign-owned plantation production rides most of the more recent public outrage following pesticide accidents in banana production. About half of all pesticide imports in Honduras are used in banana production (Jansen, 2002).

In the early 1990s, Dole was accused of having continued the use of the nematicide DBCP until the late 1970s, even while the management knew that this pesticide could cause infertility. Heated public discussions followed when workers and ex-workers pursued litigation in United States' courts. In 1992, Dole also made the headlines when impressive photographs appeared in Honduran newspapers showing rivers filled with dead fish, a consequence of pollution with the insecticides ethoprophos and endosulfan near a pineapple plantation.

As a response to such environmentalist critique, the fruit companies participated in the 'Rational and Safe Use' programmes as designed by the pesticide industry. Moreover, they argued that they had always followed the concept of rational pesticide use: given the high costs of pesticide applications they would never apply pesticides unnecessarily. Furthermore, the companies contended they had been applying Integrated Pest Management, including biological control and pest monitoring, for several decades. For several years, 'Safe Use' was the key phrase. Possible flaws in the pesticide use system were attributed to the ignorance of labourers who did not practise what they had learned.

Despite these claims of 'Rational and Safe Use' of pesticides, the social pressure for governmental action against existing pesticide practices increased. Responding to this pressure several state agencies joined to initiate environmental audits of Dole's operations by an Interinstitutional Committee under leadership of CESCCO (Centro de Estudios y Control de Contaminantes, Tegucigalpa).[8] The immediate reason for sending auditing teams to Dole's plantations was the above-mentioned massive fish mortality. Eight audits were carried out between 1992 and 1998. Initially, Dole was seen as very unco-operative. For example, it did not recognize the laboratory analyses of water samples carried out by CESCCO (Munguía, 1995). However, involved officials found that its attitude changed after the first audit. Since then, the auditing teams have been well received and most visits lasted several days. The main recommendations of the environmental audits covered a wide range of issues, including unsuitable or broken spraying equipment, cholinesterase monitoring of all plantation labourers,[9] the enormous amount of plastic waste in and around the plantations and packing stations, the mixing of pesticides at the airports and the pesticide contamination of the drainage canals, lack of protective clothing as well as the lack of control to ensure that labourers wear their protective clothing, lack of adequate infrastructure such as separate canteens, showers and equipped warehouses, lack of monitoring systems of pesticide residues, training of labourers, and problems with aerial spraying and the contamination of human beings in the plantations.

Initially, Dole did not implement many recommendations and justified delay or lack of implementation by referring to the high costs they could not bear at a time of low banana prices. Nevertheless, some changes were implemented, such as more training of labourers, better availability of protective clothing and control of their use, the construction of canteens, better control of spraying equipment, collection of plastic waste and washing of clothes by the company. After the first controversies, the technicians of Dole and the various state agencies were able to collaborate rather well and at least on one occasion the technicians publicly defended Dole against specific accusations of pesticide contamination. Nevertheless, several voices within the Interinstitutional Committee wanted to discuss a restructuring of the audit process because substantial change failed to appear. However, at the same time (in 1997), the situation altered dramatically after Dole announced its plans to obtain the ISO 14001 environmental certification. From then onwards the state officials felt that Dole really wanted them to visit its plantations and to provide comments on its environmental behaviour.

In the early 1990s, state officials also visited Chiquita's plantations after complaints about its pesticide practices. The identified problems related to the use of the herbicide paraquat, applied with backpack sprayers, and the aerial spraying of mancozeb fungicides while labourers were working in the plantations. More serious environmental audits of Chiquita's plantations did not start until 1995. Many of the environmental problems corresponded to Dole's situation and, likewise, the type of recommendations in the audit reports. But in contrast to the process at Dole, officials felt that Chiquita had worked hard from the start to change its whole system of pesticide management. Although Chiquita had embarked on the auditing process much later, it soon 'seemed to overtake' Dole according to some state officials. On reason was that Chiquita was already involved in a process of environmental certification when the governmental auditing process started.

TWO ENVIRONMENTAL CERTIFICATES

Chiquita's subsidiary in Costa Rica was the first to seek certification and for this purpose it allied with the Rainforest Alliance. This organization, with experience in certifying tropical hardwood, initiated its ECO-OK Banana Project in 1991. This project was particularly aimed at halting deforestation and conserving biodiversity. The Rainforest Alliance intended to bridge the gulf between environmentalists and industry and to build trust, transparency, involvement and consensus, at a time when environmentalist and social movements mainly opposed banana corporations and were thinking more in terms of boycotts (see Wille, 1997; <www.rainforest-alliance.org>). An anti-boycott position characterized the Rainforest Alliance.

With a group of expert volunteers, the ECO-OK Project developed a set of standards for banana production which were, according to the Rainforest Alliance, 'sufficiently strict to really make a difference, but at the same time practical and realistic' (Wille, 1997: 45). These standards included, among others, the prohibition of certain pesticides, a prohibition against cutting more forest for establishing new plantations, the obligation to provide training as well as protective clothing to workers, the obligation to protect rivers with native vegetation, and adequate management of waste. Once banana producers comply with these standards they can opt for an ECO-OK certificate. A firm that seeks ECO-OK certification has to collaborate with a non-governmental organization from the same country. In Honduras, Chiquita carries out joint programmes with the environmentalist group Fundación Héctor Rodrigo Pastor Fasquelle, although, in the first half of 2000, the certification procedure was still being carried out by the Rainforest Alliance office in Costa Rica. With the Rainforest Alliance, the company developed its own evaluation and monitoring system. This system gives marks to different aspects of the production process and calculates a final score for a whole plantation. Above a specific score that plantation is eligible for certification.

The ECO-OK project was criticized for being 'too cozy with the companies it certifies' and the certification criteria for being 'too lax' and 'too narrowly limited to technical environmental criteria', excluding the welfare interests of banana workers (Wheat, 1996). In the mid-1990s, the name of the project was changed to the Better Banana Project (BBP). Since the regulation of organic agriculture in the European Union restricts the use of the notion of 'eco', these non-organic bananas could not be exported to the European Union with 'eco' on their label (CEC, 1991).[10] The name change was accompanied by a reconsideration of the standards: the Better Banana Project included three social clauses in addition to the earlier six environmental clauses.[11]

Several years later than Chiquita, Dole pursued an environmental certificate and developed an ISO 14001 environmental management system for all its plantations worldwide. The ISO 14001 standard is an outcome of the 1992 Earth Summit in Rio de Janeiro and was released in 1996 by the International Organization for Standardization (ISO). Companies that apply for an ISO 14001 certification must identify those aspects of their operation that could have an environmental impact, set goals and targets for environmental improvement, define and ensure the participation of each employee in implementing the environmental policy, and monitor the effectiveness of their environmental operations and continually look for ways to improve them. ISO 14001 does not state specific environmental performance criteria. Another major characteristic of this environmental management system is that improvements are driven from within the organization, rather than by external forces such as regulatory agencies or environmental movements. Environmental audits focus on the compliance with environmental policy and objectives and targets defined by the management itself. Ranking criteria to define priority aspects in an organization's environmental policy include, interestingly, legal compliance and concern to interest groups and other stakeholders (Horsley, n.d.). The company SGS ICS carries out audits and certification along ISO guidelines and certified a Dole plantation in Costa Rica as the first banana export company worldwide to ISO 14001 in July 1998.[12] The ISO 14001 standard builds upon the ISO 9000 model of Total Quality Management, a programme that Dole had started several years earlier. Dole's Department of Industrial Security and Environment was assigned to implement the ISO 14001 environmental management system. A huge documentation system was set up to monitor each employee, from field labourer to general manager, on the followed training sessions and other ISO 14001-related activities. The complete Honduran legislation that has any significance for banana production and trade, water management, pesticide use, labour issues and so on, was put in a database, directly accessible via Dole's intranet for all plantation managers.

In both cases of environmental certification, the companies not only had to establish new relationships with external organizations but also within their own organizations. In various interviews it was explained how difficult it was to 'to convince our own people' at all levels within the firm. Initially, Dole faced opposition from the labour unions in implementing ISO 14001; they regarded it as an extension of the ISO 9000 quality management programme, thus creating work and exertion for the labourers without any increase in wage.

[Dole] wanted ISO due to market demand ... Maybe it is now their politics to say that labour conditions should be the same as in developed countries, but this, of course, involves costs ... We live from the reality and the practical conditions. For us the policy of the company does not count but what it shows in practice. But we have seen that more things are done [to protect the worker] with ISO than in the past. Now it is more easy to negotiate. We now give them a taste of their own medicine. We say 'that is against the rules of ISO'. In last instance we even may make an accusation. (union leader of one of Dole's plantations)

Furthermore, both Dole and Chiquita intend to draw their contract growers into the certification schemes. However, this requires large investments while there is no premium price on certified bananas. Dole finances ISO required investments, thus enlarging the debt of contract growers to the buying corporation. Chiquita was at the time of data collection not in a financial position to provide such credit to Honduran contract growers.[13]

THE SCOPE FOR CHANGING PESTICIDE USE

Before further characterizing the differences between these two strategies for seeking environmental certification, they should first be related to changes in agricultural technologies and practices. The concept 'politics of technology innovation', as developed in Chapter 1, encourages researchers to go beyond earlier social studies of fruit multinationals. Most sociological treatises on banana companies debated issues of labour and labour control on banana plantations, neo-colonialism and political power exerted by foreign capital groups, as well as foreign control over land and the regional economy in the banana enclaves, while they payed much less attention to the politics of technology use and technology development within plantations.[14] Complementary to conventional approaches investigating capital–labour relations and the insertion of transnationals into globalized food regimes, more attention could be given to understanding variation between firms in their interpretation of technological options and strategizing for technology innovation.

Pesticide management is probably the most controversial environmental issue for the banana companies. Banana production units have to understand, consider, work with and combine or resist the conflicting and often incompatible demands and characteristics of yields, pests, pesticide producers, pesticides, biological control, population dynamics of pests and natural enemies, workers, environmental movements, consumers, retailers/buyers, soils, climate, pesticide registrars, certifying consultants, GPS flight-control systems, local residents, laws and so on. Although the description below may read like a technical treatise, it is central to understanding how the companies dealt with different powers. Successively, the discussion deals with the dynamics of Sigatoka control (the major fungus disease), nematode control (which involves the most toxic pesticides), weed control and, finally, the protection of the fruit itself against insects and post-harvest fungi attacks. This section intends to provide more insight into how companies think about the risks of changing conventional control methods of major diseases and pests.

Pest control is a major cost factor in banana production. Consequently, reducing and rationalizing pesticide use have received considerable attention from the companies. Initially, improvement in pesticide management was primarily a sort of end-of-pipe technology. Both companies improved transport and storage of pesticides and introduced closed systems to fill the spray planes with pesticides. They introduced new spraying equipment, better control over the proper functioning of equipment, more protective clothing, new pesticide warehouses, waste water treatment, new constructions that allow workers to take showers and to eat in special canteens, the washing of clothes on the plantations and not at home, and so on. Organizational change focused on the training of workers in the safe use of agro-chemicals. However, these changes hardly addressed the conventional planning of pesticide use in banana cultivation, and the continuous use of pesticides, questioned by environmental and solidarity movements, has kept fuelling controversy. Changes in cultivation practices, choice of pesticides and choice of pest control method turned out to be much more difficult to realize.

Sigatoka

Pictures of aerial pesticide spraying while labourers work in the plantations or while a flagman is running away to avoid being drenched with pesticides have been widely distributed and have left an impression of irresponsible business behaviour. Aerial spraying is used principally to control Black Sigatoka, a leaf spot disease caused by the fungus *Mycosphaerella fijiensis*, and accounts for the most important part of all expenditure on crop protection; the costs for Sigatoka control may well be responsible for 25 per cent of the final retail price in importing countries (Ploetz, 1999), and is about US $1,000 per hectare in Honduras.[15] Black Sigatoka was observed for the first time in Honduras in 1972 (Gowen, 1995) and became epidemic in 1973 (Stover, 1990). It turned out to be a difficult disease to control. Between 1972 and 1981 the number of aerial applications per year of Chiquita's plantations increased from 15.1 to 44 and the related costs increased seventeenfold (Alvarez, 1983). This weekly or bi-weekly 'Yellow Rain' has hampered the construction of an environmentally friendly image for banana cultivation.

An important characteristic of the fungus is its remarkable capacity to develop resistance to systemic fungicides. This makes resistance management a crucial activity. Systemic fungicides are absorbed by the plant and remain effective for a longer period, while protectant fungicides (such as mancozeb and chlorothalonil) have to make contact with the fungus outside the plant. Systemic fungicides therefore tend to control the disease more effectively. Benomyl (Benlate®) was the first systemic product and proved very effective, but after a few years of frequent and wide applications resistance appeared (Stover, 1990). Tridemorph (Calixin®) and, after 1984, triazoles (such as tebuconazole and propiconazole or Tilt®) became important alternatives. In 1992 and 1993, the fruit companies almost lost control of the Black Sigatoka epidemic; national fungicides imports doubled and the number of applications increased. Part of the solution was found in a new system of defoliation, that is manually cutting away parts of the infected leaves in order to reduce infection. Higher frequencies of application with systemics was not considered a sound solution since it would lead to more resistance. The arrival of azoxystrobin (Bankit®) in 1996, one of the first strobilurins, a new class of supposedly more environmentally-friendly fungicides, helped to avoid an increase in the number of applications. Crucial for resistance management, and for keeping the number of aerial sprays low, is the design of complex application sequences with different fungicides. The companies alternated between different systemics and protectants (in the rainy season often mixed with oil). The elimination of one fungicide, due to unwanted environmental effects of that fungicide, would complicate the design of spraying schemes and probably increase the number of sprays.

The elimination of chlorothalonil, currently the fungicide in the spraying schemes that is most questioned, is approached differently by Chiquita and Dole. Unlike Dole, Chiquita has dropped the use of chlorothalonil, even though Chiquita's technicians praised its effectiveness. Chiquita yielded to the environmentalist critique that chlorothalonil is highly toxic to fish and aquatic invertebrates.[16] Chiquita has held to its decision to comply with the Better Banana Project criteria, and, as one involved technician suggested, to evade further critiques on their pesticide use: 'There are some small fish in the drainage canals that die when chlorothalonil is sprayed. If the environmentalists see [these dying fish] they directly say that all pesticides cause this fish death and that spraying should stop. They cannot distinguish the different pesticides. It is a corporate decision not to use chlorothalonil.' Dole has continued the use of chlorothalonil, at least for the moment. One defence line presented to me was that they observed fish in the ditches in their plantations, which proved that these were sufficiently protected against contamination.

Both the type of pesticide and the method of application are highly controversial. A major problem is that of organizing frequent aerial applications without drenching workers in the plantations and contaminating adjacent rivers and residential areas. The companies are moving the people living in camps within the plantations to nearby villages or cities.[17] To increase the precision of spraying, the companies introduced GPS in their aeroplanes. This allowed Dole to switch to nocturnal spraying while Chiquita developed a form of alternate spraying by dividing its plantations into two sections and spraying only the part where no labourers are working.

These solutions to problems in crop protection are another example of how Chiquita and Dole try to solve problems differently. With its solution, Chiquita faces the new problem of how to inform all workers which specific section is being sprayed. Decisions to spray are not always planned a long time in advance. The mistakes that easily occur may arouse criticism that the company makes errors with its new spraying practice. Dole's technological solution faced other problems. First, Dole had to convince the aviation authorities to issue a permit for nocturnal spraying. Then, the people of nearby communities protested because they were convinced that Dole was spraying illegal products; nocturnal activities suggested to them that Dole had something to hide. In the context of its local history, Dole cannot easily overcome such suspicion. A major technical problem is the larger risks pilots face while spraying at night. They fly close over the crop and any unobserved difference in field level or a cable crossing the field may have fatal consequences. Finally, at night supervisors find it more difficult to observe approaching rain. If rain falls just after spraying the control effect of the chemical may be nil and a second spraying may be required. This would increase the number of applications. Chiquita's and Dole's different choices of aerial spraying systems are based on different assessments of risks and advantages, and pose new problems for both companies.

Nematicides

A second contentious issue is the application of highly toxic nematicides that expose workers to major health risks. Nematicides control nematode infestations in the soil and generally are highly hazardous as they belong to the carbamates or organophosphates, two controversial groups of pesticides.[18] Chiquita did not apply nematicides in its plantations in the Sula Valley, while Dole did so on the plantations of its contract growers. Chiquita held the view that the level of nematode infestation did not justify nematicide application, claiming that the use of nematicide did not lead to statistical differences in yield even though it had an effect on the number of nematodes. According to Dole technicians, losses were considerable: in the order of 15–20 per cent. Nematicides were applied two to three times per year and different types of nematicides were alternated.[19] An independent pest control scientist told me that over the last ten years *Pratylenchus* nematodes have increasingly caused a certain degree of damage, but that the specific type of damage (loss of weight of the bunch) has not been recognized by Chiquita technicians who have stuck to their old research data. Chiquita technicians stated that nematicide spraying in the Sula Valley is unnecessary; but their discourse seems to have shifted. They no longer argue that research has indicated that nematicide spraying does not increase yields.[20] Instead, they use an environmentalist narrative for explaining why they do not use nematicides in Honduras: 'We do not control nematodes [chemically]. We live together (*convivir*) with the nematodes and have therefore a margin of loss. Nematicides are very toxic and culturally we are not very gifted with obedience' (manager, Chiquita). The manager here refers to the idea that, in daily plantation practice, people tend not to follow the guidelines for safe pesticide applications. It is suggested that Chiquita does not apply nematicides merely because of environmental and health reasons and therefore accepts smaller margins. This was possibly a socially desirable comment, but environmentalist considerations may indeed have played a role. Even though nematicide application may not have been cost-effective in the past, it seems to be so nowadays.[21] Therefore, it is quite likely that the current decision not to apply nematicides is informed by environmentalist criteria. Dole faces the environmentalist critique of its use of nematicides and is urgently seeking alternatives. It currently experiments with a broad-spectrum biological nematicide (DiTera®) as a possible alternative to the highly questioned organophosphates and carbamates (Castro and Gonzalez, 1997).[22]

Weed control

Weed control is second in terms of number of applications: about six to eight applications per year in an established plantation with products such as paraquat and glyphosate (Roundup®). Many of the occupational accidents registered occur with spraying herbicides. Recently, Chiquita cancelled the use of paraquat. The Better Banana Project standards prohibit the use of pesticides on the so-called 'dirty dozen' list. Paraquat, a preferred herbicide for weed control in banana, appears on the extended list because of the health risks of occupational paraquat exposure (Wendel de Joode et al., 1996). At the time of field work, Chiquita had replaced paraquat with diquat, a herbicide of the same chemical group. Diquat was not a targeted pesticide in anti-pesticide campaigns. However, diquat has several analogous toxicological effects, although a somewhat lower acute toxicity than paraquat and a similar chronic toxicity (Morgan, 1982; Extoxnet, 1996). In its public relations activities, Chiquita referred to its ban on paraquat use. Dole did not consider the elimination of paraquat from its weed control programme. Dole technicians stated that paraquat is cost-effective, is classified only as moderately hazardous, and is not a major problem if applied safely.

Other diseases and pests

Two last controversial subjects concern post-harvest treatments with thiabendazole (Mertect®) and imazalil, to control post-harvest diseases such as fruit spot and crown rot, and insecticide use for bunch protection. The companies have sought ways to improve working conditions in post-harvest treatment with fungicides. As a main improvement bananas are now sprayed in closed spraying chambers. Chiquita furthermore introduced electrostatic application which reduces the amount of required fungicide, but Dole states that it researched this option and but had to conclude that it does not function well.

Insecticide use is now a relatively minor problem in Honduras but still arouses discussion. Spraying of chemicals to control insects has been abandoned since the early 1970s, when the banana industry realized that large-scale calendar spraying led to more pests, more applications, increased costs in banana cultivation and held down profits (Stephens, 1984). Nowadays, spraying against insects only takes place in delimited areas in case of high levels of infestation. Chemical control of fruit insects takes place by covering the ripening bunch with an impregnated polyethylene bag. Recently, Dole stopped impregnating these bags with insecticides and now ties a plastic tape with a relatively low dose of chlorpyrifos around the stalk of the inflorescence. Alternatives for chlorpyrifos are being sought, as it is possible that the United States Environmental Protection Agency (EPA) will lower tolerance levels and restrict its use in the USA in the near future.[23]

Different pest control systems

The nature of pest and diseases has changed considerably over time. This has led not only to new forms of crop protection but has to a large extent determined the history of banana production in Honduras (Ellis, 1983; Stover, 1990; Soluri, 1998).[24] Uncertainties about pests, diseases and chemical control options continuously create diversity in responses. Dole and Chiquita may interpret technical problems in contrasting ways, as we have seen, for example, with their approaches to nematode control. They also choose different technical control solutions. Other issues, such as Sigatoka control, however, seem to be less poly-interpretable. The frequent and alternating application of fungicides is, for example, presented as a sort of 'natural necessity'. Considering the characteristics of Black Sigatoka and other pests and diseases, it is difficult, at this moment, to imagine a response to pest and diseases in banana plantations other than chemical spraying.[25] The cultural and organizational adoption of environmentalism has not affected the basic thinking about spraying. It has, nevertheless, affected some of the spraying activities.

Focusing on these spraying activities, it follows from the description above that Chiquita and Dole make different choices. Chiquita was influenced more by the popular views on pesticides. It took paraquat and chlorothalonil off its pesticide list and decided not to use nematicides, even though regulations in Honduras and importing countries approved the use of these products. Dole did not let itself be influenced by such populist demands and argued that it follows all official regulations and best scientific practice. In contrast to Chiquita, Dole seeks changes through large investments in agricultural research. In its view it is the latter that should drive technological innovations, not 'uninformed environmentalist opinions'. The question that emerges is to what extent is self-regulation by these banana companies able to bring about the requested but difficult transformation of banana production. The following sections will discuss the nature and limitations of these forms of self-regulation.

FORMS OF SELF-REGULATION

Evolution of environmental strategies

The evolution of Chiquita's and Dole's environmental strategies over the past decade have roughly coincided with the different phases in the greening of industry distinguished elsewhere (here I follow Simons et al., 2000). In the first phase, Chiquita and Dole reacted defensively or even with hostility to national criticism of pesticide accidents, such as the

DBCP affair, the chemical spills and massive fish deaths, accidents with paraquat sprayers and people drowned by aerial pesticide spraying.

In the second phase, technological innovations were introduced to reduce environmental and worker contamination with pesticides. Responsibility for environmental performance within the firms grew and to win back the public's confidence the companies little by little collaborated with environmental auditing by the Honduran government. Most technological improvements in this phase did not go beyond end-of-pipe technologies. Solutions were sought for the most pressing contamination of workers (safe spraying equipment, protective clothing and so on) and the environment (waste water run off on airports). Most recommendations made by the state's auditing team remained within the discourse of Rational and Safe Use of pesticides. In this phase, recommendations were regularly rejected as too costly. Technological innovations hardly touched upon the system of banana cultivation itself; the choice of specific pesticides was not really questioned. The companies were still able to shift responsibility for accidents and death to the workers, that is to the people's 'cultural ignorance' about risks. This is in line with Beck's observation (1992: 42) that management can issue strict safety regulations, knowing they will be unenforceable, and insist that they be obeyed.

In the third phase the companies went beyond prevention programmes and Safe Use approaches and introduced organizational and process changes. More actors became involved; internally, it was no longer a selected group of environment managers or doctors but also researchers, production managers, workers at many levels and top management. Externally, the companies had to become more transparent to, and collaborate with, certifying agencies, auditors, consumers and other stakeholders. Chiquita wrote its environment charter and code of conduct, and Dole wrote its environmental policy statement. Formally, the companies now assume responsibility for all accidents, independent of the direct cause. Investments in environmental management systems were made to improve priority setting, monitoring and reporting. The general change to a proactive environmental strategy was possible because environmental branding was identified as a strategic asset, particularly to gain, or at least maintain, market share in Europe.

Different ways Chiquita and Dole institutionalized environmentalism

Apart from the general similarities in the evolution of environmental strategies, some remarkable differences can be identified in the way Chiquita and Dole institutionalized environmentalism. I will conceptualize Chiquita's environmentalism as a populist-entrepreneurial approach and Dole's environmentalism as a science-driven, bureaucratic approach. This conceptualization is partly based upon narratives in existence within the companies. The reader should keep in mind that the characterized differences are only gradual and relative.

Chiquita's alliance with the ECO-OK/Better Banana Project can be called populist because it takes the environmental wisdom of non-expert rainforest conservation activists and ordinary people as the starting point for action.[26] It does so in a rather ad-hoc, pragmatic style with simple targets and procedures, which I call entrepreneurial. This is clearly reflected in the following quotation from a Chiquita manager:

> ISO 14001 is very exigent in methodology, the whole office is filled with beautiful files, but the test is in the field. Those guys of BBP are maybe a bunch of cowboys and BBP is a mess.[27] But these fellows are entrepreneurs. They have their Smartwood certification for over ten years. They did not know anything of bananas but came to talk and to consult before deciding what should happen ...
>
> BBP requires every year an evaluation while ISO has only one evaluation each three years. With our Latin culture I believe that BBP is better. With ISO 14001 you have to define your own targets and indicate the time schedule, but then it is very easy to slow down afterwards. BBP is more a benchmark. It indicates exactly what should be done and below the line you do not get the certification. Only if you come above the line. BBP is from an NGO and they do not only look at papers, which can appear very nicely. An NGO goes into the field to look what has happened. The test is in the field.

The environmental management system of Dole is different. It puts documentation and procedures first and is less interested in externally imposed, simple performance criteria. Dole's staff consider ECO-OK as 'only a few standards' you have to comply with, such as no plastic waste in the plantation. In contrast, ISO is seen as a 'total and deep affair'. ISO 14001 requires a much larger documentation system and is linked through the auditing system to a large 'scientific' bureaucracy of standards; 'scientific' in the sense that it is entirely based on expert reviews. This bureaucracy defines what the system is but not how effective the system will be (Godshall, 2000). In contrast, the auditing procedure of the Better Banana Projects intends to set clear technical production criteria with which the producers have to comply. While ISO 14001 responds to an internationally negotiated compromise between scientists, administrators and businesses about procedures for improving environmental management, the BBP standards stem from a relatively small environmentalist group and a few invited scientists who developed practical performance criteria.[28] ISO 14001 certifies the *process* whereas BBP certifies the *performance*.

Why did Chiquita and Dole opt for a specific certification programme? Most likely, it is a combination of two main factors, which will be elaborated below. The reason for a particular alliance, that is the choice of who should set the standards, is first of all an issue of assessment of the credibility of a specific label in the marketplace. A second factor is how a particular option fits into the organizational culture or cultural matrix of a company.

Market credibility and the choice for alliances

Chiquita was initially convinced that it needed NGO involvement to regain its credibility (Bendell, 2000). The choice of an NGO working on rainforest issues was not illogical, given the many public campaigns for rainforest conservation in the early 1990s. The Rainforest Alliance invited all banana producers to join their initiative, but Chiquita's main competitors, Dole and Del Monte, declined; both would opt for ISO labelling later on. With hindsight, a Del Monte director in Costa Rica suggested that the ECO-OK label would not automatically grant credibility: 'We decided that ECO-OK was largely a PR exercise. We wanted something that would defend itself and not have to be defended. ISO's new system fulfilled these aspirations, as it involves a third party assessment and is an internationally recognised standard' (cited in Bendell, 2000).

Similarly, Dole sought a credible third party that, according to one manager, would merely justify what they were already doing: 'The ISO programme started in 1997, but the whole process of change had actually started in 1992. Our system [of safe use management of pesticides] was already good, but time and again we were criticized. We could not explain [our work] – as a transnational – to our critics. That must be done by an organization with more credibility. In 1996–1997 we started with ISO 14001, a certification organization that could explain what Dole is doing.'

Chiquita's competitors thus suggested that the ISO label stands for independent assessment. This implied that the ECO-OK/BBP label does not stand for an independent environmental audit.

Credibility is furthermore related to the type of market and there is a difference in what creates credibility in the US and European markets. The Rainforest Alliance is a United States NGO with experience in awareness-raising among US citizens. But what was at stake was mainly the European market, where the quota system resulted in higher margins, where the battle of market shares took place, and where green consumption was gaining a place in the supermarket. Despite several efforts, the Rainforest Alliance did not succeed in effective network-building with European NGOs working on banana issues (Bendell, 2000). The Rainforest Alliance was viewed as a dependent ally of Chiquita, who laid too much emphasis on environmental conservation and had too little thought for the social issues that motivated much of the anti-multinational activism in Europe. It would take a lot of effort to change this view. One can draw a parallel here with Chiquita's strategically erroneous assessment of the future of the European trade regime. The unlucky choice of a label with 'ECO' in the name exemplifies the distance to the European context and legislation. The BBP label intends to attract environmentally conscious consumers. In contrast, the ISO label merely focuses on retailers, is hardly known to consumers and rather difficult to explain.

Dole was well aware that an ISO label was not very important in the US market, but had 'got quite a name' in Europe. It probably had contributed to the rise of their market share. This is not to say that the BBP label did not bring benefits to Chiquita. According to an internal communication, Chiquita recognized the BBP project as a main asset for the company; estimates circulated that without BBP the company would have lost 80 per cent of its yearly gross sales of US $250 million in Europe. Nevertheless, Chiquita set up activities to develop an environmental management system according to ISO standards, primarily for the European markets where 'ISO is better known and has more credibility'. But now Chiquita was lagging behind several years and managers indicated that it would take at least until 2003 to certify the Honduran plantations.[29]

Organizational culture and the choice for alliances

A second factor explaining why Chiquita joined the Rainforest Alliance initiative and Dole the ISO system was the difference in organizational cultures. In an entrepreneurial spirit, Chiquita was the first company to plunge into environmentalist adventures. At that time, ISO 14001 even did not exist and was not an option. The first initiatives to work together with an NGO came from below; managers at COBAL, a Chiquita subsidiary in Costa Rica, participated in ECO-OK discussions. Initially, the Chiquita bosses in Cincinnati were confused about the proposed NGO–business relationship and concerned that the certification of one division only would reflect badly on produce from other divisions (Bendell, 2000). Later they gave in to this bottom-up leverage, but the programme started only after Chiquita Brands International decided to turn all its Latin American operations into certified farms. Such bottom-up leverage tends to be less likely within Dole, given its stronger top-down management style.

Dole's choice for the ISO 14001 standard was a logical sequel to its ISO 9000 quality management system. Dole could make use of an already existing actor-network involved in ISO standards. Furthermore, ISO coincides with Dole's strong belief in the role of science-driven research for improving banana cultivation.[30] In the late 1970s, Chiquita closed down its world-famous research facility in La Lima, Honduras. The company leaders at that time did not expect major technical improvements from research. In contrast, Dole increased its investments in research in the 1980s and 1990s.[31] The current organizational culture within Dole prescribes that its Research Department should lead technological change. This department plays a decisive role in planning production activities and has kept a dominant influence in environmental issues, even after the foundation of a special department for environmental affairs. Recommendations from government auditors were directly translated by Dole's agronomists in the Research Department in terms of practical feasibility and cost increases. A ban on paraquat and chlorothalonil, as upheld by Chiquita, was a difficult proposition for the agronomy researchers of Dole to accept. These pesticides are essential for good farming, according to the agronomist perspective. Unlike Dole, Chiquita delegated its environmental issues mainly to its medical team, to which some environmental experts were later added. Chiquita considered pesticide problems in the first place as a workers' health issue. This may explain the lower level of resistance within Chiquita against eliminating certain pesticides.

Dole believes more strongly than Chiquita that innovations arise from within the company. Dole's researchers are proud of the advanced level of their research. This strong focus on internal knowledge-generation is reflected in the career perspectives of employees. Most higher-level employees I talked to in Chiquita had worked for the company for a short time and were thinking about job possibilities outside the company in the future. In contrast, most of the Dole employees clearly expressed their hopes of a long future within the company and strongly identified themselves with its professional research culture.

Dole's strong belief in internally driven technological change dovetails with the choice of the ISO 14001 standard with its focus on process as well as the definition and shaping of environmental change from within the firm. Paradoxically, this belief also inspires the view that ISO is not a major source of technological innovation. According to Dole technicians, ISO did not change the process already underway before the ISO standards of environmental management were applied: 'With ISO we only document what we were doing; eight years ago we already had a Manual for Management and Safe Use of Pesticides. It included training on all levels. We did much to use returnables [pesticide containers] and to do cholinesterase tests. We have already practised Integrated Pest Management for thirty years.'

In a similar vein, governmental audits were viewed as technically not really important for Dole's management process.[32] The audits were primarily an additional source of defence against environmentalist criticism, and, in the view of getting ISO certification, a test of whether the operations complied with all the laws.

Unlike Dole, Chiquita simply buys the technologies it needs and does not generate new knowledge itself. It implements new technologies with less rigorous testing than Dole does. It started rapidly with azoxystrobin, then it introduced electrostatic fungicide application in post-harvest treatment, a technology that never passed the test phase in Dole, and it casts anxious looks at how others study the issue of soil health. Unlike Dole, it delegates crucial production tasks to others. Spraying, for example, is not done by Chiquita itself but by a contracted firm. The relative ease and swiftness with which Chiquita introduces external technologies have a parallel in its rapid start with an environmental label. Within Dole, change takes more time and investment in research.

GREEN BANANAS AND THE LIMITATIONS OF SELF-REGULATION

In the world of bananas, self-regulation has considerably changed the internal organization of firms as well the infrastructure of plantations. Can one conclude on the basis of these cases of environmentalism in corporations that self-regulation is a good alternative to conventional command-and-control regulation? A closer look at these cases suggests that it is too early too draw such a conclusion since they reveal four important limitations.

First, there is the question of whether the standards developed in self-regulation are really comprehensive when it comes to addressing major environmental problems. In the case of Dole-ISO, ISO as a standard does not change the type of pesticides Dole is using, nor the number of applications or the amount. The impact of the ISO 14001 standard is severely limited by its lack of performance standards. It does not define concrete criteria for environmentally-friendly banana production. This leads some to argue that ISO should involve third-party certifiers who apply concrete performance standards (Godshall, 2000). Egger (1998) proposes that parallel work with non-governmental organizations should influence the ISO and make eco-labels a require-ment for ISO certification of bananas.

The current intentions of Chiquita to combine the Better Banana label with the ISO certification show, however, a major pitfall of such an approach. Local technicians estimate that current work to certify Costa Rican plantations according to ISO standards has slackened the efforts to comply with BBP standards as attention has been shifted from changes in the field to fulfilling administrative requirements in the office. This confirms the general suggestion of some authors that ISO 14001 may lower environmental performance instead of improving it (e.g. Clapp, 1998; Krut and Gleckman, 1998). This raises the question to what extent corporations are willing to yield decisive influence to external bodies setting real technical limits to their production system.

The Chiquita-BBP case shows how such an alliance with NGOs may turn out to focus on rather 'touchable' issues: trees, birds and the 'dirty dozen' pesticides. The more subtle differences between pesticides such as paraquat and diquat remained hidden. It can be questioned whether an NGO like the Rainforest Alliance is strong enough to set, independent of a large corporation, new standards that are complex, less 'touchable' and more difficult to understand.

A second limitation concerns the exaggerated importance given to self-regulation, which conceals the importance of governmental regula-tions for setting the real benchmarks. The question 'Who sets the real pesticide standards?' remains a crucial one. Dole foresees that some pesticides may not be used in the near future. That will mainly be a result of the EPA (or its European equivalent) questioning specific pesticides rather than because of the green label environmental stand-ards. Dole rejects populist critiques of pesticides and only acknowledges formalized standards by official regulatory bodies as decisive pesticide standards. Important here is the observation that, with regard to Dole's pesticide use, the bottom line is still defined by state regulation, particu-larly the EPA norms. Self-regulation of the ISO form does not lead to the restriction of hazardous pesticides; tightened state regulation may do so. The BBP criteria may seem different as these are explicit in banning a number of pesticides that are still EPA-approved. However, this attention concerns only a few pesticides and the BBP system is never capable of regulating all other pesticides or evaluating all kinds of new pesticides currently introduced. Its issue-based approach cannot replace a comprehensive regulation by government agencies.

A third limitation is the expected influence of self-regulation on innovation. The impact of BBP on R&D innovation by the company is limited. New technologies are applied but they predominantly consist of products and instruments acquired from others. Apparently, the impact of ISO on actually stimulating innovation seems more prominent. ISO standards require that firms keep innovating in order to improve their environmental performance. Dole is doing that, for example by exploring more extensively than Chiquita the usefulness of all kinds of biological agents, investigating ways to monitor weed growth and experimenting with cover crops (both may reduce herbicide use), and studying biological control (cf. Castro and Gonzalez, 1997; Wielemaker, 1997). As we have seen, however, technological innovation is more driven by Dole's research culture than by ISO.

A fourth limitation is the unresolved issue of transparency and accountability. The idea in both versions of environmental certification that local laws have to be obeyed sounds positive but does not address the question of control nor the question of proper law-making. It is still difficult for government agencies and civil society organizations to get all the information they need to make a sound judgement about the industry's performance. For example, the Honduran law obliges firms to report labour accidents, but these data remain hidden from any transparent public control. Efforts by the national government to improve auditing were initially not welcomed and did not lead to real changes since any adaptation had to be cost-neutral. Later, this auditing process improved but was principally made instrumental to the process of getting the plantations certified. More recently, auditing efforts slackened and some involved people stated that they are no longer needed. In this account, the companies appear to be more sensitive to consumer demands than to the regulatory efforts of the Honduran state. This issue of who and what transforms the corporations thus points at a more general problem of democratic control in the globalized free market ideology, where the world's elite consumers seem to have more power than democratically elected Third World governments.

This chapter has shown that fruit multinationals respond to consumers' environmental awareness and social activism, and change production processes on their banana plantations. Companies have combined organizational change, technical change, change in infrastructure, change in communication (transparency, codes of conduct), new relationships with partners (certifying and audit organizations, relationships with NGOs) and shifts in older relationships, such as between company and workers, in order to improve the image of the banana. Even during a world-market banana crisis, with pressure on profits and the need to reduce costs, remarkably large investments were made in operations that neither reduced costs nor increased yields. It also did not lead to a new product. The driving force behind these investments was the need to secure market shares and to protect the image of the banana, the brand and the firm.

Chiquita and Dole opted for different certification schemes due to different assessments of stakeholder roles, of the organizations that could improve credibility in the market, particularly the European market, and of the importance of technology innovation from within the company. Chiquita chose the populist path and linked with a NGO producing public discourses of deforestation and environmental protection. It adhered to clear and understandable performance standards. Dole put more trust in the credibility of science-driven, bureaucratic environmental management. The chosen alliance influenced the technical outcomes. For example, while Chiquita abolished the use of chlorothalonil and paraquat in line with the demands of environmentalist NGOs, Dole argued that no changes in pesticide choice are required as they comply with all national registration requirements and international regulation.

These cases show that self-regulation is able to enhance environmental performance. It is too early to judge whether the banana is now a 'healthy' fruit, since the amount of pesticide residues on the banana has probably not changed very much. The most important improvement seems to be a more healthy working environment for banana workers resulting from changed forms of pesticide use and new infrastructure. This observation of real changes within banana production does not mean, however, that self-regulation can now be proclaimed as an alternative to governmental or other forms of mandatory regulation. First, the case of bananas is special because of the huge image problem banana corporations faced. Changes were initially not driven by responsible behaviour, as a cornerstone of self-regulation, but by external pressure groups that combined environmental and social demands. They held the 'stick' of possible boycotts. Second, this case of self-regulation has revealed several limitations to self-regulation. It is highly questionable whether it leads to comprehensive performance standards. Even in these cases, governmental regulatory agencies remain the core entities for setting real benchmarks. The quality of mandatory regulation, law-making and law implementation therefore remains crucial for the outcome of this process of improving environmental management. Furthermore, self-regulation has a rather limited influence on the development of new technologies. A final limitation concerns the continuous lack of transparency and accountability, particularly towards Honduran society.

The central role of the reconstructed image of the banana within environmental discourse means that Dole and Chiquita are both drawn into a new technology regime in which pesticides have been defined as a problem. They cannot deviate from the chosen path of pesticide reduction even while pesticides have not yet been substantially reduced. This explains why they seek with conviction biological agents that can replace synthetic pesticides. The fruit companies will also have to confront the problem of how to obey all laws and labour regulations. The responses of the companies to an environmentalist critique have created new rule-sets that make them even more prone to future environmental and social critiques.

NOTES

1. Data were gathered through interviews with managers, researchers, technicians and union leaders of both companies, non-company organizations, as well as with state officials of various agencies in 1999 and 2000. Other data resulted from an extensive review of published and unpublished documents, reports, newspaper articles and web pages. Following anthropological practice to protect informants, no names are given. I am grateful to all informants, including those whose information could not be used for this publication. All translations from original Spanish-language sources were made by the author. The research was supported by the Netherlands Foundation of the Advancement of Tropical Studies (WOTRO). This chapter's main focus is on pesticide use as this is the key element of environmental performance of banana production. Mentioning product names does not mean any endorsement or validation of the product. This chapter does not evaluate quantitatively the environmental appropriateness of the certification procedures since that would require additional research.

2. See, for example: <www.bananalink.org.uk>, <www.banafair.de> and <http://bananas.agoranet.be/>

3. For example: <www.chiquita.com>: 'We committed more than $20 million of capital expenditures to a comprehensive environmental strategy, along with millions of dollars of annual operating costs and expenses for environmental programs'; <www.dole.com>: 'Environmental stewardship is an integral part

of Dole's concept of "quality", embodied in our label … Some companies treat the environment as a public relations issue. At Dole, it's an operations issue. We strive to integrate consideration for the environment into everything we do. We invest in environmental protection – in making real improvements in our people, our facilities and our operations – not in boasting about what we do.'

4. The area with export-oriented banana plantations in Latin America increased 92 per cent (to 280,554 ha) between 1985 and 1996 (Arias, 1997).

5. However, the EU trade regime allowed for higher margins in Europe (Kasteele, 1998).

6. According to Kasteele (1998), Chiquita's market share dropped, between 1992 and 1995, from more than 30 per cent to 19 per cent, at a time when total imports in the EU also decreased. In the same period, Dole's share grew from 12 per cent to 15–16 per cent, while Fyffes (including Geest) grew from a mere 10 per cent to 17–18 per cent. An unknown proportion of Fyffes' bananas were sourced from Dole's plantations.

7. The expansion of banana production since the late nineteenth century considerably reshaped the Honduran landscape. The area under production reached its peak in the late 1930s when the United Fruit Company (now Chiquita) alone cultivated about 38,000 ha of banana (Soluri, 1998: 130). In the mid-1980s, Dole and Chiquita owned about 10,000 ha planted with bananas which provided work to about 13,400 labourers (Andrade et al., 1987). Yields varied somewhat according to this source: Chiquita produced 3,220 boxes of 40 pounds per hectare, Dole about 2,660 boxes per hectare, and national producers about 2,540 boxes. In the 1990s, the total area of all banana production just exceeded 22,000 ha (FAOSTAT, 2000), about half of it cultivated directly by Chiquita and Dole and the other half by independent producers and co-operatives. The export value of bananas in 1992 was US $256 million and in 1993 $229 million and by then about 22,000 labourers found full-time employment in banana cultivation (SECPLAN, 1994). Chiquita's plantations are located along the Ulua river in the Sula Valley in the north, while Dole cultivate its bananas more to the east, in the Aguán Valley. Most so-called 'independent' producers, who have contracts with Dole or Chiquita, are located in the Sula Valley.

8. The auditing teams also included officials of the Ministry of Environment (SERNA), the Ministry of Agriculture (SAG, through SENASA, the Servicio Nacional de Sanidad Agropecuaria), the Ministry of Health and the Ministry of Work.

9. Organophosphate and carbamate pesticides, the most common ones, cause cholinesterase inhibition. Cholinesterase is an important enzyme in the nervous system and its activity can be measured in blood samples.

10. Another reason for modifying the project's name was a change in the organization. A wider network called Conservation Agriculture Network, which linked the Rainforest Alliance to other groups involved in certification work across Latin America, ran the Better Banana Project. Bendell (2000) offers a good and detailed account of the evolution of the Better Banana Project, its special relation with Chiquita and its problematic relations with other stakeholders.

11. The nine principles include: (i) ecosystem conservation, (ii) wildlife conservation, (iii) minimal, strictly managed use of agrochemicals, (iv) complete,

integrated management of wastes, (v) conservation of water resources, (vi) soil conservation, (vii) fair treatment and good conditions for workers, (viii) community relations, and (ix) environmental planning and monitoring.

12.   Del Monte Bananas in Costa Rica were ISO certified in December 1998 by BVQI.

13.   A Dole technician stated that investments in ISO-related activities are about US $800–1,000 per hectare or 30 dollar cents per box of bananas. An informant from Chiquita stated that investments in ECO-OK/BBP-related activities may exceed US $170,000 to prepare a plantation of 400 ha for certification (i.e. $425/ ha). These data are not comparable because we do not know what is included and excluded in these numbers. Furthermore, these informants were not the persons who do the accounting. Specific cost data are generally firm secrets. These data obtained through hearsay give, however, as gross estimates an impression of the magnitude of environmental investments. Formally Chiquita states that it invested US $20 million in infrastructure improvements to get certified all its 127 owned banana farms (26,500 ha), that is $755 per hectare (Chiquita, n.d.). Again, we do not know what is included in these data.

14.   Good exceptions are Ellis (1983) and Soluri (1998).

15.   Rough estimate by Mauricio Rivera, phytopathologist, FHIA-Honduras (personal communication).

16.   Chiquita had to face complaints by Zeneca, its supplier of chlorothalonil, which pushed Chiquita to reconsider its decision. Zeneca is one of Chiquita's partners in educational programmes about environmental issues.

17.   In 1998, Hurricane Mitch destroyed most banana plantations as well as the camps in Honduras. These camps are not being included in the reconstruction work.

18.   Important nematicides imported in 1998 or 1999 and used in banana production in Honduras were fenamiphos (Nemacur®), dichloropropene (Telone®), cadusafos (Rugby®), terbufos (Counter®), ethoprop (Mocap®), oxamyl (Vydate®) and carbofuran (Furadan®).

19.   Alternation is required; not so much because nematodes develop resistance against these pesticides, but because the nematicides are increasingly biodegraded by micro-organisms in the soil.

20.   Like Dole, Chiquita is experimenting with biological nematicides.

21.   This, at least, is the view of the independent scientist mentioned above, as well as Dole.

22.   The search for environmentally friendly alternatives may have a second more direct reason than environmental awareness alone. Top priority in Dole's research programme is the question of soil health. In the 1990s, yields stagnated or even declined and problems with soil management and root health were seen as the causes. It is supposed that nematicide use may influence negatively the life of beneficial soil organisms such as certain mycorrhiza.

23.   The USA Environmental Protection Agency has set a 'tolerance level' of acceptable residue of a particular pesticide for crops, including bananas. Fruits sprayed with pesticides without an 'EPA tolerance' cannot be imported into the United States. Europe and Japan follow a similar procedure.

24 The word 'determined' is used here deliberately. It does not mean a comprehensive determination, nor over-determination by technology, and thus is far off technological determinism; but it expresses a position different from social constructivism, which would approach pests, diseases and pesticides as social constructs only. Conceptually, the essential characteristics of pests, diseases and epidemics are seen here as contingently related to social structures. These non-social 'powers' can, in that sense, influence or 'determine' social structures and practices.

25. In this sense the companies share the views of some of their opponents who argue that large-scale monocultures can never produce high yields without pesticides.

26. This does not mean that Rainforest Alliance representatives had no expertise at all or did not gain expertise during the process. What is meant here is that, at the start of the process, they were not experts in all aspects of banana production, although they may have had expertise in the ecology and the biology of rainforests.

27. See Bendell (2000) for a description of the lack of clarity in the ECO-OK/Better Banana Project.

28. Flexibility is built into the certification systems in different ways. The ISO standards permit Dole to formulate its own environmental targets while Chiquita has to comply with the ECO-OK/BBP standards. However, as the Rainforest Alliance developed a one-to-one relationship with Chiquita (Bendell, 2000), the company was closely involved in developing the standards and in formulating how to adhere to these standards.

29. More recently, Chiquita (n.d.) stated that it had achieved the certification of the Costa Rican division to the ISO 14001 standard in 2000. It does not plan to certify other banana divisions to the ISO 14001 standard since it believes that the BBP standard is more valuable in driving real performance improvement.

30. The Dole Europe website reflects the scientific bent: 'Inspections, tests and sampling: they are a way of life at Dole'.

31. One difference with Chiquita's past research is that its researchers were actively producing scientific publications, while the results of Dole's current research are mostly kept secret and are not published.

32. The government auditors often felt that they could not manage the technical arguments used by Dole's staff.

REFERENCES

Alvarez Arguetab, R. C. (1983) 'Análisis de los métodos de evaluación para la detección del avance de Mycosphaerella fijiensis var. difformis, causante de Sigatoka Negra en banano'. La Ceiba, Honduras: Informe del servicio social, UNAH.

Andrade, D. A., L. Avila, M. Velásquez, M. Chávez, J. L. Martínez and A. Reyes (1987) 'Uso y comercialización de agroquímicos en Honduras'. Tesis de Licenciatura en Economía, UNAH.

Andreatta, S. L. (1997) 'Bananas, are They the Quintessential Health Food? A Global/Local Perspective', *Human Organization* 56 (4): 437–49.

Argueta, M. R. (1992) *Historia de los sin historia*. Tegucigalpa: Guaymuras.

Arias, O. (1997) 'Current Advances in the Biotechnology of Banana', in J. Yglesias Luconi (ed.), *Memoria primer taller internacional sobre control biológico y producción integrada en el cultivo de banano*, pp. 171–9. Costa Rica: EARTH.

Barahona, M. (1994) *El silencio quedó atrás. Testimonios de la huelga bananera de 1954.* Tegucigalpa: Guaymuras.

Beck, U. (1992) *Risk Society: Towards a New Modernity.* London: Sage.

Bendell, J. (2000) 'Growing Pain? The Lessons of Allying with a Transnational Company to Lessen the Environmental and Social Impacts of Banana Monocultures'. Paper presented at the 4th ISTR Conference, Dublin, July 2000.

Bennett, P. (1999) 'Governing Environmental Risk: Regulation, Insurance and Moral Economy', *Progress in Human Geography* 23 (2): 189–208.

Bruno, K. (2002) 'Greenwash + 10: The UN's Global Compact, Corporate Accountability and the Johannesburg Earth Summit'. CorpWatch/Tides Center <www.corpwatch.org/campaigns/PCD.jsp?articleid=1348> (7 October).

Castro, M. and J. Gonzalez (1997) 'Biological Control Options in an Integrated Pest Management Program for Banana Nematodes and Insects', in J. Yglesias Luconi (ed.), *Memoria primer taller internacional sobre control biológico y producción integrada en el cultivo de banano*, pp. 71–82. Costa Rica: EARTH.

CEC (Council of the European Communities) (1991) 'Council Regulation (EEC) No. 2092/91 of 24 June 1991 On Organic Production of Agricultural Products and Indications of Referring Thereto on Agricultural Products and Foodstuffs', *Official Journal of the European Communities* 34 (L 198): 1–15.

Challenger, D. and C. Friend (2001) 'Fruit of the Poisonous Tree: Journalistic Ethics and Voice-Mail Surveillance', *Journal of Mass Media Ethics* 16 (4): 255–72.

Chambron, A. C. (1999) 'Bananas: the "Green Gold" of the TNCs', in J. Madeley (ed.), *Hungry for Power. The Impact of Transnational Corporations on Food Security*, pp. 46–65. London: UK Food Group.

Chiquita (2002) '2000 Corporate Responsibility Report'. Chiquita Brands International <www.chiquita.com/chiquitacr2/References/pdfs/English.pdf> (9 October).

Clapp, J. (1998) 'The Privatization of Global Environmental Governance: ISO 14000 and the Developing World', *Global Governance* 4 (3): 295–316.

Del-Cid, J. R. (1976) 'Aproximacion al estudio de las clases sociales en el agro hondureño', in Departamento de Ciencias Sociales (ed.), *Lecturas sobre la realidad nacional*, pp. 75–100. Tegucigalpa: Editorial Universitaria.

Egger, M. (1998) 'Are ISO Standards a Sustainable Instrument for Supporting a Sustainable Banana Economy?' <http://www.bananalink.org.uk/resources/resmain.htm> (8 May).

Ellis, F. (1983) *Las transnacionales del banano en Centroamerica.* San José, Costa Rica: Editorial Universitaria Centroamericana.

Extoxnet (1996) 'Pesticide Information Profiles: Paraquat'. <http://ace.orst.edu/cgi-bin/mfs/01/pips/paraquat.htm?8#mfs> (10 October).

FAOSTAT (2000) 'FAOSTAT Agricultural Data'. <http://apps.fao.org/cgi-bin/nph-db.pl?subset=agriculture>

Flores Valeriano, E. (1979) *La explotación bananera en Honduras*. Tegucigalpa: Editorial Universitaria.

Gallagher, M. and C. McWhirter (1998) 'Chiquita Secrets Revealed', *Cincinnati Enquirer* (3 May).

Godshall, L. E. (2000) 'ISO 14001: A Case Study in Certification at Bayer Pharmaceuticals in Berkeley, California'. Paper presented at the 2nd POSTI meeting and the ESST Annual Scientific Conference, Strasbourg, 27–28 May 2000.

Gouldson, A. and J. Murphy (1998) *Regulatory Realities. The Implementation and Impact of Industrial Environmental Regulation*. London: Earthscan.

Gowen, S. (1995) *Bananas and Plantains*. London: Chapman and Hall.

Greer, J. and K. Bruno (1996) *Greenwash: The Reality Behind Corporate Environmentalism*. Penang, Malaysia: Third World Network.

Horsley, V. (n.d.) 'Implementation of the ISO 14001 Environmental Management System'. <www.sgs.ca> (11 July 2000).

Jansen, K. (2002) 'Plaguicidas y su regulación en Honduras', *Ceiba* 43 (2): 273–89.

Jiménez, J. N. (1995) *Plaguicidas y salud en las bananeras de Costa Rica*. San José: ASEPROLA.

Kasteele, A. v. d. (1998) 'The Banana Chain: The Macro Economics of the Banana Trade'. <www.bananalink.org.uk/resources/resmain.htm> (8 May 2000).

Korten, D. C. (1999) *The Post-Corporate World: Life After Capitalism*. San Francisco, CA: Berrett-Koehler.

Krut, R. and H. Gleckman (1998) *ISO 14001: A Missed Opportunity for Sustainable Global Industrial Development*. London: Earthscan.

Lewis, S. (1992) 'Banana Bonanza: Multinational Fruit Companies in Costa Rica', *The Ecologist* 22 (6): 289–90.

MacCameron, R. (1983) *Bananas, Labor, and Politics in Honduras: 1954–1963*. New York: Maxwell School of Citizenship and Public Affairs, Syracuse University.

Midttun, A. (1999) 'The Weakness of Strong Regulation and the Strength of Soft Regulation: Environmental Governance in Post-modern Form', *Innovation* 12 (2): 235–50.

Morgan, D. P. (1982) *Diagnostico y tratamiento de los evenenamientos con plaguicidas*. Washington, DC: EPA (United States Environmental Protection Agency).

Munguía Guerrero, L. (1995) 'Caso estudio: Normatización empresa Standard Fruit Company con su subsidiaria Agropor, dedicada al cultivo de piña, en el Porvenir, Atlantida, Honduras, Centroamérica', *Cuaderno sobre el estado sanitario ambiental de Honduras* 3: 3–7.

Murga Frassinetti, A. (1978) *Enclave y sociedad en Honduras*. Tegucigalpa: Editorial Universitaria.

Ploetz, R. (1999) 'The Most Important Disease of a Most Important Fruit'. APSnet feature. <www.scisoc.org/feature/banana/top.html> (28 April 2000).

Posas, M. (1985) 'In the Jaws of the Standard Fruit Company', in N. Peckenham and A. Street (eds), *Honduras: Portrait of a Captive Nation*, pp. 152–6. New York: Praeger.

— (1992) *La autogestión en el agro hondureño. El caso de la Empresa Asociativa Campesina 'Isletas' (EACI)*. Tegucigalpa: Editorial Universitaria.

SECPLAN (1994) *IV Censo Nacional Agropecuario 1993*. Tegucigalpa: Graficentro Editores.

Simons, L. P., A. Slob and H. Holswilder (2000) 'The Fourth Generation: New Strategies Call for New Eco-indicators'. Unpublished paper. Delft: TNO-Institute of Strategy, Technology and Policy.

Slutzky, D. and E. Alonso (1980) *Empresas transnacionales y agricultura: el caso del enclave bananero en Honduras*. Tegucigalpa: Editorial Universitaria.

Soluri, J. (1998), 'Landscape and Livelihood: An Agroecological History of Export Banana Growing in Honduras, 1870–1975'. PhD dissertation, University of Michigan.

Stephens, C. S. (1984) 'Ecological Upset and Recuperation of Natural Control of Insect Pests in Some Costa Rican Banana Plantations', *Turrialba* 34 (1): 101–5.

Stover, R. H. (1990) 'Sigatoka Leafs Spots: Thirty Years of Changing Control Strategies: 1959–1989', in R. A. Fullerton and R. H. Stover (eds), *Sigatoka Leaf Spot Diseases of Bananas*, pp. 66–74. Montpellier: INIBAP.

Wendel de Joode, B. N. van, I. A. M. de Graaf, C. Wesseling and H. Kromhout (1996) 'Paraquat Exposure of Knapsack Spray Operators on Banana Plantations in Costa Rica', *International Journal of Occupational and Environmental Health* 2 (4): 294–304.

Wheat, A. (1996) 'Toxic Bananas', *Multinational Monitor* 17 (9).

Wielemaker, F. (1997) 'Banana Production with "Pinto's Peanut" (*Arachis pintoi* cv. amarillo) and "Oreja de Raton" (*Geophila repens*) as Cover Crops', in J. Yglesias Luconi (ed.), *Memoria primer taller internacional sobre control biológico y producción integrada en el cultivo de banano*, pp. 84–9. Costa Rica: EARTH.

Wille, C. (1997) 'Los programas de certificación ECO-O.K. y BETTER BANANA PROJECT: acuerdos entre ambientalistas y agricultores', in J. Yglesias Luconi (ed.), *Memoria primer taller internacional sobre control biológico y producción integrada en el cultivo de banano*, pp. 43–9. Costa Rica: EARTH.

World Bank (2000) *Greening Industry: New Roles for Communities, Markets, and Governments*. Oxford: Oxford University Press.

seeking access to justice to make agribusiness
accountable in the global economy

ERIKA ROSENTHAL

§ Although only a small percentage of global pesticide use takes place
in the developing South, the vast majority of pesticide poisonings occur
there. For the victims in these countries, there is no access to justice at
home: they have no money to hire a lawyer; jury trials and pre-trial
discovery do not exist; local statutes cap the amount they may recover
at miserably low amounts; court systems are often inefficient or outright
corrupt. This chapter examines a sixteen-year legal battle, by thousands
of banana plantation workers who were made sterile by exposure to the
pesticide DBCP,[1] to win the right to bring a suit in the United States
against the US transnational agro-chemical and agribusiness companies
whose products and production decisions caused their injuries.

Although internal company documents show that the pesticide's
manufacturers, Dow Chemical and Shell Oil, knew of the product's
reproductive toxicity in the late 1950s, they marketed DBCP as safe in
dozens of countries around the world. Even after DBCP was banned
in the USA, these companies continued to export the product for use
on plantations owned by Dole and Chiquita in over a dozen Southern
developing countries. This chapter tells the history of DBCP litigation
in the US courts, the home country of these transnational corporations
(TNCs), initiated by thousands of workers from the South. It shows
the centrality of the *forum non conveniens* doctrine to corporate defence
strategies: to evade liability the corporate defendants used this arcane
procedural doctrine (FNC, or 'inconvenient forum') to prevent the case
from being heard by a US jury, and to avoid responsibility for injuries
to thousands of foreign banana workers.

The FNC doctrine allows the court, at its discretion, to dismiss a
case if it finds that the US court is an 'inconvenient' forum for the
defendant, for example because the plaintiffs are citizens of a foreign
country and sources of evidence are found in the foreign country.

Although the doctrine also theoretically requires a finding that the foreign country's legal system is an adequate alternative, in practice the courts have conveniently turned a blind eye to the realities of the justice systems in the South, ignoring the vast differences which make it virtually impossible for injured plaintiffs to receive a fair hearing in countries such as Nicaragua, Nigeria or the Philippines.

This chapter argues that the doctrine of *forum non conveniens* has been critical to the economic calculus of globalization[2] for agribusiness and other transnational corporations. The FNC doctrine has effectively ensured that there will be two standards of justice: one for the victims in the North and another for those in the South. FNC has been a reliable shield allowing corporations successfully to avoid liability for health and environmental damages caused by their products or operations overseas.

The last part of this chapter discusses how several Latin American countries, international institutions such as the Organization of American States, and a few US courts have responded to the crisis of justice and jurisdiction caused by FNC. FNC is a contentious doctrine that in many cases has led to patently unfair results – the denial of access to justice for citizens of the developing South.

THE RISE AND FALL OF DBCP

[I]ndustry studies … were kept secret … Now, tragically, twenty years later, the sterilization that had been predicted by laboratory tests became a reality – increasing numbers of workers in the manufacturing plants and the banana fields found they could not have children. EPA [the US Environmental Protection Agency] finally banned DBCP from nearly all domestic farm uses, but the companies then dumped their unused stocks overseas where it continued to be used. As a result, more banana workers … were sterilized. The tale of DBCP is an appalling one.

Senator Patrick J. Leahy. Hearings before the Committee on Agriculture, Nutrition and Forestry, Circle of Poison: Impact of U.S. Pesticides on Third World Workers, 102nd Cong.; 1st Sess. (5 June 1991)

DBCP (1,2-dibromo-3-chloropropane) is a nematicide that was developed in the 1950s by Dow and Shell. It proved to be a very effective product on numerous crops, and was adopted by farmers across the United States, generating significant profits for the agro-chemical companies (Murray, 1983: 115). Both corporations' medical researchers quickly detected the high toxicity of DBCP and the reproductive effects on rat testes. Exposure of rats to a low 5 ppm caused organ damage and shrank the testes; at 20 ppm all the rats were sterile (Murray, 1983). In the mid-1950s, Shell's consultant, Dr Charles Hines, conducted a series of tests to satisfy data requirements under the USA Food, Drug and Cosmetic Act and FIFRA labelling requirements. In 1958 he wrote a confidential report stating, 'among the rats that died, the gross lesions were especially prominent in lungs, kidneys and testes. Testes were usually extremely atrophied' (Murray, 1983: 117). At the same time, Dr Theodore R. Torkelson was carrying out similar tests for Dow that clearly indicated dermal exposure to DBCP was a hazard. A Dow in-house report published in the autumn of 1958 concluded that DBCP was 'readily absorbed through the skin and high in toxicity in inhalation'. Dow's data also showed that 'liver, lung and kidney effects might be expected' and that 'testicular atrophy may result from prolonged, repeated exposure' (Misko et al., 1993: 10).

Working for both Dow and Shell, Dr Hines drafted a report in May 1961 in support of Food and Drug Administration registration, calling for workplace concentrations of DBCP to be kept at less than 1 ppm, and recommending impermeable protective clothing if skin contact was likely. Louis Lykken, the person in charge of registration of chemicals for Shell, commented that the suggestion was 'impractical' in internal company documents obtained through discovery during the course of the case (Misko, 1993: 19).

These laboratory results in no way slowed the marketing of DBCP. In fact, the results were never made public, not even to the Environmental Protection Agency (EPA) during the registration process, but were obtained only years later as a result of litigation. The final product label did not provide complete information about the product's toxicity or its dramatic effect on the male reproductive system. The strongest language on the label read: 'Do not breath vapors.' Once registered in 1964, DBCP was marketed as a safe and effective nematicide in over a dozen countries in Central and South America, the Caribbean, Africa and the Philippines.

By 1975, DPCP had been targeted as a suspected carcinogen by the EPA. The United States National Cancer Institute began tests on selected chemicals in 1968 to determine what potential they had for causing cancer. In 1973, scientists found tumours developing in test animals. The final report published in 1975 identified DBCP as a potent cancer-causing agent (Murray, 1983).

In 1977, workers at an Occidental Chemical company DBCP-formulating plant in California discovered that many of them were having problems concerning children. The Chemical Workers' Union brought their case to the attention of health specialists. In the testing that followed, 35 of 114 workers at the plant were found to be sterile. Both California and the EPA ordered an immediate temporary ban on the sale of DBCP. Politically powerful California growers argued strenuously for the continued use of DBCP in the state. In a public hearing held by California authorities, growers threatened that multi-million-dollar crops such as grapes and almonds would disappear from the state without the pesticide. The workers were represented at the hearing by the non-profit law firm California Rural Legal Defense. Their attorney, Ralph Lightstone, argued that the 'real question for the State of California has to do with how to respond to the pressure. The known facts about DBCP – its incredible toxicity, its power to penetrate known protective materials, its persistent residues in the soil – weigh in on the side of human health.'[3] California upheld the prohibition, and Californian agriculture has prospered without DBCP.

The federal EPA banned DBCP for almost all uses in 1979.[4] But pesticides that are banned or never registered can still be legally manufactured in and exported from the USA. The EPA does no review of occupational health or environmental impacts of pesticides produced for export only. Under the main US pesticide law, the Federal Fungicide, Insecticide and Rodenticide Act (FIFRA), exporters are required to notify foreign country importers if a pesticide is not registered for use in the USA. The importer must sign a purchaser acknowledgement statement, which the EPA then sends to the importing country government. The EPA is also required to notify foreign governments when a pesticide is registered, restricted or cancelled. The effectiveness of this notification has often been questioned. Notices often languish on the desk of the Ministry of Agriculture; workers, health professionals and farmers rarely if ever see them.

During the 1980s the sterile workers at the California Occidental Chemical plant sued for health damages and won large jury verdicts, ranging from $500,000 to $4 million (Siegel, 1991). Californian cities also brought successful suits against Dow and Shell when they discovered that their potable water supplies had been contaminated by DBCP run-off from legal use on nearby fields.[5] The question then emerges: Why shouldn't citizens from the South, who were injured by the same pesticide manufactured by the same companies, be able to seek justice in the US courts as well?

> A child is priceless. Big corporations must know that we, too, are people
> with feelings, just like the people of the first world.
>
> Victoria Zumbado, wife of a sterilized banana worker in Costa Rica
> (Misko et al., 1993: 3)

Working and living conditions on industrial banana plantations are
atrocious. Pesticide applicators are given little training and usually do
not have protective equipment or cannot wear it because of the extreme
tropical heat. The chemical stench can be overpowering. Pesticides are
often mixed by hand in open barrels. The workers' kitchen and lunch-
room are often adjacent to the pesticide storage shack. Many workers
and their families live on the borders of the plantations; children play in
pesticide-contaminated drainage ditches. Workers are sent into recently
sprayed areas to prune and cut fruit; pesticides drip down directly on
them. Workers and neighbouring residents suffer myriad health problems related to pesticide exposure, which is often compounded by poor
nutrition and grinding poverty. Chronic skin rashes and respiratory ailments are almost epidemic, and acute poisonings are common. Although
more difficult to document, anecdotal evidence suggests an elevated
incidence of spontaneous abortions and cancers as well.

DBCP use began at Standard Fruit plantations (later purchased by
Dole Fresh Fruit Co.) in Central America and around the world in 1969.
Between the late 1960s and the early 1980s, workers on banana plantations in Central America, Ecuador, Africa and the Philippines applied
DBCP. It was applied both by workers who injected the chemical into
the root system of the banana tree, as well as via the plantation irrigation system. Field applicators, irrigation tower workers, pesticide mixers
and others had regular exposure to DBCP through skin absorption
and inhaling the vapours (Misko, 1993: 17). DBCP splashed on workers during irrigation or when the injectors hit rocks or other objects.
Run-off from applications through the irrigation system contaminated
drainage canals that local children played in. The workers wore no
gloves, protective clothing or respirators because no one told them
that the product was dangerous. Workers in a dozen countries around
the world have stated that they received no warnings. Standard Fruit's
production manual contained no warnings of the testicular effects of
DBCP, and did not recommend the use of safety equipment.

The DBCP cases are unique because the signature health damage caused by the pesticide, male sterility, is both rare in nature and not a common health effect of exposure to other pesticides. This makes it straightforward to show legal causation even where workers have been exposed to multiple pesticides and other chemicals. In other words, the causal connection between exposure to this one particular pesticide among many, and a rare health consequence, can confidently be made.

In 1984 Domingo Castro Alfaro and eighty-one other Costa Rican banana workers filed suit in Texas state court for health damages, primarily sterility, suffered because of exposure to DBCP on US-owned plantations. Local doctors helped the affected workers contact US lawyers because the Costa Rican legal system, which for example does not have mechanisms for pre-trial discovery and mandates low statutory caps on potential awards, made it very difficult if not impossible to bring such a case in Costa Rica. Typical compensation for a worker sterilized on the job in Costa Rica was $1,500 (Hosmer, 1990: 10). Nicaragua's worker compensation system was worse – it didn't even recognize sterility as a possible injury, and therefore offered no compensation (Dra. Margarita Ramírez, personal conversation, 1991).

According to documents obtained by the lawyers for the banana workers during discovery, even after the product was banned, Standard Fruit Co. (now Dole), which owned many of the Central American banana plantations, threatened a breach of contract action against Dow Chemical if they failed to deliver the product as per their contract. Eventually Dow agreed to continue to ship DBCP to Standard in Costa Rica, which in turn promised to indemnify Dow in the event of any injuries. Standard was so intent on continuing to use DBCP that it was willing to promise to protect Dow in any future suits arising from the use of DBCP in Costa Rica (Siegel and Siegel, 1999). After all, DBCP was a cheap and effective product. Since DBCP was now banned in the USA, Dow sent a revised manual on safety procedures, recommending that the user not apply DBCP unless 'all people have been evacuated from the area to be treated and those surrounding areas which may be exposed to the liquid or vapors' (Misko et al., 1993: 19). Jack DeMent, who was in charge of Standard's worldwide banana pest control programme, reviewed the new Dow manual. He thought the new precautions were unnecessary, and wrote to all field managers: 'This is not operationally feasible and does not need to be implemented' (Misko et al., 1993: 19).

In other words, in a calculated action the banana companies knowingly exposed thousands of workers in the developing South to a banned pesticide likely to incur health risks. Whether Dole would have done the same to US workers knowing that the likelihood of enormous legal liability was high is an open question. But the companies certainly knew that the likelihood of Latin American workers facing them in a US court, or any other court for that matter, was vanishingly small. For foreign victims, this was the calculus of personal and family tragedy.

At the petition of the defendants – some of the largest corporations in America including Dow Chemical, Shell Oil, Dole and Chiquita – the local Texas court dismissed the cases based on FNC. Defendant corporations that take refuge in the theory of FNC ask the judge to close the courthouse doors to the plaintiff and send them back to their home country's court system. The companies were betting that the foreign country court system would impose only a fraction of the damages award that could be won in the USA, or that the plaintiffs, faced with the shortcomings of the developing country legal system, would simply give up altogether.

During the following six years the dismissal was appealed up to the Texas Supreme Court. Happily for the Costa Rican workers, although the majority of US states had adopted the FNC doctrine, in 1984 Texas still had a unique 1913 statute[6] that expressly granted foreign citizens access to Texas courts if they were injured by a Texas company, that is a company that had the required links to the state to establish jurisdiction. When the DBCP case reached the Texas Supreme Court, the court ruled in favour of the plaintiffs, stating that FNC would not block foreign citizens from bringing cases for health damages in Texas. Supreme Court Justice Doggett wrote in the decision:

> Shell Oil Company is a multinational corporation with its world headquarters in Houston, Texas ... Dow operates this country's largest chemical manufacturing plant within 60 miles of Houston in Freeport, Texas. The district court where this lawsuit was filed is three blocks away from Shell's world headquarters, One Shell Plaza in downtown Houston ... The banana plantation workers allegedly injured by DBCP were employed by an American company on American-owned land and grew Dole bananas for export solely to American tables. The chemical allegedly rendering the workers sterile was researched, formulated, tested, manufactured, labelled and shipped by an American company in the United States to another American company. The decision to manufacture DBCP for distribution and use in the third world was made by these two American companies in their corporate offices in the United States. Yet now Shell and Dow argue that the one part of this equation that should not be American is the legal consequences of their actions.[7]

What is really involved is not convenience but connivance to avoid corporate accountability. Abolishing *forum non conveniens* will provide a check on the conduct of multinational corporations. Some will undoubtedly continue to endanger human life and environment … until the economic consequences … are such that it becomes unprofitable to operate in this manner.

Threatened with the possibility of landing in front of a jury in Texas with compelling evidence of their negligence, the companies settled the first 1,000 cases from Costa Rica for a significant amount. These workers were able to settle their cases because of the very real possibility of a lawsuit in an American court decided by American jurors. This result, had it been predictable in 1979, is likely to have served the deterrent function of law, discouraging the export and use of a banned pesticide known to cause severe health problems.

When the Texas Supreme Court issued the ruling in 1990, refusing to apply *forum non conveniens*, Texas business reacted strongly. Dozens of Fortune 500 companies have their headquarters in Texas, including giant oil, chemical and agribusiness companies such as Exxon and Conoco. The Texas Supreme Court ruling threw out a doctrine that had become the chief way that these transnational corporations avoided lawsuits arising out of harm caused in foreign countries. The Texas Association of Business warned that: '[A]llowing foreign workers to sue Texas companies could drive industry from the state or keep new companies from moving in,' calling it a 'significant blow' to Texas business (Hosmer, 1990: 11).

These companies mounted a powerful lobbying campaign in 1991 that resulted in the adoption of law that reinstated FNC in Texas, closing the doors to Texas courts to foreigners as of September 1993 (Hosmer, 1990; Siegel and Siegel, 1999). The new law passed by the Texas legislature came into force on 1 September 1993. Cases filed prior to that date would not be blocked by the FNC doctrine in Texas courts. Cases filed after that date could be.

The success of the early Costa Rican cases prompted banana workers in other countries to join the case. Thousands of injured banana workers, who had been exposed to DBCP in Central and South America, Africa and the Philippines, were later identified. In Nicaragua, for example, agricultural workers' unions such as the Asociación de Trabajadores del Campo (Rural Workers' Union) helped US lawyers communicate with workers who had been exposed to DBCP.[8]

By 1993, more than 26,000 workers injured by DBCP had filed civil lawsuits (Siegel and Siegel, 1999). These cases were grandfathered under the old Texas statute and protected from dismissal by the FNC doctrine in Texas courts (Schemo, 1995). Individual actions were joined together at the request of the court into groups of similarly situated plaintiffs based on their country of residence. These workers, in sixteen countries around the world, consistently stated that they never received any warning of DBCP's dangers. Here it's important to note that US federal courts recognized FNC all along, that is to say during the period during which the case was being tried in Texas. As described below, the companies therefore set their legions of attorneys to the task of moving the case into the federal courts.

AVOIDING LIABILITY WITH A SUBVERTED *FORUM NON CONVENIENS* DOCTRINE

Rooted in nineteenth-century British Common Law, FNC is a Scottish legal doctrine originally created to protect defendants from harassment by being sued in a distant jurisdiction other than his/her domicile (i.e. where he resides or the principal place of business). In addition to the USA, it has been applied in the UK, the EU, Canada and Australia. In a case in 1947 called *Gulf Oil C. v. Gilbert*,[9] the US Supreme Court upheld the original interpretation of the doctrine stating that a plaintiff should not be able to 'harass' or 'oppress' a defendant by putting it to the expense or trouble of defending itself in an inconvenient forum where the plaintiff was unfairly suing in an 'inconvenient' forum.[10]

The FNC doctrine was rarely invoked until the mid-1970s when the US federal courts, facing an increasing number of complex multinational tort actions, began using it with greater frequency. When the Supreme Court next considered the issue, in 1981,[11] in a case called *Piper Aircraft Co. v. Reyno*, it turned the original interpretation of FNC on its head. Earlier cases had held that a plaintiff's choice of forum was entitled to deference, and that FNC should be applied sparingly and only where the foreign country court system provided an adequate alternative forum to hear the case and would better serve the interests of justice. The 1981 ruling held that the traditional deference to the plaintiff's choice of forum did *not* apply if the plaintiff was a foreigner.[12] In the Piper case the Supreme Court held that the possibility that less favourable laws would be applied in the foreign country should also not prevent dismissal on FNC. The Court added that only in those cases where the remedy provided by the foreign country, or 'alternative forum', is so totally inadequate that it is the practical equivalent of no remedy at all, should the court give substantial weight to this factor in deciding whether to retain the case in the USA or dismiss the case back to the foreign country.

A defendant seeking an FNC dismissal must first establish the existence of an available and adequate alternative foreign forum. A foreign forum is considered available when the second country's court system can legally exercise jurisdiction over all parties and the case. The foreign forum is considered adequate when the parties will not be deprived of all remedies, even though they might not have remotely the same procedural or substantive rights that they would have received in a US court. If the court determines that an available and adequate alternate forum exists, it then balances a series of 'public' and 'private' interest factors, such as access to evidence and witnesses, and concerns about burdening the court system, to arrive at a decision. In the last twenty years, conservative judges have dominated the American legal system. These judges have been receptive to the arguments of corporate defendants, and have frequently used the FNC doctrine to dismiss cases and clear their dockets, thus closing the doors to the courthouse to foreign plaintiffs – workers, consumers or those representing a contaminated environment – injured by US corporations' products or operations overseas. TNCs have found the doctrine a reliable tool to shield them from liability in US courts for harm caused overseas by their business decisions.

Such decisions severely limit access to the US judicial system, with its modern procedural and substantive advantages, for citizens of the South. The USA's legal system offers numerous fair-minded procedural advantages including jury trials, strong pre-trial discovery, contingency fees and mechanisms for class action litigation[13] among other mechanisms that do not exist in Latin America.[14] The ability to go to court and secure damage awards for injuries caused by dangerous products or production processes has been shown to be an effective way to get companies to change their behaviour – that is, to modify a defective product or take it off the market.[15]

It is a tribute to the effectiveness of the US court system that, during the long legal process, the mere possibility that the DBCP cases would get into an American court prompted a partial settlement with the chemical companies in the late 1990s, while the FNC appeal was pending.[16] But because at the time the probability of the case ever being heard by an American jury was already small, the settlement amount was only a fraction of what the plaintiffs would have likely received if the case had gone to trial in the USA.[17] FNC gives the defendants a huge advantage at settlement negotiations; playing off the huge obstacles that plaintiffs must overcome to get a foot in the door of the US courthouse, defendants are often able to settle the case for pennies on the dollar.

When the plaintiffs are forced to re-file their cases at home, in Nicaragua or Guatemala for example, their chances of ever seeing their day in court are slim. In many countries in the South, where laws and law enforcement are lax, judicial systems weak and the people overwhelmingly poor, corporations are able reliably to assume that an injured worker or contaminated environment won't cost them much. Because multinationals are so important to the economies of small countries, it is that much harder to get a court to rule against them. And in the rare event that the case actually makes it to the court, under many countries' legislation, damage awards for injury and even wrongful death can be as little as a few thousand dollars. This becomes an incentive for corporations to discount the value of the health and environmental protection overseas, forgoing investments in safeguards because they know that the likelihood of ever being made to pay damages and thus internalize these costs is slim.

The Bhopal tragedy is perhaps the most notorious example of the use of FNC to shield a corporation from liability. The explosion at Union Carbide's shoddily maintained pesticide plant resulted in a release of massive amounts of deadly methyl isocyanate, killing thousands and injuring hundreds of thousands more.[18] An internal Union Carbide document acknowledged that the company regarded the dangers of sub-standard plant management as an acceptable 'business risk ... in view of the desired long term objectives of minimum capital and foreign exchange expenditures' (Pesticide Action Network-UK, 2002). The Bhopal victims originally filed their cases in a US federal court where they could hope to receive a just recovery, but at the petition of Union Carbide they were dismissed on FNC and sent back to Indian courts.[19] Union Carbide eventually settled with the Indian government for a paltry $470 million, their insurance limit. Individual settlements have been in the range of $500 for a permanent disability and $3,000 for loss of life (Noronha, 1999).[20]

This chapter profiles litigation that is taking place in the USA, but it is important to note that these issues are being considered by UK, Canadian and Australian courts as well. Defendant corporations in these countries have also successfully used the doctrine as a shield against liability. For example, an action brought in Canada against the Canadian mining company Cambior by victims of a collapsed tailings dam in Guyana was dismissed in 1998 on the grounds that Guyana was the more appropriate legal forum. A case against Texaco filed in the USA by Ecuadorian citizens,[21] claiming that Texaco had released huge quantities of toxic petroleum wastes into surface and groundwater that local people use for drinking causing health and other damages, was dismissed by a US federal court on grounds of *forum non conveniens* in 2001. A US transnational copper corporation[22] invoked FNC to avoid liability in the USA for health damages caused to local residents by toxic releases from its copper smelter in Peru. And a US glue company, H.B. Fuller Co., avoided liability for the death of Guatemalan children who sniffed their addictive product, even where it would have been easy and cheap to modify the product to prevent the injury (Malamud, 1996).[23]

CORPORATE DEFENDANTS SEEK AN FNC DISMISSAL

Although the defendants could not get the banana workers' case dismissed on FNC in Texas state courts, a FNC dismissal was still available in the federal courts.[24] A series of complicated legal manoeuvres by the companies eventually succeeded in removing the case to a federal court where FNC was applied to dismiss the case, sending the plaintiffs back to their home countries, but with a surprising twist described below.

The aggressiveness with which the defendants litigated the FNC issue is a testament to the fear that these companies had of ever finding themselves in front of an American jury. With many millions of dollars of liability at stake, the companies set their legions of attorneys to the task of getting the cases out of Texas courts and into federal court. These legal manoeuvres were made possible by the unusual fact that DBCP had also been manufactured and sold in tiny quantities in Latin America by an Israeli-owned company that had been partly owned by the state of Israel in the 1970s: Dead Sea Bromine proved willing to be a complicit partner in the defendants' strategy.

The US Foreign Sovereign Immunities Act gives foreign countries or entities owned or controlled by them special procedural rights in the USA. These rights include the right to remove to federal court any civil litigation brought against it in a state court. The Foreign Sovereign Immunities Act also gives foreign sovereigns the option to then exercise sovereign immunity in federal courts – that is, to be dismissed from the lawsuit. Usually this is what happens: a foreign sovereign wants to be in federal court so that it can be immune from liability. If the foreign sovereign chooses to waive immunity, though, it still has the right to choose to move the case from a state to a federal court, where a dismissal based on FNC is still available to the corporations.

Shell and Dow brought the Israeli company Dead Sea into the lawsuit with the express purpose of getting the cases out of the Texas courts – where FNC did not apply – and into a federal court, where FNC did apply. This was the long sought-after result desired by the defendant corporations, because, as Judge Doggett stated in his decision: 'A *forum non conveniens* dismissal is often, in reality, a complete victory for the defendant.' According to one university analysis, less than 4 per cent of cases dismissed in the USA on grounds of FNC ever make it to courts overseas (Robertson, 1987).

The defendant corporations brought Dead Sea into the litigation, and at the same time convinced them not to exercise sovereign immunity, but instead to remain part of the case and demand removal of the case to the federal court under the FSIA.

In short order the federal court dismissed the case on FNC – but with one novel and important condition. After dedicating 101 pages to a discussion of the applicability of FNC, the penultimate paragraph on page 102 said that if the highest court of the foreign country refuses jurisdiction, the banana workers could return to the US courts.[25]

LATIN AMERICA TAKES A STAND

The DBCP case was a clarion call to Latin American countries about the discrimination their citizens experienced under the FNC doctrine. In response, several countries passed laws affirming that FNC contravenes basic constitutional principles, including the principle of sovereignty found in many Latin American constitutions. From a Latin American legal perspective, a US judge has no authority to impose unilaterally an obligation to hear a case on a Latin American court. Additionally, because it discriminates openly against the foreign plaintiff, FNC violates the Charter of the Organization of American States.[26] FNC also contravenes constitutional and international law principles establishing that all nations are equal, and that every nation must guarantee access to justice for all. Moreover, most Latin American countries have signed bilateral treaties of Friendship, Commerce and Navigation with the USA, which typically include an article that assures the access by nationals of one country to the courts of another. Similarly, a host of multilateral treaties guarantee free access to justice, including the Universal Declaration of Human Rights,[27] which states: 'Everyone has the right to an effective remedy by the competent national tribunals for acts violating the fundamental rights granted him by the constitution or by law' (Art. 8).

After the federal court decision, the banana workers returned to re-file their cases in their home countries. By 1999, the Supreme Courts of Honduras, Ecuador, Costa Rica, Panama, Nicaragua and the Philippines had all refused jurisdiction, effectively ruling in favour of their citizens' rights to choose a forum in the United States.

Several countries' attorneys general issued official opinions against FNC. Other countries produced congressional resolutions and even laws specifically enacted to counter FNC.[28] For example, in 1995 the Congress of Ecuador issued a public declaration stating:

> Companies of highly industrialized countries import technical procedures and goods capable of causing accidents of catastrophic proportions, with hundreds or thousands of victims, or causing severe damage to the environment. Our judicial system, in responding to a socio-economic reality that is different from that of highly industrialized countries, is not designed to resolve massive accidents of catastrophic proportions as a result of the application of dangerous industrial techniques or the use of a highly noxious substance.
>
> It is not just, or proper, that the harm caused by products or highly noxious techniques from societies of great industrial development be redressed only by our Judiciary Power, which, logically, is not adequately equipped with the infrastructure or mechanisms necessary for these cases.[29]

Ecuador's attorney general added: 'It would then seem that citizens of my country, just for being foreign, are considered as second-class citizens and receive a less favourable treatment than that afforded to American nationals.'[30]

In 1997 the Guatemalan Congress unanimously adopted the Law for the Defense of Procedural Rights of Nationals and Residents, which declared that FNC was in violation of the constitution of Guatemala, and therefore the theory 'is declared unacceptable and invalid, when it intervenes to prevent the continuation of the lawsuit in the domiciliary courts of the defendants'.[31]

The Honduran Congress issued a Resolution in the Defense of Legislative Sovereignty, Judicial Independence and Procedural Rights in 1996,[32] stating:

> It is a fact that certain enterprises of highly industrialized countries eventually market or use products and/or technical procedures that

constitute an enormous source of danger. There are even some enterprises capable of marketing or using products in our nation after they have been banned in their country of origin once their unreasonably dangerous nature has been scientifically proven ... It sometimes happens that when our people file a lawsuit abroad, in the domicile of the responsible enterprises, the latter seek refuge in the theory of *forum non conveniens* to dodge facing liability in their own country ... It is not just, nor proper, that the harm and conflict caused by catastrophic products, manufactured by highly industrialized countries, be only redressed by our Judiciary Power which, logically, was not equipped to deal with cases of catastrophic destruction and massive harm.

In late 2000 Nicaragua adopted Law No. 364,[33] a special statute designed to redress the unfairness caused when the defendant corporations used FNC to deny affected banana workers access to the US courts. In an effort to level the playing field, the law requires that defendant corporations in DBCP litigation filed in Nicaragua post a large bond if they want to remain in Nicaraguan courts. The intent of the law is to force the defendants to post a bond in Nicaragua or submit unconditionally to the jurisdiction of the US courts and expressly renounce FNC.[34] The first 130 cases were filed in Nicaragua under the new law in mid-2001, against Chiquita and Standard Fruit (now Dole), and Dow, Occidental and Shell Oil (Lanchin, 2001). The companies will have the option to defend the case in Nicaragua and pay the bond, or to ask the court to dismiss the case in Nicaragua and agree not to challenge the cases in US courts on FNC.[35]

Two years earlier, the Latin American Parliament, which brings together parliamentarians from across Latin America, had issued a model law[36] on FNC. The preamble states: 'This law would benefit the victims of ecological wrongs and, in general, those who have suffered damages caused in or from another country ... In summary, what the law clarifies is that those who incur in international tort liability, will not be able to escape their domiciliary courts ... One hopes that the enactment of the bill will help toward the respect of the environment and the health of our Peoples.'

Two other international fora are currently considering conventions that would reaffirm the plaintiff's choice of jurisdiction, thus greatly weakening FNC. The first is the Organization of American States, whose judicial committee issued a paper entitled: 'Proposal for an Inter-American Convention on the Effects and Treatment of the Forum Non Conveniens Theory'.[37] The OAS committee report identifies FNC for what it is: a mechanism by which TNCs can pollute or commit torts overseas and escape jurisdiction and liability.

The second international forum considering the issue is The Hague. The 'Preliminary draft convention on jurisdiction and the effects of judgment in civil and commercial matters'[38] reaffirms the principle that corporations can be sued in their domiciliary forum (Art. 3). It also reaffirms that a suit is properly brought either where the injury arose (i.e. where the banana plantations are) or where 'the act or omission that caused injury occurred' (Art. 10), in other words, where the corporate decisions to export DBCP were made in the United States. The draft states that the US courts cannot discriminate 'on the basis of the nationality or habitual residence or seat of the parties' (Art. 24) as US courts routinely do when ordering FNC dismissals of suits brought by foreign plaintiffs.

In the meantime, in several cases US courts have quietly begun to balance the FNC factors more realistically, denying corporate defendants motion for dismissal on FNC due to a new understanding of Latin American law, and a new willingness to look at the reality of developing country legal systems. In England and the European Union as well, recent decisions have held that FNC will not bar injured foreign plaintiffs from filing suit in the corporate defendant's home country.[39] For example, in a case where Costa Rican farmers alleged that the pesticide Benlate made by the US company DuPont harmed their plants, a Florida judge rejected the petition for dismissal on FNC based on an analysis of the weakness of Costa Rican law, including the inability to compel the production of documents.[40] And in 2002 a federal court judge in one of the consolidated DBCP actions from Honduras, the Philippines and Costa Rica for the first time denied the defendants' motion for an FNC dismissal,[41] agreeing with the Latin American position that foreign courts were neither available nor adequate alternative fora.

The steps taken by Latin American countries to defend their citizens' right to access to justice had an important influence on the decision. The 2002 DBCP decision recognized that civil law countries such as Latin America and the European Union reject the doctrine of FNC. The decision also notes that previous groups of DBCP cases had been dismissed by Costa Rican courts for lack of jurisdiction following dismissal from US courts on FNC, showing that under Latin American law plaintiffs' choice of forum is determinative and the domicile of the defendant is a correct forum.

The court also analysed the important question of the adequacy of the foreign country fora, and found that in the case of Honduras and the Philippines, those countries' courts were not adequate alternatives. The decision quotes reports from the United States Department of State, stating that in Honduras the judiciary is 'often ineffective, and subject to outside influence ...' and that 'powerful special interests still exercise influence and often prevail in the courts (US Dept. of State, Country Report on Human Rights Practices, Honduras, 2001 [released March 4, 2002])'. The US Department of State report on the Philippines states, 'the judicial system suffers from corruption and inefficiency' (p. 49).

This kind of more realistic evaluation of the ability of Southern country court systems to hear injured workers' claims fairly has also been voiced in recent decisions in England that have held that FNC should not apply to block a series of cases filed by injured workers from South Africa. The English appellate court, the House of Lords, based its decision on a determination that 'substantial justice will not be done in the alternative forum'. In a leading case settled in 2001, over 7,000 South African workers forced Cape Plc, a British company with a South African subsidiary, Cape Asbestos, to offer an out-of-court settlement after a four-year battle to have the case brought before the English court. The claimants alleged that working conditions in the South African subsidiary caused thousands of people to contract asbestos-related illnesses in the 1970s. The case led to a landmark decision in the House of Lords in July 2000 that permitted the claimants to proceed against the parent company in England for the practices of its foreign subsidiary, based on a determination that 'substantial justice' could not be obtained there.[42]

A GLOBALIZED ECONOMY REQUIRES GLOBALIZED ACCESS TO JUSTICE

Globalization is opening up markets and resources in the South to transnational corporations at an ever-increasing speed. These corporations make operational decisions for their global operations, accrue profits and pay shareholders in the USA. The only part of the equation that they don't want to take place in the USA is legal responsibility for the injuries or pollution caused by their products or procedures in other countries.

The DBCP cases are instructive because they demonstrate the lengths to which corporations will go to obtain a dismissal from US courts and prevent the substantive claims against them from being heard in their home country's courts. Corporations routinely make calculations weighing safety against the cost of compensating health injuries or environmental damage. The threat of liability acts as a deterrent, prodding companies to institute better environmental protection and health and safety measures to avoid expensive liability down the road. But if corporations can be reasonably sure that they will be able to evade liability for overseas activities, the deterrence factor vanishes. The legal doctrine FNC gives corporations who export dangerous products or operations to the developing South significant assurance that they will not be held legally liable, or economically accountable, for injuries to health or damage to the environment. Sales to, and operations in, foreign countries, represent profit without any corresponding liability for any injuries or environmental contamination.

There will always be a conflict between the profit motive and the cost of measures to implement high standards of worker and environmental protection. FNC therefore becomes an incentive for certain companies to commit dangerous acts in developing countries – for example, selling products that were prohibited in their home country or running factories without proper emergency safeguards – that they would probably never do in the USA for fear of massive liability in the event of injury. *Forum non conveniens* gives these corporations the opportunity to keep a lawsuit out of a Northern country court where liability for wrongdoing is expensive, and send it back to a foreign country where it is cheap. By allowing companies to avoid being held responsible at home for harm caused abroad, FNC helps remove the economic incentive for companies to invest in safety measures and pollution prevention. TNCs profit not only by exploiting Southern countries' comparative advantage of low wages and abundant resources, but also the comparative 'advantage' of poverty and the absence of a rule of law culture.

Clearly, litigation is an end-of-the-pipe solution, albeit an effective one that can serve to deter future bad acts as well as to compensate victims. Litigation as well as regulation helps to shape corporate behaviour. If corporations know that they could be forced through the courts to internalize the cost of injuries or environmental damage caused by their products or operations in foreign countries, they might be compelled by their own bottom line to act more responsibly.

It would, of course, be far preferable if Southern governments had greater ability to effectively to regulate the activities of transnational companies within their borders, or if corporations would voluntarily agree to be held to the strictest Northern standards in their operations in the South. Or if the US government would change its policy of allowing US companies to export pesticides that have been banned for domestic use for health or environmental reasons.[43] But unless and until these and other measures are taken to better govern corporate activities in the globalized economy, end-of-the-pipe remedies will remain crucial. Experience shows that the threat of large damage awards to injured workers and consumers, or in response to environmental harm, has precipitated changes in corporate behaviour and removed dangerous products, from asbestos to DES, from the market. The US courts should accept increased responsibility for reviewing the negative impacts of US corporations' activities in foreign countries, where corporations knowingly expose workers to dangerous products or life-threatening conditions that could be easily avoided, often with minimal investment.

FNC should be abolished to help remove the economic benefit from corporate decisions that deliberately elevate profits over health, the environment and human life in the developing South. Today's globalized economy, in which products, technologies and corporations circumnavigate the globe freely, requires access to justice that is equally globalized.

NOTES

1. 1,2-Dibromo-3-chloropropane.

2. Globalization is used to denote the economic strategy pursued by the industrialized, Northern countries and the transnational corporations (TNCs) whose interests they represent. Globalization seeks to ensure open, unregulated access to the world's markets for these TNCs. The economic liberalization upon which globalization is founded has caused national governments to force down labour and environmental standards to attract foreign investment with the promise of low costs.

3. Ralph Lightstone, California Rural Legal Assistance, 1978.

4. Use on pineapples received a temporary extension under severely restricted conditions.

5. DBCP is a persistent organic pollutant, and highly mobile in both surface waters and groundwater. For example, the city of Sanger, where six of the eleven potable water wells were contaminated, received approximately $16 million from the chemical companies to instal a water purification system (Holding, 1993). Similarly in 1995 Dow, Shell and Occidental paid the city of Fresno $21 million to help clean up contaminated city wells, at least half of which had been contaminated with DBCP, and agreed to make additional payments for water treatment units for forty years (PANUPS, 1995). Dozens of CA city water supplies were contaminated by DBCP; the total cost of decontaminating the water was estimated at over $600 million (Holding, 1993).

6. Texas Civil Practice and Remedies Code, Sec. 71.031.

7. *Dow Chemical v. Castro Alfaro*, 786 SW 2d 674 (Tex. 1990) cert. denied, 498 US 1024 (1991).

8. In all cases a standard contingency fee contract was offered to potentially affected workers. The advantage of the contingency fee arrangement is that the plaintiffs pay their lawyers nothing unless they receive a money award in the case. Although this is a typical arrangement in the USA, there is no such similar scheme in Latin America.

9. *Gulf Oil Co. v Gilbert*, 330 US 501 (1947).

10. In the Gilbert case, the US Supreme Court set forth a three-part standard for determining whether a suit should be dismissed under *forum non conveniens*. First the court must ascertain whether there is an available and adequate alternative forum that will provide the parties with certain procedural safeguards and the plaintiff with an adequate remedy. If the court finds that an adequate alternative foreign forum exists, the second part of the analysis directs it to balance 'private interest factors', including the relative ease of access to evidence, the availability of a compulsory process for forcing an unwilling witness to attend a trial; the possibility of visiting the site, etc. The third step requires the court to consider 'public interest factors', including the burden of imposing the case on a court that has no relation to the litigation; the local interest in having local controversies decided at home; and administrative concerns such as congested courts. Overall the plaintiff's choice of forum is entitled to deference.

11. *Piper Aircraft Co. v. Reyno*, 454 US at p. 235, 1981. In this case the US Supreme Court dismissed to Scotland a wrongful death action based on FNC, even though Scottish law was much less favourable to the plaintiff than US law, depriving him of the right to assert the strict liability claim which was available under US but not Scottish law.

12. Since 1981 more than forty US states have endorsed the US Supreme Court decision (Siegel, 1991).

13. The concept behind class actions and contingency fees, and other procedural mechanisms that are favourable to plaintiffs in the USA, is to give incentives to individuals and groups that can act as watchdogs and take up cases that individual victims themselves aren't able to bring alone.

14. For example, in some countries such as Nicaragua the companies tried to buy releases from liability from plaintiffs who were key union leaders in the hopes that they could sow discontent within the banana workers' community. In the USA, if a plaintiff is represented by a lawyer, the defendant may not communicate directly with the plaintiff but rather must communicate only through the lawyer. Breaching this rule in the USA can lead to disbarment and other severe penalties.

15. In fact, many corporations routinely do 'cost-benefit' accounting, analysing potential financial liability for deaths and injuries caused by a defective product against the costs of taking corrective action, such as redesigning the product or taking it off the market. The case that brought this practice into the open in the USA was the Ford Pinto fuel tank case (*Grimshaw v. Ford Motor Company*, 174 Cal. Rptr. 348, 1981). In this case a Ford exploded after a rear-end collision, killing the driver and causing severe burns on her child's face and body. The Ford Pinto was known to explode in rear-end collisions because of a defectively designed gas tank, but Ford refused to fix this problem because an analysis determined that its financial exposure to lawsuits was less than the cost of adding a device that would prevent the fires. As one judge wrote, Ford 'engage[d] in cost-benefit analyses which

balanced life and limb against corporate savings and profits'. By the time the US government finally forced Ford to recall the Pinto cars, fires caused by collisions rupturing the fuel tank had killed at least twenty-seven people and injured many others (Public Citizen, 2002). There are numerous documented cases of this kind of corporate cost-benefit analysis that have come to light in litigation over defective industrial machines, pharmaceuticals, baby clothes and many other products.

16. The settlement was negotiated with the four chemical companies – Dow, Shell, Occidental and Amvac – and was distributed proportionally among more than 20,000 workers worldwide (Lanchin, 2001). The injured workers received payments according to a schedule based on their degree of sterility, according to World Health Organization classifications, and the number of children they had between one and three. (Workers with more than three children had been deemed ineligible to join the litigation.)

17. Although pains were taken to explain the US legal process to the workers, much confusion remained. Many workers were pleased that their injury had been recognized and compensated at all, but many others were rightly angry at that the awards distributed under the partial settlement with Dow and Shell were so small. In countries such as Costa Rica and Nicaragua where the workers were better organized, they went on to petition their country's Human Rights Ombudsman office and Parliaments to take action on their behalf.

18. Bhopal victims suffer from blindness, permanent lung damage, cancers, post-traumatic stress disorder and other ailments.

19. In *Union Carbide Corporation Gas Plant Disaster at Bhopal, India in December 1984* (SDNY 1986) 634 F. Supp. 842, the court found that the Indian legal system provided an adequate alternative forum and granted Union Carbide's petition for dismissal.

20. Union Carbide is now a fully owned subsidiary of Dow Chemical. When asked about the settlement amount, Dow public affairs leader Kathy Hunt stated: '$500 is plenty good for an Indian.' In stark contrast to the Bhopal settlement, Dow/Carbide paid out a $10 million settlement to one US child who suffered a brain injury after exposure to their pesticide Dursban. Dow has withdrawn Dursban from the market in the USA, but still markets it as safe in India (International Campaign for Justice in Bhopal, 2002).

21. *Aguinda et. al. v. Texaco*, 142 F. Supp. 2d 534 (SDNY 2001).

22. *Arias Torres v. Southern Peru Copper Corporation*, No. 96–4023 (5th Circuit, May 19, 1997).

23. Fuller chose not to reformulate or otherwise protect children from the toxins in its products. Resistol is highly addictive; sniffing glue can cause neurological and kidney damage, liver disease and death. Fuller did not put a warning on the cans. The judge dismissed the case on FNC and also held that Fuller was not responsible for the actions of its subsidiaries (Malamud, 1996).

24. In the USA legal remedies available in the federal court system and state court systems can vary significantly.

25. *Delgado v. Shell Oil*, 890 F. Supp. 1324 (SD Tex. 1995).

26. 'Proposal for an Interamerican Convention on the Effects and Treatment of the Forum Non Conveniens Theory'. Dr Gerardo Trejos Salas, 55th Regular Period

of Sessions, August 1999, Rio de Janeiro, Brazil. OEA/Ser.Q, CJI/doc.29/99, 14 July 1999.

27. Universal Declaration of Human Rights, Art. 7 and 8, 10 December 1948, Paris, France.

28. These resolutions and statutes were passed when American judges continued to order FNC dismissals even after the attorneys general of several Latin American countries had expressly told the US judge that their countries did not have jurisdiction after the initial filing in the USA.

29. Public Declaration of the President of the International Affairs Commission of the Honorable National Congress of Ecuador, Don Gustavo Larrea, signed on 25 January 1995 (Dahl, 1999).

30. Official Opinion of the Attorney General's Office of Ecuador, signed by Don Leonidas Plaza Verduga, 15 January 1997, in a letter addressed to the US Attorney General, Ms Janet Reno (Dahl, 1999).

31. Law for the Defense of Procedural Rights of Nationals and Residents, Guatemala, 14 May 1997 (Dahl, 1999: 225 et seq.).

32. Resolution in the Defense of Legislative Sovereignty, Judicial Independence and Procedural Rights, Honduran Congress, March 1996 (Dahl, 1999: 227 et seq.).

33. Ley No. 364, Ley Especial para la Tramitación de Juicios Promovidos por las Personas Afectadas por el Uso de Pesticidas Fabricado a Base de DBCP [Special Law for Proceeding with Lawsuits Filed by Persons Affected by the Use of Pesticides Manufactured Based on DBCP]. La Gaceta, *Diario Oficial*, No. 12. Managua, Miércoles, 17 de Enero 2001.

34. Artículo 7, Ley 364: 'Las empresas que dentro de los noventa (90) días de notificada … no hayan depositado la suma establecida en el Artículo 4 de la misma, deberán someterse incondicionalmente a la jurisdicción de los tribunales de los Estados unidos de Norte América para la decisión definitiva del caso en cuestión, renunciando de manera expresa a la excepción de "Forum No Conveniente" alegada en aquellos Tribunales.'

35. The Nicaraguan court heard the first set of DBCP cases filed in Nicaragua under the new law in late 2002.

36. Model Law on International Jurisdiction and Applicable Law to Tort Liability. Permanent Forum of Regional Parliaments for the Environment and for Sustainable Development, PARLATINO [Latin American Parliament], 27 January 1998, in Dahl (1999: Law 239 et seq.).

37. 'Proposal for an Interamerican Convention on the Effects and Treatment of the Forum Non Conveniens Theory'. Dr Gerardo Trejos Salas, 55th Regular Period of Sessions August 1999, Rio de Janeiro, Brazil. OEA/Ser.Q, CJI/doc.29/99, 14 July 1999.

38. The Hague Conference on Private International Law, 'Preliminary draft convention on jurisdiction and the effects of judgments in civil and commercial matters'. Adopted provisionally by the Special Commission on 18 June 1999. The Hague Academy.

39. In the European Union, the Brussels Convention on Jurisdiction and Enforcement of Judgments in Civil and Commercial Matters governs (Brussels

Convention on Jurisdiction and Enforcement of Judgments in Civil and Commercial Matters 1968 as amended by the Accession Conventions of 1978, 1982 and 1989). The convention establishes the principle that defendants can be sued in the courts of the EU member states where they are domiciled, and therefore FNC does not apply. As recently as 2000, though, the Court of Justice of the European Communities dealt with a case involving questions of FNC.

40. *Super Helechos, S.A., et. Al v. E.I. Du Pont de Nemours and Company Inc.*, Case No. 01–6932, 01–6935 and 01–23796. 11th Judicial Circuit, in and for Miami-Dade Country, Florida, 20 May 2002.

41. *Lucas Pastor Canales Martinez, et al. v. Dow Chemical Company, et al.*, US District Court Eastern District of Louisiana, 16 July 2002. Civil Action N: 95–3212.

42. Other cases include the Thor Chemicals litigation, in which twenty-eight workers who suffered severe mercury poisoning in a South African factory argued that the UK parent company should be held liable because it was directly responsible for setting up and maintaining the wholly-owned subsidiary in South Africa, and knew or should have known that it would be unsafe for the people who worked there. The court found that England was an appropriate forum and allowed the case to proceed. These cases were eventually settled out of court. In another case the plaintiff, Edward Connelly, alleged that the British company Rio Tinto Zinc failed to provide adequate protection against radioactive dust in the Rosin Uranium Mine in Namibia, a Rio Tinto subsidiary, and that he contracted throat cancer due to exposure to the dust (Schoonakker, 1998). The House of Lords allowed the case for personal injuries to go forward in 1997, although the case later failed for other procedural reasons (Ward, 2001).

43. The US agro-chemical industry has successfully opposed proposed federal legislation to prohibit the export of banned and never-registered pesticides from the USA on several occasions during the last decade. US Customs records reveal that 3.2 billion lbs of pesticide products were exported between 1997 and 2000, an average rate of 45 tons per hour. Nearly 65 million lbs of the exported pesticides were either banned or severely restricted in the United States (Smith, 2001).

REFERENCES

Dahl, H. S. (1999) *Dahl's Law Dictionary: An Annotated Legal Dictionary (Spanish-English/English-Spanish)*, 3rd edn., Buffalo, NY: William S. Hein.

Holding, R. (1993) 'Pesticide Makers Sued for Water Cleanup Costs', *San Francisco Chronicle* (1 March): A5.

Hosmer, E. (1990) 'First World Justice: Costa Rican Farmworkers in Texas State Courts', *Texas Observer* (13 July): 10.

International Campaign for Justice in Bhopal (2002) *Fact Sheet: The Double Standards of Dirty Dow*. <www.bhopal.net> (July 2002).

Lanchin, M. (2001) 'Poisoned Plantations: Ex-workers in Nicaraguan Banana Fields Sue U.S. Firms over Illness Linked to Toxic Fumigant', *San Francisco Chronicle* (115 March).

Malamud, S. (1996) 'A Double Standard? H. B. Fuller: A Different Record Home and Abroad', *Business and Society Review* (August).

Misko, F. et al. (1993) 'DBCP: The Legacy'. Dallas, TX: Misko, Howie and Sweeney.

Murray, D. (1983) 'The Politics of Pesticides: Corporate Power and Popular Struggle Over the Regulatory Process'. PhD thesis, University of California Santa Cruz.

Noronha, F. (1999) 'Union Carbide Sued in U.S. for 1984 Bhopal Gas Release', *Environment News Service* (16 November). <http://ens-news.com/ens/nov 1999/1999-11-16-02.asp> (31 January 2003).

PANUPS (1995), *Pesticides in California Groundwater*. Pesticide Action Network North America Updates Service (26 May). <www.panna.org>

Pesticide Action Network-UK (2002) *Carbide's Guilty Secret Found in Bhopal Factory Papers*. Press Release (16 November). <www.pan-uk.org/press/bhopsec.htm> (November).

Public Citizen (2002) *Smoking Guns: Corporate Behaviour and the Harmful Impact of a Punitive Damages Cap*. <www.citizen.org/congress/civjus/tort/tortlaw/ articles.cfm?ID=919> (31 January 2003).

Robertson, D. W. (1987) 'Forum Non Conveniens in America and England: "A Rather Fantastic Fiction"', *Law Quarterly Review* 103: 398–432.

Schemo, D. J. (1995) 'Pesticide from U.S. Kills the Hopes of Fruit Pickers in the Third World', *New York Times* (6 December 1995).

Schoonakker, B. (1998) 'SA Employees of UK-based Firms Face New Threat', *Sunday Times Business Times* (22 November).

Siegel, B. (1991) 'Going an Extra Mile for Justice', *Los Angeles Times* (21 March): A1.

Siegel, C. S. and D. S. Siegel (1999) 'The History of DBCP from a Judicial Perspective', *International Journal of Occupational and Environmental Health* 5 (2): 127–35.

Smith, C. (2001) 'Pesticide Exports from U.S. Ports, 1997–2000', *International Journal of Occupational and Environmental Health* 7 (4): 266–74.

Ward, H. (2001) 'Governing Multinationals: The Role of Foreign Direct Liability', Briefing Paper New Series no. 18. London: Royal Institute of International Affairs.

NINE | Business and biotechnology: regulation of GM crops and the politics of influence

DOMINIC GLOVER AND PETER NEWELL

§ Public regulation of agribusiness has become a particularly controversial issue in the field of biotechnology, in both the North and the South. A potent combination of high levels of public anxiety, elite scientific discourse, an intimate connection with international trade concerns, and the prominent role of a handful of powerful multinational enterprises, makes decisions about how to manage modern crop biotechnologies the subject of strongly contested political debate the world over.

This chapter assesses the effectiveness of different approaches to the regulation of the social and environmental risks associated with genetically modified (GM) crops. We argue that public regulation at the national, regional and international level suffers from a number of flaws and limitations and fails to address key public concerns about modern biotechnology. We show that biotechnology regulations have responded more to commercial and trade concerns than to public anxiety about environmental and social risks. In this sense much contemporary regulation provides regulation *for* business rather than regulation *of* business.

The perceived limitations of public regulation have prompted civil society actors to resort to alternative means to contest the commercialization of GM crops, to influence debates about the appropriate scope and scale of regulation, and to put pressure directly on the biotech firms. These means include the use of civil liability litigation, direct action against GM crops and forms of 'civil regulation'. We examine what contribution these techniques and strategies make to the overall regulatory environment and suggest that they help to plug 'governance gaps' in the existing public regulatory system, as well as perform broader political functions. These broader functions include democratizing and politicizing the biotechnology debate by challenging the hegemony of prevailing scientific and technicist discourses, and drawing companies into a debate about their social responsibilities as well as economic rights. Our aim is to assess critically the role of these strategies in holding the biotech companies to account for their actions and providing for the more effective regulation of business.

REGULATION FOR BUSINESS

The scope of regulatory activity in relation to crop biotechnology covers areas as diverse as the regulation of laboratory research, intellectual property protection, oversight of field trials, the trade in genetically modified organisms (GMOs), issues of food and feed safety, and product labelling. The structures that exist to regulate genetic technologies include 'a mass of legal regulations, non-legal rules, codes, circulars, practice notes, international conventions and ethical codes' (Black, 1998: 621). These are generated and overseen by an enormously complex set of advisory bodies, committees, professional organizations and industry associations operating at the international, national and sub-national level. Though many countries developed their own regulations independently during the 1990s, in 2000 the Cartagena Protocol on Biosafety – an international agreement on the management of the international trade in GMOs – gave new impetus to many governments to develop national bio-safety laws.

A key point of contention in the biotech debate is how far existing regulations, for example those relating to chemical pesticides, are sufficient to cover the potential risks arising from GM technologies. In this regard, the United States and the European Union have taken strikingly different approaches to the development of regulatory regimes for GM crops (Cantley, 1995; Dunlop, 2000; Endres, 2000), and these two approaches have emerged as predominant models that frame the global debate on regulating GMOs.

The USA adopted a product-oriented system that focuses on the characteristics and intended use of the end product rather than the recombinant technology deployed to create it. The US stance has been to regard GM crops as products that are 'substantially equivalent' to their conventional counterparts, that pose no special risks and do not require a special regulatory regime. Regulatory oversight is, therefore, left to the authority of existing laws and agencies. In contrast, the EU adopted a process-oriented approach, in which regulatory oversight of a GMO is triggered by the genetic engineering process by which it was created (Cantley, 1995; Dunlop, 2000). It regulates all products that have been produced using modern biotechnology techniques. EU regulation implements this approach by requiring prior consent and risk assessment for every proposed release and by applying broad ecological criteria on a case-by-case basis both before and after a GM product's release into the environment or a market (Dunlop, 2000: 151). This precautionary approach means that controls are put in place even in the absence of definite information about the risks posed (Black, 1998: 629).

Despite these differences in approach, broadly speaking, regulation performs three key and closely related functions in the biotechnology context. These are: (i) risk management, (ii) facilitating commercial transactions, and (iii) generating public trust in the new technologies (Newell, 2002). In this section we argue that the imperative of facilitating the commercialization of GM products has been allowed to override a fuller consideration of the potential environmental and socio-economic risks associated with GM crops. This has undermined public trust and confidence in the regulation of biotechnology products.

Any public regulatory system designed to establish and enforce environmental safeguards is likely to have weaknesses that undermine its effectiveness or legitimacy. Some may be peculiar to developing countries, where capacity and resource issues represent serious constraints. Others may be related to the nature of the technology in question, or the strategic importance attached to it by the state or by industry. Collectively, these factors help us to understand the limits of effective public regulation and provide the context for the alternative strategies adopted by opponents of biotechnology, who perceive existing forms of public regulation to be weak, poorly enforced and corrupted by private interests. The next sections explore these different factors.

State capacity

Governments and regulatory authorities anywhere struggle to keep up with the pace and fluidity of change in the biotech sector. Regulatory systems are slow to evolve and modify, and governments often react to technological change in the private sector rather than drive it. The practical difficulties of tracking the cross-border trade in GMOs, monitoring where such crops are being grown and enforcing bio-safety regulations at farm level present technical, logistical and administrative challenges to even the most developed countries. Human and financial constraints magnify these problems for developing countries.

A related issue is the ability of biotech companies to evade the regulatory authority of governments. NGOs in particular have expressed concern that developing countries, which may lack the resources and capacity to oversee field trials and enforce regulations, may be viewed by biotech firms as attractive regulatory havens (Brac de la Perrière and Seuret, 2000). There have already been allegations that GM crops have been grown illegally in parts of sub-Saharan Africa, Latin America and South and East Asia. In India recently, Bt[1] cotton was found to have been cultivated without authorization in Gujarat, highlighting the degree of micro-surveillance that is required for effective enforcement (Srinivas, 2002).

The state's capacity to manage the demand for approvals of GMOs is also questioned by biotech firms. Regulators in developing countries, in particular, have been subject to industry pressure to speed up application procedures for biotech developments, to avoid 'undue delay'. For example, the Indian government has been under pressure to create a 'one-stop' approval process, thereby consolidating the existing sequential series of regulatory steps (AIBA Report, 2000). Similarly, in Canada, 'thorough assessment of environmental hazards and meaningful public dialogue have been sidelined by the imperative to market GE crops quickly and competitively' (Barrett and Abergel, 2000: 7). Companies also express frustration at the lack of know-how and experience among government regulators, especially in developing countries, and the delays caused by the 'excessive' caution of officials responsible for risk assessments and approvals. For example, the pharmaceutical company Ciba-Geigy[2] expressed their distrust of the competence of the national regulatory authorities in Thailand. Their objection was that the biotech regulations were not understood by all parties, including the public and private sector researchers and government officials controlling and approving experiments.

The industry has also raised concerns over the security andconfidentiality of commercially sensitive data submitted to regulators, especially where decision-making is fragmented across different government departments. In this regard, firms view with suspicion regulatory scientists who, as fellow biotechnology researchers, are potentially in competition with the private sector. By virtue of being regulators, public sector scientists have access to information and data that may be useful to their own research and would be unavailable by other means (AIBA, 2000). In the USA and Canada, applicants have made extensive use of exclusions on grounds of commercial confidentiality (Barrett and Abergel, 2000; NAS, 2002). This is an important barrier to the free sharing of information and, while some information is made public, there remains a tension between transparency on the one hand and protecting the commercial interests of those being regulated on the other (Black, 1998: 627). The reluctance of firms to disclose information about their research and development work inhibits a more participatory and deliberative policy process. It forms a barrier to the exercise of broader and more inclusive forms of public scrutiny and control over the direction and applications of the technology.

Public regulation for private interests

Although businesses tend to have strong views about preferred forms of regulation, it is important to acknowledge that many firms also benefit from clear and transparent regulations that help to make their activities more certain, stable and predictable. Regulation plays an important role in enabling firms to make more informed, and long-term investment choices. Regulation can bring order to commercial interactions and lower transaction costs, as well as confer legitimacy upon business transactions. Internationally, harmonized regulation can reduce barriers to trade by creating common standards and rules of conduct, and prevent the growth of obstacles to investment. However, firms also want regulatory procedures that are quick, entail low transaction costs and create minimal interference with their commercial goals. For these reasons the private interests that are meant to be the subject of public regulation have been proactively shaping the form and scope of that regulation.

Businesses are often keen to ensure that decision-making is as technical and devoid of political conflict as possible. Therefore industry has expressed concern about widening the regulatory circle too far, both in terms of the actors involved and the range of issues considered. For example, during the negotiation of the Biosafety Protocol, industry sought to resist the attempt by countries such as Ethiopia and Malaysia to insert language that would have allowed states to evaluate the socio-economic impacts of GMOs in their risk assessments (Newell and Mackenzie, 2000). While the European Commission conceded that, in special cases, it may consider socio-economic aspects of the technology, the European biotech industry has insisted that product regulation should 'assess only safety, quality and efficacy for man and the environment on the basis of objective scientific criteria' (Levidow and Tait, 1995: 134). 'From industry's standpoint social need [for the technology] should be determined by the free choice of consumers in the market' (ibid.).

One of the ways in which firms have sought to restrict the scope of systems of public regulation for GM crops is by invoking international trade rules. Where GM risk assessments do not conform to industry's preferred standards, and especially if they are considered to include 'political' elements, they are prone to be condemned as 'illegitimate' trade barriers. For example, US industry spokespeople attacked the EU's de facto moratorium on GM crops as a WTO-illegal restriction on trade. From industry's perspective, the WTO has the advantage that its dispute settlement mechanism can adjudicate on trade disputes and gives priority to trade considerations in all its deliberations. An essential feature of this approach is that regulation on environmental and food safety risks should be founded on the principles of 'sound science'. For example, the Technical Barriers to Trade (TBT) and Sanitary and Phyto-Sanitary (SPS) agreements of the WTO stipulate the use of 'sound science' criteria as the only legitimate basis on which risks may be invoked as grounds for restricting trade. This narrows the opportunities available to countries to justify restrictions on trade according to other criteria.

The appeal to trade rules also reinforces the effort to harmonize risk assessment procedures internationally. Increasingly there is a set of global pressures for establishing common means of identifying and managing the risks associated with GM products, that emanates from the OECD, the 'Miami Group'[3] and leading companies in the biotech sector. The biotech industry has lent its support to initiatives such as the OECD guidelines, which are aimed at reducing barriers to trade by making regulatory requirements more transparent, predictable and universal, thus helping to reduce transaction costs for business (OECD, 1992). As Levidow et al. note (1996: 140), 'harmonisation efforts gained impetus from many sources: from free-trade imperatives, from applicants operating across national boundaries and ultimately from marketing applications, which stimulated regulators to try to reconcile their data requirements.'

The use of 'scientific' principles, which compare the novel aspects of technologies with what we already assume to be safe, has been one device for projecting confidence that any undesirable effects are under control. For example, the principle of 'substantial equivalence' (SE) is used to compare the risks associated with products containing GMOs with those produced with traditional plant-breeding techniques. It is designed not as a substitute for risk assessment, but rather as a means to provide reassurance that a new food product is comparable in terms of its safety to its conventional counterpart (Barrett and Abergel, 2000). The OECD has sought to get SE accepted as an international regula- tory concept by establishing a programme on the harmonization of regulatory oversight in biotechnology. The idea is to provide policy- makers with science-based and predictive capacities in any political and ecological setting, thereby encouraging harmonized regulations that facilitate trade.

The concept of 'familiarity' is also used in many regulatory regimes for the dual purposes of projecting confidence in the regulatory process, as well as facilitating the trade in GM products. It has been incorporated into the regulations of several countries as a 'trigger' for risk assessments. Because the only way to gain familiarity with commercial releases is by allowing for commercial releases, 'familiarity closely binds regulatory oversight with industrial interests and market imperatives' (Barrett and Abergel, 2000: 10). These authors find that in practice both substantial equivalence and familiarity 'support decisions to deregulate GE crops by promoting biotechnology as an innovative and competitive technology, while simultaneously downplaying concerns for environmental hazards' (ibid., p. 2). For them, familiarity and SE function as a type of 'international currency that facilitates the trade and exchange of GE crops' (ibid., p. 3). The principles act as powerful gate-keeping tools, in so far as risk assessments are mandatory only for GE crops not considered to be familiar or substantially equivalent. Ironically, of course, while trade barriers are to be removed on the grounds that there is essentially nothing new about GM products, for the purpose of protecting intellectual property, they have to be seen as novel and innovative.

The high level of start-up capital that is required in crop development drives companies to seek intellectual property protection. This is in order to cover the substantial research and development costs of crop innovation and, for many firms, to satisfy the demands of venture capitalists, on whom they are dependent for start-up money, for a short-term return on their investments. Biotech firms claim that intellectual property protection is crucial to their business strategies and innovation. This commercial imperative explains the support biotech companies have lent to the TRIPs[4] agreement of the WTO which requires member countries to put systems of patent protection in place at the national level. Sell (1999) has described how major US-based transnational companies stimulated demands for the TRIPs agreement and at the same time mobilized their 'home' governments to apply bilateral pressure on 'host' countries to tighten and strengthen their national patent regimes.

Regulation for business brings other commercial benefits for firms. For example, Miller (1999) argues forcefully that major biotech companies have lobbied for more restrictive regulation than could be justified on 'scientific' grounds, in order to create a market-entry barrier to smaller competitors that are less able to afford the costs of compliance.

Moreover, as Levidow and Tait suggest: 'Even those who downplay the risks favour such regulation, if only in order to establish clear rules for commercial competition and to allay public fears' (Levidow and Tait, 1995: 132). In this regard, the biotech firm Aventis[5] notes the potential usefulness of labelling: 'Aventis supports labelling of GMO produced food products, viewing it as a fundamental step in the future acceptance of biotechnology and genetically improved foods' (Aventis, 2000).

Perceived harmony between the interests of business and the state

The nature of the relationship between the state and business is crucial to understanding why governments have been so responsive to the pressures and demands made by biotechnology companies of public regulators that we have described above. The relationship is intensified in the case of biotechnology because the interests of industries coincide strongly with governments' own definitions of their national interest, envisaged as generating growth through hi-tech development in the biotech sector (Levy and Newell, 2000: 13). The biotech industry has been able to present itself as a key component of the knowledge economy, invoked as a major driver of growth by both European and North American governments, especially the USA and UK. To encourage companies to engage in biotechnology R&D, governments have provided a range of financial incentives, soft loans and other subsidies, supportive infrastructure and policy frameworks, as well as sponsoring public–private partnerships.[6]

Leading individuals within the policy process have also used their positions to support the development of the industry. UK science minister Lord Sainsbury, for example, with his own commercial interests in biotechnology companies, produced a report advocating support for the development of 'biotechnology clusters'.[7] There is also evidence of a 'revolving door' between the biotechnology industry and government agencies. In the USA, for example, government officials have moved into industry jobs and vice versa (Ferrara, 1998). While Val Giddings went from being responsible for biotechnology regulation within the US department of agriculture and part of the US negotiating team in the bio-safety negotiations to become vice president for food and agriculture of the Biotechnology Industry Organization, Michael Taylor, the FDA's deputy commissioner for policy responsible for drafting the labelling guidelines on the GE cattle drug rBGH, was formerly a Monsanto lawyer for seven years (AgbioIndia, 2002). There are important implications here for governments' responsibilities as regulators, when promoting an industry is equated with removing regulations.

The Thatcher government in the UK, for example, issued a White Paper stating the government's desire to support the biotech industry by removing 'regulatory constraints inhibiting biotechnology development, such as the burdensome health and safety regulations' (Gottweiss, 1995: 205).

The degree of industry mobilization around the GMO issue also helps to account for the distinct regulatory approaches that have emerged in the USA and Europe. While in the USA during the 1980s the industry was already pressing government officials on biotechnology regulation, in Europe the biotech lobby came together too late to influence the 1990 European Deliberate Release Directive (90/220) which sought to establish harmonized procedures and criteria for all genetically-modified organisms. 'The very existence of directive 90/220 undoubtedly reflects the absence, for most of the 1980s, of any powerful biotech lobby organisation in Europe' (Dunlop, 2000: 152). Consequently the European industry organization EuropaBio spent most of the 1990s attacking what they refer to as 'Catch 220' and its protracted approval processes. By contrast, Dunlop attributes the US regulatory focus on end products to the 'undeviating pro-product pressure from both the scientific lobby and that of the biotech industry' (Dunlop, 2000: 151). The public mood in Europe, on the other hand, makes it more likely that a precautionary approach will be retained, despite industry claims that wealth creation is being stifled by process-based legislation, putting the EU at a competitive disadvantage in relation to the USA and Japan in particular (Levidow et al., 1996).

If there is to be any convergence between the two regulatory approaches, the initiative may well come from industry itself. Increasingly, biotech firms on both sides of the Atlantic are combining to press for similar approaches to regulation in Europe and the USA with a clear preference for product-oriented rather than process-oriented regulations. As long ago as June 1998, AgrEvo's[8] CEO Dr Gerhard Prante urged an audience of 100 high-level politicians and government officials to 'seize the chance to "harmonise" regulatory frameworks internationally [presumably down to the US standard], before differences had time to solidify' (Corporate Watch, 2000). Companies are now co-ordinating their lobbying internationally through transatlantic business dialogues which bring together senior public regulators in Europe and North America and leading industrialists from the biotech sector (Levy and Newell, 2000). Their efforts are aided by the increasingly transatlantic integration of biotechnology investment (Levidow et al., 1996: 140).

Firms are also key actors in the international institutions engaged with this issue. Much of the capital and knowledge about GMOs is tied up in the private sector and so it is unsurprising that those with the expertise whose products are the subject of regulation, are heavily involved in the international governance of crop biotechnologies. For the purposes of presenting a unified position at the international negotiations on bio-safety, national and regional industry bodies have formed a Global Industry Coalition. The coalition brings together groups such as EuropaBio, BIO (Biotechnology Industry Organization [US]) and the BioIndustry Association (UK), and works closely at national level with organizations such as the All India Biotech Association that have played a prominent part in articulating industry concerns within state-level policy processes.[9]

As a result of these forms of political mobilization, the biotech sector provides further evidence of what has been called the 'privatization' of the United Nations (Lee et al., 1997) whereby standard-setting is increasingly conducted by corporate representatives working alongside other governmental and non-governmental specialists. For example, life science industries are described as 'hugely influential' in the work of the Codex Alimentarius Commission and the Intellectual Property Committee of the WTO (Barrett and Abergel, 2000: 10). The SPS and TBT agreements are particularly important to industrialists because they describe the least trade discriminating path to risk assessment and standard-setting. The prominent role of industry groups in building the capacity of governments to engage in the trade in GMOs, and working with the Global Environment Facility (GEF) on pilot bio-safety programmes, also indicates a high level of engagement. The Biosafety Protocol itself reads in places rather more like an investment agreement for biotechnology, confirming the entry and exit options of MNCs, than an environmental accord. This is attributed by some observers to the influence of biotech firms on the positions of key players in the negotiations, such as the USA and Canada from the Miami Group, in ensuring that the agreement was consistent with the free trade principles of the WTO (Stabinsky, 2000).

Implications for effective public regulation

The limitations of state capacity, pressure from the private sector and powerful governments, the constraints placed by international trade rules and demands for harmonization, and the tendency of many politicians to equate key strategic national interests with the interests of private companies, raise questions about the extent to which public policy-makers can exercise a degree of autonomy in determining what regulations are appropriate and desirable for their own country. Again, because of their economic weakness and dependence on firms for inward investment and aid from donors in GMO-exporting countries, the autonomy of developing countries is likely to be particularly circumscribed.

One key challenge is the apparent tension in the politics of regulation, between the potentially conflicting goals of promoting a strategic industry and, at the same time, regulating the ecological and social impacts of that industry. This tension between governments' role as *promoter* of biotech and *protector* of the public interest is manifested in competing bureaucratic mandates. In Germany, for example, these functions are also combined in a single law, affirming 'the state's presumed capacity to undertake these potentially conflicting tasks without compromising the rights or values of its citizens' (Jasanoff, 1995: 323). As states have sought to reconcile these tasks, Gottweiss argues that '[r]ather than inhibiting genetic engineering, the emergence of risk and its regulation turned out to be critical for the diffusion of the new technology into research and industry' (Gottweiss, 1995: 153). In the European case this was certainly driven by a fear that the USA was stealing a commercial lead.

The extent to which this tension will impact upon the effectiveness of public biotechnology regulation will depend partly on the extent to which a government has sufficient capacity for autonomous action. It will also depend on the extent to which there is an active civil society contesting the predominant framings of regulation for business. Nevertheless, the European and Indian experiences suggest that vocal protest movements may be more effective at engaging with consumer concern than they are at reorienting regulatory systems towards meeting broader notions of the public interest. Concessions may be made, decisions delayed and outcomes contested but, as Levy and Newell (2000) show, most regulators have been successful at accommodating dissent and modifying aspects of policy without fundamentally altering systems geared towards meeting the needs of producers rather than consumers of biotechnology products. Those governments that have sought to take a more restrictive stance on the trade in GMOs, such as Croatia, Sri Lanka and China, have encountered intense opposition from GMO exporters and in many cases have been forced to back down following intense bilateral pressure and the threat of a case being brought at the WTO.

For the various reasons discussed here, public regulation is in many respects, at this stage, a blunt and ineffective instrument for managing the social and environmental impacts of biotechnology that reflects the privileging of trade and commercial concerns. We have also seen how the scope and nature of regulations adopted by international organizations are often shaped by market needs and the pressures exerted by market actors. The emphasis by bodies such as the OECD on harmonization of risk assessments, as a means to facilitate trade, and the preference of UNIDO for a code of conduct on biotechnology[10] (as opposed to more restrictive and binding regulations), both indicate the ways in which the policy preferences of international organizations and their autonomy of operation are conditioned and affected by prevailing ideologies about what constitutes an acceptable form of regulation, which accord with the preferences of leading market actors.

Regulation of business

Partly in response to the limited scope and effectiveness of public regulation, opponents of GM crops and actors whose interests are threatened by biotechnology have resorted to alternative strategies to contest the policy process and make their voices heard. In the following sections we examine the role and effectiveness of these approaches to regulation that are based on civil society action. These include the tactical use of litigation as well as the various techniques of 'civil regulation' which have been used to scrutinize and discipline the conduct of firms (Bendell, 2000; Newell, 2000, 2001a). The key questions we seek to address here are: What political functions do these interventions serve in the debate? What extra checks and balances do they introduce on the activities of biotechnology companies in particular?

Liability and redress as elements of a regulatory framework

There is a substantial degree of scientific uncertainty over the magnitude of risks associated with GM crops, and the probability that they will materialize. Given the plausibility and seriousness of these risks, however, questions arise about what mechanisms may be used to manage them and how society should insure itself against possible harm. Equally, the widespread introduction of transgenic crops to agriculture entails a likely redistribution of costs and benefits among the actors in the sector. If transgenic technology is seen to conflict directly with the legitimate and lawful interests of other existing agricultural producers, such as organic farmers, this raises questions about how the state should arbitrate between the players. The legal concept of liability provides one way of addressing these issues. A liability regime gives rights to injured parties to sue those responsible for causing the harm, and imposes obligations on others to limit the risk, mitigate the harm and provide redress. Liability law is often considered to be merely a mechanism for resolving disputes '*ex post*' and obtaining compensation after damage has already occurred (Wilde, 1998). However, it can also help to prevent harm from occurring in the first place, because it creates incentives for both potential plaintiffs and defendants to keep hazardous activities under control. A system of civil liability can therefore contribute to the effectiveness of a regulatory regime by providing 'an additional sanction for infractions, thus ensuring stronger compliance incentives' (EU Commission Working Paper on Environmental Liability, quoted in Wilde, 1998: fn 47). From a public policy perspective, liability rules can also be used as a tool to help strike a balance between competing collective and individual social interests. By allocating responsibility for managing risks and insuring or indemnifying against potential harms, liability rules can alter the distribution of benefits and risks between different actors or groups.

It is because the allocation of legal responsibility entails such important, and potentially costly, consequences that liability is such a critical strategic node in the struggle between the competing interests that are ranged around the application of modern biotechnology in agriculture. The potential legal liabilities for harm caused by GMOs have attracted strategic attention from both proponents and opponents of the technology. For example, two anti-GM organizations, the Institute for Agriculture and Trade Policy (IATP) and Genetically Engineered Food Alert (GE Food Alert), recently issued a report warning US farmers about the risks of being sued by their neighbours for genetic contamination (Moeller, 2001). Meanwhile, the US law firm Faegre & Benson has prepared legal briefings to alert American seed companies to the range of possible claims that might arise out of genetic drift, and defences that might be used to resist them (Mandler and Eads, 2000).

There are two dimensions to the confrontation over liability. On the one hand, anti-GM NGOs such as Friends of the Earth and Third World Network and organic farmers' organizations such as the UK's Soil Association, are campaigning at national and international levels for the elaboration of a new, special liability regime for GM crops. The fiercely contested struggle over the liability issue has meant that the elaboration of a settled liability regime for GM crops, especially the harmonization of norms internationally, is proving difficult. On the other hand, we find evidence that dissatisfaction with the prevailing modes of biotech regulation is prompting opponents of GM crops to resort to other types of strategy to promote their claims. In the absence of a special liability regime for GMO-caused damage, liability claims under existing legal frameworks, such as torts in the United States, are being used instrumentally as a tool for direct resistance against the introduction of GMOs in agriculture. We discuss these two dimensions in turn below.

Formal public regimes for liability and redress

In accordance with the product-oriented approach adopted in the USA, no special provision has been made for civil liability for harm caused by GM crops. 'Neither the regulatory agencies nor citizens may use the various federal laws regulating biotechnology to recover for GMO-caused damage' (Endres, 2000: 481). Consequently, those wishing to sue for GMO-caused damage must fall back on existing areas of the law, notably product liability regulation, contract law and the common law of torts (specifically trespass, nuisance, negligence and potentially also claims under the theory of 'strict liability') (Endres, 2000; Moeller, 2001). The process-oriented approach in the EU is much more open to the development of a special liability regime. Inevitably, however, the design of such a regime has been controversial and time-consuming. As Wilde has noted: 'It is likely to be some years before any EC environmental liability regime is actually implemented. In the meantime it would be necessary for an aggrieved conventional or organic farmer [in Britain] to rely on existing common law torts' (Wilde, 1998: 167). We discuss the implications of this conclusion in the next section.

At the international level, a liability framework for GMOs is envisaged under Article 27 of the Cartagena Protocol on Biosafety (CPB) (CBD Secretariat, 2000) which oversees the 'transboundary movement' of GMOs.[11] One of the major struggles over the proposed liability regime is between those countries and interest groups that favour a narrow interpretation of its scope, and those who would prefer a broader construction. A narrow interpretation would restrict the application of the Protocol's liability rules strictly to harm caused to biodiversity and only to GMOs in transit across borders. Under such a strict interpretation, harm not directly pertaining to loss of biodiversity, or which occurred after the consignment had been safely delivered and stored at a destination in the receiving country, might be excluded. On the other hand, many developing countries and environmental NGOs are pressing for a more liberal interpretation of the Protocol's ambit that would include a broader range of activities and harms including 'socio-economic' impacts (Stabinsky, 2000). There is no agreed definition of what 'socio-economic impacts' might include but loss of income, livelihood displacement and impacts on food security, especially in developing countries, would be among the factors considered. However, the very notion that 'socio-economic impacts' have any place alongside a scientific bio-safety risk assessment is fiercely contested by GMO producers and exporters.[12]

The focal points of this struggle can be seen in the discussions that took place during a 'dialogue workshop' in September 2001, in advance of the second meeting of the Intergovernmental Committee on the Cartagena Protocol (ICCP-2). The workshop was convened to discuss the key issues relating to the implementation of the Article 27 liability and redress regime (Meridian Institute, 2001). Discussion centred on the question of whether the definition of 'damage' under the Protocol would have to be restricted only to damage to biodiversity, or could be expanded to include 'damage to human health, property, other economic losses resulting from [GMOs], and harm to the environment' (ibid., p. 6). Similarly, participants were divided on the question of imposing liability for legal deliberate releases of GMOs into the environment (as opposed to accidental or unintentional releases), and whether states or civil actors should be held liable for the resulting harm. A related issue was whether the Protocol calls for the elaboration of a new international GMO liability regime, or existing national laws on civil product liability could suffice (ibid., pp. 5, 8). Also controversial was the discussion of the appropriate grounds for liability, with some participants arguing for a 'strict liability' regime (ibid., pp. 8, 9).

The principle of 'strict' or 'no-fault' liability is an area where the stakes are particularly high for the opposing sides in the GMOs debate. This principle exists in common-law jurisdictions such as the United States and the United Kingdom, and may also be imposed by statute or treaty. Strict liability may be applied to activities that are judged to be inherently hazardous, so that it is not necessary for an injured party to prove fault (e.g. negligence) by the party in control of the activity. It is necessary to show only that damage has occurred and to establish a causal link between the harm and the hazardous activity (see Repp, 2000: 616–20). If the parties to the CPB were to adopt a strict civil liability regime, this could have a serious disincentive effect on firms contemplating commercializing or trading in GMOs. Anti-GMO campaigners may feel that in strict liability they have identified a powerful tool for resisting the commercialization of GMOs. However, the burden of proof may be prohibitive because of the degree and extent of uncertainty in knowledge about genetic modification, the complexity of mechanisms of gene transfer in the environment, as well as the time it may take for damage to manifest itself or be noticed and quantified (Meridian Institute, 2001: 8, 9; Endres, 2000: 486–91).

The disagreements rehearsed by the participants in the dialogue workshop were reflected in the negotiating positions adopted by the parties during the ICCP-2 meeting, and also in the positions of lobbyists from NGOs and the biotechnology and seed industries who attended the meeting. For example, the World Wide Fund for Nature (WWF) circulated a document urging the parties to develop 'effective provisions on liability and redress as a high priority for the Protocol' (WWF, 2001: 4). In particular, WWF called for the provisions on liability and redress to apply the principle of strict liability, to be based on civil liability, and to channel liability to private actors: 'There is no justification for leaving states to assume liability concerning the activities of private parties' (ibid.). The Global Industry Coalition, a lobby group representing biotech and seed firms, intervened during one of the sessions on liability to argue that, since the CBD and the CPB agreements are between states, the responsibility for liability and redress ought to rest with states. In the event, the parties were unable to agree on the substantive issues during ICCP-2, and instead worked to develop a process for elaborating a liability regime (CBD Secretariat, 2001: 10–12, 27–9). The debate on the possible contents of a transnational liability regime, therefore, continues to unfold.

Liability as a tool of resistance: litigation in North America
In the absence of a statutory liability regime that addresses public concerns, private actors are resorting to existing regimes of civil liability law and public law as alternative methods for raising their objections to GM crops and defending their interests. These private actors include those campaigning against GM technology on principle, as well as interested parties such as organic or conventional farmers who claim their rights or interests have been damaged by GM crops. For example, at the time of writing, several private liability (tort) cases have been brought or are being considered in the US and Canadian courts, by producers of organic or 'conventional' crops who have been affected by 'genetic drift'.[13] Tort is a branch of law that provides redress for wrongs or injuries caused by a breach of legal duty to do or refrain from doing something. It derives from the English common law, a body of traditional law developed by the courts consisting of principles which are embodied in precedents set by previously decided cases. Duties and liabilities under tort law therefore exist independently of statutory provisions that provide for civil liability.

The North American tort cases include class action[14] cases against Monsanto and others in North Dakota, Minnesota, Iowa and Illinois in the USA and Saskatchewan in Canada (Agence France Presse, 2002; Cropchoice.com, 2001a, 2001b; Knight, 2000; Kossick, 2002; Shadid, 2001), as well as a counter-suit filed by the Canadian farmer Percy Schmeiser in his defence in a patent-infringement case brought against him by Monsanto (Mandler and Eads, 2000).

These cases are worth examining for a number of reasons. First, although the specific provisions of civil liability law differ from one jurisdiction to another, these North American cases serve to illustrate the types of conflict that can occur between interest groups over the introduction of biotech crops. Second, they demonstrate how recourse to law is sometimes used as a form of strategic political intervention by civil society groups. Third, they serve as an example that enables us to assess critically the additional forms of regulatory control and restraint that private actors are able to exercise in the North American context. Finally, the global importance of North America as a seed market and as a grain-exporting region, combined with the geo-political weight of the United States in the global biotechnology debate, means that the eventual outcomes of these ongoing legal struggles may have impacts worldwide. Their example cannot simply be extrapolated across other jurisdictions, however. In particular it should be remembered that citizens' ability to resort to the civil law depends on having access to an effective justice system. In developing countries especially, this factor may be missing or compromised by a lack of resources, corruption, intimidation or a lack of legal literacy.

Suits for torts like trespass and nuisance have certain limitations, including a heavy burden of proof, and are best suited to resolving disputes between farmers and landowners in cases where property rights have been infringed and economic losses incurred. For example, a tort suit may be a suitable vehicle for an organic farmer to seek redress if it can be shown that the crops cannot be marketed because of genetic drift from a neighbouring GM farm (although if the financial losses are construed to be a 'pure economic loss', damages cannot be recovered [Endres, 2000: 502–3; Wilde, 1998: 169]). But torts are not ideally suited to claims relating to general environmental harm or general public interest claims, or for deciding matters of general principle about the environmental release of GMOs. On a procedural level, environmental pressure groups will find it difficult to establish standing in such cases, although instead they may try to catalyse suits by potential plaintiffs and link up with class actions (Mandler and Eads,

2000). Class action cases in North America suggest that this strategy is indeed being adopted.

The tort of 'public nuisance' may offer some scope for public interest groups to challenge GMO releases to the environment. A 'public nuisance' may be found where an activity 'unreasonably interferes with the public use of land or … unreasonably endangers the health, safety and welfare of the public as a whole' (Mandler and Eads, 2000: 13; see also Endres, 2000: 491–2). A class action suit alleging a public nuisance, as well as claims under anti-trust law and international customary law, was filed in an American court in December 1999 against Monsanto by the Foundation on Economic Trends (FET) and the National Family Farm Coalition (NFFC) (FET, 1999). The suit seeks damages from Monsanto for failing adequately to test GM crops for human health and environmental safety before releasing them on to the market.

The cases mentioned above suggest that tort claimants are targeting the biotech and seed companies rather than the individual farmers who grow the GM crops or the government agencies responsible for regulating them. This may be because of the difficulties of proving causation against an individual farmer (Endres, 2000; Repp, 2000), the deeper pockets of major transnational companies as compared with farmers, the lack of insurance cover against genetic drift claims (Gaia Trust, 2000; Minnesota Planning, 2001; Shadid, 2001), or perhaps an unwillingness on principle to hold individual farmers responsible for the environmental release of GMOs.

The latter concern helps to explain the actions of Terra Prima, a Wisconsin-based organic food processor and wholesaler which decided to recall and destroy 87,000 bags of tortilla chips when they were found to contain GM corn. The company sustained a substantial loss, including the cost of destroying the affected bags, damaged consumer confidence and ongoing costs involved in instituting new testing procedures intended to avoid similar incidents in the future. However, the affected corn had come from a long-standing organic supplier to the company whom Terra Prima declined to hold responsible. The farmer believes the contamination resulted from cross-pollination from neighbouring farms. Instead of suing their own supplier, the farmer's neighbours or the firms responsible for developing and marketing the GM corn, the company joined environmental and consumer groups, organic farmers, processors and certifiers in a public interest lawsuit against the US Environmental Protection Agency claiming that it had violated the law in giving its approval to the release of GM crops (Center for Food Safety, 1999; Chase, 1999; Cropchoice.com, 2001a; Repp, 2000: 591).

None of the cases discussed here has yet reached a final resolution and therefore it is impossible to draw definite conclusions about their likely implications. It remains to be seen whether the tensions and stresses exposed by the GMO liability cases may build pressure for the development of more comprehensive and effective forms of public regulation. One possibility is that, by giving the appearance that these new issues can be managed effectively within existing legal frameworks, pressure for reform may be muted, allowing regulators and policy-makers to justify inaction and shelter from controversy.

The above examples show that, in the absence of a comprehensive liability and redress regime for agricultural biotechnology, tort law provides at least a partial and incomplete avenue for those seeking redress. It may also appear to be a relatively efficient mode of regulation because it adapts an existing regime of civil liability, which already provides a framework for settlement of disputes and redress between citizens. However, tort law provides an unsatisfactory framework for determining whether and under what conditions genetically modified crops may be cultivated. In particular, by framing the potential problems arising from the environmental release of GMOs as essentially disputes between property-owners and market actors, tort rules out a wider consideration of the ethics, ecological risks or socio-economic impacts involved.

The effectiveness of tort as a means of restraining the uncontrolled environmental release of GM crops is very limited. For example, proof of causation is extremely difficult in genetic drift cases. The doctrine of strict liability may help to address this problem, but it will apply only if the courts judge cultivation of GMOs to be an inherently hazardous activity. In addition, it may prove to be relatively easy to mount a legal defence against a genetic drift claim. For example, the farmer may escape liability if he can show that he followed all the relevant agronomic guidelines and took the recommended precautions, such as notifying his neighbours and planting a buffer zone of conventional crops between his GM plants and his neighbours' fields.[15] Similarly, if statutory regulations stipulated what precautions were legally required, a defendant GM farmer would be able to avoid liability if he had followed them, even if the mandated precautions were not actually sufficient to prevent the harm (Wilde, 1998).

These examples illustrate the reliance that courts or legislators must place on scientific expertise to help determine the probability and magnitude of risks and what precautions are reasonable (Repp, 2000). The premises and evidence on which this scientific advice is based must therefore be regarded as critically important. Equally, however, it is questionable whether lawyers and judges are well equipped to evaluate scientific evidence about risks, or whether a court is the most desirable forum for determining what level of risk society should be willing to accept. The judicial system is insulated from democratic accountability and there is no scope for public consultation regarding the wider implications of a judgment in a specific tort suit.

The decision by some plaintiffs to target the biotech firms instead of farmers or regulators needs to be understood in the context of their broader strategy and goals. If improved enforcement were the main priority, a legal challenge against government regulatory authorities, as in the Terra Prima case, makes better sense. If it were a question of targeting the party with the best ability to pay, then the corporations might be a good bet, except that torts such as nuisance and trespass are likely to be easier to bring against neighbouring farmers than the companies which sold them the seed they planted on their land. The decision to go after the biotech corporations makes sense as part of a wider strategy for delaying GM commercialization, by adding costs, creating uncertainty and generating adverse publicity that frustrates the plans of the biotech firms. Seen in this light, even failed cases matter to the anti-GM campaigners, provided they succeed in causing delay and drawing attention to inadequacies in the current system of public regulation by highlighting issues that have been overlooked or incompletely addressed. Complainants also tend to be animated by a strong sense that, regardless of what the law may judge, the biotech corporations ought to accept the moral responsibility for the risks involved in releasing novel varieties into the environment.

The FET/NFFC anti-trust case against Monsanto provides a striking illustration of the way that anti-GM activists are using lawsuits tactically as one element in a broader strategy of resistance to GM crops. The press release announcing the lawsuit makes this connection explicit:

> FET and NFFC are launching a parallel public campaign to accompany this litigation and are quickly reaching out to Civil Society Organizations (CSOs) – farm, environmental, trade, animal protection, health, consumer, and social justice organizations – as well as political parties and government and business leaders to mobilize world wide support. Our aim is both to use the litigation to raise the critical environmental, health and economic issues surrounding GMO food and to secure a court ordered injunction prohibiting Monsanto from marketing its corn and soy. (FET, 1999)

Similarly, the Center for Food Safety uses litigation alongside a range of other activities and campaigns, as part of a wider strategy aimed at securing a strict testing and labelling regime for GMOs, as well as ensuring that rigorous organic standards are maintained (Center for Food Safety, 2002). Recourse to litigation should therefore be seen as a useful weapon in the armoury of those resisting the commercialization of GMOs, but one which is deployed alongside other methods and tactics of influence and resistance. These are discussed in the next section.

NGOS AND CIVIL REGULATION

The previous section looked at the extent to which civil litigation strategies can either improve compliance with existing systems of public regulation or generate new mechanisms of regulation. In this section, we consider a range of other strategies that have been adopted by civil society actors assessing what they contribute to the strengthening of existing systems of regulation or the creation of new forms of 'civil regulation'.

The term 'civil regulation' provides one way of describing the purpose and means of these strategies (Bendell, 2000; Newell, 2000). It denotes actions taken by civil society actors that have the intention or effect of restraining, regulating or resisting the actions of private actors that are thought to be beyond state control. We use the term here to capture pressures and expectations upon firms that force them to act in new ways which go beyond the requirements of compliance with state-based regulation. Other civil society actions of direct resistance to the technology, mentioned below, may express a dissatisfaction with the regulatory process but do not necessarily contribute new mechanisms of governance as such. Indeed, the intention is often to ensure that the technology is not used at all, rather than ensuring that it is better regulated.

Resistance

NGO opposition to GM crops and the regulatory processes by which they have been approved has been expressed in the form of media-friendly spectacles in which activists uproot the crops in full view of watching journalists. In 1999, twenty-eight British Greenpeace activists were arrested and later acquitted for pulling up GM maize plants being tested at a site in Norfolk (UK) on behalf of AgrEvo (Greenpeace UK, 2002). Activists invoked the notion of 'civil responsibility' to justify their efforts to 'decontaminate' field sites by removing GM crops (Levidow and Carr, 2000: 262). The combined effect of public protests, according to Levidow and Carr, was that the two ministers responsible for safety regulation 'sought to accommodate public protest through more stringent regulation' (ibid., p. 264). Similar actions have taken place in Australia, France, Germany, Ireland, the Netherlands, New Zealand and the Philippines, among others (Goldsmith, 1998; MASIPAG, 2001; Robson, 2002). In India in 1998, the Karnataka State Farmers' Association (KRRS) initiated Operation Cremate Monsanto, in which activists, including farmers, landless peoples and members of 'untouchable' castes, tore up and burned test plots of Monsanto GM crops (Kingsnorth, 1999).

A second, less prominent approach has been to try and undermine the market for GM crops by encouraging farmers to conclude that the benefits are too slight or the risks too severe to justify their use. Good examples are reports by Moeller (2001), which warn farmers about the legal liability risks they assume by planting GM crops, and Benbrook (2001a, 2001b), who undermines the claims of the biotech firms about the cost savings, yield increases and environmental benefits associated with their transgenic Bt products. By seeking to undermine the demand for GMOs in this way, they aim to impose additional risks, delays and costs on the biotech companies. In doing so, they are taking advantage of the technical, financial and competitive pressures under which the major biotech TNCs are operating. For example, during the late 1990s, adverse publicity and consumer reaction had a damaging impact on the share prices of major biotech firms like Monsanto, AstraZeneca and Novartis. In response to this pressure, company managers instigated a series of divestments and mergers that were designed to insulate their profitable pharmaceuticals and chemicals divisions from their struggling agricultural businesses (Levy and Newell, 2000).

Confronting public regulation, constructing civil regulation

Some groups have sought to confront the elite and technicist nature of policy discourses around biotechnology by subjecting expert claims to public scrutiny. Groups such as ActionAid have used 'participatory' methods to enable poor farmers to assess for themselves the professed benefits of GM crops by cross-examining 'experts' from the scientific, corporate and government community (Newell, 2001b). These methods include 'citizens' juries' and 'scenario workshops', facilitated and organized by NGOs and academic institutions, and involving associations of farmers and landless peoples in Karnataka and Andhra Pradesh (India), Brazil and Zimbabwe. These events have made it possible to broaden the debate about the impacts of GM crops beyond ecological risks, to include socio-economic questions; they have also served to highlight issues of power, access and affordability, as well as the liability of biotech firms to provide compensation if the crop fails to deliver the claimed benefits (Pimbert et al., 2001). In doing so they have helped to highlight issues of concern to the ultimate users of GM seeds and contributed to a more inclusive public dialogue about the appropriate social control of the technology. In India, members of the government's Department of Biotechnology attended the meeting to provide an account of government actions and hear the concerns expressed by the jurors. Even if such events do not result in an immediate change in public regulation, they help to create a bridge between the formal and informal regulatory arenas, as well as drawing these broader issues into public debate through the media coverage they attract.

In addition to engaging with corporations directly and facilitating alternative policy processes, civil society groups have also played an important role as watchdogs for the effective monitoring and enforcement of public biotechnology regulations. In August 2000, Friends of the Earth US was instrumental in identifying the contamination of the human food chain by StarLink, an Aventis variety of Bt maize that was not approved for human consumption. The contamination turned out to be pervasive throughout the US food supply. Hundreds of food products had to be recalled, and USDA was forced to institute a massive buy-back programme in an effort to prevent the contaminated seed from being planted. Environmental NGOs claimed the StarLink affair 'showed a major regulatory failure. The tests that detected [StarLink's] presence were administered not by any biotech company, nor by government inspectors, but by a non-governmental organization' (Villar, 2001: 11).

In December 2001, the British environmental groups the Gaia Trust and Friends of the Earth UK (FOE) demanded action from government regulators when volunteer oil-seed rape plants on a former Aventis test-plot unexpectedly came into flower during mild winter weather, thus breaching the terms of the field-test consent. When the Department of Environment, Farming and Rural Affairs (DEFRA) ordered Aventis to remove the plants, NGOs claimed the credit for having effectively monitored the company's compliance with its permit. Pete Riley of FOE said: 'Quite obviously these sites have not been properly monitored by Aventis, even though it is legally responsible. If it hadn't been for the alert behaviour of a local farmer and Friends of the Earth these GM weeds would still be polluting the local environment' (Friends of the Earth UK, 2001).

An example from India illustrates both the potential weakness of formal public regulation in developing countries, as well as the role of NGOs in demanding enforcement action from public authorities. In November 2001 the Indian NGO Gene Campaign asked the Delhi High Court to order a criminal investigation into the illegal selling of an unauthorized Bt cotton variety, Navbharat 151, in Gujarat. The illegal plantings had been discovered in October, but despite orders from the government of India that the crop should be destroyed, it was known to have been harvested and sold on the open market. It was feared that the GM seeds had also been marketed in three other Indian states (*The Hindu*, 2001; *Times of India*, 2001). The cotton seed in the Gujarat case appears to have been obtained illegally by a seed firm. However, the fact that it was possible for the planting to go unnoticed for up to two seasons gives credence to the concerns of environmentalists, consumer groups and farmers, who fear that the whole apparatus of bio-safety regulation may be irrelevant if enforcement is practically impossible and GM 'contamination' becomes a widespread fact (Srinivas, 2002).

Civil regulation should be seen to be as much about contesting the rights and responsibilities of firms as it is about disciplining their activities through legal means. NGOs have succeeded in generating a climate of scepticism about the safety of GMOs. Through consumer boycotts, alliances with supermarkets willing to declare their foodstuffs GM-free, and media battles with biotech companies, they have succeeded in drawing companies into a public debate about the environmental and human safety of GMOs and their ability to address the food insecurity of the poor. This has created new demands of the companies and expectations regarding their conduct. Consequently, many of the companies find that even where they are in compliance with statutory bio-safety regulations, they cannot afford to ignore the extra-governmental demands being articulated by media-savvy and politically influential NGO groups. Levidow and Carr (2000: 261) show how 'Political protest has led to strategies of precautionary commercialisation' and prompted industry to devise voluntary guidelines to ensure segregation of GM crops and to limit the spread of GM herbicide-tolerance. The voluntary guidelines were developed by the Supply Chain Initiative for Modified Agricultural Crops, a group representing biotech companies, agricultural suppliers and farmers. Toft (2000: 227) also shows how in Denmark public concerns regarding risk, sustainability and ethics, concerns which 'lay beyond the regulatory expertise [of government]' encouraged industry to accept begrudgingly a voluntary agreement that only GM fodder beet would be grown on a large scale in Denmark in 1999.

The media have been a key battleground for the biotech debate, from Monsanto's full-page newspaper advertisements claiming to offer 'food, health and hope', to NGOs' success in stigmatizing 'Frankenstein foods' and 'terminator' seeds. The history of the terminator technology is a good illustration of the ways in which NGOs have succeeded in holding companies publicly to account for their actions where public regulation has failed to. 'Terminator' is the label originally used by activists at the Rural Advancement Foundation International (RAFI)[16] to describe a genetically engineered trait in which a plant is designed to produce sterile seeds. RAFI and other NGOs launched a high-profile international campaign challenging the morality of sterile-seed technology, focusing in particular on its likely impact on poor farmers who would normally save seed for replanting. The NGOs were able to stimulate a bruising public backlash against companies promoting this technology (Charles, 2001), but despite calls for public authorities to ban its use, governments did not act. Instead, various firms, including major players Monsanto, DuPont and Novartis,[17] publicly and unilaterally declared their intention not to commercialize terminator. They appeared to do so out of fear of the damaging public relations consequences of being associated with a technology that had been so roundly condemned.

Hence, while their behaviour was legitimate in a narrow legal and regulatory sense, company strategy was altered by public protest that was ignited and fanned by media-savvy NGOs. Indeed, from the quiet beginnings of biotechnology regulation, when the regulatory process was essentially an elite, technical and collaborative process that took place out of the public eye (Cantley, 1995), NGOs have succeeded in opening it up to the scrutiny of much wider publics. This informal regulation by civil society actors has served to articulate a set of social demands and create normative boundaries within which corporations are expected to act, providing an extra set of non-legal checks and balances on the activities of companies. In so far as firms internalize the expectations and anticipate the reactions of NGOs and consumers, then a degree of social control over the development of GM technologies can be said to have been exercised, that goes beyond the requirements of formal legal compliance. The examples above suggest that this is already occurring. However, as with civil regulation in general, it fails to meet the tests of predictability and enforceability, operating instead at the level of socially-constructed expectations which companies will find hard to anticipate and pre-empt (Newell, 2000).

In so far as micro-surveillance of GMO testing grounds and exposure of illegal growing by NGOs helps to compensate for the state's own lack of capacity to monitor the trade in and trials of GMOs, civil regulation may be said to lend support to the infrastructure of public governance. Where informal regulatory arenas are created through citizen juries and the like, the basis for new social contracts between firms and publics is created. In so far as firms change their behaviour in light of these encounters, a form of civil regulation has been constructed that extends control beyond what the public system provides.

CONCLUSION

This study of competing approaches to the regulation of the biotechnology sector suggests some important broader lessons for managing the impacts of global agribusiness on the environment. In an area of high technology, where elite expertise dominates and considerations of commercial confidentiality often make decision-making closed and unrepresentative, opening up the process to broader forms of social control represents a key challenge for civil society. Our discussion suggests that the key factor that drives actors to resort to tort litigation, public law challenges, strategies of civil regulation and even civil disobedience, is a disaffection with the prevailing modes by which environmental and social risks are identified and managed by states. This disaffection undermines the effectiveness and legitimacy of public regulation. It challenges not only the technical aspects of the process, such as the range of scientific tests and field trials employed to gauge crop and food safety; much more fundamentally, it also raises questions about who gets to make decisions about the future of agriculture, and the appropriate role of new technologies in addressing complex social problems that may not be amenable to technological fixes. As we saw above, strategies of civil regulation help to place questions of responsibility and liability, access and control and the power to determine levels of acceptable risk, at centre-stage.

Civil society demands for a more open and responsive regulatory process pose important questions about the way in which commercial interests and scientific experts are charged with the responsibility for tackling issues that are, in essence, moral and ethical (Levidow and Tait, 1995). Underpinning this concern is a breakdown of public trust in the ability of regulatory bodies to adjudicate on the merits of new technologies in the public interest, especially when the boundaries between the scientific community, industries and regulators appear porous at best. This challenge is clearly not exclusive to biotechnology, though in the case of agricultural biotechnology the potential for elite control of the debate about the technology and its implications for society is perhaps heightened.

To some degree, public regulation protects firms from the pressure of civil regulation, and certainly provides a more comfortable and predictable arena for companies to negotiate the terms of regulation because of the high levels of access and influence that firms enjoy. Nevertheless, broader public engagement appears both inevitable and desirable, even from the perspective of corporate strategy. Rather than pulling in different directions, civil and public regulation may interact in a mutually supportive way with each approach building on the limitations of the other. While civil regulation constructs new normative frameworks, generates fresh expectations and brings into the regulatory process a wider circle of stakeholders, it can never replace the authority, legitimacy and enforceability of public regulation. In many ways, the regulatory functions that we attribute to public and civil regulation aim to achieve different things. Some are clearly meant to encourage or deter particular types of investment, whereas others aim to manage the existing trade and development of GMOs in a balanced and responsible manner. Resort to litigation under civil law may seek only compensation for victims of harm. More broadly, civil litigation can be seen to fulfil an intermediate role between the public and private spheres that, when it functions well, can bolster the effectiveness of public regulation while simultaneously providing an avenue for the expression of particular civic interests or concerns.

The future regulation of biotechnology products is likely to be characterized by a complex and increasingly dense and interrelated set of competing pressures to bring the conduct of the biotech industry into conformity with a broad range of both social expectations and formal regulatory requirements. Firms that perceive themselves to be immune from various forms of civil regulation may find that their intransigence in the face of social pressure harms their public credibility and leads to calls for more stringent public regulation to discipline their conduct. Even where social expectations eventually translate into state-based regulation, it seems to be the case that pressures on companies to take on a broader range of ethical responsibilities will continue to outstrip those obligations enshrined in law. Hence, while civil regulation may have the effect of 'ratcheting up' public regulation, the process is an iterative one in which the boundaries of rights, duties and entitlements are always being contested in the courts, in the boardroom and in the media.

NOTES

The authors would like to thank Farhana Yamin, Ruth Mackenzie and the editors for their comments on earlier drafts of this paper.

1. *Bacillus thuringiensis*, shorthand for an insecticidal toxin.

2. Now part of Novartis.

3. The Miami Group is made up of the USA, Canada, Australia, Argentina, Uruguay and Chile.

4. Trade-Related Intellectual Property rights agreement.

5. Now part of Bayer.

6. See Gottweiss (1995) on the extensive efforts made by governments in Europe and the USA to promote biotechnology as a technology key to growth.

7. 'Biotechnology Clusters', report of a team led by Lord Sainsbury, Minister for Science, August 1999.

8. Later part of Aventis, itself now part of Bayer.

9. Interviews in India with AIBA and with industry representatives at ICCP-2, Nairobi.

10. Voluntary Code for the Release of Organisms into the Environment, 1991.

11. In the Biosafety Protocol, GMOs are known as 'Living Modified Organisms' or 'LMOs'.

12. See the exchange of views between Crompton and Wakeford (1998) and Miller and Huttner (1998).

13. 'Genetic drift' describes the contamination of one crop by seeds or pollen from another, related crop.

14. A class action is a lawsuit in which a number of plaintiffs sharing a common characteristic or with similar claims, are permitted by the courts to combine their legal challenges into a single case.

15. See Mandler and Eads (2000) for a discussion of possible defences.

16. Now the Action Group on Erosion, Technology and Concentration (ETC).

17. Now part of Syngenta.

REFERENCES

AgbioIndia (2002) 'Welcome to the Revolving Door'. <www.agbioindia.org> (15 July).

Agence France Presse (2002) 'Western Canada Organic Farmers Sue Monsanto, Aventis Over Modified Canola', <biotech_activists@iatp.org> (11 January).

AIBA Report (2000) *Biotechnology Parks*. Delhi: AIBA.

Aventis (2000) 'Aventis CropScience. Our position on … ' <www2.aventis.com/cropsc/position/position.htm>

Barrett, K. and E. Abergel (2000) 'Breeding Familiarity: Environmental Risk Assessment for Genetically Engineered Crops in Canada', *Science and Public Policy* 27 (1): 2–12.

Benbrook, C. (2001a) *When Does It Pay to Plant Bt Corn? Farm-Level Economic*

Impacts of Bt Corn, 1996–2001. Institute for Agriculture and Trade Policy and Genetically Engineered Food Alert. <www.gefoodalert.org/pages/home.cfm> (3 January).

— (2001b) 'Do GM Crops Mean Less Pesticides?' *Pesticide Outlook* 12 (5): 204–7, and at <www.mindfully.org/GE/GE3/Benbrook-Less-Pesticide.htm> (28 February 2002).

Bendell, J. (2000) 'Civil Regulation: A New Form of Democratic Governance for the Global Economy?', in J. Bendell (ed.), *Terms for Endearment: Business, NGOs and Sustainable Development*, pp. 239–66. Sheffield, UK: Greenleaf.

Black, J. (1998) 'Regulation as Facilitation: Negotiating the Genetic Revolution', *Modern Law Review* 61 (5): 621–60.

Brac de la Perrière, R. A. and F. Seuret (2000) *Brave New Seeds: The Threat of GM Crops to Farmers*. London: Zed Books.

Cantley, M. F. (1995) 'The Regulation of Modern Biotechnology: A Historical and European Perspective', in D. Brauer (ed.), *Volume 12: Legal, Economic and Ethical Dimensions*, of H.-J. Rehm and G. Reed with A. Pühler and P. Stadler (eds), *Biotechnology*. Weinheim: VCH.

Carr, S. and L. Levidow (2000) 'Exploring the Links Between Science, Risk, Uncertainty, and Ethics in Regulatory Controversies about Genetically Modified Crops', *Journal of Agricultural and Environmental Ethics* 12: 29–39.

CBD Secretariat (2000) *Cartagena Protocol on Biosafety to the Convention on Biological Diversity*. Montreal: Secretariat to the Convention on Biological Diversity.

— (2001) 'Report of the Intergovernmental Committee for the Cartagena Protocol on Biosafety on the Work of Its Second Meeting'. UNEP/CBD/ICCP/2/15. <www.biodiv.org/doc/meetings/iccp/iccp-02/official/iccp-02-15-en.pdf> (11 January 2002).

Center for Food Safety (1999) 'Greenpeace, Center for Food Safety and Organic Farmers Sue EPA over Gene-Altered Crops'. Press release (18 February). <www.centerforfoodsafety.org/li/BTpress.htm> (9 January 2002).

— (2002) 'About Us'. <http://centerforfoodsafety.org/au.html> (16 January).

Charles, D. (2001). *Lords of the Harvest. Biotech, Big Money, and the Future of Food*. Cambridge, MA: Perseus.

Chase, B. (1999) 'Gene-Altered Crops are Trouble in the Wind for Organic Foods' (11 August). <www.biotech-info.net/GE_crop_trouble.htm> (9 January 2002).

CorporateWatch (2000) *GE Briefing: Aventis*. <www.corporatewatch.org/publications/GEBriefings/aventis1.html> (13 October).

Crompton, T. and T. Wakeford (1998) 'Socio-Economics and the Protocol on Biosafety', *Nature Biotechnology* 16: 697–8.

Cropchoice.com (2001a) 'ND Farmer, Organic Certifier Calls for Farmers to Organize Against Monsanto over GM Crop Contamination'. Cropchoice guest opinion (8 October). <www.cropchoice.com> (3 January 2002).

— (2001b) 'Saskatchewan Organic Farmers Likely to Launch Lawsuit over Transgenic Contamination'. Cropchoice news (26 October). <www.cropchoice.com> (3 January 2002).

Dunlop, C. (2000) 'GMOs and Regulatory Styles', *Environmental Politics* 9 (2): 149–55.

Endres, A. B. (2000) ' "GMO": Genetically Modified Organism or Gigantic Monetary Obligation? The Liability Schemes for GMO Damage in the United States and the European Union', *Loyola of Los Angeles International and Comparative Law Review* 22: 453–505, fnn.

Ferrara, J. (1998) 'Revolving Doors: Monsanto and the Regulators', *The Ecologist* 28 (5) (September/October).

FET (Foundation on Economic Trends) (1999) 'Landmark Class-Action Antitrust Lawsuit Filed Against Monsanto'. Press release (14 December). <www.biotechcentury.org/monsantosuit.html> (9 January 2002).

Friends of the Earth UK (2001) 'GM Weeds Finally Destroyed'. Press release (7 December). <www.foe.co.uk/pubsinfo/infoteam/pressrel/2001/2001120715 20 37.html> (1 March 2002).

Gaia Trust (2000) 'NFU Mutual Won't Insure GM Crop Trial Risks'. Press release (10 March). <www.mindfully.org/GE/NFU-Mutual-Wont-Insure.htm> (27 February 2002).

Goldsmith, Z. (1998) 'Who Are the Real Terrorists?', *The Ecologist* 28 (5): 312–17.

Gottweis, H. (1995) *Governing Molecules: The Discursive Politics of Genetic Engineering in Europe and the United States.* Cambridge, MA: MIT Press.

Greenpeace UK (2002) 'The Greenpeace 28 Go on Trial in Norfolk on April 3rd 2000'. <www.greenpeace.org.uk> (16 January).

Hindu, The (2001) 'India: NGO Moves', *The Hindu* (23 November). <(biotech_activists@iatp.org> (24 November).

Jasanoff, S. (1995) 'Product, Process or Programme: Three Cultures and the Regulation of Biotechnology', in M. Bauer (ed.), *Resistance to New Technology*, pp. 311–31. Cambridge: Cambridge University Press/National Museum of Science and Industry.

Kingsnorth, P. (1999) 'India Cheers While Monsanto Burns', *The Ecologist* 29 (1): 9–10.

Knight, D. (2000) 'Who's Liable for Damages from GMO Crops?'. Inter Press Service/South-North Development Monitor (SUNS) (25 February). <www.t wnside.org.sg/title/liable.htm> (9 January 2002).

Kossick, D. (2002) 'Organic Farmers Sue Monsanto and Aventis'. <biotech_activists@iatp.org> (12 January).

Lee, K., D. Humphreys and M. Pugh (1997) 'Privatisation in the United Nations System: Patterns of Influence in Three Intergovernmental Organisations', *Global Society* 11 (3): 339–59.

Levidow, L. and S. Carr (2000) 'UK: Precautionary Commercialisation?' *Journal of Risk Research* 3 (3): 261–71.

Levidow, L. and J. Tait (1995) 'The Greening of Biotechnology: GMOs as Environment-Friendly Products', in I. Moser and V. Shiva (eds), *Biopolitics: A Feminist and Ecological Reader on Biotechnology*, pp. 121–39. London: Zed Books.

Levidow, L., S. Carr, R. Von Schomberg and D. Wield (1996) 'Regulating Biotechnology in Europe: Harmonisation Difficulties, Opportunities and Dilemmas', *Science and Public Policy* 23 (3): 135–57.

Levy, D. L. and P. Newell (2000) 'Oceans Apart? Business Responses to Global Environmental Issues in Europe and the United States', *Environment* 42 (9): 8–20.

Mandler, J. P. and K. R. Eads (2000) 'Liability Exposure to Seed Companies from Adventitious GMO Pollination Due to Pollen Drift Resulting in Cross Pollination or Outcrossing'. Legal assessment (26 January). Minneapolis, Desmoines and Denver: Faegre and Benson LLP. <http://www.faegre.com/downloads/gmo.doc> (19 December 2001).

MASIPAG (2001) '800 Protesters Uproot Bt corn in Mindanao', *Masipag News & Views* (29 August). <www.poptel.org.uk/panap/latest/masiroot.htm> (3 January 2002).

Meridian Institute (2001) 'Liability and Redress under the Cartagena Protocol on Biosafety'. Detailed summary from a dialogue workshop, 11–13 September 2001. <http://madison.merid.org/meridian/home.nsf/projectareaall/32366 1010C53EEE285256ACD00476B69> (11 January 2002).

Miller, H. I. (1999). 'The Real Curse of Frankenfood', *Nature Biotechnology* 17 (2): 113.

Miller, H. I. and S. L. Huttner (1998) 'A Baroque Solution to a Nonproblem', *Nature Biotechnology* 16: 698–9.

Minnesota Planning (2001) 'Are Farmers or Biotech Seed Companies Liable for "Genetic Drift"?', Minnesota IssueWatch agriculture briefing, June. <www.mnplan.state.mn.us/issues/scan.htm?Id=736> (28 February 2002).

Moeller, D. R. (2001) 'GMO Liability Threats for Farmers', Institute for Agriculture and Trade Policy and Genetically Engineered Food Alert. <www.gefoodalert.org/pages/home.cfm> (3 January 2002).

National Academy of Sciences (NAS) (US) (2002) *Environmental Effects of Transgenic Plants: The Scope and Adequacy of Regulation*. Washington, DC: National Academy Press.

Newell, P. (2000) 'Environmental NGOs and Globalization', in R. Cohen and S. Rai (eds), *Global Social Movements*, pp. 117–34. New Jersey: Athlone Press.

—— (2001a) 'Managing Multinationals: The Governance of Investment for the Environment', *Journal of International Development* 13 (7): 907–19.

—— (2001b) 'Biotechnology for the Poor?' *Science as Culture* 10 (2): 249–54.

—— (2002) *Biotechnology and the Politics of Regulation*. IDS Working Paper 146, Brighton: IDS. <www.ids.ac.uk/ids/env/biotechpubs.html>

Newell, P. and R. Mackenzie (2000) 'The Cartagena Protocol on Biosafety: Legal and Political Dimensions', *Global Environmental Change* 10: 313–17.

OECD (1992) *Safety Considerations for Biotechnology*. Paris: OECD.

Pimbert, M., T. Wakeford and P. V. Satheesh (2001) 'Citizens' Juries on GMOs and Farming Futures in India', *LEISA (Low External Input and Sustainable Agriculture)* 17 (4): 27–30.

Repp, R. A. (2000) 'Comment: Biotech Pollution: Assessing Liability for Genetically Modified Crop Production and Genetic Drift', *Idaho Law Review* 36: 585–620, fnn.

Robson, S. (2002) 'Raid Ruins Research Lab Crops'. <(biotech_activists@iatp. org> (14 January).

Sell, S. K. (1999) 'Multinational Corporations as Agents of Change: The Globalization of Intellectual Property Rights', in C. Cutler, V. Haufler and T. Porter (eds), *Private Authority and International Affairs*, pp. 169–97. Albany: State University of New York Press.

Shadid, A. (2001) 'Blown Profits. Genetic Drift Affects More than Biology – US Farmers Stand to Lose Millions', *Boston Globe* (8 April): G1. <www.biotech-info.net/blown2.htm> (19 December).

Srinivas, R. (2002) 'Bt Cotton in India: Economic Factors Versus Environmental Concerns', *Environmental Politics* 11 (2): 154–8.

Stabinsky, D. (2000) 'Bringing Social Analysis into a Multilateral Environmental Agreement: Social Impact Assessment and the Biosafety Protocol', *Journal of Environment and Development* 9 (3): 260–83.

Times of India (2001) 'Bt Cotton Seed Sellers Face Arrest', *Times of India* (23 November). <biotech_activists@iatp.org> (24 November).

Toft, J. (2000) 'Denmark: Potential Polarisation or Consensus?' *Journal of Risk Research* 3 (3): 227–37.

Villar, J. L. (2001) *GMO Contamination Around the World*, Amsterdam: Friends of the Earth International.

Wilde, M. L. (1998). 'The Law of Tort and the "Precautionary Principle": Civil Liability Issues Arising from Trial Plantings of Genetically Modified (GM) Crops', *Environmental Liability* 6: 163–75.

WWF International (2001) 'The Cartagena Protocol on Biosafety: Implementation Now!' Position document for the Second Meeting of the Intergovernmental Committee for the Cartagena Protocol on Biosafety (ICCP-2) Nairobi, Kenya, 1–5 October 2001.

TEN | Social struggles and the regulation of transgenic crops in Brazil

VICTOR PELAEZ AND WILSON SCHMIDT

§ The rapid and wide adoption of new transgenic, herbicide-resistant, soybean varieties in the USA, Canada and Argentina since the late 1990s illustrates the potential market for genetically modified crops. However, in Brazil, the second largest exporter of soy, the introduction of transgenic crops has been hampered by fierce social resistance and regulatory hurdles, despite the high expectations of medium and large soy producers in southern Brazil and Federal Government support for the diffusion of GM technologies.[1] The resistance to genetically modified organisms (GMOs) was particularly echoed in the decision of the government of the state of Rio Grande do Sul to place a state-wide ban on GMO farming. The decree suspending the federal government's approval of the commercialization of Roundup Ready soybeans in 1998 bore witness to the strong social resistance of environmental, consumer and small-farmer organizations.

This chapter discusses how a leading agribusiness company, Monsanto, was confronted by social and political reluctance to accept a new technology. The next section describes Monsanto's strategy for dealing with the politics and regulation of technology in general terms. This is followed by a sketch of the Brazilian agricultural economy, which would seem to be favourable to Monsanto's expansion strategy. Then we address the key issue in this chapter: why genetically modified crops have been banned in Rio Grande do Sul when so many powerful groups in Brazil were in favour of them. To understand the resistance to the genetically modified soybean in Brazil, we have to examine the contested views on agricultural development and the history of social struggles in agriculture. The next section shows that the resistance to GM crops is intertwined with a long-standing struggle for autonomous farmers' communities, which, among others, resulted in alternative views on the selection and appropriation of technology. We then address the political debates and social struggles around the introduction of Monsanto's Roundup Ready (RR) soybeans, focusing on two instructive events: (i) the transformation of the state Rio Grande do Sul into a transgenic-free territory, and (ii) the political struggles around the commercialization of RR soybeans between the federal government and Monsanto on one side and civil society organizations and government agencies on the other.

MONSANTO AND THE MAKING OF REGULATORY FRAMEWORKS

Innovation in Monsanto is tied up with the history of its interactions with the regulatory environment. The role of the lawyer Robert Shapiro has been crucial in linking Monsanto's strategies to the federal government and the regulatory bodies of the USA. In 1984 Monsanto purchased the pharmaceutical company Searle, where Shapiro started his career as an executive, developing the successful marketing of aspartame. It took ten years to get aspartame approved by the US Food and Drug Administration (FDA), a period marked by intense controversies about the toxicity levels of the new artificial sweetener. Searle went through a credibility crisis when the FDA cast doubts upon the company's test results of its medicines such as Flagyl, Aldactone and Aldactazine. The FDA went so far as to set up a special commission in July 1975 to check the validity of the toxic studies of seven products filed by Searle for evaluation, aspartame being one of them. To cope with regulatory demands, in June 1977 Searle appointed Donald Rumsfeld as president because of his wide-ranging experience in the public sector: he had been Congress member for Illinois and held important posts under Nixon and Ford as the director of the Office of Economic Opportunity, director of the Cost of Living Council, NATO ambassador, White House Chief of Staff and Secretary of Defense (*Fortune*, 1979).[2] In October 1977, Robson was hired as vice president to organize the registration of pharmaceutical products. Like Rumsfeld, John Robson had solid experience in the public sector as a legal adviser at the White House. Two years later, in 1979, a third lawyer, Robert Shapiro, who had worked on governmental consulting committees in legislation concerning anti-trust cases, was taken on as VP of one of Searle's branch offices (McCann, 1990: 39–40). After Monsanto bought Searle, the department responsible for the development and marketing of aspartame (Nutrasweet) became an independent division of Monsanto under Robert Shapiro.

With the development of such derivatives of genetic engineering as the cattle growth hormone and herbicide-resistant soy (Roundup) in

TABLE 10.1 Mobility of scientists and executives between regulating bodies and biotechnology corporations in the USA

Linda J. Fisher	Former administrative assistant of the EPA, now vice president of public and governmental business for Monsanto
Michael Friedman	Former member of the FDA Commission, now vice president of clinical affairs at Searle, pharmaceutical division of Monsanto
Marcia Hale	Former assistant to President of USA and director of inter-government affairs, now director of international government affairs at Monsanto
Mickey Kantor	Former secretary of US commerce and former US commerce representative, now member of the board at Monsanto
William Ruckelshaus	Former EPA administrative director, now member of the board at Monsanto
Lidia Watrud	Former researcher at Monsanto, now at the environmental laboratory of the EPA
L. Val Gidddings	Former biotech controller and biological safety negotiator at the USDA (United States Department of Agriculture), now vice president of the Bio-tech Industrial Organization (BIO)

Source: Edmonds Institute <www.edmonds-institute.org/olddoor.html>

the early 1980s, Monsanto began a long-term project towards building a favourable policy environment for biotechnological products. The first strategy consisted of lobbying the federal government, seeking on the one hand to gain the political support of both Republicans and Democrats, while on the other hand involving the official regulatory bodies, the Environmental Protection Agency (EPA) and the FDA. The second strategy was based on winning over possible opponents of genetic modification, for example by hiring them as consultants (Eichenwald, 2001). It also included advertising directed at consumers and financing university research as a means to guarantee the approval and legitimacy of the scientific community (Bloomberg News, 1999).

In the early 1990s, Shapiro, then director of the Agricultural Division, took over the presidency of Monsanto. He adopted a new strategy based on a more direct and incisive policy of lobbying the federal government rather than a more articulate long-term plan of winning over public opinion. This short-term strategy was successful in getting fast approval for transgenic products and guaranteeing rapid expansion in the USA. However, there was general rejection in the large consumer markets of Europe and Japan. The scientific community voiced considerable concerns about the lack of tests that demonstrated the health and biosafety of the products. Will Carpenter, former director of the company's biotechnology group, considered Shapiro's new strategy to be an act of arrogance and incompetence. Later, at a conference organized by Greenpeace in the USA in 2000, Shapiro himself would admit that his strategy was marked by overconfidence and arrogance (Eichenwald, 2001).

Independent scientists and an FDA employee protested against the irregularities in the registration procedure of the cattle growth hormone produced by Monsanto (Ferrara, 1999). Ferrara observed incompetence on the part of FDA experts as well as favouritism towards Monsanto. Such favouritism could be associated, among other things, with the so-called 'revolving-door' between biotech companies and regulating bodies in the USA, through which scientists and executives of the respective institutions commute and which reduces control on the part of public departments (see Table 10.1).

Monsanto's ability to influence regulation relied on accumulated experience acquired from the outset and turned into organizational structures and procedures:

> Our regulatory organization is comprised of over 300 scientists and regulatory affairs experts located throughout the world to support our agricultural chemical biotechnology, seed and animal health products. We employ premier scientists in several disciplines, including environmental sciences, product safety assessment, ecology, product characterization and statistics, to ensure that the safety data supporting our products meets the highest standard ... Our success in obtaining regulatory approvals for biotechnology-derived products has been clearly demonstrated. In the United States, we have obtained from the USDA more of the approvals that are necessary to permit the commercialization of our products since 1998 than all of our competitors combined ... We are actively involved in international regulatory organizations that promote the need for harmonized data requirements and the use of science-based, risk-based assessments in the regulatory decision-making process. (Monsanto, 2000: 77)

Initially GMO regulation and Monsanto's role created little controversy in the USA. This certainly contributed to the rapid acceptance of genetically modified organisms both by farmers and North American consumers. Monsanto was resolutely committed to becoming one of the world's leaders in transgenic seed production, assuming that GMOs would be rapidly disseminated on the world market. But the question soon emerged whether the company was able to transfer this combined strategy of expansion and setting the regulatory agenda to a different context.

Expansion of markets

The first significant sowing of GM crops took place in 1996, initially almost exclusively in the USA. Since then, the area planted with transgenic seed worldwide has grown rapidly, reaching 41.5 million ha by 1999 (53 per cent with soy, 27 per cent maize, 9 per cent cotton, 8 per cent rape-seed, 7 per cent tobacco). GMOs also spread quickly in Argentina: in relative terms, the expansion of soybean cultivation outstripped even the growth in the USA between 1996 and 1999. In 1999, 5.5 million ha, that is 75 per cent of the total Argentinian soybean area, were planted with GMOs (European Commission, 2001). After the introduction of RR soybean in 1996, a 'new technological paradigm composed by no-tillage systems and transgenic varieties' emerged (Craviotti, 2000). Reduced tillage and no tillage became feasible since weeds, resulting from not ploughing the soil, an increased use of fertilizers and the introduction of irrigation, could now be controlled with an increased use of herbicides. Another important aspect of the Argentinian case is that environmental and consumer pressure groups had little or no voice; the economic situation effectively put an end to the momentum of environmental or socio-economic questioning of policy (Ferrazino et al., 2000). Transgenic soybeans were seen as the response to a slump in Argentinian agricultural and livestock exports. In Brazil, however, the expansion of the RR soybean was far from successful in comparison to the Argentinian case.

CONDITIONS FOR THE INTRODUCTION OF TRANSGENIC CROPS IN BRAZIL

'The last (big) domino' in the soybean market

As in Argentina, the prospects of increased profits through GMOs attracted the interest of a section of the Brazilian farming community who, in general, found themselves in a precarious financial situation due to a drastic reduction of credits. The federal government, proponents of a free-market economic policy, the reduction of subsidies and the elimination of protectionist barriers, viewed the possibility of

Brazilian agriculture's increased competitiveness through the growth of transgenic crops as a welcome opportunity to intensify international competitiveness. A significant percentage of the large Brazilian farmers supports the quick authorization of GMOs, arguing that this would increase their competitiveness.

Brazil, the world's seventh largest exporter of agricultural products, is the second largest soybean exporter with Asia and Europe as its main markets (FAO, 2001). Soybeans account for 7.5 per cent of the country's exports. In 2000–01, Brazil was resonsible for about 20 per cent of the world's soybean production, assuming second place in the world, and for more than 26 per cent of soybean grain exports worldwide.[3] Production is still growing and, according to the United States Department of Agriculture, Brazil has sufficient land resources to expand its soybean area and production to challenge the USA as the largest soybean producer (USDA, 2001a).[4]

Together, the United States, Brazil and Argentina account for about 90 per cent of soybean exports. Bulk shipments from the United States and Argentina are predominantly GMO, while Brazil is the primary source for non-biotech soybeans and soybean meal. This makes the Brazilian position towards the commercial plantation of GMOs a highly strategic marketing issue. As Barboza (2001) emphasizes, 'if Brazil legalizes biotech production, Europe and Asia – the world's two biggest purchasers of soy – would have almost nowhere to turn for adequate supplies of non-biotech soybeans'. Barboza quotes Bob Callanan, a spokesman for the American Soybean Association, a trade group that supports the use of gene-altered crops, who said a propos of Brazil legalizing the planting of GMOs: 'We are very hopeful that last domino will fall.' Furthermore, he believes that environmentalists, who appear to be the main opponents of GMOs, also take this strategic advantage into account: 'that's why the environmentalists are putting up a stink down there in Brazil. They know if that goes, it's all gone' (Barboza, 2001).

From 2000 to April 2001 demand for certified biotech-free soybean meal grew from near zero to 20 to 25 per cent of the EU market. This growth in demand is pushed by the retail food sector, driven by consumer demand for products based on non-biotech ingredients along with pressure from environmental organizations (USDA, 2001b). Nearly 50 per cent of the soybean meal consumed in the EU is currently obtained from regions where the planting of Roundup Ready soybeans is prohibited. Much (44 per cent) of this is supplied by Brazil. Continued growth in demand for non-biotech soybean meal could eventually have a negative impact on US soybean sales to the EU (USDA, 2001b).

Changes in the Brazilian seed market

Like elsewhere, the prospect of making profits with transgenic seeds led to mergers, purchases and joint ventures in the Brazilian seed market in the mid-1990s (Wilkinson and Castelli, 2000). Monsanto followed this strategy internationally to become the second biggest seed company in the world and the biggest foreign seed company in Brazil, controlling 60 per cent of the national market of maize seed and 18 per cent of soybeans. The lower percentage for soybeans was related to the fact that farmers themselves can produce soybean seed. Furthermore, the state agency EMBRAPA (the Brazilian Agricultural Research Corporation) controlled 60 per cent of the national production of soybean seed. Recently, private companies have succeeded in enlarging control over the soybean seed market. Restricted by lack of funds for research, EMBRAPA started partnerships with foreign companies, particularly Monsanto, to develop new varieties of Roundup Ready soybean better adapted to climate and soil conditions in Brazil (Paula, 2000). By controlling the production of the bestselling herbicide in the country (Roundup) and a large percentage of the Brazilian seed market, Monsanto became one of the largest suppliers of agricultural inputs. Pesticide use (including herbicides) in soybean cultivation, the second crop in terms of pesticide consumption in Brazil, contributes to the fact that Brazil is the fifth largest market in the world for agrochemical products (Campanhola et al., 1998).

The regulation of genetically modified organisms in Brazil

Compared to other Latin American countries, Brazil was relatively early in developing regulations on two major GMO issues: intellectual property rights and bio-safety. In 1997, the Cultivation Law (*Ley de Cultivares*)[5] guaranteed intellectual property rights on plant varieties and made patenting of transgenic varieties possible, thus making it more interesting for companies to gain more control of the Brazilian seed market (Wilkinson and Castelli, 2000).

The Cultivation Law followed the Bio-safety Law, adopted in 1995, which regulates the inspection of institutions and activities dealing with the manipulation of genetic material in order to establish safety rules protecting people and plant life as well as the environment. This law also created the National Technical Biosafety Commission (CTNBio), linked to the executive secretary office of the Ministry of Science and Technology, and defined the jurisdiction and composition of the Commission.[6] The Commission is responsible for the National Policy of Bio-safety, for reviewing technical reports before releasing any GMO into the environment, and for preparing technical reports about the registration and handling of products containing GMOs for the designated authorities. Environmental impact studies might be requested by the Commission, but are not a prerequisite for the registration of GMOs (Araújo and Mercadante, 1999). This would lead to a juridical polemic about the Commission and its positions (see below).

The composition of the Commission (CTNBio) shows the power of the Minister of Science and Technology, who nominates its eighteen members: eight technical and scientific specialists, eight representatives of the ministries (Science and Technology, Health, Environment, Foreign Relations, Agriculture [animal and plant sectors], and Labour and Health); one representative of the private biotechnology sector; and one representative of the Institute for Consumer Defence. Araújo and Mercadante (1999) comment that the minister's power is almost absolute, as long as the criteria of specialist knowledge for the selection and nomination of the scientists are extremely subjective.

The soliciting company is responsible for demonstrating to CTNBio the bio-safety of genetically modified organisms. In July 2001, a new labelling regulation was issued, requiring a specification on the label when a product contains more than 4 per cent transgenic material (either by weight or volume).

ALTERNATIVE PERSPECTIVES ON DEVELOPMENT AND
TECHNOLOGY

GMOs were first introduced in Brazil in June 1998, after CTNBio approved the marketing of Roundup Ready soybeans at the request of Monsanto. In the same period, the consumer organization IDEC (the Institute for Consumer Defence) and environmental groups related to Greenpeace presented a petition to ban transgenic soybeans to the Federal Court. In September 1998, the Court decided in favour of the suspension of the cultivation of RR soybeans until an environmental impact study had been conducted and labelling rules had been issued.

It would be wrong to conclude, from the lawsuits brought by IDEC and Greenpeace, that resistance to GMOs in Brazil is recent and mainly fomented by urban organizations of consumers and environmentalists. Instead, we argue that this resistance is a direct outcome of a movement that challenged the Green Revolution model of agricultural modernization at the end of the 1970s. This section intends to recover the main elements of the history of this movement, its concepts and its importance to the Brazilian institutional-political debate as counterweight to corporate appropriation of seed. This movement was active on two fronts: the establishment of a network of non-governmental organizations with the objective of recovering farmers' autonomy in the production of seeds; and the struggle against industrial property laws which permitted the patenting of life forms.

Farmers' autonomy and alternative technology programmes

In the mid-1970s, various associations and non-governmental farmers' support organizations developed the idea of preserving the social and productive category of 'family farming' and wanted to strengthen the economic capacity and practice of an 'alternative agriculture' (Almeida, 1999; Brandenburg, 1999). Important was the anti-establishment action of a group within the Association of Agronomists in the state of São Paulo in 1977 (Ehlers, 1996). This group provoked a debate that would influence an entire generation of students and agronomists and which was brought to national attention by the *Journal of Agronomists*. Further critical discussions concerning the agricultural model introduced by international agribusiness took place in the 1980s at the Brazilian Encounters for an Alternative Agriculture (EBAA: I–1981; II–1984; III–1987; IV–1988). These were organized by the Brazilian Federation of Agronomists (FAEAB) and by certain non-governmental organization (NGOs), notably the Alternative Technologies Project (PTA). Central to these debates was the dependency of farmers on inputs produced by industry, particularly seeds. John Wilkinson underlined this during the EBAA conference in the following terms:

> If we think about the input industry, we must not limit the analysis to questions of the use of plant protection products and herbicides. Why do we see an increase in needs? Because the industry is progressively appropriating the raw agricultural material, i.e. seeds. The great challenge that we must meet is the appropriation of the whole circuit of agricultural production through the control of the seed industry by the multinationals. (EBAA, 1984: 75–6)

Wilkinson considers that the elaboration of an alternative agricultural policy must take into account specific legislation to prevent the monopolization of seed production and the research related to it. Wilkinson warns, in fact, against the technical and scientific capacity of the multinationals in agricultural biotechnology. Three years later, in the III EBAA of 1987, Pat Roy Mooney's conference was well attended. He had just published the Brazilian edition of his book *Seeds of the Earth – a Private or Public Resource?*, written in 1979, in which he expressed his concerns about the growth of the seed industry and the development of varieties that resist agrochemical products (EBAA, 1987: 202).

Both scholars influenced a considerable number of agronomy students, technicians and Brazilian agronomists, some of whom would later form, or reinforce, the extensive network of agro-environmental NGOs in the south of Brazil (Rede TA/Sul, 1997) and connect technical support with political militancy (Almeida, 1999).[7] They developed influential positions in the debates on the course of agrarian change in the three states in the south of Brazil. Criticism of the growing power of the major agro-supply industries in the 1980s strengthened the non-governmental organizations committed to the movement for family farming in Brazil (Byé and Schmidt, 2001).

After generating criticism of 'industrial' agricultural practices, these associations and NGOs turned to developing alternative propositions, i.e. alternatives to the technological package offered by the major agro-supply industries. The idea took root that the movement of alternative agriculture should not limit itself to criticizing the Brazilian model of agricultural modernization that excluded small farmers, but should move to a phase of 'propositions'. These propositions had as a general denominator the insertion of small-scale agriculture into the economy and the development of agro-ecology through the implementation of local projects (Brandenburg, 1999; Von der Weid, 1994). The propositions took small family agriculture as a model of cultural and social organization that had to be associated with techniques of minimal use of agro-industrial inputs. To increase the independence of the small farmer in relation to the big agro-business companies, the aim was to create market niches suited to the real production capacities of those farmers. The focus was on a variety of products which embody the value of pesticide-free, regional, family production.[8]

Since 1990, NGOs active in the south and south-east of the country – regions with an intense process of agricultural modernization – have defined a common work strategy in the PTA network. A principal element was the development of endogenous plant varieties and the participation of small farmers in the preservation and development of knowledge related to plant improvement. This would help to limit the dependency of farmers on external seed supply (Cordeiro and de Mello, 1994). The first results came out of work on maize. Maize is one of the main Brazilian crops and is cultivated on the majority of small farms. Important work was carried out on the conservation of local varieties and seed improvement, and a network for knowledge exchange was created among family farms and NGO research centres. This 'maize network' was extended to other crops including beans and soybeans.

The NGOs of Rio Grande do Sul are well known for their effectiveness, notably through their support of Centres for Small Farmers (CAPA) and the Centre for Popular Alternative Technologies (CETAP). The emergence of these movements aiming at the reinforcement of small farmers' autonomy improved the bargaining power of social organizations in the rural sector and provided the necessary legitimization for NGOs to represent the political interests of the rural sector in congressional disputes. The struggle around, and the NGO involvement in, the elaboration of the Patent Law and Plant Variety Protection Bill, presented below, exemplifies this.

Patent law and the Plant Variety Protection Bill[9]

Three laws regulate the intellectual property rights of plants in Brazil. The Industrial Property Code approved by Congress in 1971 excluded chemicals, metal alloys, food and pharmaceutical products and processes from patenting. The Paris Convention – the only international agreement for patents operating at the time – allowed such exceptions aimed at promoting national technological development in developing countries. The 1971 law made no provision regarding biotechnology or living organisms. The federal government patent office – the National Industry Property Institute (INPI) – did not approve any of the patent requests filed in this area.

In 1989 the United States announced economic retaliation against Brazil because of the absence of patent protection for pharmaceuticals, thus defending the interests of US companies expanding in developing countries whose legislation on intellectual property rights was labelled as 'rudimentary'. In January 1990, the recent elected government of President Fernando Collor had the US retaliations suspended after promising to draft a new patent bill. It was sent in April 1991 to the National Congress as the Industrial Property Law (IPL). The first critical reactions came from Brazilian-owned pharmaceutical companies and trade unions in the health sector. A few months later, organizations concerned about the possible negative social and ethical impacts of patents on seeds joined the opposition to this bill: agro-ecology and environmental NGOs, as well as the Catholic Bishops Conference.

A special commission created to report on this bill to the plenary of the Congress held public hearings in November and December 1991. Instead of including the views of the opposition, the Commission's rapporteur modified the original draft of the bill essentially to include further US demands. The new administration of Itamar Franco presented a compromise draft almost entirely satisfactory to US demands, which was approved by the Congress on 2 June 1993. However, once discussed in the Senate the bill again inspired heated debates. On the one hand, Brazilian biochemical companies, while pushing for approval of the bill, demanded even more extensive rights and fewer restrictions on their patents. On the other hand, a majority of Senators did pay attention to arguments presented by social movements. They were tired of being labelled either as 'outdated nationalists' or people willing to 'sell out the country' and appreciated the chance to seek a pragmatic 'middle ground'. A negotiation process took place in the Constitution and Justice Commission of the Senate with the active participation of the Forum for the Free Use of Knowledge (Forum pela Liberdade do Uso do Conhecimento). This umbrella organization, joined by more than a thousand organizations from civil society, including unions, professional organizations, churches, scientific societies, NGOs and the national pharmaceutical industry, co-ordinated the lobbying efforts. Their campaign centred on no patent on life, but also voiced strong concerns about pharmaceuticals and the 'pipeline' for stronger compulsory licensing provisions. It also advocated shorter patent terms and a longer transition period before the law would come into force. In the end, however, US political pressures and the government's 'steam roller' tactics ensured approval in the final vote on the Senate floor. After it passed in Congress, the final version was signed into law on 14 May 1996.[10]

The third bill regulating intellectual property rights resulted from the existing Industrial Property Law which announced the creation of an Intellectual Property Law specific to the plant varieties. In June 1991, the Ministry of Agriculture created a working group in EMBRAPA, which drafted a Plant Variety Protection (PVP) bill adapted to the terms of the UPOV-1978 Convention (UPOV – International Union for the Protection of New Varieties of Plants). However, another working group with representatives from the Ministry of Agriculture, other ministries and the seed industry met intermittently in the following years. The bill (the Cultivation Law) it finally presented to Congress in January 1996 was fully compatible with the much more demanding UPOV-1991.[11]

During the elaboration and parliamentary discussions of the new Cultivation Law, big seed companies, both national and foreign, lobbied intensively among the members of Congress and the Executive Power (Hathaway, 1997). Opposition to the bill was led by one congress member and the Advisory to Project on Alternative Agriculture (AS-

PTA). This NGO working with small producers considered the law to be harmful to national interests and family farming. Amendments resulting from the AS-PTA opposition finally led to changes in the law (Araújo, 1998). The major advance in Brazil's PVP Law compared with laws in other countries, is Article 2 which explicitly incorporates the UPOV-1978 prohibition of double protection of plants by both PVP and patents. In addition, the 'farmer's privilege' to save seeds from his own crop is extended from an individual right (as in UPOV-1978) to small farmers' associations. They also may reproduce and share (but not sell) seeds from protected varieties.

While contesting the various bills, the action range of NGOs and NGO networks supporting small family farming has thus extended beyond the rural community. The experience of these NGOs in the political areas of decision-making in the National Congress provided important lessons for mobilization against the approval of introducing transgenic seeds in Brazil and deepened the sustained conflict around the introduction of GM technology. The two most conflicting cases are analysed below: the case of Rio Grande do Sul, whose government tried to transform the state into a transgenic-free territory, and the political struggles about the approval of transgenic soybeans between the federal government and Monsanto on the one hand and civil society organizations and the Republic Attorney's Office on the other hand.

THE DEVELOPMENT OF THE CONTROVERSIES

Problems of restrictive regulation: farmers' autonomy and corporate evasion

The left-wing Workers' Party (PT) came into office in the state of Rio Grande do Sul after the 1998 elections and, simultaneously, increased its number of representatives in the Legislative Assembly. Technicians linked to the NGOs working for family farming became part of the government, assumed posts as parliamentary advisers or were given other key positions in public agencies in the fields of agriculture and rural development.

In March 1999, a few months after its installation, the new government explicitly supported a legislative initiative of Elvino Grass of the Workers' Party to transform Rio Grande do Sul into a 'state free of transgenic products'. The State Secretary Office of Agriculture supported this ban on transgenic crops in order to safeguard public health as well as to strengthen soybean exports to the European market (Araújo, 2001). The economic argument underlying this ban viewed that the rejection of GMOs by European consumers would create new export opportunities for producers from Rio Grande do Sul. Several major agro-industrial groups were interested in gaining back a market share that had been lost to producers in central and west Brazil, covering two-thirds of the national soybean production.

From 1999, seminars to debate the GMO issue were held all over the state with participation from, among others, the Movement of the Rural Landless Workers (MST), and the Agricultural Federation of Rio Grande do Sul (FARSUL) – a rural organization of employers, NGOs active in rural development and environmental movements (Menasche, 2000). Moreover, the government of Rio Grande do Sul launched an important media campaign with the slogan: 'Transgenics: don't plant this idea!' When the campaign was launched, the Secretary of Agriculture of Rio Grande do Sul clearly defined the official position of the state government, reaffirming their opposition to the Federal Government by stating: 'the farmers cannot be slaves to the purchase of seeds from one single multinational' (*Jornal do Brasil*, 1999). Based on the initiative of Rio Grande do Sul, various proposals for similar laws appeared in other Brazilian states.

From the start, Monsanto responded strongly to the development in Rio Grande do Sul. In a first attempt to disqualify and isolate this kind of regulation of transgenic crops, Monsanto's director of regulatory affairs, Luiz Abramides do Val, declared in the newspaper *Folha de São Paulo* (9 March 1999): 'This is an ideological measure. The government of Rio Grande do Sul is left-wing and is linked to non-governmental organizations which associate biotechnology with the power of large multinational companies.' The federal government supported Monsanto. The fact that a left-wing party was governing Rio Grande do Sul, in public opposition to the federal government, has been of great importance. In the past, the post of Minister of Agriculture had mostly been occupied by politicians from a right-wing party (Brazilian Progressive Party – PPB).

The ban on growing transgenics in Rio Grande do Sul triggered disputes between the government inspectors, trying to prevent the cultivation of RR soybeans, and those producers in favour of transgenics. This opened up a third battlefield, besides the struggles about law-making and the ideological struggles within the state and with Monsanto. On 13 May 1999, the federal police seized illegal transgenic seeds. Rumours circulated that many producers were growing soya from Monsanto and its subsidiary Monsoy with seeds smuggled from Argentina through Paraguay. Several reports on the Internet mentioned the persistent presence of Monsoy technicians marketing RR soybeans to farmers (Giuliani, 2000). The precise involvement of Monsanto in illegal planting, however, remains unclear. What is a fact is that transgenic soybeans are illegally planted in Rio Grande do Sul and cause severe problems of governance. Reports from Monsanto and the Brazilian Association of Seed Producers (ABRASEM) stated that the amount of transgenic soybeans would correspond to one-third of the planted area in 1999. The country would harvest 1 million tons of GM soybeans from an area of 2 million ha in the state in the following year (Menasche, 2000; *Zero Hora*, 1999b, 2001; *Valor Econômico*, 2001a). The Association of Producers and Seed Traders of Rio Grande do Sul (APASSUL) estimated the cultivation of transgenic soy on 1.4 million ha. People opposing transgenics consider these data to be exaggerated. In the media, Monsanto tried to remove all suspicion, suggesting that the large scale of illegal planting was the choice of farmers. However, by referring at the same time to the magnitude of the planted area, they tried to present the public with a fait accompli (Araújo, 2001).

Concerning the smuggled material, the government of Rio Grande do Sul took measures to prevent its dissemination among farmers, by means of fiscal action, police repression and legal action against the farmers implicated. These measures resulted in direct confrontations with the farmers that had an adverse political effect on the government, since most of the actions turned out to be ineffective in stamping out the spread of GMOs. In the light of the intense political disputes, the repressive policy was changed into a new approach which no longer targeted illegal crops but considered a guidance programme for the certification of conventional, non-transgenic crops. This new policy aims to improve international competitiveness among rural producers interested in creating a special market for non-transgenic soybeans (Pelaez and Dalto, 2002).

Federal policy and the justice system: lobby, resistance and the powers of the state

The regulatory environment at the federal level (the Industrial Property Law, the Cultivation Law and the Biosafety Law) seemed favourable to transgenic crops and Monsanto's strategy in Brazil. However, controversies arose as soon as Monsanto asked the CTNBio for permission to sell Roundup Ready soybeans in Brazil in June 1998.[12] Several organizations, including the Brazilian Society of Scientific Research (SBPC) and IDEC, opposed the approval of RR soybeans, pointing out the lack of studies on the possible effects on health and the environment. After

IDEC and Greenpeace environmentalist groups petitioned the Federal Court to ban transgenic soybeans, the Court decided on 16 September 1998 to suspend the cultivation of RR soybeans until environmental impact studies had been carried out (Sant'anna, 1998).

CTNBio did not comply with this judicial decision and disregarded civil society opposition when, on 24 September 1998, it allowed Monsanto to trade RR soybeans, with thirteen votes for, one against and one abstention (Falcão, 1998). According to the CTNBio report: 'the specialists understood that genetically modified foods do not offer risks to the environment or to health' (Weber, 1998). A debate within the environmental committee of the Congress followed. Warned by non-governmental organizations, the opposition cast doubt on the impartiality of the decisions taken. A case was presented which suggested that Monsanto was lobbying in state agencies to change regulations and standards in its favour. The Brazilian Sanitary Surveillance Agency had allowed an increase from 0.2 ppm to 20 ppm in the tolerated residue level of the herbicide Roundup in transgenic soybeans. This happened on the same day that the CTNBio had authorized the cultivation of RR soybeans.[13] However, despite Monsanto's efforts to get support from the executive power and regulatory agencies, the writ of 16 September 1998 by the Federal Court kept preventing Congress from allowing Monsanto to register transgenic crops in Brazil.

The pressure by opponents of GMOs further increased when IDEC commenced a public civil action on 16 October 1998, this time aimed at extending the writ to all biotechnology companies. IDEC demanded that the CTNBio would attend all stipulations in the law, that is to elaborate the rules related to food safety, labels and trade of transgenics, to abstain from expressing opinions about any application before having elaborated the referred rules, and to demand environmental impact studies before taking any final technical decision. IBAMA, the Brazilian Institute of Environment and Renewable Natural Resources (part of the Ministry of the Environment), requested the Federal Court to authorize its participation in the legal action started by IDEC and Greenpeace against the approval of RR soybeans. IBAMA wanted Monsanto to carry out environmental impact studies on its GMOs.

Meanwhile, the federal government reinforced its support for Monsanto by creating a special co-ordinator to handle the disputes at the judiciary level with respect to the authorization of GMOs. The first act of this federal government's attorneys was to point out that IBAMA as a federal institution could not oppose government decisions and instead should defend in court the authorization of GMOs. Besides, the Minister of Agriculture declared that he would approve the registration of transgenic soybeans as soon as Monsanto had petitioned it (*Rural Business*, 1999a). One month later, the Minister of Science and Technology confirmed the decision of the CTNBio to allow the growth of transgenic soybeans in Brazil. For him, 'the decision of the CTNBio is definite and any discussion is out of the question' (*Rural Business*, 1999b). In this favourable situation, Monsanto requested the National Plant Varieties Protection Service (SNPC) to register five transgenic soybean varieties on 5 May 1999. Ten days later, the Ministry of Agriculture confirmed the registration. According to the newspaper *Zero Hora* (1999a) from Porto Alegre, the news 'surprised even the multinational, which did not expect such a quick reply'.

The decision sparked a lot of new legal actions, which would soon reverse the favourable environment for introducing GMOs. The government of Rio Grande do Sul decreed an agricultural moratorium that prohibited the entry of transgenic seeds to this state for five years. The federal government had to give way to civil society pressure and proposed that GMOs were labelled. A team was appointed to write the regulations. Still in May 1999, IDEC and Greenpeace announced a new writ – added to the earlier civil action – intending to prevent the registration of Monsanto's transgenic GM seeds.[14] As a result, the Federal Court pronounced on 18 June 1999 a ban on the growth and trade of RR soybeans as long as no environmental impact studies were carried out and no labelling standards were established. The federal government and Monsanto questioned the legal procedure, but in a second-tier trial in August 2000 the federal justice unanimously ratified the previous decision.

A final judgment of the Federal Court in the civil action against CTNBio started by IDEC in October 1998, was pronounced on 26 June 2000. The verdict banned the cultivation and trade of GMOs in Brazil, except for experimental areas, and stated that the government had to demand environmental impact studies before authorizing releases of GMOs (Bahia, 2000; Weber, 2000). Moreover, the judge considered unconstitutional two of the CTNBio decisions that exempted GMO releases from environmental impact studies. The government was ordered to demand that CTNBio make new rules about food safety, trade and consumption of transgenic food within ninety days (Weber, 2000). During this time, the CTNBio was not allowed to express any final technical opinion.

Despite this verdict, the government continued to defend transgenic products and alleged in a note on 7 July that the activities of CTNBio expressed government policy concerning GMO safety.[15] According to this note, 'the Government understands that Brazil cannot be outside this technology (of transgenics) or any other which might bring benefits to the country and its citizens' (Mendes and Beck, 2000; Sato and Weber, 2000). The week after, the Minister of Agriculture announced the results of the 1999/2000 crops, saying that it would be the 'last Brazilian non-transgenic harvest'. In a press interview, the minister accused non-governmental organizations opposing transgenics of being sponsored by multinationals that would lose revenue when herbicide use was reduced and that served countries competing with Brazilian producers in the global agricultural market (Lacerda and Trindade, 2000).

Besides this political support to GMOs, the federal government tried to escape from previous judicial decisions through provisory measures and decrees. On 28 December 2000, during the holiday period when Congress was in recess, the President of Brazil issued a 'provisional remedy' (MP 2137) to alter the Brazilian policy of bio-safety.[16] This MP re-created CTNBio and changed its parameters, aiming to overcome the legal impositions pronounced by the federal justice. The new CTNBio was permitted to leave out environmental impact studies if it considered these unnecessary. According to Zanatta (2001), the federal government believed that the new attributes of CTNBio would resolve the doubts about the committee's competence to make decisions without these studies. The lack of environmental impact studies was the main reason why the federal justice banned the GMO trade in the country.

To respond to the second issue in the judicial sentence, the labelling issue, the President of Brazil issued a decree on 18 July 2001 stating that foods with a residual GMO content higher than 4 per cent should have indicated this on the label. IDEC criticized the decree, since with a tolerance level of 4 per cent only a few processed foods would be subject to labelling.[17] IDEC also questioned the lack of scientific arguments for setting the percentage at 4 per cent. IDEC claimed that the government seemed to privilege transgenics above other additives, such as chemicals and artificial sweeteners, which must be mentioned on the labels even when used in infinitely small amounts. Moreover, IDEC warned against a failing of the rule: when the product contains more than one transgenic ingredient, each below the maximum of 4 per cent, the total can exceed 4 per cent without being mentioned on the label. IDEC insisted that the decree was illegal because it contradicted the Consumer Defence Code, which states that information on products has to be 'correct, clear, precise' (IDEC, 2001; *Estado de São Paulo*, 26 July 2001).

Besides all the struggles around the environmental impact studies and the labelling issue, the credibility of federal policies, particularly regarding CTNBio, was brought into the discussion for two other reasons: the cosy relationship between regulators and multinationals and the non-compliance with technical norms when authorizing field experiments. The suspicion that biotechnology regulation benefits only multinationals was aroused when IDEC and Greenpeace questioned the organization of the First Brazilian Congress on Bio-safety in September 1999. Monsanto, Novartis, Agrevo and DuPont sponsored this event organized by CTNBio. According to the environmentalists, these four multinacionals had definite interests and the CTNBio should have maintained its independence as a regulating organ of public health and the environment (Giuliani, 2000).

The discussion about non-compliance with technical norms focused on the irregularities in hundreds of authorized experiments – totalling an area of 703 ha in January 2001 – and in the number and qualification of bio-safety inspectors (Araújo, 2001). A report from the Federal Deputy Fernando Ferro of the Labour Party and non-governmental organizations (including Greenpeace) showed that more than 90 per cent of the experimental area was managed by Monsanto (*Agra Presse Hebdo*, 2000). The number and size of these experiments was called to the attention of the Federal Public Ministry. A new controversy emerged when CTNBio authorized experimental Bt maize cultivation on 60 ha in Cachoeira Dourada (MG). Bio-safety specialists claimed that the cultivation of 60 ha could only be meant for commercial purposes (which was still not allowed). In a civil public action, Republic Attorney Aurélio Rios suspended all authorizations for experiments with pesticidal transgenics which did not have the Special Temporary Register (RET) as stipulated in the Pesticide Law (Law no. 7802, 1990). One of the conditions for obtaining a RET is that the size of the experiment must be less than 1,000 square metres. Moreover, each RET has to be issued simultaneously by the Ministry of Agriculture, IBAMA (the Ministry of Environment) and the Brazilian Sanitary Surveillance Agency (the Ministry of Health). This was not the case in all of the 900 authorizations CTNBio had issued. The attorney also considered that the government had neglected earlier recommendations by the federal Public Ministry to cancel or suspend experiments with transgenics without a RET (Gonçalves, 2001). The federal justice respected the public civil action and issued a writ suspending field experiments with transgenics considered as pesticidal or alike (Aliski, 2001). Besides the so-called Bt plants, the measure also affected RR soya, which is resistant to glyphosate, the active ingredient of the Roundup herbicide and classified as a product similar to pesticides (Quadros et al., 2001).[18]

During all these controversies Monsanto followed multiple strategies, several of which have been reviewed above: direct political lobbying, pressure on regulators, sponsoring CNTBio seminars, PR activities, legal struggles and, possibly, supporting illegal planting of GMOs in Rio Grande do Sul. A strategy of Monsanto not yet mentioned was the announcement of an investment of $550 million for a new plant to manufacture Roundup. Its construction started in the state of Bahia in January 1999 (*Folha de São Paulo*, 2000). In a country where free-market policies strongly discourage industrial investments, the probability of attracting international capital for economic development was very important. The major investments for the building of the Roundup herbicide factory can be seen as part of a political strategy to persuade the federal government to approve RR soybeans. Apart from the signal it gave to policy-makers, the plant also had a direct economic objective. As Belmiro Ribeiro, Monsanto's director of communications in Brazil, says: 'despite the non-release of soybeans, there is a great potential for the use of this herbicide in Brazil' (Cardoso de and Cesare, 1999).

Recently, it turned out that the partnership between Monsanto and the public sector was even stronger than expected. In an extraordinary session on 6 December 2000, the Superintendence of Development in the Northeast (Sudene), a development agency financing investments, authorized a subsidy of nearly $100 million for building the above-mentioned plant.[19] When a parliamentary inquiry commission revealed this agreement, protests followed because only very few jobs were generated (319 direct jobs) by this subsidy (Seabra and Fernandes, 2001).

Further pressure also resulted from contracts signed with other new allies. In April 2000, Monsanto conceded to EMBRAPA and OCEPAR (Organization of Co-operatives in the state of Paraná) the right of scientific and commercial use of the gene that gives resistance to the active ingredient of Roundup (Carmo, 2000). Together, these organizations controlled 80 per cent of the soya seed market in Brazil. OCEPAR started to advertise in major newspapers the release of transgenics in Brazil.

These strategies of Monsanto probably play a role in the continuing support of the federal government for creating a favourable regulatory environment for GMOs, in spite of all the negative pronouncements of the federal justice and the resistance in Brazilian society. Brazilian politicians were willing publicly to support Monsanto's case for transgenics at strategic moments. In a speech to entrepreneurs and investors in New York on 26 July 2001, the Minister of Agriculture and Supply, Pratini de Moraes, said that he was liberating five types of transgenic soya, ignoring all the existing judicial prohibitions (Salvador and Godoy, 2001). Brazilian NGOs reacted immediately as they considered that the timing of this announcement of RR soybean release as well as the decree on labelling discussed above were suspiciously synchronized with a meeting in Saint Louis (USA) on 25 July, where Monsanto would announce its financial results for the second quarter of the year. The Monsanto director of communications in Brazil remarked that Latin America and Brazil were fundamental to the long-term development plans of the company (Lopes, 2001). The NGOs restated their disposition to a new 'judicial battle' pointing out the illegality of the labelling decree according to the Consumer Defence Code and vigorousness of the judicial decisions which do not authorize the release of GMOs. The minister's speech also had a strong effect on the Brazilian judiciary. The Federal Judge Association regarded this declaration as a direct confrontation of powers and warned in a public note that 'if the Government takes this measure, it will disobey a judicial decision and create conflict with the Judiciary' (Zanatta and Basile, 2001). In this adverse context, the Minister of Agriculture withdrew and stated that his ministry would register transgenic soya varieties only after the justice had solved GM soya issues (*Valor Econômico*, 2001d). Monsanto could not trade its transgenic seeds for at least three consecutive harvests. The most important consequence certainly was the postponing of the expected returns on its investments in purchasing seed companies.

At the time of finalizing this chapter, the release of GMOs is still an unresolved issue in Brazil and its solution depends on power politics in society and the powers of the state (executive, legislative and, mainly, judiciary). The halted judiciary decision process has to be restarted following the nomination of the recently elected President Luis Inacio Lula da Silva (of the left-wing Workers' Party) in January 2003. Although the Workers' Party has rejected the release of GMOs without being validated by environmental impact studies, the choice of state ministers is a complex combination of different political interests and divergent views on the regulation of GMOs. It is likely that social struggles concerning GMOs will remain on the political agenda throughout the mandate of the new president.

CONCLUSION

From 1995 onwards, Brazil has created the institutions that would make the legal authorization of GMOs possible. Targeting the potential market for GM seed in Brazil, Monsanto initiated a series of mergers with and acquisitions of Brazilian seed companies. However, despite the promising prospects for the Brazilian soy seed market, the efforts to introduce GM crops resulted in a series of disputes and conflicts which would hinder a definitive introduction. NGOs initiated political and juridical struggles around patent laws as they were aware of the importance of preventing regulations that would be purely favourable to the expansion strategies of large agro-industrial companies. They had constructed an alternative development view based on a culture of farmer autonomy. An example of their search for alternative technological trajectories which support farmer autonomy was the production of 'creole' varieties, better adapted to local conditions and requiring few inputs of industrial origin.

NGO pressure on the one hand and Monsanto's lobbying on the other hand resulted in a heterogeneity of views on the GMO issue within the state apparatus. While the state of Rio Grande do Sul undertook various efforts to ban GMOs, the federal government took measures to support the introduction. In this context, the position of the Brazilian judiciary appeared to be crucial. Despite attempts of the executive to create legal artifices to overcome several pronouncements of the judiciary, which put limits on the release of GMOs, the federal justice has been trying to uphold the laws on the preservation of the environment, health and consumers' rights. The justice resolutions weakened the position of the federal government *vis-à-vis* those states where the principle of precaution had led to bans or moratoria on the introduction of GMOs. It is at the federal justice level that the organized opposition has shown that it has learned from its past experiences in political and social disputes and has adroitly questioned the proposals, decisions and methods of the public and private sectors involved in introducing GMOs.

The court decisions limiting the use of transgenics in Brazil were unusual for Monsanto. The company was used to favourable regulatory environments in countries such as Canada and the United States, which were apparently more stringent when it came to environmental hazards and risks to human health. In Brazil, Monsanto had to respond to regulation based on the principle of precaution, demanding additional safety tests as well as studies on environmental impact. Support from the federal government and close ties with the regulatory agency on bio-safety, CTNBio, could not prevent the judiciary from again insisting that the precautionary principle should be applied and proper safety studies be carried out. With all its privileged technical and scientific knowledge, its experience in approaching regulators in other countries, and with its considerable financial resources to establish a large marketing network and invest in 'economic pressure', Monsanto could not get authorization for the release of its RR soybeans. Could this failure to have transgenic seeds legalized in Brazil then be related to overconfidence on the part of Monsanto in its ability to convince regulatory authorities?

Although the arrogant attitude of the company may have contributed to this remarkable ban, any more comprehensive analysis has to do justice to the role of the social resistance movement that has sprung up against GMOs in Brazil. We have argued that the blocking of GMOs in Brazil is due not only to a flaw in the powers of persuasion or overconfidence on the part of Monsanto, but is also the result of long awareness and the learning process in certain sectors of Brazilian society. This process was underway in the 1970s when resistance movements were consolidated both socially and politically to defend the autonomy of the farmer and the country at large in the face of nationwide capital. These movements have acquired much experience in disputes and are established at all power levels (executive, legislature and the courts). They were also able to mobilize parts of the scientific community to question the technical arguments presented by companies.

In this complex scenario of disputes, the possibilities of defining a new technological trajectory, based on the use of GMOs, remain uncertain. In our analysis of the controversies around GMOs, we have emphasized the importance of the non-economic variables (social and political) that determine the pace and the direction of technological innovations. The resistance to GMOs in Brazil has shown that the future of GMOs is not yet the fait accompli that the interests behind biotechnology intend to make us believe. Technology is, in its essence, a product of society, whose development and adoption results from a continuous process of agreements and disputes between different social agents.

NOTES

1. Brazil is generally viewed as a country with 'large husbandry': the large rural farm, monocultures of export crops and slavery. The last farming census (1995/96) shows, however, that 85 per cent of the 4,859,864 Brazilian agricultural holdings are family farms. These family businesses, averaging 26 ha, use 30.5 per cent of all farm land and produce 37.9 per cent of the gross value of animal and vegetable production (Bittencourt and di Sabbato, 2000). In southern Brazil this pattern is even stronger: family businesses contribute to 47 per cent of the production value, part of which is soybean production.

2. Rumsfeld returned as Secretary of Defense in the current administration of George W. Bush.

3. For soybean meal and soybean oil Brazil had a world market share of 25 and 16 per cent respectively. The internal market for soybean and its derivatives is also important: only 27 per cent is directly exported while 66 per cent of the harvest is destined for crushing (the remainder is for stock, seeds and others). Of the obtained soybean oil and soybean meal, approximately 33 per cent and 58 per cent respectively is for export (Altoé et al., 2001).

4. Yields in Brazil, Argentina and the USA do not differ very much and vary between 2.5 and 2.7 tons per ha (cf. USDA, 2001c).

5. We use 'Cultivation Law', the translation according to INPI, although 'Cultivar Law' would probably be a better translation.

6. Decree law 1752, 20 December 1995 and decree law 2577, 30 April 1998.

7. To name a few of the organizations which today form part of this network: Opaco, small farmers' association from the west of Santa Catarina; Assessoar study association, orientation and rural support; Cae-Ipe, Ecology Agriculture Centre; Capa, small farmer support centre; Cetap, Popular Alternative Technological Centre; Vianei Centre of Popular Education; Rureco, Economical Development Foundation from the centre-west of Paraná.

8. Schmidt (2001) and Byé and Schmidt (2001) discuss the potentials and limits of these propositions in the south of Brazil, as well as the challenges faced by NGOs.

9. Except for the passages where we quote other sources, this section is based on D. Hathaway (2001), 'Paper on IP Rules in Brazil' (unpublished paper), an excellent history of the making of the Industrial Property Law and Plant Variety Protection 'Cultivation Law' in Brazil. The authors gratefully acknowledge the permission given to use this unpublished work.

10. Some changes were made in the original bill, which was even more demanding than requested by the TRIPs Agreement (Trade Related Aspects of Intellectual Property Rights), accepted by Brazil after having ratified the GATT agreement in late 1994.

11. The Convention of UPOV from 1991 allows for plant patenting. Compared with UPOV-1991, UPOV-1978 gives a country more possibilities for safeguarding farmers' rights to reproduce seeds of protected varieties. Moreover, UPOV-1991 allows for two systems of property rights protection (patenting and traditional protection), while UPOV-1978 accepts only one or the other.

12. Earlier requests had been for experimental cultivation only.

13. Later on, the Administrative Rule no. 888 of 06/11/98 established the limit at 2.0 ppm, still ten times higher than the original value (Araújo and Mercadante, 1999).

14. The provisory registration of the Ministry of Agriculture was insufficient, since the Health Ministry and the Environment Ministry also had to approve any release of transgenic seeds, which they never did. Even though the Minister of Agriculture announced the release of GMOs more than once, these declarations were subsequently denied (Menasche, 2001). Wary of possible repercussions, the publication of the definitive registration of Monsanto's transgenic soya was postponed each time. This reflects the internal struggle and pressure on the government.

15. Confronting the judicial sentence, the CTNBio expressed a favourable

opinion on the importation of transgenic maize for animal feed on 30 June, with the approval of the Ministry of Science and Technology. The federal government used this opinion to authorize the unloading of 38,000 tons of Argentinian transgenic maize from a ship in the port of Recife.

16. The Provisional Remedy is an instrument foreseen in the Brazilian constitution. It allows the executive to legislate and then submit it to the legislature for approval. Even if it is not approved, it is valid for thirty days. The instrument is meant to anticipate emergencies. Its abusive use by the President of Brazil has caused a real confusion of powers. Since there are political and operational difficulties for approving these remedies by the legislature, the executive can indefinitely re-edit them month after month. Currently, a proposal to regulate this situation is being drafted in the Brazilian Congress.

17. In research undertaken by IDEC and Greenpeace, only three out of the seventeen food products which contained transgenic substances exceeded this 4 per cent (*Indústria e Comércio*, 2001). At the time of writing, the European Union requires labelling when food contains more than 1 per cent GMO; in Japan, it is 5 per cent (*Valor Econômico*, 2001c).

18. At the time of writing, the General Solicitor of the Federal Union was planning to request an appeal against the writ.

19. This amount practically equals all funding of the Investment Fund in the Northeast (Finor) in 1999. It is almost four times higher than the federal government budget for fighting the drought in the north-east ($31million), destined for 600,000 families of rural workers.

REFERENCES

Agra Presse Hebdo (2000) 'Le Brésil hésite à franchir le pas', *Agra Presse Hebdo* 2788 (11 December): 27–9.

Aliski, A. (2001) 'Veto a transgênicos surpreende multis da biotecnologia – Todos os testes serão destruídos', *Gazeta Mercatil* (25 May). <www.gazetamercantil .com.br> (15 July).

Almeida, J. (1999) *A construção social de uma nova agricultura: tecnologia agrícola e movimentos sociais no sul do Brasil*. Porto Alegre: Ed. UFRGS.

Altoé, S. M., N. Tanaka and S. Hisano (2001) 'Soybean Production and GMO Issues in Brazil', *The Review of Agricultural Economics* 57: 135–55.

Araújo, J. C. de (1998) *A Lei de Proteção de Cultivares; análise de sua formulação e conteúdo*. Brasília, Rio de Janeiro: UFRJ (Monografia ao Curso de Especialização em Políticas Públicas e Governo).

— (2001) 'Produtos transgênicos na agricultura – questões técnicas, ideológicas e políticas', *Cadernos de Ciência & Tecnologia* (18) 1: 117–46.

Araújo, J. C. de and M. Mercadante (1999) *Produtos transgénicos na agricultura*. Brasília: Consultoria Legislativa da Câmara Federal.

Bahia, C. (2000) 'Mantida proibição de transgênicos', *Zero Hora* (29 June). <www. zerohora.com.br> (4 January 2001).

Barboza, D. (2001) 'As Biotech Crops Multiply, Consumers Get Little Choice', *New York Times* (10 June). <www.nytimes.com> (16 August).

Benson, T. (2001) 'Monsanto Sees Breakthrough for GMO Soybeans in Brazil', *Dow Jones* (2 February).

Bittencourt, G. A. and A. di Sabbato (2000) *Novo retrato da agricultura familiar; o Brasil redescoberto*. Brasília: MDA/Incra.

Bloomberg News (1999) 'Plantio de milho transgênico deve ser menor nos EUA', *Gaṣeta Mercantil* (31 August). <www.gazetamercantil.com.br> (25 May 2001).

Brandenburg, A. (1999) *Agricultura familiar, ONGs e desenvolvimento sustentável*. Curitiba: Ed. UFPR.

Byé, P. and W. Schmidt (2001) 'Agriculture familiale au Sud du Brésil; d'une exclusion productiviste à une exclusion certifiée?', Paper presented at the XIXth Congress of the European Society for Rural Sociology, Dijon, 3–7 September.

Campanhola, C., G. Rodrigues and W. Bettiol (1998) 'Biotechnology and Crop Protection in Brazil, EMBRAPA/CNPMA', in J. Richter, J. Huber, B. Schuler and D. Joerdens-Roettger (eds), *Biotechnology for Crop Protection: Its Potential for Developing Countries, Proceedings of an International Workshop*, Berlin, 9–13 December 1996. Feldafing: ZEL.

Cardoso, D. and C. F. de Cesare (1999) 'Monsanto mantém orçamento no Brasil', *Gaṣeta Mercatil* (23–26 December). <www.gazetamercantil.com.br> (25 May 2001).

Carmo do, A. J. (2000) 'EMBRAPA vai pesquisar soja transgênica', *Estado de São Paulo* (7 April). <www.estado.estadao.com.br/editorias/2000/04/07/ger364.html> (15 May).

Cordeiro, A. and B. de Mello (1994) 'La experiencia de la Rede Milho', *Biodiversidad* 1 (1): 18–22.

Craviotti, C. (2000) 'Pampas Family Farms and Technological Change: Strategies and Perspectives Towards Genetically Modified Crops and No-Tillage Systems', Paper presented at the Xth World Congress of Rural Sociology, Rio de Janeiro, Brazil, 30 July to 5 August.

EBAA (Encontro Brasileiro de Agricultura Alternativa) (1984) II *Anais* ... (Proceedings). Petrópolis: Faeab.

— (1987) III *Anais* ... (Proceedings). Cuiabá: Faeab.

Ehlers, E. (1996) *Agricultura sustentável; origens e perspectivas de um novo paradigma*. São Paulo: Livros da Terra.

Eichenwald, K. (2001) 'Biotechnology Food: From the Lab to a Debacle', *New York Times* (25 January). <www.nytimes.com/2001/01/25/business/25 FOOD.html> (2 March).

European Commission (2001) 'Economic Impacts of Genetically Modified Crops on the Agri-Food Sector'. <http://europa.eu.int/comm/agriculture/publi/gmo/fullrep/ackn.htm> (14 July).

Falcão, D. (1998) 'Soja transgênica tem parecer favorável', *Folha de São Paulo* (25 September), Cad. Mundo, p. 9.

FAO (2001) *FAOSTAT Agricultural Database*. <http://apps.fao.org/cgi-bin/nph-db.pl?subset=agriculture> (14 July).

Ferrara, J. (1999) 'Les vases comunicants entre Monsanto et l'administration',

Courrier International 452 (1-7 July). <www.courrierinternational.com> (20 July 2001).

Ferrazzino, A., A. Bochicchio and J. Souza (2000) 'Impact of the Transgenic Plants in Argentina and Brazil', Paper presented at the Xth World Congress of Rural Sociology, Rio de Janeiro, Brazil, 30 July to 5 August.

Folha de São Paulo (2000) 'Monsanto investe US$ 550 mi na Bahia', *Folha de São Paulo* (14 January): 2–4.

Fortune (1979) 'A Politician Turned Executive', *Fortune* (10 September): 88–94.

Giuliani, G. M. (2000) 'O dilema dos transgênicos', *Estudos Sociedade e Agricultura* 15: 13–38.

Gonçalves, J. A. (2001) 'Aberto caminho para soja transgênica', *Gazeta Mercatil* (5 June). <www.gazetamercantil.com.br> (14 July).

Hathaway, D. (1997) *Lei de Cultivares: Impactos e Horizontes*. Rio de Janeiro: Ibase.

IDEC (2001) 'Governo decide não rotular os transgênicos'. <www.uol.com.br/ IDEC> (21 July).

Indústria e Comércio (2001) 'Risco de transgênicos não está descartado' (24 July).

Jornal do Brasil (1999) 'Destruição de lavouras', *Jornal do Brasil* (2 September).

Lacerda, A. and R. Trindade (2000) 'ONGs são usadas pelas indústrias', *Jornal do Brasil* (17 July).

Lopes, F. (2001) 'Lucro líquido global da Monsanto tem alta de 5% no trimestre', *Valor Econômico* (26 July). <www.valoronline.com.br/valoreconomico/ materia.asp?id=747192> (4 August).

McCann, J. (1990) *Sweet Success: How Nutrasweet Created a Billion Dollar Business*. Illinois: Richard Irwin.

Menasche, R. (2000) 'Legalidade, legitimidade e lavouras transgênicas clandestinas', Paper presented at the Seminário Democracias sustentáveis?: roteiros para a ecologia política latino-americana, CLACSO, Rio de Janeiro, 23–24 November.

— (2001) 'Cronologia da luta contra os transgênicos', Rio de Janeiro: LabConsS/ FF/UFRJ. <http://acd.ufrj.br/consumo/transgenicos.htm> (31 July).

Mendes, V. and M. Beck (2000) 'Overno sai em defesa de transgênicos', *O Globo* (7 July). <www.oglobo.com.br> (30 July 2001).

Monsanto (2000) 'Read Monsanto's Prospectus'. <www.monsanto.com> (30 July 2001).

Paula, N. de (2000) 'Produção e comercialização de sementes: um novo modelo de regulação', Paper presented at the Xth World Congress of Rural Sociology, Rio de Janeiro, Brazil, 30 July to 5 August.

Pelaez, V. and F. Dalto (2002) 'The Establishment of a GMO-Free Zone in Brazil: Identifying Inter-Institutional Boundaries', in *Proceedings of Tercer Congreso Europeo de Latinoamericanistas*, Amsterdam, 3–6 July 2002.

Quadros, M., A. Aliski and J. A. Gonçalves (2001) 'Aumenta o cerco aos transgênicos', *Gazeta Mercatil* (9 May). <www.gazetamercantil.com.br> (25 May).

Rede TA/Sul (Rede Tecnologias Alternativas/Sul) (1997) 'Interconectando idéias e ideais na construção da agricultura do futuro', in J. Almeida and Z. Navarro (eds), *Reconstruindo a agricultura; idéias e ideais na perspectiva do desenvolvimento rural sustentável*, pp. 169–85. Porto Alegre: Ed. UFRGS.

Rural Business (1999a) 'MA deve aprovar soja transgênica' (18 March).

— (1999) 'Decisão sobre soja transgênica é definitiva' (19 April).

Salvador, F. and F. Godoy (2001) 'Transgênicos: órgão protestam em Brasília', *O Estado de São Paulo* (26 July). <www.estado.com.br/editorias/2001/07/27/ger013.html> (4 August).

Sant'anna, L. (1998) 'Liminar impede cultivo de soja transgênica', *O Estado de São Paulo* (17 September). <www.estado.estadao.com.br/edicao/pano/98/09/16/ger626.html> (4 January 2001).

Sato, S. and D. Weber (2000) 'Governo defende produção de transgênicos' *O Estado de São Paulo*, (7 July). <www.estado.estadao.com.br/editorias/2000/07/07/ger639.html> (14 July 2001).

Schmidt, W. (2001) 'Agricultura orgânica; entre a ética e o mercado?' *Agroecologia e Desenvolvimento Rural Sustentável* 2 (1): 62–73.

Seabra, C. and D. Fernandes (2001) 'Multinacional tem maior incentivo da Sudene', *O Globo* (9 June). <www.oglobo.com.br> (30 July).

Teece, D. (1986) 'Profiting from Technological Innovation: Implications for Integration, Collaboration, Licensing and Public Policy', *Research Policy* 15: 285–305.

USDA (1999) 'U.S. Soybean and Soybean Meal Exports to the European Union: Are GMO Worries Resulting in a Drop in U.S. Sales?', *USDA International Agricultural Trade Report* (Special Report) (17 December). <www.fas.usda.gov/oilseeds> (4 January 2000).

— (2001a) 'Soybeans: South American Production Expanding Despite Lower World Prices'. <www.fas.usda.gov/oilseeds> (14 July).

— (2001b) 'Demand for Certified Non-Biotech Soybean Meal Expands in the EU', *USDA International Agricultural Trade Report* (23 May). <www.fas.usda.gov/oilseeds> (14 July).

— (2001c) 'Oilseeds: Worlds Markets and Trade', *Circular Series – FOP* (1 August). <www.fas.usda.gov/oilseeds> (14 July).

Valor Econômico (2001a) 'Área semeada com soja modificada pode passar de 50% no Rio Grande do Sul', *Valor Econômico* (8 June). <www.valoronline.com.br/valoreconomico/default.asp?edicao=110> (14 July).

— (2001b) 'Biossegurança: começam as mudanças na CTNBio', *Valor Econômico* (15 June). <www.valoronline.com.br/valoreconomico/default.asp?edicao=114> (14 July).

— (2001d) 'Pratini desiste de liberar soja transgênica', *Valor Econômico* (9 August). <www.valoronline.com.br/valoreconomico/default.asp?edicao=153> (21 August).

— (2001c) 'Brasil, Estados Unidos, Europa e transgênicos' (23 July). <www.valoronline.com.br/valoreconomico/default.asp?categ=83&edicao=140> (21 August).

Von der Weid, J. (1994) 'Da agroquímica para a agroecologia', Paper presented at the Seminário Nacional sobre políticas públicas e agricultura sustentável, Rio de Janeiro, August.

Weber, D. (1998) 'Aprovada soja transgênica da Monsanto', *O Estado de São Paulo* (25 September). <www.estado.estadao.com.br/edicao/pano/98/09/24/ger954.html> (4 January 2000).

— (2000) 'Decisão sobre transgênicos é adiada para agosto', *O Estado de São Paulo* (29 June). <www.estado.estadao.com.br/editorias/2000/06/29/ger447.html> (14 July 2001).

Wilkinson, J. and P. Castelli (2000) *A transnacionalização da indústria de sementes no Brasil*. Rio de Janeiro: Actionaid.

Zanatta, M. (2001) 'MP dá mais autonomia para a CTNBio', *Valor Econômico* (2 January). <www.valoronline.com.br> (4 January).

Zanatta, M. and J. Basile (2001) 'Juízes Federais combatem liberação de soja alterada', *Valor Econômico* (30 July). <www.valoronline.com.br/valoreconomico/default.asp?edicao=145> (21 August).

Zanatta, M. and L. Herrison (2000) 'Governo fecha posição a favor de transgênicos', *Valor Econômico* (7 July). <www.valoronline.com.br> (7 July).

Zero Hora (1999a) 'Ministério da Agricultura anuncia liberação de soja transgênica', *Zero Hora* (15 May). <www.zerohora.com.br> (4 January 2001).

— (1999b) 'Abrasem prevê 1 milhão de hectares com soja modificada' (2 September). <www.zerohora.com.br> (4 January 2001).

— (2001) 'Volume de sementes certificadas deverá cair', *Zero Hora* (15 June). <www.zerohora.com.br> (14 July).

ELEVEN | Private versus public? Agenda-setting in international agro-technologies

PAUL RICHARDS

§ Environmentalism is concerned not only with the impact of technologies on nature and society, but also with how sustainable futures are envisaged. Several chapters in this volume explore the current one-sidedness of this imaginative effort. The present chapter is concerned with the imaginative effort itself. Agenda-setting is often viewed by technologists as an issue of rational calculation. Send for the economists. Here a different line is taken. The approach to technology is cultural, and makes use of a Durkheimian analytical perspective (Durkheim, 1964, 1995; Stedman Jones, 2001) focused on the (often rather small) task groups generating the technologies in question. Technological agenda are treated, in the first place, as manifestations of will shaped by task group concerns (Richards, 2000). Forming a commitment to a particular technological path bears comparison with the shaping of religious belief. Commitment is summoned in moments of group excitement ('effervescence'; Durkheim, 1995), and regulated by collective representations (symbols, ideas, models, agreed procedures). These representations are impressed on members of the group through ritual (including induction of new initiates into the mysteries of a science or craft). The result is a relatively stable formation – a technological culture. Questions about a clash of (technological) cultures can then be posed (Douglas and Ney, 1998; Perri 6, 1999; Schwarz and Thompson, 1990; Tranvik et al., 2000). The chapter takes three agro-technological cultures – the Green Revolution, public–private partnerships for biotechnology, and the food security concerns of transnational humanitarianism – briefly indicating the ways in which each culture selects its distinctive research agenda.[1] The three cultures compete vigorously for societal attention. Which is the right approach to food security? The chapter argues that the wider interest is best served by vigorous competition among real alternatives. In technology as in religion, differences of dogma are less important than clarifying shared human ends.

In an interesting and provocative paper the plant breeder Norman Simmonds once reviewed evidence that breeders are no better than random at making an initial selection of potential breeding materials (Simmonds, 1989). Breeders tend to explain their choices in terms of judgement based on long experience, but Simmonds found little supporting evidence for this. His data suggested that breeders might make just as much progress if forced (by some mix-up) to breed from their reject bin. What he shows is not that there was anything wrong with the (science-guided) technology of breeding, but that the crucial first 'cut' – the decision about what material to work with – lies outside science. It is a division based not on genetic knowledge but on inspired guesswork.

This seems a widespread condition in science and (science-based) technology. Harré (1972) notes that virus theory 'describes a [real] causal mechanism', but it had to be conjured up in the imagination before it could be observed. Harré suggests this is a characteristic of (causal) mechanisms in general. In technology the decision to take a radically new approach is likewise often based on little more than hunch. MacKenzie (1992) cites such an example in the case of a new generation of super computers. The guess was wrong – the projected leap was too large – but it became locked in place as the industry standard for a number of years through tracking among business rivals. Other stories circulate of figures plucked from the air which mysteriously turn into actual achievements. An oil palm geneticist (Hardon, personal communication, 1993) tells of an off-the-cuff estimate of the potential benefit from hybridization quoted 'as gospel' in technology assessments for a number of years which turned out to be close to the figure eventually achieved. New technology, in short, begins in self-belief. It is a triumph (in its earliest stages) of will over idea.

And yet will alone – except among absolute dictators – is not enough to keep a technology programme moving for long. Money has to be found, teams have to be deployed, setbacks overcome, accountants or politicians and a restive public, persuaded. This is to say, in other words, that the technological vision begins sooner or later to live a full social life. The lonely inventor disconnected from the social world is an unrealistic stereotype. It was one aspect of the genius of Samuel F. B. Morse (the opposite of a lonely crank) to realize that the telegraph would not take off – that people would simply not 'get it' – until a rudimentary network was put in place, upon which users would then stretch their social imaginations and so make his invention work. The clever thing was to drum up the funds for the skeletal network. Very rapidly thereafter the telegraph spread worldwide as the Victorian version of the Internet (Standage, 1998).

How do will and idea (self-belief and social acceptance) interconnect? In *The Elementary Forms of Religious Life* (first published in 1912), Durkheim shows how the human will to achieve or make is first summoned in moments of special revolutionary fervour and then bridled by social concerns (Richman, 2002). The key is ritual. The ritual process shapes collective representations (e.g. totems, flags, badges of office). These are symbols imprinted with group values. Collective representations serve to recapitulate and render reproducible commitments entered into in moments of founding excitement. Durkheim based his argument on ethnographic data relating to the Australian aboriginal 'corroboree' but, against the grain of opinion among intellectuals writing at the time of the great social changes brought about by industrialization, drew no distinction between religion and science. Through his 'ethnographic detour' (Richman, 2002), Durkheim establishes that the religious festival and the mould-breaking scientific conference, clan totems and glittering marks of scientific distinction are essentially no different. Human energies are harnessed to group ends through revolutionary excitements, and shaped through ritual and the collective representations that rituals produce. A culture (an enduring way of thinking, a solidarity) results.

An alternative word for 'culture', in this context, is Kuhn's coinage 'paradigm'. Kuhn's influential sociology of science is Durkheimian in conception (even though no direct link to the *Elementary Forms* is acknowledged). In a postscript to the second edition of *The Structure of Scientific Revolutions*, Kuhn (1970: 175) defines 'paradigm' as 'an entire constellation of ideas, values, techniques ... shared by members of a given community' (i.e. as a culture). Kuhn is as insistent as Durkheim on the special part played by initiation and ritual in the binding process. Paradigms are formed in moments of revolutionary ferment. But Kuhn notes a second and more specific use of his term, referring to 'the concrete puzzle solutions ... employed as models or examples [to] replace explicit rules as a basis for the solution of the remaining puzzles of normal science'. This second usage seems compatible with – indeed to be a manifestation in scientific terms of – the Durkheimian notion of collective representation (as a socially-shaped shorthand of symbols and other mental constructs guiding collective action, and through which the group functions).

This Durkheimian/Kuhnian theory of scientific culture is here used to provide a standpoint from which to explore technological projects. We are prompted to inquire systematically into the initial mobilization of such projects, and the cultures which sustain them. The focus of the present chapter is upon post-1945 international food security. The three projects briefly analysed are the Green Revolution, market-led biotechnology and humanitarian food security. Each technological culture is associated with a specific moment of founding excitement (global security concerns at the beginning of the Cold War, the market enthusiasm associated with Cold War victory, and the post-Cold War challenge of 'new war' and global terrorism). Each develops its own set of collective representations, i.e. shared ways of talking about values (food security through an ethic of international public service, via [market-led] pursuit of efficiency and profit, as a human right) and a specific organizational modality (international public sector institutes, public–private partnerships and non-governmental volunteer activism). Each generates distinctive output (e.g. 'miracle' [broadly adapted, fertilizer-responsive but non-hybrid] seeds, 'facultative apomicts' [bioengineered seed types conceived as public-interest opposites of commercial 'terminator' seed types], and locally-adapted 'emergency' planting materials). Despite different historical triggers the three cultures are better regarded as parallel and competing modes of technology generation, than as successive stages. Each sustains its own flow of innovations via different task group organization and solidarities, reinforcing distinctive technological agenda.

It would be foolish to ignore the competitive tensions between the approaches, since these relate to wider issues of global inequalities and injustices. The question is how to handle such tensions. Must we battle on until it is clear which approach is right? This risks conflating issues of freedom and justice with issues of technological potential. Neo-liberals favour public–private partnerships because they believe in economic freedom. Human rights activists favour 'humanitarian' solutions because they believe in justice. The international institutions continue to forge Green Revolution answers because they believe in an ethic of public service. If one culture were to win out we would be faced with a technological monoculture. An approach that restricted itself to rights-based or public-interest solutions might be as limited in capacity to realize technological potentials as the single-minded privileging of market solutions. Thus it seems better technology policy to seek to open a space in which the different approaches both co-exist and struggle against each other. This is to make the case for complex articulation, i.e. multiculturalism in technology as well as in religious belief. For as Durkheim saw, in regarding the technological societies formed by the first industrial revolution, it is only in wrestling with such complexity that the wider social interest becomes fully apparent. There is something important beyond the opposition of public and private in the food-security sphere – and that is an emergent, and less fractured, sense of transnational human interests.

THE GREEN REVOLUTION: INTERNATIONAL AGRO-TECHNOLOGY AND THE COLD WAR

The roots of the Green Revolution lie in Rockefeller Foundation support for agricultural change in Mexico from *ca*. 1940. But a global programme supported by the US private foundations and later by Western governments for the transformation of food-crop agriculture in Southern countries threatened by the twin hazards of population pressure and communist insurgency took shape only in the 1950s. The defining moments were the spectre of post-war food shortages in Europe and the Cold War.

A new basis for agro-technology was laid by the neo-Darwinian synthesis in biology, *ca*. 1900–20.[2] The rediscovery by De Vries and others of Mendel's 'particulate' theory of inheritance, Johansen's distinction between genotype and phenotype, and the work of Fisher on the statistical basis for plant selection, contributed to a science-based technology of plant improvement that soon spread across the world, assisted by colonial rule. Science-based plant improvement took root in, for example, the Dutch East Indies and British India in the 1920s and '30s (Maat and Richards, 2000). Even small, obscure dependencies – e.g. Mauritius and Sierra Leone – followed the trend, with local researchers generating important contributions to international plant science (Storey, 1997; Richards, 1985).

Internationalism in plant sciences took longer to develop in the United States. At first the new genetic knowledge mainly served to revitalize the fortunes of the seed companies, through the remarkable success of hybrid maize. Crop technologists left the university sector to found successful seed companies, which later became transnational. One such figure was Henry A. Wallace, a founder of Pioneer Hybrid (Kloppenburg, 1988). The broader public perspective developed less in plant breeding than in cognate disciplines, and perhaps most notably in plant pathology. Elvin Stakman, of Minnesota State University, became involved in the problem of controlling wheat blight in the United States in the 1930s. Vector issues required a large-scale national (and continental) approach to control. When Stakman joined a team commissioned by the Rockefeller Foundation in 1943 to respond to a request by the Mexican government, fearing food shortages, for help in setting up a programme in scientific agriculture, he was already familiar with running large-scale public sector programmes for disease control (Perkins, 1997). He and other plant scientists dismissed the views of the Berkeley geographer, Carl Sauer, who considered the central problem to understand the best local practices in peasant agriculture. In advocating an agro-ecological approach, based on what would now be termed indigenous knowledge, Sauer was accused of wanting to keep the Mexican peasantry a 'heap of ants' for his own research purposes (Marglin, 1996; Perkins, 1997).

A key figure in the Rockefeller Mexican agricultural research support programme was a PhD student of Stakman's, Norman Borlaug. Appointed to the Mexican programme, and moving wheat varieties around the country between highland and lowland zones, for experimental purposes, Borlaug was, in effect, selecting for broad adaptation. His discovery of 'shuttle breeding' was then combined with a shift in plant architecture – the introduction of semi-dwarfing genes into wheat, thus improving the ratio of grain to straw – to create the first high-yield (fertilizer-responsive) broadly adapted varieties. A disadvantage of conventional tall varieties with high fertilizer use was that the plant lodged (fell over in the field due to the greater weight of grain). Short straw varieties were less likely to lodge. They became prototypes for the 'miracle' seeds later to transform agricultural output in large parts of South Asia (notably the Punjab) and, as Perkins (1997) notes, Europe.

Post-Second World War food shortages in Britain and continental Europe in 1945–47 placed food security issues on the international agenda. The issue was debated between President Truman in the USA and Prime Minister Attlee in Britain and contingency plans laid. In the event, shortages were not as severe as anticipated, but world political leaders had been made aware of the potential threat to public order in, for example, occupied Germany, should food supply be disrupted (Perkins, 1997). A second development, to which Perkins's path-breaking study of the political and technical origins of the Green Revolution draws attention, was an intellectual panic, especially in the USA in the late 1940s, over the issue of world population (Perkins, 1997). A number of widely read books, such as one by William Vogt, predicted Malthusian crisis. Meanwhile the Cold War had started, and Western leaders were preoccupied with containing the communist threat. The threat of Soviet expansion in Western Europe became especially apparent in the blockade of Berlin in 1948, the same year the Maoists took power in China. Communist expansion took on a global aspect, with concerns over left-wing insurgent movements in India and South-east Asia. Connections were drawn between issues of international military and food security in a report to the president of the Rockefeller Foundation by Warren Weaver and others. They outlined a version of what Perkins (1997) terms the Population National Security Threat – population pressure causes famine causes revolution. The key argument was that the plant sciences, as developed in the Mexican agricultural programme, could help buy time, to develop defences against the twin threats of communist expansion and the population 'bomb'. The Foundation committed itself to a second programme, for India. This laid the institutional and scientific foundations for the subsequent Green Revolution.

The global architecture of the Green Revolution emerged in the 1960s. With funding from the Rockefeller and Ford Foundations, but later with World Bank and bilateral donor support, a global network of international agro-technology research centres, modelled on the initial Mexican Wheat and Research Programme, was established. The first of these units, IRRI, founded in 1960, applied itself to transferring the lessons of the wheat and maize programme to Asian rice (Anderson et al., 1991). The Japanese occupation of Taiwan provided a technological template. Japanese researchers had worked out ways of producing two crops of rice a year in tropical conditions on occupied Taiwan for export back to Japan, by adapting short-duration japonica rices. Taiwanese researchers adapted the scheme for local indica rices. As with wheat, the plant ideotype was changed to a semi-dwarf aspect. The Taiwanese exported their new rice technology directly, in competition with the communist Chinese, to Africa, for example. But IRRI director Robert Chandler recognized that the technology might be better separated from such obviously ideological packaging. IRRI internationalized the Taiwanese package, and spread it widely through the better rice-growing wetlands of South and South-east Asia, and to parts of Africa, during the 1960s and '70s (Bray, 1986). Double cropping of high-yield IRRI rices sharply increased the productivity of both labour and land over large parts of the Asian wet rice region.

Soon other international agricultural research facilities were set up, to comprise a network of sixteen centres in all, with mandates covering all major tropical food crops and underdeveloped regions, under the management of a joint World Bank–FAO-donor committee known as the

Consultative Group on International Agricultural Research (CGIAR), with headquarters in the World Bank in Washington, DC. The aim was to replicate the success of applied plant sciences in transforming yields of wheat, maize and rice. Most Western aid donors eventually subscribed to the consortium, and international recruitment policies brought together not only internationally-minded American researchers and their Dutch, British and French peers in tropical crop sciences, but also an international cohort of the best-qualified plant scientists from the recently independent former colonial territories.

The successes and failures of the Green Revolution have been widely debated. Attention has centred on the positive impact on food prices, especially of benefit to the urban poor (Lipton with Longhurst, 1987), dispossession of marginal farmers (Griffin, 1974), and ecological damage caused by fertilizer and pesticide dependencies. While some critics deplore the adverse social and ecological impact of Green Revolution crops (Pearse, 1980), others regret their inapplicability to rain-fed areas of Asia or large parts of Africa (Greenland, 1984). The point here is not to revisit these debates, but to underline the way the research agenda for the Green Revolution were set by the excitements infecting the international politics of its era. Without the security concerns of the Cold War – specifically the belief that communist insurgency was fed directly by rural poverty in overpopulated South and South-east Asia – the Stackman–Borlaug version of how to translate the potential of the new plant sciences into agro-technology might never have become so dominant a model for international public sector research. The Green Revolution was designed to have impact quickly, and over a wide area (Borlaug, 1972). The idea was to buy time to address other security and developmental concerns; sustainability issues were of lower priority. In scale and sense of urgency, the approach then matched the preoccupations of the major donor, the World Bank under the presidency of Robert McNamara (from 1968). Hunger-reducing packages of high-yield seeds and fertilizer, bundled by the World Bank with cheap rural credit to break the grip of a supposedly usurious class of village money-lenders forcing impoverished peasants into the hands of leftist insurgents, to be delivered via Integrated Agricultural Development Projects, promised to address lessons of agrarian politics learnt by Mr McNamara when he was handling the Vietnam War as US Secretary for Defense.

Sometimes the history of (science-based) technology is 'read' as if it was an inevitable consequence of certain trends in scientific development. But with the Green Revolution we can see clearly that there was nothing inevitable about the path traced by the international public sector. In other circumstances the same science would have supported different technological approaches. We can draw this conclusion from two distinct developments.

The first is the success of the commercial seed companies with hybrid technology in US and European agriculture during the Cold War period. Such commercial solutions to agro-technological transformation were little emphasized in developing countries at the same period, but involve essentially the same scientific foundations as supported the Green Revolution. This is seen clearly from the most intriguing case of China where, after the 1958 famine, the government emphasized the acquisition of American hybrid commercial seed technology (Song, 1998). Borlaug's institute CIMMYT set its face against hybrids, preferring open-pollinated varieties for small-scale farmers, so they would not be forced into a dependent relationship on seed companies. Borlaug accompanied President Nixon to China in 1973, and CIMMYT began to supply the Chinese with superior seeds. These were used not as CIMMYT had envisaged, but mainly as raw material for inbred lines to produce hybrids (Song, 1998). Dependence of the farmer on the supplier (the one-party state) was not a problem for the regime. Later Chinese researchers applied hybridization techniques to wheat and rice (in-breeding varieties where the commercial sector had hung back). There can be no clearer (if ironic) instance of politics pushing the same science towards different applications.

The second case provides us with evidence that the approach of Sauer (building from what the best small-scale farmers already did) was, in fact, also a perfectly viable development path. It was tried in a number of places. One especially well-documented instance is colonial Nigeria, where wartime low-input conditions fed a lively process of discovery and indigenous innovation. This 'with farmer' integrated approach to crop and land management was well documented in a local journal, *Farm and Forest* (1940–52). Many of the issues first raised in the pages of *Farm and Forest* have never entirely disappeared from the scientific literature. Their revival and development in the 1970s and '80s continues to feed a healthy debate in both ecology and the plant sciences today. An important figure in this revival was the Cambridge- and Trinidad-trained plant breeder Norman Simmonds, who developed, mainly after retirement from a Chair in Edinburgh, the potential of a population genetics approach to plant improvement basic to what is now sometimes called 'farmer participatory' crop improvement. In particular Simmonds published important papers on the idea of systematic genetic base broadening as a platform for plant improvement, and theoretical arguments for expecting exploitable genetic potential in low-yield cultivars adapted to 'poor' environments (Simmonds, 1991, 1993). This work contributed a new impetus to the on-farm and 'with farmer' experimental approaches now generally termed 'participatory plant improvement' (Almekinders and Elings, 2001; Atlin et al., 2001; Sperling et al., 2001). Increasingly these ideas have become mainstream in plant science, and are well represented in the work of the CGIAR centres (e.g. through the system-wide programme on gender and participation).

With the ending of the Cold War much of the 'steam' went out of international public sector agro-technological research, resulting in space for private sector and populist expansion. But market forces are a far stronger influence over the shaping of new agro-technological agenda than any political alliance for 'participatory' development. The dominance of the market sector has made it a matter of some urgency to consider what happens in cases of market failure. Specifically, low-resource farmers are often caught in a trap. They remain poor because they cannot afford agro-chemicals or proprietary seeds. Companies are not interested in penetrating, or developing suitable products for, areas where farmers are too poor to buy. So the circle of agrarian poverty persists. In the search for ways of extending new agro-technologies to producers who lack purchasing power, one much-canvassed idea is that of public–private partnership (PPP). For instance, public sector crop research institutions might buy licences to exploit commercial technologies in order to develop relevant innovations for low-income producers. In the next section we will look more closely at options for PPP. It offers the advantage of retaining some control over technology agenda relevant to the poorest of the poor where market opportunities are limited.

THE GENE REVOLUTION: INTERNATIONAL AGRO-TECHNOLOGY AND THE MARKET

The wind-down to the end of the Cold War in the 1980s was accompanied by 'the triumph of the market', the neo-liberal enthusiasm associated with the Reagan presidency in the USA and the advent of Mrs Thatcher in Britain. Neo-liberalism is here counted a moment of genuine Durkheimian collective effervescence. A fuller discussion (for which there is no space here) would stress how neo-liberal reform was pushed with some of the fervour of a crusade, helping to lock in place institutional beliefs that market forces are the main or only drivers of useful technological innovation (except in the defence industry). Apparently frustrated in an ambition to 'modernize' British universities, Mrs Thatcher, in an act of some symbolic force, focused on public technology. One of her decisions was to privatize 'near-market' research in the plant sciences. Venerable, and university-linked, institutes, such as the Plant Breeding Institute at Cambridge, were sold to newly-organized 'global' life sciences companies. It was only after this transition that the issue of PPP began to come to the fore.

The theory and practice of public–private partnership has been extensively debated in Britain, where PPP is an important aspect of the Labour government's 'third way' (an attempt to go beyond the neo-liberal revolution). In UK there is broad political consensus that provision of some key services – notably health and education – remains a state responsibility, with provision free at the point of use. But this is not to exclude the private sector from a role in providing such services. The argument is that the private sector has relevant specialist knowledge and experience, and can make cost-effective contributions to public services, provided the state or local authority retains control over contracting, and workers and users are involved in assessing the quality of services offered. *Building Better Partnerships* (CPPP, 2001), the final report of the Commission on Public Private Partnerships, offers extensive advice on lessons learnt from a range of activities, from hospital cleaning to the involvement of private specialists in running low-performing schools. Careful specification of contracts, transparency in accountancy and evaluation procedures, effective co-operation between partners (commissioning agencies, private providers and the voluntary sector), participation of clients in designing and assessing programmes, and attempts to ensure that citizens and staff have a stake in programmes, are all highlighted as important areas for attention if programmes are to prove acceptable and sustainable. Criteria for success include (i) social equity and response to need; (ii) value for money and high quality of service; (iii) accountability and redress. Participation of clients in the selection of service providers is especially important in some areas, such as housing. The role of the private sector in PPP is to provide management and commercial skills, and not basic finance. Participation is seen to be an area that needs strengthening (the report notes a need 'for bite and concrete vision in community involvement in public services'). Leaving aside the strong arguments of the 'old left' that PPP is big business's way of extending the benefits of defence contracting into 'civil' spheres (government pays promptly, and is lenient on cost overruns), it is conceded, even by proponents, that 'making a success of partnerships is difficult'.

To return to the plant sciences, the neo-liberal revolution coincided with the transformation of the plant sciences through rapid developments in molecular biology and genetic knowledge. Molecular methods offer ways both to improve conventional breeding and to transfer genes across species, and most assessments conclude that application of the new molecular knowledge is an inescapable component of future global food security. But it is also an area of technique largely paid for by venture capital and subsequently 'enclosed' by private intellectual property regimes. The international seed companies quickly proclaimed their role in deploying the new molecular knowledge for the public good, not least through advertising angled towards the issue of food security. Analysts riposted (plausibly) that many millions of impoverished, self-provisioning farmers (often growing crops for their own food security as part of a diverse livelihood strategy) were too poor to gain access to new technologies through the market (Stone, 2002). These opposing arguments represent an important cultural shift. The issue was no longer whether or not technology possesses the means or knowledge to solve the problem of hunger but whether or not a problem of 'market failure' can be overcome. The international public sector was deprived of the financial means to attempt to develop major new areas of poverty-alleviating technology on its own account when donors scaled back funding, convinced the market would provide. To access the benefits of the molecular revolution the international public sector was forced to adjust to the cultural values of neo-liberalism. PPP was envisaged as one way to proceed.

The arguments are well laid out in a valuable review of access to agricultural biotechnology in developing countries by Byerlee and Fischer (2002). They emphasize the dramatic dominance of the private sector in molecular technology, and reject go-it-alone options, even taking into account the combined resources of the international public sector and the larger national programmes in developing countries (notably China, Brazil, India and South Africa). The issue is more than research capacity within the public sector or access to genomic information. The Rockefeller Foundation invested heavily in the 1980s and 1990s in building up public sector biotechnology capacity in poorer countries, especially in Asia. One result is that the rice genome – the grain crop of greatest global significance to the poor – has been mapped largely by public sector initiative, due in part to major investments by the Japanese government (Hindmarsh and Hindmarsh, 2002). But functional genomics (working out what genes actually do, once chromosomes have been mapped) involves privately-owned techniques and procedures protected by complex nets of intellectual property rights (IPR). The public sector, Byerlee and Fischer argue, has to brace itself to pay for licences, negotiate material transfer agreements (MTAs – instruments that protect the rights of original owners in any discoveries or innovations subsequently made), and contract out key aspects of molecular investigation to private sector specialist companies. In their view, co-operation across the public–private divide is inescapable.

The context in which Byerlee and Fischer (2002) discuss PPP – global plant improvement dominated by the new molecular knowledge – is very different from the Blair government's 'third way' (improved health and education service provisioning Great Britain). The task envisaged for the international public sector and national agricultural research system (NARS) partners is to gain access to private sector knowledge or skills in order to develop innovations on behalf of the poor. This might be through licensing, contracting out research, or mutually advantageous knowledge-sharing agreements, in which the public sector knowledge, protected via defensive patenting, is set up as a bargaining counter. The idea of a defensive patent is not to make money on public sector discoveries, but to ensure co-operation on favourable terms from private sector players. One resource Byerlee and Fischer point to is the large amount of germplasm and genetic information the international public sector institutes hold, in trust, on behalf of the poor farmers from whom it was collected. In some quarters it has been suggested that protective patenting might cover not only advanced molecular research but also farmer knowledge, including the selection efforts that have gone into shaping farmer varieties or crop land races (Gupta, 1995).

One rather dramatic instance of PPP in international plant sciences is embodied in the 1998 Bellagio Declaration on apomixis. Apomixis is the ability of some plants, in certain circumstances, to form embryos without going through sexual reproduction. Where it exists in nature – in dandelions, for example – the characteristic appears sometimes associated with stress, e.g. drought escape. If the genetic basis of apomixis were better understood it might be possible to introduce it into high-quality crop plant types (Bicknell and Bicknell, 1999). Seeds would in effect be clones of superior maternal lines. They would reproduce true-to-type indefinitely. The life sciences companies have some interest in apomixis research, but mainly from the perspective of work on variety use restriction technologies (VURT).[3] VURT research is concerned with how to switch on and off the viability of proprietary seeds. It is envisaged as an alternative to the cumbersome procedure of taking 'free riders' to court for unauthorized copying of seeds (Visser et al., 2001). The approach envisaged in the Bellagio Declaration is rather different. Here the idea would be to leave facultative apomixis permanently switched on. In principle control of apomixis would mean being able to create and fix new varieties more easily than through the current lengthy processes of back-crossing in conventional breeding. Varieties of value to poor farmers might then more readily circulate farmer-to-farmer, without need to revert to a formal seed source (whether seed company or government extension project).

The motivation of the Bellagio Declaration (<http://billie.btny. purdue.edu/apomixis/>), signed by a leading group of apomixis researchers during a conference (*Designing a Research Strategy for Achieving Asexual Seed Production in Cereals*) held in 1998 at the Rockefeller Foundation's facility on Lake Como, Italy, was that facultative apomixis is potentially too valuable to low-resource farmers to risk it being researched and tied up in patents by life sciences companies (especially if these companies would want to own the technology largely as a spoiling tactic, to undermine the idea of free copying of seeds). The signatories had in mind defensive patenting as a means to protect their own work on facultative apomixis. Aid donors might not be willing to fund the five-to-ten-year research programme envisaged (requiring perhaps $50 million). An alternative, therefore, was to consider getting venture capitalists to fund the research, and for these investors to recover their investment by licensing the technology (maybe in VURT formats) to life science companies operating in countries with well-developed seed markets, while reserving the technology for free use in poor countries without seed markets.

Some CG centres have begun to apply the idea of licensing agreements built on such defensive patents. CIMMYT, for example, has developed a model agreement with several life sciences companies to license CIMMYT discoveries and materials for use in commercial markets in order to guarantee free (i.e. subsidized) use by poor farmers in countries subject to 'market failure'.

What is immediately obvious from these cases is that PPP as conceived by Byerlee and Fischer, or as expressed in CIMMYT licensing agreements, operates in very different circumstances from the PPP of the Blair government in Britain. In the latter case PPP is based on a clear democratic mandate, with the state drawing up or supervising contracts. In Byerlee and Fischer's analysis the global technology market is an overriding factor, with poor farmers at risk of exclusion through market failure. There is no 'world government' to draw up contracts on behalf of the poor, nor is there any clear way to determine what users expect, or prefer. Mandates for the international agricultural research centres are still largely set by 'expert' committees in interaction with aid donors. If client consultation is still a weak point of British PPP, then the same could be said, only more so, for the CG system, despite recent experiments with a more 'participatory' approach (limited mainly to 'with farmer' experimentation, rather than user control over research agenda). The international public sector in plant molecular research, as characterized by Byerlee and Fischer, no doubt realistically, will have to operate as a niche player, bargaining cleverly for whatever its limited funds and resources permit in a vast field dominated by private sector interests. When the Bellagio apomixis project envisages the private sector as a source of funding, it contravenes one of the IPPR's basic tenets for successful PPP (the private sector provides management and commercial skills but not funding). In PPP in the British health and education sectors the aim is to get the best the private sector can provide, but within a framework strongly regulated by democratic politics. In PPP as envisaged by Byerlee and Fischer, the public sector has little option but to operate in a global 'free market' dominated not by social considerations and the needs of the poor, but by the interests of stockholders. It is an operation that is adaptive rather than agenda-setting.

Thus, we should perhaps not expect too much from PPP in the international agricultural research sector. Its problems are generic to those of an international 'order' in which regulatory instruments are often weak (or contradictory in effect) and 'citizen' views (as distinct from consumer preferences) hard to establish except through very indirect means (e.g. votes of national governments in the UN General Assembly). Just as the problem of voting cycles ('whatever option the people chooses, there is another which a majority of the people would rather have ... [thus seeming] to rule out direct democracy in any large group of people' [McLean, 1991: 181]) so it would be an impossibly complex task to establish a popular mandate for a far-reaching international public sector technology such as facultative apomixis. And yet some stiff 'democratic' test would seem desirable for a technology that cannot be switched off, and which is intended to spread contagiously through poorer agrarian communities. Even if successful apomicts benefit poor farmers, and at very low transaction costs, there seems some danger that these results would be achieved at the expense of undermining other (perhaps currently rather ill-defined) genetic goods. Of concern is what happens to the gene flow seemingly basic to farmer-based plant improvement. Farmer selection often appears to flourish after the introduction of exotic material enriches local gene pools. Dennis (1987) describes one such case for Thailand after the introduction of Green Revolution rice varieties.[4] There is as yet very little exact research of the kind pioneered by Dennis, but seemingly where exotic genes cross into local populations it appears to become more worthwhile for low-income and subsistence-oriented farmers to embark on, or continue, intense selection activities. The fact of such activities has been extensively reported (Jusu, 1999; Longley, 2000; Richards, 1997; Tchawa et al., 2001; Zimmerer, 1996). Wide up-take of apomicts would seem to imply the end of this 'natural' process of gene pool enrichment. No one knows what longer-term local adaptive potential might thereby be forgone.

We might regard apomixis research, along Bellagio lines, as not very different from market solutions in general, in insensitivity to longer-term outcomes. We should perhaps regard the Bellagio declaration as a dialectic challenge to current market concern with VURT – i.e. as representing an inversion of market thinking, rather than striking out in a radically different direction. Some might even prefer the market solution to its 'inversion'. Apomicts might be safer wrapped up in VURT. A fast machine that splutters to a halt when run without licence might be safer than one without brakes and no means of switching off the engine.

The conclusion of this section is that in transnational crop research PPP as described by Byerlee and Fischer the market is very definitely the 'dog', and thus the converse of arrangements found in British public services sector PPP, where agenda based on democratic mandates firmly wag a private sector 'tail'. For genuinely different 'agenda-setting' approaches to plant sciences, reflecting the needs of the world's poorest, we may have to consider shifting out of the market framework altogether, while at the same time seeking to avoid some of the more obvious traps of 'populist' approaches (lack of true representativeness in consultation exercises). The final case study will consider agenda-setting in plant sciences from the perspective of humanitarian discourse on needs and rights.

FOOD AS A RIGHT: INTERNATIONAL AGRO-TECHNOLOGY IN AN ERA OF 'FAILED STATES'

The slogan for President Clinton's second term was 'it's the economy, stupid'. His successor as President of the United States of America, George W. Bush, came to power vowing to make the continuation of the high-technology economy his priority. Within months the World Trade Center in New York lay in ruins (11 September 2001) and the Bush presidency was engaging the al-Qaida terrorist network in Afghanistan, one of the poorest places on earth. Neo-liberal *laissez faire* lost impetus. The British Prime Minister Tony Blair argued that tackling global poverty could no longer be postponed.

This is easier said than done. Conventional development programmes presuppose a state. Afghanistan was a failed state – a polity which had imploded under the weight of Cold War intrigue and post-Cold War neglect. The existence of swathes of the globe similar to Afghanistan – abandoned to war-lord rivalries or terrorist groups – had throughout the 1990s posed a challenge to established thinking about economic development (Duffield, 2001). The challenge provoked an outburst of social and institutional innovation focused on trans-boundary humanitarian intervention, seen at its most dramatic in the work of agencies such as Médicins Sans Frontières (MSF) and Action Contre la Faim (ACF).

Post-Cold War trans-boundary humanitarianism sustains its own research activities, based on addressing problems apparent only from the heart of the crisis. Food security is one of the issues addressed. But the task-group culture – and thus technology agenda – tends to be very different from the international public-service ethic of the Green Revolution, or the marketplace manoeuvres of biotechnology patent holders. The food security experts in trans-boundary humanitarian task groups tend to be volunteers and not career scientists (even though often medically or scientifically trained and highly competent). They seek technologies for immediate applicability in war zones where the writ of states or the international community does not run. Human rights thinking, and concern with transnational justice, not issues of profitability or environmental sustainability, form the standards against which technological approaches are screened.[5]

In conventional political and diplomatic thinking the state is duty holder granting human rights, backed by the international institutions. In trans-boundary humanitarianism there is no state, and the humanitarian agency itself becomes the duty holder. This has led to an intense internal debate about how humanitarianism maintains the right to food in contexts where neither the state or state-oriented international institutions function.

Trans-boundary humanitarian organizations are not free simply to 'do their best' and 'give what they can'. They are required to ensure that all their activities are compliant with the basic idea of a right to food security. This has brought a great deal of attention to modalities of food distribution, and the accountability and transparency of food distribution procedures. There is considerable evidence that giving out food without paying detailed attention to record-keeping and accountability to all sections of the population discriminates against needy elements, and undermines fragile social solidarities in war-zones (Archibald and Richards, 2002a, 2002b).

In responding to these kinds of criticisms many international humanitarian agencies have signed up to a process, the Sphere Project, which tries to establish humanitarian principles and standards for rights compliance. The food protocol has yet to be finalized (Sphere Project, 2000), but it will include some consideration of food and seed quality and safety standards. A basic idea of the Sphere Project is that there should be participatory engagement of assisted populations in determining the kind of assistance offered. It is common for humanitarian organizations to give out planting materials as part of second-stage food security reinforcement to refugee and war-affected populations (Sperling and Longley, 2002). There are cases where populations are attempting to resettle having been equipped with the wrong seed (lowland types where upland types were needed, or 'out-of-date' groundnut seeds with very low germination potential). Judged by human rights standards, the duty holder is liable for such failures. Where there is corruption, incompetence or simply a failure to consult over what is appropriate, an abuse of rights may have been committed. Humanitarian agencies have not been slow to respond to the implications. They know they need to improve their consultative procedures and at the same time to acquire better technological advice. It is common to find crop researchers from national agricultural research services in war-affected countries working as consultants or on full-time secondment in the humanitarian food security sector.

To summarize the situation, the crisis of failed states is having far-reaching impact on the food security field. In a good number of cases it is no longer the international and national institutions, or the market, but the humanitarian agencies setting the agro-technology agenda. This extends to having firm guidelines on what biotechnologies can and cannot be permitted in the field of humanitarianism, according to what best preserves or guarantees a right to food to needy populations. An example is a recent set of guidelines issued by Action Contre la Faim. A paper, *Technical Positioning Towards GMOs* (ACF, 2002), focuses, in regard to seeds, on the aim 'to restore or maintain agricultural autonomy within communities just after, or in prevention of, critical situations', with clear riders to the effect that this might allow 'novel, high-yielding or resistant varieties, but only ones which are proven in the local environment'.

How do agro-technology agenda change when humanitarian considerations come to the fore? Some answers can be gleaned by comparing parallel Green Revolution and humanitarian projects to make use of the genetic potential of African rice (*Oryza glaberrima*). This plant is cultivated widely, if not very intensively, in the West African coastal rice zone, a region badly affected by state collapse and the spread of non-state war since 1989. These conflicts comprise insurgencies in the Casamance region of Senegal, Guinea-Bissau, Sierra Leone, Guinea, Liberia and most recently La Côte d'Ivoire. Of two competing rice seed projects for the region launched during the 1990s, one stems from a task group operating out of the re-formed West African Rice Development Association, and is shaped by Green Revolution assumptions. The other project began in the same year (1991), but was conceived as a response to the start of the civil war in Sierra Leone, and has been shaped by the assumptions of trans-boundary humanitarianism. The differences of approach illustrate the divergences in agenda of the two different institutional cultures.

Anthropological fieldwork by Richards (1986) established that a significant part of the 'hungry season' food security of low-resource rice farmers in central Sierra Leone came from maintaining a portfolio of rice types adapted to different soil types and planting regimes. Farmer interest centred, in particular, on a range of early rices planted in low-lying rainfall run-off plots before the main planting season. These were 'hunger breakers', harvested during the middle part of the rainy season when other food supplies were exhausted. Some of these 'hunger breakers' belonged to the African rice species, *Oryza glaberrima*. Most breeders had hitherto rejected *O. glaberrima* as a crop for improvement because of its inherently low yield potential (unlike Asian rice the African species has simple branched panicles, and thus a low harvest index). One breeder in Sierra Leone, Malcolm Sellu Jusu, disagreed with this opinion. Daily in contact with low-resource farmers, he could see that the earliness and weed-competitiveness on poor soils of these rices allowed farmers to claim a crop under low-intensity management where other rices failed. Farmers preferred a smaller amount of timely rice to a larger amount of rice later in the year when they had incurred debts from running out of food.

Monde, Jusu and others proposed a research scheme (summarized in Monde and Richards, 1992) to collect and characterize these 'hunger breaker' rices, including (centrally) ones belonging to the African species. The aim of this proposal – in the face of a looming war – was to preserve crucial planting material, to understand better how farmers used such planting material to fight hunger, and to explore the scope there might be for improvement of rices in the 'hunger breaker' class, with a view to having suitable material on hand for relief and rehabilitation activities by humanitarian agencies. A funding application (to the European Union) was rejected on the grounds that the proposal offered nothing new from a scientific perspective. The rejection note specifically mentioned that the West African Rice Development Association (WARDA, an African inter-governmental research agency recently reorganized as a Green Revolution centre funded by the Consultative Group on Agricultural Research) was proposing to start a research project on African rice. WARDA had become interested in *O. glaberrima* as a potential source of germplasm for an inter-specific hybridization programme using molecular methods. This biotechnology-oriented approach, it was implied, would be a more effective use of the genetic potential of African rice than the humanitarian scenario.

The focus of the WARDA inter-specific breeding programme (funded by Japanese aid) during the 1990s was on transfer of *glaberrima* features into Asian rices. The resulting 'nerica' (new rices for Africa, i.e. *sativa* × *glaberrima* crosses) are disease-resistant replacements for inferior Asian types used in the main planting season (Walsh, 2001; Linares, 2002). This means that the significance of the earliness of low-yield African cultivars in a portfolio of farmer planting activities to ease hungry-season indebtedness has been lost, notwithstanding the fact the African rice parentage in the 'nerica' set is from one of the region's war-zones (CG14, a variety from the Casamance), and that research by other WARDA scientists established, contemporaneously, that early season and main season upland rices in West Africa often have different drought escape mechanisms, a reason for farmers in the region continuing to use a portfolio of different seed types (Dingkuhn and Asch, 1999).[6] The agronomic considerations keeping *O. glaberrima* varieties in use were set aside in the breeding programme's more general interpretation of the genetic potential of African rice, thus obscuring the survivalist concerns of the impoverished and vulnerable farmers who had contributed the genetic material.

This is not to argue that the WARDA strategy will not benefit large numbers of farmers in regions far beyond the localities in which the parent African rice material was collected. But the WARDA agenda ignored the issue at the heart of the humanitarian project: to offer war-afflicted farmers an immediate buffer against food insecurity by preserving, purifying and re-releasing materials locally developed for such a purpose. In short, the key to the technology agenda of humanitarian groups was disaster preparedness, not capitalization upon longer-term development opportunities (Monde and Richards, 1992). Shaping of *glaberrima* material by the WARDA rice-breeding task group, by contrast, reflected the concern of the Green Revolution for cultivars with widespread, long-term and sustainable impacts (Walsh, 2001). The difference is, as Douglas (1987) suggests, the institution doing the thinking. In the one case this is shaped by an ethic of international public service, and a preference for large-scale solutions. In the other case, the thinking is that of an emergencies-oriented team, seeking to protect the rights of a rather limited group (the war-vulnerable and war-afflicted) and seeking immediate solutions.

Events have since confirmed the technological relevance of what the humanitarian group had proposed. Fieldwork on the Liberian border in southern Sierra Leone, in an area surrounded by fighting, encountered a farmer growing an African rice type acquired in central Sierra Leone and introduced to displaced farmers in the south of the country on earlier advice from Jusu and colleagues (Richards and Ruivenkamp, 1997). The owner of the field explained his family had three times been driven by fighting to hide in a nearby *sokoihun* (corner in the bush) and this was the only variety of several planted to survive weed and bird damage from these periods of neglect.

There is no suggestion here that we should pick and choose between the two research agenda. The issue of concern is to create space for technological agenda informed by humanitarianism in a world where, otherwise, project selection tends to be guided by the extent of 'normal' impact, and not by considerations of justice to the most vulnerable. Here it is relevant to reflect on the potential reach of human rights thinking in opening the required space. A clear instance of the right to food is the obligation on governments not to starve the enemy by preventing the passage of relief supplies. A rights-based approach may also impose on duty holders the obligation to sustain the technological bases of local hunger coping mechanisms in zones of war or refugee displacement. This suggests that the issue will be to build sufficient technical capacity to understand, sustain or rehabilitate such systems within trans-boundary humanitarian field organizations. The present section will be concluded with a few remarks on this issue.

In relation to the case study described above, Malcolm Sellu Jusu now advises the agency CARE in Sierra Leone on technological aspects of seed within the context of a rights-based agricultural rehabilitation in central Sierra Leone, in which resettled households have an acknowledged right to those varieties which they judge will best serve their food security needs. Jusu's work is now concerned with identifying such needs, tracking, recovering and screening lost varieties, and assessing (with farmers) progress in re-establishing pre-war levels of seed system agro-biodiversity. Much of this activity depends on gene banking and crop characterization data, but it might also evolve into a crop development programme based on ideas of participatory plant improvement (cf. Almekinders and Elings, 2001). It is, in effect, an application of the technology agenda discussed above, but in a new and more enabling institutional setting. An important aspect of this project is to understand how local ideas about food security and seed exchange reinforce notions of solidarity and rights (Archibald and Richards, 2002a, 2002b). Local seed systems do not just yield food; they also 'grow' communities. Unthinking disruption of these processes (e.g. by aggressive introduction of 'modern' varieties, an activity pursued by some agencies in war-zones) might – in conditions of post-war social recovery – be an abuse of the rights of the vulnerable, as suggested in the ACF stance on GMOs (ACF, 2002).

Some of the international public sector crop sciences institutes have already shown considerable interest in the issue of seeds, war and social rehabilitation, notably activities by IPGRI (Richards and Ruivenkamp, 1987) and a collaborative programme for bean farmers in Rwanda (Buruchara et al., 2002). Given a general shift of international mood, this type of activity seems likely to become more general within the public sector institutes. It is possible to envisage rights-based approaches spreading beyond immediate zones of conflict. The right to the food is at the heart of the debate about global poverty. This would make it difficult for public sector research programmes, or life sciences companies, to avoid issues of rights compliance, before launching seed innovation programmes that might have far-reaching, and potentially damaging, consequences for the survival strategies of the poor. The oil companies have had to confront human and cultural rights in the Niger Delta. It can be envisaged that the life sciences companies will have to address the challenge of the right to food, and that this might, in the end, modify many technological agenda (Krattiger, 2002).

CONCLUSION: AGRO-TECHNOLOGICAL MULTICULTURALISM

This chapter has argued that more is at stake than a simple opposition of public and private agro-technological spheres. Via a

Durkheimian perspective it has been shown that a range of different agro-technological agenda are formed in moments of crisis and endure as competing cultures. Green Revolution, public–private partnership and humanitarianism reflect the moments of excitement through which three specific technological cultures were formed: the start of the Cold War, its ending, and the post-Cold War crisis of 'new war' and terrorism. A detailed example (utilization of the genetic potential of African rice) has been used to illustrate ways in which the technological cultures of the Green Revolution and humanitarianism differ in their thinking about technological challenges associated with African food security. The question is 'Where does this take us?' In Kuhn's argument about cultures of science, the 'paradigm' is presented in progressive terms. Paradigms shift; old and less supportable cultures of science wither and die. The case with technology is different. Old technologies are less clearly outmoded by the new – everything depends on whether they continue to work, and for whom. Thus a complex interpenetration of technologies emerges, in which the old and the new may be vigorously hybridized (cf. Richards, 1985). Seeds, and genetic constructs, apparently travel freely. At times a problem (cf. claims concerning transgenic constructs in Mexican landraces of maize) it is also a strength. Useful seeds penetrate barriers of race, religion and nationality. But usefulness is defined in the use, and not by research or development agenda. A significant proportion of the food security of the world's poorest rural peoples rests on planting materials escaped, borrowed or rescued from long-forgotten formal interventions. Much of Africa's food security today rests on two crops from the Americas – cassava and maize – largely adopted outside the confines of formal government initiatives or market inducements. This is where a Durkheimian perspective has advantages over a stress on paradigm replacement, for technology studies at least, since it allows us to relate technological task group cultures to the bigger picture. Technological cultures are embedded within a wider – emergent, and as yet very imperfectly formed – transnational field, the field of common humanity. This was at the core of Durkheim's stress on 'organic' solidarity – recognition of the value of a specialized division of labour in modern society. It mattered that there should be freedom to specialize, to obviate a 'forced' division of labour leading in the direction of civil strife. Applied to education this meant struggle to create the structural conditions to make real a freedom of opportunity; people should not be limited to certain occupational paths, as in societies based on slavery or extremes of wealth and poverty (cf. Sen, 1999). Applied to technology it becomes a case for technological multiculturalism. Technological monocultures reinforce the social solidarities through which they have been created, and (even if unintentionally) devalue otherwise effective ways of binding people into groups. Technological monoculturalism also stimulates a dangerously misguided reaction. Technology itself seems to be the enemy. Anti-GM protesters imagine they are fighting a technique, whereas (arguably) their battle should be mounted against a system that monopolizes potential ways of viewing the knowledge gains of modern genetics. Historically, agro-technology has been good at spreading across borders and finding a diversity of homes. But we now see future versions of this scenario undermined by the threat of technological monoculture. The struggle is to sustain the competition between differently configured cultures of technology, and to expect new projects to arise, triggered by new crises, shaped by new social energies and commitments. Nor should the world be so tied up in intellectual enclosures that the results of differently configured projects cannot spread freely and create their own unpredictable webs of interconnection and interdependency. The agro-technological infrastructure laid in battling extreme poverty may be one of the most important ways of fostering and protecting an emergent, if tentative, sense of shared human destiny. It is concluded that so long as technological monocultures prevail, the power of technology to emancipate, i.e. to underpin new, adaptive societal arrangements in a divided and fragile world, will remain latent rather than effective.

NOTES

1. The present discussion, for reasons of space, is limited strictly to agenda-setting (how each culture selects its topics). A fuller account would also consider the ethnography of the three cultures (including discussion of task-group recruitment, initiation, practices, solidarities and beliefs, cf. Knorr-Cetina, 1999).

2. This was the second science-based agro-technical revolution. The first was based on soil chemistry of Liebig in the mid- to late nineteenth century.

3. It is important to distinguish VURT (variety use restriction technology) and GURT (gene use restriction technology). The former is a commercial goal. The latter is a tool or methodology, which could be vital in switching on apomixis and leaving this as the default state, to provide free copy options for food-insecure farming communities. Thanks to Professor Stephen G. Hughes (ESRC Centre for Genomics in Society, University of Exeter) for clarification.

4. Dennis's material directly contradicts the often-stated idea that crop plant genetic diversity correlates with cultural diversity. He found the rices planted by culturally diverse hill populations less genetically diverse than the rices planted in districts transformed by the Green Revolution (Dennis, 1987).

5. For a good exposition of the emergent junction between human rights

and basic needs thinking see Klein Goldewijk and de Gaay Fortman (1999). On transnational justice and food security see O'Neill (1991).

6. Many West African rices are photo-periodic, i.e. flowering is determined by day length. But some African rices from mid-latitude West Africa are non-photo-periodic. They can be used at any time of year, and flower a fixed number of days from germination. Planting of these varieties can be varied to match early rainy season soil moisture conditions. It is this temporal flexibility that farmers use to alleviate hunger.

REFERENCES

ACF (Action Contre la Faim) (2002) 'Technical Positioning towards GMOs', Position paper, Technical Department ACF. Paris: ACF.

Almekinders, C. J. M. and A. Elings (2001) 'Collaboration of Farmers and Breeders: Participatory Crop Improvement in Perspective', *Euphytica* 122: 425–38.

Anderson, R. S., E. Levy and B. Morrison (1991) *Rice Science and Development Politics: IRRI's Strategies and Asian Diversity 1950–1980*. Oxford: Clarendon Press.

Archibald, S. and P. Richards (2002a) 'Seeds and Rights: New Approaches to Post-War Agricultural Rehabilitation in Sierra Leone', *Disasters* 26 (4): 356–67.

— (2002b) 'Converts to Human Rights? Popular Debate about War and Justice in Rural Central Sierra Leone', *Africa* 72 (3): 339–67.

Atlin, G., M. Cooper and A. Bjornstad (2001) 'A Comparison of Formal and Participatory Breeding Approaches Using Selection Theory', *Euphytica* 122: 463–75.

Bicknell, R. A. and K. B. Bicknell (1999) 'Who Will Benefit from Apomixis?', *Biotechnology and Development Monitor* 37: 17–20.

Borlaug, N. E. (1972) 'Breeding Wheat for High Yield, Wide Adaptation, and Disease Resistance', in IRRI (ed.), *Rice Breeding*, pp. 581–92. Los Baños, Philippines: International Rice Research Institute.

Bray, F. (1986) *The Rice Economies: Technology and Development in Asian Societies*. Oxford: Basil Blackwell.

Buruchara, R. A., L. Sperling, P. Ewell and R. Kirkby (2002) 'The Role of Research Institutes in Seed-Related Disaster Relief: Seeds of Hope Experiences in Rwanda', *Disasters* 26 (4): 288–301.

Byerlee, D. and K. Fischer (2002) 'Accessing Modern Science: Policy and Institutional Options for Agricultural Biotechnology in Developing Countries', *World Development* 30 (6): 931–48.

CPPP (Commission on Public Private Partnerships) (2001) *Building Better Partnerships: The Final Report of the Commission on Public Private Partnership*. London: Institute for Public Policy Research.

Dennis, J. V. (1987) 'Farmer Management of Rice Variety Diversity in Northern Thailand'. PhD thesis, Cornell University.

Dingkuhn, M. and F. Asch (1999) 'Phenological Responses of *Oryza sativa*, *O. glaberrima* and Inter-specific Rice Cultivars on a Toposquence [sic] in West Africa', *Euphytica* 110: 109–26.

Douglas, M. (1987) *How Institutions Think*. London: Routledge.

Douglas, M. and S. Ney (1998) *Missing Persons*. Berkeley: University of California Press.

Duffield, M. (2001) *Global Governance and the New Wars*. London: Zed Books.

Durkheim, E. (1964 [1893]) *The Division of Labor in Society*, trans. G. Simpson. New York: Free Press.

— (1995 [1912]) *The Elementary Forms of Religious Life*, trans. Karen E. Fields. New York: Free Press.

Greenland, D. J. (1984) 'Exploited Plants: Rice', *Biologist* 34 (4): 219–25.

Griffin, K. (1974) *The Political Economy of Agrarian Change: An Essay on the Green Revolution*. London: Macmillan.

Gupta, A. K. (1995) 'Ethical Issues in Protecting Biodiversity', in Agrarian Questions Organising Committee (ed.), *Agrarian Questions: The Politics of Farming anno 1995: Proceedings*, pp. 537–44. Wageningen: Wageningen Agricultural University.

Harré, R. (1972) *The Philosophies of Science: An Introductory Survey*. London: Oxford University Press.

Hindmarsh, S. and R. Hindmarsh (2002) *Laying the Molecular Foundations of GM Rice across Asia*. Penang, Malaysia: PAN AP Policy Research and Analysis.

Jusu, M. S. (1999) 'Management of Genetic Variability in Rice (*Oryza sativa* L. and *O. glaberrima* Steud.) by Breeders and Farmers in Sierra Leone'. PhD thesis, Wageningen University.

Klein Goldewijk, B. and B. de Gaay Fortman (1999) *Where Needs Meet Rights: Economic, Social and Cultural Rights in a New Perspective*. Geneva: WCC Publications.

Kloppenburg, J. R. (1988) *First the Seed: The Political Economy of Plant Biotechnology, 1492–2000*. Cambridge: Cambridge University Press.

Knorr-Cetina, K. (1999) *Epistemic Cultures: How the Sciences Make Knowledge*. Cambridge, MA: Harvard University Press.

Krattiger, A. F. (2002) 'Public–Private Partnerships for Efficient Proprietary Biotech Management and Transfer, and Increased Private Sector Investments. A Briefing Paper with Six Proposals Commissioned by UNIDO', *IP Strategy Today* 4: 1–46. <www.bioDevelopments.org>

Kuhn, T. S. (1970) *The Structure of Scientific Revolutions*, 2nd edn. Chicago, IL: University of Chicago Press.

Linares, O. (2002) 'African Rice (*Oryza glaberrima*): History and Future Potential', *PNAS (Proceedings of the National Academy of Sciences)* 99 (25): 16360–5.

Lipton, M. with R. Longhurst (1987) *New Seeds and Poor People*. London: Hutchinson.

Longley, K. (2000), 'A Social Life of Seeds: Local Management of Crop Variability in North-Western Sierra Leone'. PhD thesis, University College London, Department of Anthropology.

MacKenzie, D. (1992) 'Economic and Sociological Explanation of Technical Change', in R. Coombs, P Saviotti and V. Walsh (eds), *Technological Change and Company Strategies*, pp. 25–48. London: Academic Press.

McLean, I. (1991) 'Forms of Representation and Systems of Voting', in D. Held (ed.), *Political Theory Today*, pp. 172–96. Cambridge: Polity Press.

Maat, H. and P. Richards (2000) 'Colonial (and Post Colonial) Plant Scientists as Knowledge Brokers: From Mendel to Bio-Informatics'. Unpublished paper, Technology and Agrarian Development Group, Wageningen University.

Marglin, S. (1996) 'Farmers, Seedsmen, and Scientists: Systems of Agriculture and Systems of Knowledge', in F. Apffel-Marglin and S. Marglin (eds), *Decolonizing Knowledge: From Development to Dialogue*. Oxford: Clarendon Press.

Monde, S. S., and P. Richards (1992) 'Rice Biodiversity Conservation and Plant Improvement in Sierra Leone', in A. Putter (ed.), *Safeguarding the Genetic Basis of Africa's Traditional Crops. Proceedings of the CTA/IBPGR/KARI/ UNEP Seminar, Nairobi, October 1992*, pp. 83–100. Wageningen and Rome: CTA and IPGRI.

O'Neill, O. (1991) 'Transnational Justice', in D. Held (ed.), *Political Theory Today*, pp. 276–304. Cambridge: Polity Press.

Pearse, A. (1980) *Seeds of Plenty, Seeds of Want: Social and Economic Implications of the Green Revolution*. Oxford: Clarendon Press.

Perkins, J. H. (1997) *Geopolitics and the Green Revolution: Wheat, Genes and the Cold War*. Oxford and New York: Oxford University Press.

Perri, G. (1999) *Morals for Robots and Cyborgs: Ethics, Society and Public Policy in the Age of Autonomous Intelligent Machines*. Brentford: Bull Information Systems.

Richards, P. (1985) *Indigenous Agricultural Revolution: Ecology and Food Production in West Africa*. London: Hutchinson.

— (1986) *Coping with Hunger: Hazard and Experiment in a West African Rice Farming System*. London: Allen and Unwin.

— (1997) 'Towards an African Green Revolution?: An Anthropology of Rice Research in Sierra Leone', in E. Nyerges (ed.), *The Ecology of Practice: Studies of Food Crop Production in Sub-Saharan West Africa*, pp. 201–52. Amsterdam: Gordon and Breach.

— (2000) 'Food Security, Safe Food: Biotechnology and Sustainable Development in Anthropological Perspective', Inaugural lecture, Wageningen University.

Richards, P. and G. Ruivenkamp (1997) *Seeds and Survival: Crop Genetic Resources in War and Reconstruction in Sierra Leone*. Rome: IPGRI.

Richman, M. (2002) *Sacred Revolutions: Durkheim and the College de Sociologie*. Minneapolis: University of Minnesota Press.

Schwarz, M. and M. Thompson (1990) *Divided We Stand: Redefining Politics, Technology and Social Choice*. Hertfordshire: Harvester Wheatsheaf.

Sen, A. (1999) *Development as Freedom*. New York: Anchor Books.

Simmonds, N. W. (1989) 'How Frequent are Superior Genotypes in Plant-Breeding Populations?', *Biological Review* 64: 341–65.

— (1991) 'Selection for Local Adaptation in a Plant Breeding Programme', *Theoretical and Applied Genetics* 82: 363–7.

— (1993) 'Introgression and Incorporation: Strategies for the Use of Crop Genetic Resources', *Biological Review* 68: 539–62.

Song, Y. (1998) '"New" Seed in "Old" China'. PhD thesis, Wageningen University.

Sperling, L., J. Ashby, M. Smith, E. Weltzien and S. McGuire (2001) 'A Framework for Analyzing Participatory Breeding Approaches and Results', *Euphytica* 122: 439–50.

Sperling, L. and K. Longley (2002) 'Beyond Seeds and Tools: Effective Support to Farmers in Emergencies', *Disasters* 26 (4): 283–7.

Sphere Project (2000) *Humanitarian Charter and Minimum Standards in Disaster Response*, ed. I. McConnan. Oxford: Oxfam.

Standage, T. (1998) *The Victorian Internet: The Remarkable Story of the Telegraph and the Nineteenth Century's Online Pioneers*. London: Weidenfeld and Nicolson.

Stedman Jones, S. (2001) *Durkheim Reconsidered*. Cambridge: Polity Press.

Stone, G. D. (2002) 'Both Sides Now: Fallacies in the GM Wars, Implications for Developing Countries, and Anthropological Perspectives', *Current Anthropology* 43 (4): 611–19.

Storey, W. (1997) *Science and Power in Colonial Mauritius*. Rochester, NY: University of Rochester Press.

Tchawa, P., N. T. Jean-Baptiste, A. M. Ze and E. Mujih (2001) 'Farmer Innovation and Plant Breeding: The Case of Maize K5252 Created by Emmanuel Kamgouo of Bandjoun, West Cameroon', in C. Reij and A Waters-Bayer (eds), *Farmer Innovation in Africa: A Source of Inspiration for Agricultural Development*. London: Earthscan.

Tranvik, T., M. Thompson and P. Selle (2000) 'Doing Technology (and Democracy) the Pack-Donkey's Way: The Technomorphic Approach to ICT Policy', in C. Engel and K. H. Keller (eds), *Governance of Global Networks in the Light of Differing Local Values*, pp. 155–96. Law and Economics of International Telecommunications, vol. 43. Baden-Baden: Nomos.

Visser, B., D. Eaton, N. Louwaars and I. van der Meer (2001) *Potential Impacts of Genetic Use Restriction Technologies (GURTs) on Agrobiodiversity and Agricultural Production Systems*. Rome, Italy: FAO.

Walsh, J. R. (2001) *Wide Crossing: The West Africa Rice Development Association in Transition, 1985–2000*. Aldershot: Ashgate (SOAS Studies in Development Geography).

Zimmerer, K. (1996) *Changing Fortunes: Biodiversity and Peasant Livelihoods in the Andes*. Berkeley: University of California Press.

Notes on contributors

DAVID BURCH is a Professor in the School of Science, Griffith University, Brisbane, Australia, and Director of the Science Policy Research Centre. He is a political scientist with a particular interest in science and technology studies related to agriculture and social change in Australia and South-east Asia. He is a co-editor of *Restructuring Global and Regional Agricultures: Transformations in Australasian Agri-food Economies and Spaces* (Avebury, 1999), and a special edition of *Rural Sociology* entitled *Antipodean Visions* (June 1999). He is also a co-editor of the *International Journal of the Sociology of Agriculture and Food*.

DOMINIC GLOVER is a Research Officer at the Institute of Development Studies at the University of Sussex, Brighton, UK. His research interests are in the areas of policy processes and regulatory systems surrounding agricultural biotechnology, corporate responsibility and the impacts of globalization at the local level. He is currently researching the role of transnational corporations in the development and commercialization of biotechnologies internationally, with a focus on the implications for developing country agriculture and smallholder farmers.

JULIE GUTHMAN is a lecturer and researcher in the Department of Geography at the University of California, Berkeley, USA. Her current research focuses on the politics of consumption in shaping agrarian change. Her forthcoming book, *Agrarian Dreams? The Paradox of Organic Farming in California* (University of California Press, Berkeley) reports on this study more thoroughly.

MARK HARVEY is Senior Research Fellow at the ESRC Centre for Research in Innovation and Competition, University of Manchester, UK. He is a co-author of *Exploring the Tomato: Transformations in Nature, Economy and Society* (Cheltenham: Edward Elgar, 2002).

KEES JANSEN is a lecturer in the Technology and Agrarian Development Group at Wageningen University, the Netherlands. His current research focuses on expert knowledge in biotechnology regulation and international crop protection regimes. Recent publications include: *Political Ecology, Mountain Agriculture, and Knowledge in Honduras* (Amsterdam: Thela,

1998), 'Devil Pact Narratives in Rural Central America: Class, Gender, and "Resistance"', *Journal of Peasant Studies* 29 (3/4): 270–99 (with E. Roquas, 2002); and 'Crisis Discourses and Technology Regulation in a Weak State: Responses to a Pesticide Disaster in Honduras', *Development and Change* 34 (1): 45–66 (2003).

GEOFFREY LAWRENCE is Professor of Sociology and Head of the School of Social Science at the University of Queensland. He has written widely in the areas of rural social change, regional restructuring and the sociology of agriculture and the environment. Among his recent co-authored/co-edited books are: *A Future for Regional Australia* (CUP, 2001); *Altered Genes II* (Scribe, 2001); and *Globalization, Localization and Sustainable Livelihoods* (Ashgate, 2002).

STEWART LOCKIE is Director of the Centre for Social Science Research at Central Queensland University. His current research addresses food production and consumption, natural resource management in agriculture, social impact assessment and coastal zone management. He is co-editor of *Rurality Bites: The Social and Environmental Transformation of Rural Australia* (2001), *Consuming Foods, Sustaining Environments* (2000) and *Environment, Society and Natural Resource Management: Theoretical Perspectives from Australasia and the Americas* (2001).

KRISTEN LYONS lectures in Science, Technology and Society at Griffith University in Australia. Her current research interests include the sociology of organic agriculture, international trade and regulation of organic food, community supported agriculture and local food networks. She has recently published in *Sociologia Ruralis, International Journal of Sociology of Food and Agriculture* and *Agriculture and Human Values*.

PETER NEWELL is a Fellow at the Institute of Development Studies at the University of Sussex, Brighton, UK. He is the author of *Climate for Change: Non-state Actors and the Global Politics of the Greenhouse* (CUP, 2000), co-author of *The Effectiveness of EU Environmental Policy* (Macmillan, 2000), and co-editor of *Development and the Challenge of Globalisation* (ITDG, 2002). His current research interests lie in the area of corporate regulation and responsibility and the politics of GMO regulation in developing countries.

VICTOR PELAEZ is Assistant Professor in the Economics Department at the Federal University of Paraná (Brazil). His research focus is the role of regulation as a determinant of the pace and the direction of technical progress. He has written about the political disputes over the regulation of GMOs in Brazil. Recent publications include: 'The Dissemination of

Genetically Modified Organisms in Brazil', *International Journal of Biotechnology* 4 (2/3): 211–27 (2002); 'Genetically Modified Organisms: The Side Not Revealed by Science', *International Journal of Technology Management* (forthcoming), and 'The Search for a Perfect Substitute: Technological and Economic Trajectories of Synthetic Sweeteners from Saccharin to Aspartame', in R. Munting (ed.), *Competing for the Sugar Bowl* (St Katharinen, Germany, 2000).

PAUL RICHARDS is Professor and Chair of the Technology and Agrarian Development Group at Wageningen University, the Netherlands. His research interests are participatory technology development (especially crop improvement), resource conflicts, agro-technology and human rights, and food security issues. He is author of *Fighting for the Rain Forest: War, Youth and Resources in Sierra Leone* (Oxford: James Currey, 1996 and 1998); 'Are Forest Wars in Africa Resource Conflicts? The Case of Sierra Leone', in N. Peluso and M. Watts (eds), *Violent Environments* (Cornell University Press, 2001); 'Converts to Human Rights? Popular Debate about War and Justice in Rural Central Sierra Leone', *Africa* 72 (3), 339–67 (2002, with Steven Archibald).

ERIKA ROSENTHAL has been a local Nicaraguan counsel on the DBCP cases in Nicaragua and is now based at the Red de Acción en Plaguicidas y sus Alternativas para América Latina, USA/Perú and the Earthjustice Legal Defense Fund, California.

WILSON SCHMIDT is Assistant Professor at the Department of Animal Husbandry and Rural Development, Universidade Federal de Santa Catarina/Brazil. His current research interests include organic agriculture, its regulation in Brazil and the gap between two phenomena: the endogenous building of organic agriculture techniques and the external public recognition of their development. He has recently published with Victor Pelaez on the dissemination of genetically modified organisms in Brazil in *International Journal of Biotechnology*, *Économie et Sociétés* and *La Questione Agraria*.

SIETZE VELLEMA is a researcher in Technology Management and Policy in the Institute for Agro-Technological Research (ATO), Wageningen University and Research Centre. He works in foresight studies in food provision and in the industrial use of renewable resources, with a focus on improving innovation management and engaging diverse stakeholders in transitions of agro-food chains. He is also research fellow at the Technology and Agrarian Development group of Wageningen University. His research centres on organizational configurations in international agribusiness, especially in South-east Asia, and on learning process in contract farming. He is the author of *Making Contract Farming Work? Society and Technology in Philippine Transnational Agribusiness* (2002).

WILLIAM VORLEY is senior research associate at the International Institute for Environment and Development (IIED) in London. His current research focuses on how small-scale agricultural producers can deal with agri-food industrial concentration. He is co-editor of *Bugs in the System: Redesigning the Pesticide Industry for Sustainable Agriculture* (London: Earthscan, 1998).

Index